Riders of the Apocalypse

Riders of the Apocalypse

German Cavalry and Modern Warfare, 1870–1945

David R. Dorondo

NAVAL INSTITUTE PRESS
Annapolis, Maryland

This book has been brought to publication with the generous assistance of Marguerite and Gerry Lenfest.

Naval Institute Press
291 Wood Road
Annapolis, MD 21402

Library of Congress Cataloging-in-Publication Data
Dorondo, D. R., 1957–
  Riders of the apocalypse : German cavalry and modern warfare, 1870–1945 / D. R. Dorondo.
    p. cm.
  Includes bibliographical references and index.
  ISBN 978-1-61251-086-6 (hbk. : alk. paper) 1. Germany. Heer—Cavalry—History—20th century. 2. World War, 1939–1945—Cavalry operations. I. Title.
  UA714.D67 2012
  357'.1094309041—dc23
                                                                    2011051956

20 19 18 17 16 15 14 13 12   9 8 7 6 5 4 3 2 1
First printing

And their horsemen shall come from afar: they shall fly
as the eagle that hasteth to devour.
They shall come all for violence.

The Book of Habakkuk, I, 8–9

From all the villages, along all the roads, they come together: wagons, horses, refugees with handcarts. Hundreds. Thousands. Endlessly they stream from north and south to the great east–west road and crawl slowly away, day after day, as though the hoofbeat of the horse were the metronome of the hour, the measure of the ages. . . . Behind us crash the waves of war. Before us stretches the infinite succession of wagons. But here there is only the rhythm of the horse's gait, just as it has always gone, imperturbably, for all time.

Marion Gräfin Dönhoff, "Ritt gen Westen"
Die Zeit, 21 March 1946

CONTENTS

ACKNOWLEDGMENTS

I do hope readers will take a few moments with what follows, for while whatever deficiencies there are in this work remain mine alone, a number of individuals and organizations provided important support to me in the writing of this book. My colleagues in the Department of History at Western Carolina University, notably my Head of Department, Richard Starnes, sustained me throughout with research assistance, kindness, and good humor. CuChullaine and Basha O'Reilly of The Long Riders' Guild gave unfailing encouragement in many ways and opened doors that I did not even know existed. Jeremy James, in *The Byerley Turk*, wove a tale that has, for reasons of my own, touched me more deeply than he knows. Serena Herter, Tenzin Frisby, and Don Wood placed great trust in me over the years in many ways. They exhibited unfailing generosity to me and my family, and I shall always be grateful. Adam Kane of the Naval Institute Press saw something worthy in this undertaking. To him I owe a particular debt of gratitude, as I do to both Chuck Grear for his fine cartographic skill and Wendy Bolton for her sharp eye and keen instinct for the best words. Seven Meadows Archery of Tacoma, Washington, and Cold Steel, Inc., of Ventura, California, allowed me access to extraordinary mounted weaponry both for this book and for my university course, "The Horse in European History." Ashley Evans and Mark Haskett at WCU's Office of Public Information supplied valuable photographic assistance. Much closer to home, Cheri and India endured my equine enthusiasms with more patience, grace, and equanimity than I deserve. I love them dearly and thank them with all my heart. Finally, there are the horses: Grey Action (Frosty), a gentle soul of a Quarter Horse; PMX Tuxedo Junction (Buster), the quintessential Morgan; Midnight's Roxanne (Roxy), a delightfully headstrong Anglo-Arab; and—standing above them all—My Victory (Buddy), a magnificent Irish Thorougbred. As only a horse can, Buddy sees clearly what remains hidden from my sight. He already knows, as of old, what lies beyond those horizons I have yet to cross. His voice comes to me from that distant place, gently urging me on. When the time comes, I pray that I may follow after him and that he will remember me.

CHAPTER 1

The Day of the Horseman

Until its final passing in the 1940s, European mounted warfare constituted a reflection, however distant, of the inheritance of the steppe. Though occurring on battlefields usually very different from the endless grassland stretching eastward from the Black Sea to the Tian Shan and Altai Mountains of China and Mongolia, this warfare nevertheless retained characteristics derived from the horse-cultures of the East: aggression typically paid off; riders could usually outflank fixed defenses; speed and maneuverability remained critical to victory.[1] Well into the twentieth century, the presence of the mounted warrior exerted a profound effect not only on Western military thought but also at deeper levels such as politics, religion, literature, and the heraldic arts. In the seventh-century *Lex Baiuvariorum*, for example, the tribal duke of the Bavarians would not be required to name a co-regent so long as he could mount his own horse unaided and effectively wield his weapons.[2] In the *Heliand*, an inculturated Saxon version of the Gospel written in the first half of the ninth century, there appears to be a recurrent apprehension about the ever-present threat of mounted attack. Even in the original Christian scriptures, in this case the Book of Revelation, there would also seem to be reference to the much earlier terror evoked in the eastern Roman world by the Parthian horsemen of the first century AD, a terror that the Romans frequently attempted to counter by recruiting non-Roman horsemen of their own.[3] As is too well known to require elaboration here, the whole of medieval chivalry centered upon the mounted warrior. Later, in the early modern period, the age-old specter of the Ottoman Turkish horseman inspired European emulation not only in the formation of units of hussars and uhlans in Hungary, Poland, and Prussia, but also in the very terminology to describe them and their uniforms. Indeed, after 1870 "uhlan" became a synonym across Europe for the much-feared German cavalry, regardless of an individual unit's actual designation, while the Polish lancer's *czapka*, with its flat top and decorative cordage, became perhaps the most distinctive helmet of the modern age. Not even the world wars eliminated the iconic status of the mounted warrior, for horse-cavalry vocabulary carried on in armored formations' names in Great Britain and France. In today's Germany the official heraldic shields (*Länderwappen*) of two federal states reflect these ancient equestrian traditions. There one sees very prominently displayed the "Saxon Horse" and the "Westphalian Horse" in the armorial bearings of Lower Saxony and North Rhine-Westphalia, respectively.

To be sure, the military and social importance of the horse was also recognized far beyond Europe's bounds. In China, to note but one very distant example, horses, their chariots, and—unfortunately—their drivers were buried in royal Shang tombs,[4] and in post-Soviet Turkmenistan the horse has been conspicuously adopted as reflecting the very essence of Turkmen identity. Closer to Europe's home, in Istanbul's Topkapi Palace, twentieth-century Turkish sultans still sat in tents that nomads would have recognized, tents at whose entrances stood horsetail standards. Interestingly enough, this same Turkish adornment was adopted by Prussian and other German armies and police forces in the form of the standard called the *Schellenbaum* or "jingling Johnnie," along with Turkish kettle drums and cymbals.[5] The *Schellenbaum* is still used in the Federal German Armed Forces.

Of course, today's most famous remnant examples of mounted soldiers are also to be found in Europe, namely the Household Cavalry of the British Army and the Republican Guard in France. There are also less-well-known European examples to be found in the very successful Irish Defence Forces' Equitation School and the riding curriculum at the

Theresianische Militärakademie, Austria's West Point. However, one should also certainly note non-European units such as the Indian Army's President's Bodyguard. The Indian Army also enjoyed, at least as of 2008, the distinction of fielding the only remaining horse-mounted, un-mechanized cavalry regiment in the world: the 61st Cavalry, not surprisingly home to some of the world's best polo players. In the United States, too, the (armored) 1st Cavalry Division still maintains an official Horse Cavalry Detachment for ceremonial purposes, and in the wake of the fighting in Afghanistan in 2001, the U.S. Army's Command and General Staff College at Ft. Leavenworth temporarily instituted a military horsemanship program for Special Operations personnel.

In addition to certain armies' retention of horses, a number of paramilitary law-enforcement agencies around the world also still employ them. Among others, these forces include the South African Police Service, the Royal Canadian Mounted Police, and the U.S. Border Patrol. Then, too, the metropolitan police forces of many major cities throughout the world still include mounted units and not merely for ceremonial purposes. In the United States the most famous such unit by far is New York's, which was substantially expanded as recently as 2006, but other cities as varied as Honolulu, Las Vegas, and Washington, D.C., were also enjoying what the *New York Times* then called "a resurgence in horseback policing."[6]

For more than three thousand years, whether in enforcing the law or, more importantly, waging war, the horse was the means by which the warrior gained true mobility, range, and striking power. Either by riding the horse or by having it pull his chariots, supply wagons, or, later, machine guns and artillery, he harnessed the strength, endurance, and above all the intelligence of the horse for his own military purposes; and, despite the horse's flight-response to danger, he even managed make use of its occasional aggressiveness. This latter trait became particularly useful in the massed attack when the horse's herd-instincts could effectively mask threats from which even cavalry mounts trained to the sound of gunfire might otherwise flee. Equine aggressiveness among stallions and late-gelded males could also be brought to bear in the melee of individual combats wherein the horse would see another mount, and not its rider, as the enemy.[7] Such innovations "brought to warmaking the electric concept of campaigning over long distances and, when campaigning resolved itself into battle, of manoeuvering on the battlefield at speed— at least five times the speed of men on foot."[8] It also brought fear: the fear of an enemy able to appear at times and in places of his own choosing, often completely unexpectedly. Indeed, given the context of the present work, it seems worth noting that this pervasive fear rooted itself very deeply in the European psyche. As late as the 1940s, the German government's propaganda consciously attempted to evoke the terror still latent in the folk memory of the menace of the steppe horsemen. The purpose was to encourage resistance to the advancing, and by then largely mechanized, Red Army. Emphasis on the specific ideological threat posed by Communism only overlaid and reinforced the much more ancient dread. The essential element was the fear itself, the perception of Germany's being overrun by "Asiatic hordes." Ironically, the fact that the Red Army still employed large units of horse-mounted Cossacks only further reinforced the propaganda.

The centrality, the emotional pre-eminence, of the mounted warrior even down to the twentieth century's beginnings was not quite as old as the Western way of war itself. From approximately the fifth century BC to the fifth century AD, that way of warfare consisted primarily in the face-to-face fight to the death of the infantry phalanx with cavalry acting (occasionally brilliantly, as under Alexander's command, or as with the Thebans at Leuctra in 371 BC) as an adjunct to the main battle. Nevertheless, the transmission of the mounted warrior's role from the Eurasian steppe and Persia via Greece and Rome to Europe proper created a powerful impetus for the future. This force found its first true expression in the post-Roman, Germanic successor-kingdoms of early medieval Europe. In them the Greco-Roman tradition combined itself with the power of the horse to create an essentially new style of mounted warfare, one aiming at the immediate destruction of the enemy rather than hit-and-run harassment and graduated attrition typical of the steppe warrior.

To the extent that Western cavalry now gave primacy to rapidly closing with and destroying the enemy, the widespread use of the stirrup constituted an important contributory technology. As with the idea of the cavalry itself, the stirrup's use also gradually migrated from East to

West. By the tenth century AD it was commonly used by Western European horsemen and, among cavalrymen, helped provide a more stable platform from which to drive home attacks with a couched lance or to strike heavier, downward blows with handheld weapons such as the mace, sword, or axe.[9] It is also suggested that the increased striking power made possible through the combination of effective bits, stirrups, and deeper-seated saddles encouraged the breeding of heavier horses in Western Europe from the Carolingian period forward, ones capable of withstanding the greatly increased collision-impact of lance-wielding heavy cavalry. It should, for example, be remembered that two armored knights' chargers, each weighing at least one thousand pounds (not including the weight of the rider, his weapons, and armor) and moving at speeds approaching 15–20 mph (25 km/h), would generate a tremendous shock.[10] As such face-to-face combat became the idealized norm in Western mounted warfare, breeds possessing a heavier, though not necessarily "cobby" or "carty," conformation followed. Indeed, they helped drive the cycle: the heavier the horse, the greater the weight of man and armor it could carry and impact it could withstand. This capability, in turn, necessitated still heavier breeds to absorb ever-greater collisions, and so on.

Insofar as German cavalry is concerned (but not only there), the long-term consequence of this equid-and-technology evolutionary spiral in the early-modern period was the increasingly rigorous and state-supported breeding program of the sort that produced such fine military horses as the Hanoverian and the Trakehner. And, though lance-on-shield combat eventually disappeared, the essential physical dynamics of Western European cavalry combat from AD 870 to 1870 did not. As a result, into the twentieth century Western European cavalry horses, German horses among them, would remain generally taller and of heavier conformation than, for example, their Cossack counterparts. Nevertheless, one never really sees a clear break between a Western way of war involving nothing but infantry and a Western way of war wholly dominated by mounted knights by circa AD 750–800. Rather, there appears to have been a steady, and steadily growing, influence of the concept of mounted warfare permeating Western Europe from the East, undergoing modification and culminating in the full flowering of the chivalric ideal in the High Middle Ages[11] and then continuing through the early-modern period with its introduction of gunpowder weaponry.

In the latter age, however, one of the primary conundrums facing cavalrymen in the Western world was what their role would become given the advent of firearms. The employment of long-range missile-weapons by horsemen was, of course, already of ancient lineage. The tactically successful use of such weapons against riders was a crucial military evolution even before the common use of gunpowder. One need only mention Crecy (1346) and Agincourt (1415). The introduction and rapid refinement of firearms merely compounded the range at which common foot soldiers might visit destruction upon their chivalric social betters. To a certain extent, firearms also added to the perceived insidiousness of the foot soldier's shooting the rider from the saddle before the latter could even strike a blow or, more likely, simply killing his horse. The horse did, after all, present a much larger target than the man riding it, and killing the horse automatically stopped the cavalry charge. For example, the nobly born Gaston de Foix, commander of the French army at Ravenna in 1512, and some twenty of his courtly fellows were unceremoniously "gunned down to a man" when they sportingly attempted to pursue already defeated Spanish arquebusiers.[12] Furthermore, if such factors were not already sufficient to make socially refined horsemen unsure about facing mere mechanics on a gunpowder-dominated battlefield, there was the occasional accusation that gunmen used an early equivalent of dum-dum bullets in the form of rounds dipped in poisonous substances such as green vitriol (likely an oily metallic sulfate), a charge specifically made during the siege of the English city of Colchester in 1648.[13]

In the late fifteenth and throughout the sixteenth century the principal firearm was, in one version or another, the arquebus. For the time being this weapon, though dangerous, did not truly threaten to displace cavalry from the battlefield. The arquebus did not, for example, possess a high rate of fire. Estimates range from one shot every thirty to forty seconds under ideal conditions (unlikely in a battle) to one shot every "several minutes." Perhaps the best estimate is one shot every two minutes, though this, too, may be generous.[14] Under such circumstances, cavalry could very likely close with opposing infantry before the latter's arquebuses inflicted unacceptable losses of men and horses. Moving at the trot, cavalry on sound horses could cover perhaps 270 yards (approximately 250 meters) per minute, while at the gallop the distance covered would approximately double.[15] Consequently, infantry armed with arquebuses faced unpalatable options. They could fire a volley at the weapon's maximum effective range of about one hundred yards and hope to reload and fire again before the horsemen were upon them. Conversely, they could wait until the range had decreased to a much more lethal fifty yards or so, fire, and then see whether the horsemen survived in sufficient numbers and with sufficient impetus to ride them down. Precisely for this reason, pikemen remained an integral feature of infantry formations throughout the period. The pike—as much as eighteen feet in length—provided close-in protection for arquebusiers who were otherwise doomed, as were artillerymen, if the cavalry got in amongst them.[16] The pikemen were therefore essential to the infantry's survival until the invention of the socket bayonet. That device transformed the shoulder-fired weapon into a means by which infantrymen could defend themselves from cavalry attack while reloading, provided they had the nerve. Large numbers of horses moving at the gallop not only present a tremendous visual spectacle. For anyone standing nearby, they also literally shake the earth. A wall of such creatures, hundreds or even thousands strong, ridden by shouting cavalrymen and running full tilt directly into one's face, would certainly seem to be unstoppable. The adverse psychological effect upon infantrymen, even when they formed the vaunted infantry square, could be enormous.[17]

Of course, the cavalry forces of European armies also attempted to adapt themselves to the use of firearms, most notably in the form of the pistoleers of the mid-sixteenth century.[18] The *caracole*, through a complicated tactical evolution, resulted precisely from the effort by cavalrymen to make use of firearms themselves to break up opposing infantry formations and thus render possible a battle-winning charge with cold steel. "Cavalry," writes historian Jeremy Black, thus continued to provide "mobility, and that was crucial for strategic, logistical, and tactical reasons. It enabled forces to overcome the constraints of distance, to create equations of numbers, supplies and rate of movement that were very different to those of infantry, and also to force the pace of battle in a very different fashion to that of infantry."[19] The arquebus, the wheel-lock horse-pistol, and, eventually, the eighteenth-century flintlock musket did not render that utility nugatory. Indeed, if the carbine musket and cannon could be fully incorporated into the cavalry, as in fact they were, then the cavalry would continue to have, as in fact it did, a viable combat role on the battlefields of Europe.

According to Michael Roberts, the Swedish king and royal innovator Gustavus Adolphus nevertheless forbade the *caracole* and instead insisted that the cavalry always charge home with swords drawn, relying on the combined weight of man and horse for tactical success. In place of his horsemen's firearms, or at least supplementing them, he also "was able to arm his units with a light and transportable field piece designed to supply close artillery support for infantry and cavalry alike."[20] Herein one may see the beginnings not only of the vaunted horse-artillery of the Napoleonic era but also what late-twentieth-century military writers would have termed an organic artillery capability for the cavalry. Unsurprisingly, however, not all historians agree that this incorporation of artillery with the cavalry constituted a solution to the cavalry's problem of how to break up firearms-carrying infantry formations. David A. Parrott, for one, maintains that Gustavus Adolphus' effort created no real solution. On the contrary, he writes that the Swedish king's artillery was not "capable of the same degree of mobility as cavalry." While the Swedes had developed cannon firing 3-pound shot over an effective range of some three hundred yards, these "were not mobile as a matter of course" owing to a lack of good-quality horses and easily portable stocks of ammunition. Therefore, "the vaunted reforms of Gustavus Adolphus produced nothing capable of approaching this [mobility] requirement."[21] Parrott therefore concludes that, absent the aforementioned and truly revolutionary innovation that highly mobile horse-artillery would have provided in smashing prepared infantry formations, the cavalry's tactical importance became increasingly that of turning the flanks of opposing armies so that the latter could be taken from the side or rear while pressure was maintained front and center by one's own infantry. Of course, the opponent's own cavalry would be tasked with preventing just such a turning movement, thus setting up the continued face-to-face clash of horsemen employing not only handheld firearms but cold steel, both at pointblank range. It would, therefore, not be "new" tactics deciding the issue in a given cavalry battle but the resolution of the combatants,[22] and at least implicitly the quality of the winners' mounts. In precisely this respect, the importance of secure, high-quality breeding stock for supplying large numbers of remounts assumed a strategic significance.

In Germany the eighteenth century witnessed the establishment or expansion of a number of State studs whose mission was to develop and maintain breed-stock suitable for military and agricultural employment. Two of the most famous of these would eventually play major roles in the breeding of the modern German military horse. These were the East Prussian State Stud at Trakehnen and the Hanoverian State Stud at Celle. These studs and others contributed greatly to the establishment of a solid breed-stock of horses that, if not quite as finely athletic as the English Thoroughbred of the day, were nonetheless very well suited for employment as cavalry mounts. To that extent, they helped revamp the capabilities of a Prussian and, later, German cavalry that no less an observer than Frederick the Great dismissed upon his accession as being "not even worth the devil coming to fetch it away."[23] Nevertheless, the development of more stringent breeding standards, combined with more effective training in individual and close-formation galloping and other exercises by Frederick's cavalry commanders such as Johann Joachim "Papa" von Ziethen and Friedrich Wilhelm von Seydlitz, soon honed the Prussian cavalry into a force of European renown. No longer would the Prussian cavalry be good only for parading, a fact demonstrated for all to see in battles such as Seydlitz' crushing victory over the French at Rossbach in 1757.[24]

Firearms of all kinds had indeed made the battlefield more lethal. That was true enough. Cavalrymen, such as the Prussians at Rossbach, recognized "that a well-timed musket volley could destroy an entire regiment." They also knew, however, that musketry, rifle-fire, or artillery could create opportunities for the cavalry's decisive engagement, provided that cavalry commanders appreciated "the complexity of the [late-eighteenth-century] battlefield." More than ever before, "precise maneuvers, speed, boldness, and timing" would determine the mounted arm's success on battlefields where "the margin of error separating cavalry success and failure" grew ever narrower.[25] This lesson applied not only to

Prussian or other German cavalry, but to all the military horsemen of Europe.

These issues became acute between 1800 and 1815, for European cavalry "reached its apotheosis" during the reign of Napoleon I.[26] In his campaigns, cavalry performed those functions—often with consummate skill—that still remained to it on battlefields now coming to be dominated by the emperor's beloved artillery, if not quite yet by truly accurate, long-range volleys from rifled firearms. These roles consisted of screening the French armies' movements and strength from spies and opposing forces. The cavalry also carried out reconnaissance and prepared the conditions for the concentration of divergent French columns at the point of contact with the enemy. Finally, the French horsemen became the ultimate pursuers of broken enemy formations, though the latter were almost never broken by the cavalry itself. Despite the awful psychological effect of a massed cavalry attack made at the gallop, Napoleonic-era infantry squares, bristling with bayonet-tipped muskets and often supported by guns, could only rarely be smashed by direct mounted assault.[27] Nevertheless, Napoleon may be said to have resurrected the cavalry's operational role from its relative diminution in the eighteenth century as reflected in the declining ratio of cavalry to infantry, despite the cavalry's contributions in such famous early eighteenth-century battles as Blenheim (1704) and, later, Rossbach.[28] Napoleon added skirmishing to the cavalry's remit and, in the 1790s, was one of the first French commanders to employ effective horse-artillery. The latter innovation gave genuine speed and mobility to the "king of battle," greatly increasing the striking power of mounted formations.[29] Furthermore, by disrupting the enemy infantry's formations, a properly coordinated artillery barrage, whether from field guns or horse batteries, could still make possible the European cavalry's ultimate self-expression, namely the pressing home of attacks with the *arme blanche*. At the very least, it was assumed that dragoons and carabiniers could close sufficiently to employ their own shoulder-fired weapons or pistols.[30] Nevertheless, even Napoleon's superb cavalry could not overcome the iron logic of gunpowder weaponry, as demonstrated with such terrible magnificence in the futile attack by fully 10,000 French horsemen against the allied squares at Waterloo. Not even such a grand failure, however, served to dislodge the cavalry from the armies of Europe, if for no other reason than that no substitute for it existed in the missions noted above. Only the cavalry could rapidly execute the vital tasks of long-range reconnaissance, screening, flanking, liaison, and pursuit. Nothing less than the advent of reliable wireless communications and internal-combustion propulsion would truly change that calculus; and even then, the cavalry's departure from the scene "was slow, uneven, and reluctant."[31]

Thus, throughout the second half of the nineteenth and well into the twentieth century, the cavalry—indeed military horsepower generally—could still claim a place on the battlefields of Europe. In the last great cavalry war of Western European history, the Franco-Prussian War, both France and the German States routinely employed light and heavy cavalry at both the tactical and the operational level, though not, as shown below, with equal effectiveness. Later, in World War I, all of the major European armies still marched with huge numbers of cavalry fully integrated into their combat formations, though as the reader will see, nascent motorization (particularly armored cars)—not to mention more effective, long-range artillery and machine guns—vastly restricted what the cavalry might still accomplish, at least on the Western Front. By contrast, on the Eastern Front from Courland and East Prussia to Rumania, horsemen still enjoyed a considerable prestige and found themselves usefully employed both tactically and operationally.

Nevertheless, not even the events of 1914–1918 completely removed cavalry and horse-powered transport from European armies. We are particularly concerned with the fact that this remained so in Germany. Throughout the 1920s and 1930s, the *Reichsheer* of the Weimar years and, later, the *Heer* still conceived of important tactical and operational roles for the horse, both in combat and in logistics. Both organizations would plan accordingly, notwithstanding a great deal of propaganda to the contrary. Consequently, when Hitler's government willfully plunged Europe into the greatest war in its history, the German Army still possessed hundreds of thousands of horses in its establishment and not just for pulling supply-wagons, field-kitchens, artillery, and ambulances. German cavalry also went to war in 1939, not as a mere horse-mounted anachronism but as a matter of some necessity. As will be shown, that necessity would only grow before 1945.

One might well argue that that reliance on horses by the *Reichsheer* and the Nazi-era *Heer* was misplaced. Germany's military leaders, so the argument would run, ought to have done otherwise. Such an objection is fair enough in the abstract. In this matter, however, as in all historical inquiry, the primary question—as formulated by a noted authority in German military history—should not necessarily address what the German army *ought* to have done regarding the cavalry's employment. Rather, the question should account for *why* the German army did what it did. Why still use horse-mounted troops after 1918? Why after 1925, when motorization was becoming a reality? Why after 1935, when the first panzer divisions were being raised? Why, ultimately, even in 1945, when literally thousands of horse-soldiers still found themselves in action? This work constitutes the beginning of an attempt to answer these questions.

Of course, cavalrymen were only as good as their horses, and this treatment of the German cavalry therefore also touches upon one of the great and enduring bonds in the human experience: that between the horseman and his mount.[32] Having moved steadily away from regular, close contact with large animals since the middle of the twentieth century—except among a continuously dwindling number of farmers or perhaps from the safe side of a zoo's enclosures—Western society has become largely ignorant of the profound interaction between horses and humans. Notwithstanding the undoubted commercial successes of recent occasional books, plays, and feature films (the British National Theatre's 2009 triumph *War Horse* and the U.S. films *Seabiscuit* and *Secretariat* come most immediately to mind), horses since 1945 have become the perceived preserve of a "horsey set" of racing owners and/or breeders, huntsmen, or the simply rich. This perception remains current despite the fact that in the United States alone the equine population stood at well over five million at the beginning of the twenty-first century. In the United Kingdom the figure totaled perhaps one million at the same date, though it remains somewhat unclear whether that number resulted from recent natural accretion or severe undercounting in earlier surveys. Given such numbers, particularly in the United States, and based upon the author's own experience, it seems clear that very substantial numbers of horses certainly do not live a life of luxury in racing stables and hunt clubs, nor do they live quite so far apart from their human companions as one might think. Nevertheless, actual contact between those huge numbers of horses and the larger human population in whose midst they live remains minimal for human society as a whole.

Of all the ties binding humans and horses, surely the most poignant and nearly the oldest is the one existing between the military horse and the mounted warrior. If not quite as ancient as warfare itself, this bond is nearly so. But war remains, and has always been, a hard business. Physical destruction abounds. Men, women, children—and animals—die. Of course, no moral equivalence between the death of a horse and that of a man, woman, or child is intended. The assertion of any such equivalence would be grotesque. Nevertheless, the deaths of horses can be piteous. They know real fear. They feel real pain. They seem to suffer real loss. Their size and their very nearness to their riders make their suffering all too palpable, all too visceral, when they are seriously or mortally injured. That nonquantifiable but vivid characteristic called "heart," the inner quality possessed by so many horses that drives them on even at the risk of injury or death, can show itself most heroically when they die. Horses worn out by their lives' exertions can be utterly composed and evidently ready when they go to their graves. The author has seen this firsthand. Those not yet ready to die can fight for life and very often do. The author has seen this as well. Cavalry horses' training could itself sometimes be brutal, but so was the task to which they were set by their human masters. The numerous instances of those same horses' noble behavior in combat (other words simply do not fit) nevertheless attest to a quality far beyond simple, enforced obedience. Just as many of their riders did, just as many soldiers have always done, such horses often showed their most profound dignity when their own lives hung in the balance. Is this mere cavalry romanticism, mere horseman's anthropomorphism? Perhaps it is. Certainly many cavalrymen viewed their mounts merely as equipment to be discarded without further ado when injured or to be replaced without a second thought when killed.[33] Others evidently felt differently. If not, why have war horses, so far as we can reckon, always had individual names from the earliest times down to the vast mounted forces of the late nineteenth and early twentieth century? Beginning in the Napoleonic period, most cavalrymen were literate.

Consequently, it was "the first period where the personal relationship between the military horse and the soldier was recorded"[34] in substantial numbers of accounts. The relationship could prove, and was shown to be, as intense as any between humans. Those accounts also provide the first substantive indication of a tale quite likely as old as the military horse itself, a tale of a very special bond forged in the crucible of war, a tale of fierce joy in life and unbearable heartache in death.

CHAPTER 2

The Legacy of 1870

Prior to the dawn of mechanized warfare in the early twentieth century, and indeed for several decades thereafter, no element of the Western world's armies so evoked the exotic and romantic aspects of war as the cavalry. For centuries the cavalryman's kettle-drums and bugles were the sine qua non of martial music. For pageantry, nothing could surpass the panoply of the cavalryman: the sheer mass of his horse, his flowing regimental standards, snapping guidons, jingling tack, polished leather, and flashing steel.[1] But it was not all mere show. Cavalry still evoked real fear. The shock value—and therefore the fear—of a massed cavalry attack was as old as the weapon itself and still persisted in the late nineteenth century. As he had for centuries, the mounted warrior still appeared to be forever "uncatchable, inescapable, unapproachable."[2] Long before the defeat of the foot-slogging Anglo-Saxons by the Norman horsemen at Hastings in AD 1066 and the great flowering of the Age of Chivalry, so fearsome were the mounted charge and its practitioners that they transformed not only European warfare but even European culture itself, as seen as early as the ninth-century Saxon Gospel, *The Heliand*.[3] Indeed, historian H. R. Trevor-Roper, among others, placed the horseman at the epicenter of a fundamental societal change in the chivalric ideal; and no less a military historian than John Keegan speaks of a "cavalry revolution," one in which massed horsemen literally reinvented warfare as a "thing in itself," a means not merely to dominate one's enemy but to annihilate him. War could now become, though it was not always in fact, a product of "militarism."[4]

Perhaps the last great hurrah for this view of the cavalry was the Franco-Prussian War. Though all of the major European armies would still possess huge cavalry forces in World War I, and though the German army, for one, was still fielding new cavalry forces as late as 1943–1944, the last significant and sustained cavalry-versus-cavalry operations occurred in 1870–1871. The romance of the cavalry had yet to be blown away by the full mechanization of European warfare. Feats of the nineteenth-century mounted arm—indeed all arms—could still be celebrated in verse, prose, and song: Tennyson and, later, Kipling come first to mind for English-speakers. More germane, however, was the fact in the aftermath of 1870, German lights such as Theodore Fontane, Richard Wagner, and Johannes Brahms celebrated the Reich's victory over France in moving words and music. The "gigantic historical canvases" of painter Anton von Werner depicting German commanders on the field at Sedan or the proclamation of the German Empire at Versailles could still effectively disguise the battlefield's carnage at Spicheren and Wörth, Metz and Mars-la-Tour.[5] Socially, sartorially, psychologically, European cavalry remained wedded to this military romanticism in spite of the rapidly changing technological world surrounding it.

Curiously, even earlier manifestations of the cavalry's attempted adaptation to technology in the early-modern period, whether in the form of so-called horse-pistols, carbines, or even horse-artillery and the resultant designations of light cavalrymen as hussars, dragoons, uhlans, or chausseurs, did not succeed in permanently or completely divorcing the cavalry from the idea that cold steel remained the ultimate weapon. Very frequently, light-cavalry formations, such as those mentioned above, evolved into versions of their heavy-cavalry rivals—the cuirassiers in France and the *Reiter* regiments in Prussia—and became possessed of the same dictum, namely that the "consummation of the cavalryman's purpose in life [remained] the charge *en masse*."[6] Notwithstanding the hussar's braid-encrusted pelisse and rakish busby—a uniform that gave Prince Friedrich Karl von Hohenzollern (commander of the Prussian

Second Army in 1870) the nickname "The Red Prince" because he wore it all the time—light cavalry also tended to aspire to the social status and panache of the heavy cavalry regiments, especially that of the armor-plated cuirassiers, a status that remained attractive to even the upper-most crust of European society, particularly on the Continent. Even Otto von Bismarck, Prussian and, later, imperial chancellor, held a major's commission in the 1st Heavy Reserve *Reiter* Regiment and often wore its uniform, much to the serious annoyance of many professional officers around him, one of whom commented "acidly" that wearing a cuirassier's greatcoat was no particular aid to military understanding.[7] And perhaps no mounted regiment in Europe surpassed the splendor of French emperor Napoleon III's "Hundred Guards" cuirassiers, though their flamboyant uniform was not atypical with its mirror-finish steel cuirass and helmet, the latter with gilded crest; two helmet-plumes (white horsehair and red feathers); a sky-blue tunic trimmed with red collar, cuffs, and lapels; gold epaulettes; white trousers; black top-boots; and white gloves.[8]

Fancy or not, the cavalry faced an uncertain future at mid-century. In Prussia and elsewhere after 1850, the cavalry's role in modern armies was being re-examined. Following the victorious war against Austria in 1866, Prussia's leading commander, Helmuth von Moltke the Elder, did something rather unusual for victorious commanders: he analyzed what he and the Prussian army had done wrong. Insofar as the cavalry was concerned, several items were of note. On 27 June 1866 at Langensalza on the River Unstrut in Thuringia, the cavalry of the Hanoverian army (allied with Austria) had just managed to break Prussian infantry squares, suffering severe casualties in the process. This outcome seemed to confirm the cavalry's traditional role as battle-winning shock troops. But in the very next month, on 3 July at Königgrätz, the Prussian cavalry found itself incapable not only of providing effective reconnaissance in the days before the battle but also of effective pursuit of the defeated Austrians afterwards. When Moltke subsequently critiqued his and his armies' performance in a "sensitive memorandum" to the Prussian king in 1868, he gave vent to his views of what the Prussian (and eventually the German) cavalry's future role should be.[9] He stressed that the cavalry could and should still work in tactical concert with artillery and infantry as had the

Hanoverians at Langensalza and the Prussians at Königgrätz. Nevertheless, the cavalry should no longer be held back primarily in order to deliver a massed charge at a decisive moment that might never come. While not entirely discounting the latter possibility, he wrote that cavalry should instead be used more extensively for screening, reconnaissance, and security. All these were missions for which horsemen remained uniquely suited. Precisely two years later, in July 1870, Moltke's conclusions were tested in the Franco-Prussian War.

Despite Moltke's admonitions, one roughly contemporaneous observer of the events of 1870–1871 wrote that German cavalry didn't develop effective reconnaissance and screening capabilities until well after the war against France had begun; thus it did not emulate examples such as that set by the U.S. Army's General John Buford during the Gettysburg campaign in the Civil War.[10] The same author criticized the "stubbornness" and the "ill-informed" attitudes of the Europeans in their refusal to learn what he considered the proper lessons from the Civil War.[11] Unlike their European counterparts for whom the cavalry's specialization by type was still at least nominally in effect in 1870, American cavalrymen had long ceased to be functionally divided into "heavy cavalry" (for battle-winning massed attacks delivered with the *arme blanche*), "light cavalry" (for screening, reconnaissance, and messenger-service), and "dragoons" (essentially well-mounted infantry). Instead, "the traditional [American] cavalryman has ever been the light dragoon—a soldier trained and equipped to fight mounted or dismounted, to perform screening and reconnaissance, and to act as a scout or messenger. True heavy and true light horse have been rare."[12] Thus the cavalry of the American Civil War, whether Union or Confederate, did the bulk of its fighting on its feet. It broke no fundamental tradition in adapting to increasingly effective firepower. Though saber swinging melees did occur, as at Brandy Station, Virginia, in June 1863, most cavalry action during the Civil War was on foot, the horse serving as much as a means of transport as of attack. Evidently the American cavalryman did not feel morally obligated, as one author put it, to die on horseback, whereas his European counterpart still did in 1870.[13]

Whatever difficulties they had in executing Moltke's vision, the German cavalry of 1870 tended to exhibit much better understanding of their newly important role than did the French. At the beginning of the war, for example, the French cavalry was still guided by the regulations of 1829, the arm having "learnt nothing" in the meantime regarding more modern operations and tactics, according to one contemporaneous observer.[14] Implicitly, this would mean that nothing was learned from the Crimea, the American Civil War, or even the much more recent Austro-Prussian War. Still, says this same observer, the French cavalry was conscious of its "past bravery and patriotism." The absence of effective lessons learned was exacerbated by the fact that when the war began, the French cavalry "had no reserves of horses" and an "[unspecified but evidently large] portion of the effective strength were four-year old remounts."[15]

By contrast, Prussian and other German cavalry—almost always referred to by the French as uhlans whether the cavalry in question were actually lancers or not—consistently demonstrated an ability to reconnoiter more effectively than their French counterparts, even while stubbornly insisting on the ideal of the massed attack. As early as the frontier battle at Wissembourg on the borders of the Palatinate on 4 August 1870 and the roughly coincidental battle at Spicheren near Saarbrücken some forty miles to the northwest on 6 August, the French cavalry utterly failed to determine the scope of the threat facing Napoleon III's armies. In part this was owing to the extraordinary directive of the French marshal Achille Bazaine dated 20 July wherein he stated that "our reconnaissance should not be aggressive." Unfortunately for Bazaine, cavalry still constituted the sole reliable means of gathering information about an enemy's dispositions beyond the line of sight. His directive, therefore, amounted to gouging out his own eyes during the critical phase of the armies' concentration for battle. As it was, the French cavalry remained almost "completely inactive"[16] throughout the period up to and including the Battle of Sedan as regards operational reconnaissance, even if at a tactical level French mounted forces were sometimes capable of effective action. Further, since French cavalry when it did patrol was "not accustomed to patrol far to the front," French commanders typically assumed that German cavalry patrols were followed by much larger forces immediately to the rear even when this was not the case. This misapprehension helps explain French timidity when confronted with the constant presence of far-ranging German mounted units.[17] And while perhaps the case could be made that cavalry proved to be of little practical value in the steep defiles around Spicheren, the same could not be said of the fighting at Wissembourg and the follow-on battles at Froe-schwiller, Wörth, and Morsbronn. There the French desperately tried to retrieve their infantry's fortunes through a sacrificial massed attack by General Michel's and General Bonnemain's reserve cavalry, including a full division of cuirassiers.

At Froeschwiller and Wörth, the French 2nd Cavalry Division's 1st and 4th Cuirassiers of the *Brigade Girard* charged Badenese and Würt-temberger infantry over ground broken up by palisaded hop-fields and vineyards. As the horsemen were funneled by these obstructions into the intervals between the fields, the 4th Cuirassiers had to ride over two-thirds of a mile under sustained rifle-fire. Both regiments suffered heavy losses "without having effected anything." The division's 2nd and 3rd Cuirassiers of the *Brigade Brauer* attacked over similar terrain made even worse by an "absolutely insurmountable" barricaded ditch. The 2nd Cuirassiers alone lost their colonel and 5 officers killed; more than 130 officers and men wounded; and some 250 horses killed outright or dying subsequently of their wounds. Throughout the attacks, the German infantry was "always out of reach and often out of sight" of the French horsemen.[18]

In the view of recent scholarship of the Franco-Prussian War, the German infantry's standing up to charging cavalry was still a radically new way for infantrymen to fight horsemen, dating back perhaps to Waterloo. Traditionally, infantrymen not formed in squares would tend to throw themselves to the ground to avoid blows from sabers and to make the horses shy away, presuming that the foot soldiers weren't already running for their lives. Now, however, they "simply stood in lines and blazed away."[19] The results of such tactics for the French horsemen repeated themselves elsewhere that day. At the other end of the French line on the far right, for example, the 8th and 9th Cuirassiers of the 1st Cavalry Division's *Brigade Michel* attacked German infantry in the village of Morsbronn. As earlier on the left, French troopers again charged through the intervals between hop-fields and vineyards and took heavy rifle-fire as they passed. The 8th Cuirassiers lost two-thirds of their horses

before the cavalrymen even reached the village. Of the 9th Cuirassiers—
and the supporting 6th Lancers of the division's *Brigade Nansouty*—
almost all troopers not killed before they gained the village were subsequently shot down and killed or captured along the village's main street
as the horsemen rode headlong into a blockaded dead-end. Afterward,
dead horses and men lay so thickly in the street that passage along it was
literally impossible. Witnesses and subsequent observers reported that
the German bullets had "rattled like hail" against the cuirassiers' steel
breastplates and created "a strange music" in the process.[20] The preponderance of unarmored lancers among the French dead at Morsbronn,
compared to steel-plated cuirassiers, led at least one historian of the battle to conclude, erroneously, that the breast plate would therefore always
be a part of the cavalryman's equipment.[21] Be that as it may, German
riflemen had emptied hundreds of saddles and killed and wounded hundreds of men and horses. The French horsemen, for their part, had
merely bought a bit of time for their infantry's retreat.

As disastrous as these attacks had been, the French cavalry's failure in
reconnaissance had been equally faulty. As at Spicheren, so too at Froeschwiller the French suffered "a disastrous failure . . . to appreciate the
strength and intentions of the Germans." Indeed the day before the
Bavarians attacked at Wissembourg (3 August), the local French commander, General Ducrot, reported that the Bavarians' threat was a "simple bluff."[22] Only effective employment of the French cavalry in reconnaissance could have provided timely intelligence of unimpeachable
character. By dramatic contrast, orders issuing from the Prussian Royal
Headquarters, as well as from those of Prince Frederick Charles' Second
Army, often directed the cavalry specifically to "be pushed forward *as far
as possible.*"[23] Of course, not all orders were executed as given, and war's
inevitable friction affected the reliability of the information passed back
up the chain of command. Nevertheless, in the war's crucial opening
phase, German cavalry operated consistently more effectively and widely
than the French in the critical job of providing intelligence and fixing the
enemy in place so that German infantry could be brought to bear.

In the aftermath of the fighting at Spicheren and Froeschwiller/
Wörth, and with the French armies in retreat across the board, the Germany cavalry—despite occasionally losing contact with the enemy—

nevertheless showed itself willing and able to act boldly and range widely. In these instances, its behavior sometimes appears reminiscent of the "rides" of American Civil War generals Jeb Stuart, John Hunt Morgan, Nathan Bedford Forrest, Alfred Pleasanton, and Benjamin Grierson. Perhaps the most striking example, though still somewhat paltry when compared to the distances and consequences involved in that earlier conflict, was the German advance to the Moselle between 6 and 14 August 1870. German horsemen thrust in behind the French Army of the Rhine as it fell back on the fortress of Metz, cutting the telegraph connecting Paris and the depot at Nancy.[24] The German riders thereby made cooperation with French forces still at Belfort all the more difficult. In some cases, German cavalry patrols forged as far as forty miles ahead of advancing main columns. On 12 August German cavalry reached the Moselle below Metz at Pont-a-Mousson and, farther south, at Frouard. In both places they crossed the river and again not only cut the telegraph but also the rail lines linking Metz with Nancy and, by extension, Chalons-sur-Marne where the French Government had ordered the formation of a reserve army. In point of fact, most of the German cavalrymen at Pont-a-Mousson were actually captured before they could complete their work of destruction. Nevertheless, they scored psychological victories as dramatic as in the war's opening days when, on 26 July, the young Count Zeppelin and his mounted patrol had been captured while having lunch at the Shirlenhof Inn eight miles behind French lines at Niederbronn, or when Prussian uhlans blew up a French railroad viaduct near Saargemünd on 23–24 July. These examples were now being replicated up and down the line not only at Frouard and Pont-a-Mousson but also by the German cavalrymen who rode brazenly to the very walls of the fortress of Thionville, the gates being shut virtually in their faces, or who openly scouted within one-half mile of the main French camp at Metz. For their part, the French commanders in the latter city appeared to have failed utterly to use their available cavalry for anything like effective reconnaissance. On the contrary, they limited their efforts to placing staff officers as observers in the cathedral's belfry.[25] At a so-called council of war on 10 October, at least one corps commander recognized that the cavalry remaining in the city was "incapable of service," evidently through prior mismanagement and the consequent collapse of morale.[26]

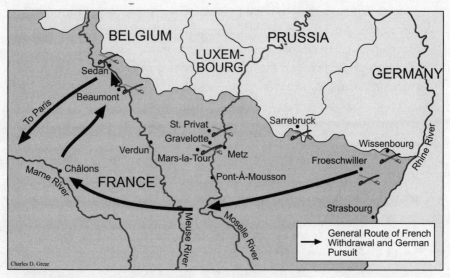

Map 1. The Franco-Prussian War, August–September 1870

Presaging 1914, or even 1940, relatively small numbers of wide-ranging German uhlans and hussars created an effect "out of all proportion to their strength and achievements." It was enough to create that terrifying picture of "'the Uhlans' [sic], ruthless, swift, and ubiquitous, which was to frighten the children of France and Europe for forty years to come."[27] Such operational success for the German cavalry most dramatically manifested itself soon thereafter with the stopping of the French withdrawal westward from Metz.

In this case the 5th and 6th Cavalry Divisions received orders to scout ahead to the Metz-Verdun road to try to determine the French army's line of retreat. On 14–15 August German mounted units encountered French cavalry and other forces headed westward along the road in the vicinity of Mars-la-Tour and Vionville. The German cavalrymen took the French under fire with horse-artillery and stopped the column in its tracks. Other German formations advanced to the sound of the guns. For their part, the French failed to push their way through what still amounted to a cavalry screen in order to keep open their line of retreat. The result was the halting of the entire French movement along the line of Mars-la-Tour–Vionville–Rezonville–Gravelotte–Metz. Here the German cavalry, materially assisted by French hesitation, played the critical function of finding and fixing the enemy while the German infantry came up to try to cut off the French withdrawal.[28] The German horsemen thus played precisely the roles assigned them by Moltke in his report to the Prussian king in 1868.

Of all the fighting along the road linking Metz and Verdun, certainly the emotional high point for German mounted troops was the so-called Death Ride at Mars-la-Tour of the 12th Cavalry Brigade under General Friedrich Wilhelm von Bredow. In this attack the 1st, 2nd, and 4th Squadrons of the 7th Cuirassiers and the 2nd, 3rd, and 4th Squadrons of the 16th Uhlans charged en masse against prepared French infantry and artillery in order to gain time for faltering German troops and guns to regroup. Taking advantage of swales to approach within several hundred yards of the French positions, the German cavalry burst from the gun-smoke obscuring the battlefield and "flashed by" endangered Hanoverian artillery batteries at the critical moment. Somewhat atypically, the attack was launched straight from the gallop with no preliminary trot to the canter. As the charge got under way, four attached Prussian horse-artillery batteries fired obliquely across the right front of the horsemen. This gunfire, "right before their [the horses'] feet," according to one student of the event, helped pave the way for a successful attack and fit perfectly with Prussian artillery doctrine in 1870 by covering the cavalry's deployment and preparing its attack by direct fire upon the enemy. Charging over a distance of some 1,500 yards (1,300 m), the Prussian cuirassiers and uhlans crashed headlong into the French gun-line, cut down at least two French artillery batteries' gunners, destroyed a mitrailleuse battery, and smashed two squares of French infantry. Unfortunately, the Germans' formations broke up as they went forward, a perennial problem for any massed cavalry attack at that or any other time. They then found themselves counterattacked in turn by French horsemen outnumbering them by a factor of about five. In the fighting that followed, described as "frenzied" and a "tornado" of violence in which all arms of both sides became completely intermingled and heedless of trumpeted commands, the Germans nevertheless managed to extricate themselves and retreat to the safety of their own infantry and covering artillery. In a similar fashion later that same day, but in an event much less well known, the Prussian 1st Guard Dragoons attacked French infantry advancing on and threatening the Prussian left flank's 38th Infantry Brigade on the heights northeast of Mars-la-Tour. Once again, the charge went in under rifle- and mitrailleuse-fire so as to allow the German infantry to disengage. The dragoons rode headlong into the advancing French infantry and accomplished the mission, but with 5 officers, an ensign, 42 men, and 204 horses dead. Six officers, 2 ensigns, 76 men, and 42 horses were wounded. Five troopers went missing. This constituted about 30 percent of the regiment's effective strength. In the case of Bredow's brigade, the losses were more than 50 percent (420 killed and wounded of 800 engaged). They would presumably have been higher still had not the badly rattled French infantry shot down more than 150 of their own counterattacking cuirassiers in the space of a few minutes' confusion. Though described as not merely a "rarity" but as perhaps the "last successful cavalry charge in Western European warfare," Bredow's attack had allowed the German infantry time and space to rally. That, in turn, kept the French from continuing their retreat to the west. The same could be said of the Guard Dragoons. Notwithstanding these terrible losses, losses soon to be far surpassed by French horsemen at Sedan, the German troopers' success buttressed arguments favoring the cavalry's continued utility for the next forty years.[29]

Despite the German cavalry's accomplishments following the war's outbreak and their frightful success at Mars-la-Tour, lessons were being learned regarding cavalry's future role. One of the most important of these lessons appeared to be that "the rifle bullet and the spade [had] made the defensive the stronger form of warfare,"[30] at least temporarily. Consequently, and as witnessed by Moltke's earlier memorandum of 1868, the classic cavalry charge against infantry was fast becoming a thing of the past. In the war of 1870, for example, the French *chassepot* rifle had a maximum range of about 1,300 yards (1,200 m),[31] while the German Dreyse "needle gun's" maximum range was about 650 yards (600 m). And while in both cases the maximum effective range would be much less, they remained a deadly threat to mounted troops. But even certain cavalry units such as dragoons now carried rifled weapons of their own. The Prussian light cavalry, for example, carried a shortened carbine-variant of Dreyse's rifle.[32] The rapid and increasingly widespread issuing of rifled weapons to both foot soldiers and cavalrymen since about 1850, when combined with the means to deliver unprecedentedly large numbers of men to the front via railroads, constituted an important change in European military affairs. What had not yet happened was a real opportunity to test the effects of this change on European battlefields. True, it may be argued that the elder Moltke's initial deployment of Prussia's armies by rail in the invasion of Saxony and Bohemia in 1866 served to show the European importance of at least one of these new technologies and on an almost American scale of distance.[33] Further, insofar as cavalry still formed an integral portion of Prussia's armies, Moltke made provision that rail cars have tether rings and removable partitions built into them so that horses and artillery of all types could be more easily transported.[34] To the extent, however, that the Prussian campaigns of 1866 and 1870 depended at least in their initial stages on deployment by rail with a view to long-distance maneuvering for a decisive *Kesselschlacht*,[35] one would have thought that the cavalry's importance would have increased and not decreased. That is, while armies deployed to their frontiers by rail, they typically marched thereafter. Only later, as the enemy's railroads were commandeered, would they be expected to bring up reserves and supplies using the iron horse.

As late as 1866 the need for more effective cavalry employment was exacerbated by the fact that Prussian mounted formations were still often placed at the end of marching columns instead of being allowed to range far ahead. Indeed at Königgrätz, the Prussian cavalry still followed behind the infantry. The horsemen did not truly bring their great numbers to bear in the fighting and did not effectively pursue the broken Austrian Army at the end of the day (in part because of late charges by the latter's heavy cavalry as they attempted to buy time for an Austrian withdrawal).[36] Once again, Moltke's report of 1868 noted such deficiencies. The war of 1870 changed all that and witnessed the combination of rail-deployment and massive cavalry operations, even though the latter sometimes had only disastrous tactical results.[37]

Consequently, German and European cavalry in 1870 was not typically used in one of its most potentially important operational spheres, namely the regular, long-range interdiction of the enemy's railways as had so often been the case during the American Civil War. In retrospect, employing cavalry for this purpose should have been self-evident given the railroads' own significance. "If railway lines were intact, the trains smoothly organized [this itself being an important prerequisite], and supply from the railhead unhampered, armies could keep the field so long as there was blood and treasure in the nation to support them."[38] Interdiction of such lines of communication and supply could have played a critical role in making the eventual German victory even more devastating to France than it turned out to be. Using cavalry for this purpose provided "the chance of disorganizing by invasion or *deep raids* [emphasis added] the mobilization of" the enemy, thus "reducing his plans to chaos, and leaving him defenceless."[39] At least one prominent American military observer in 1870, General Philip Sheridan, saw the German cavalry in action and noted the absence of such efforts. In his view, the German cavalry performed well the traditional roles of covering the front and flanks of advancing armies; and he did not fault the bravery of either the German or French troopers in the massed attack. Nevertheless, he observed, German horsemen never had the far-ranging effect their numbers should have allowed. Had the cavalry "been massed and maneuvered independently of the infantry, it could easily have broken up the French communications, and done much other work of weighty influence in the prosecution of the war."[40]

Whatever shortcomings the German cavalry may have had in Sheridan's estimation, it was nevertheless coming to grips with a salient feature of military operations in the second half of the century. Rapid technological change associated with breech-loading rifles, nascent automatic weapons, rifled artillery, and railways necessitated more effective combined-arms thinking. Defensive positions, otherwise strong and massing the defenders' long-range rifle-fire, might still be overcome by determined opponents using the combined-arms assault of infantry, cavalry, and artillery. Conversely, anything less than attack by combined arms ran the very real risk by 1870, if not by 1860, of decimation by the same massed rifle-fire.[41] Interestingly enough, at Mars-la-Tour Bredow's troopers closed successfully with the French gunners and infantry, in part, precisely because the Prussian horse-artillery fired diagonally across the front of the charging horsemen. This particular tactical doctrine still prevailed in 1914, even though an eventually stalemated Western Front had not yet been foreseen.[42]

The German cavalry of 1870 also continued a tactical employment of horsemen and horse-artillery dating back to Napoleon I. The French emperor had pioneered the combination of artillery (to weaken an enemy's infantry formations) with massed cavalry and infantry assault (to shatter them). Given the technology of the Napoleonic era, trotting horsemen covering some six hundred paces every two minutes (approximately 250 yards/228 meters per minute) could close with the typical artillery piece of the day (firing to a range of eight hundred to nine hundred paces) before the gun could fire more than one or two rounds. Of course, at the canter or gallop the distance closed much more quickly, and many charges covered the final 150 yards or so (137 m) at the latter gait provided that horses were fresh. Therefore, charging cavalry "did not suffer over-much from enemy cannon fire," an observation excepting those unfortunate men and horses who were actually blown apart or eviscerated by canister or round shot.[43] The employment of massed cavalry in corps formation at the decisive moment to defend one's own position or to attack the enemy's also dates to Napoleon. He'd established "the corps . . . as the largest organizational form for cavalry units."[44] But given the substantially increased range, hitting-power, and rate-of-fire of rifles and artillery by 1870, horsemen charging a prepared infantry formation became much more vulnerable. Indeed, cavalrymen began to experience this painful realization as early as Waterloo, despite the estimated maximum of only 5-percent accuracy for unrifled musketry fire beyond ten yards' range.[45] Unfortunately, the deadlier weapons of 1870 greatly increased the cavalryman's exposure. Assuming the height of a heavy cavalry horse to be sixteen hands or nearly five-and-a-half feet ("hands" being four-inch increments measured from the forefeet to the point of withers with the horse standing square on a flat surface), the rider's head rose to a height of not quite three yards (2.75 m) above the ground. Notwithstanding his helmet and/or cuirass, he was now extremely vulnerable at unprecedentedly long ranges; and this does not even take into account the horse itself. As a target for riflemen or artillerists, the horse possessed the terribly unfortunate combination of a thin skin and a high silhouette even when galloping for brief moments at perhaps thirty miles per hour (48 km/h).

Despite these critical vulnerabilities, cavalrymen—at least at a campaign's beginning when their horses were not yet debilitated—could cover up to 50 miles (80 km) per day when riding hard. Even 80 to 100 miles (up to 160 km) in a twenty-four-hour period were not unheard-of for well-mounted light cavalry. All the while, the horse bore an average load approaching 250 pounds (113 kg). Furthermore, given its ability to swim, not even the tactical obstacles of streams and middling rivers necessarily stood in the cavalry's way, even though rivers such as the Moselle above and below Metz demanded ferries or bridges in order for the cavalry to cross. Therefore, in a premotorized age, and indeed even later, a realistic alternative to horse-mounted units on the European battlefield simply did not exist. Scouting, patrolling, covering the flanks and rear, protecting the withdrawal, raiding—all of these missions remained the tasks of both pure cavalry formations and the mounted units attached to Prussian infantry divisions. By 1866 even the latter included four squadrons of approximately seven hundred horsemen.[46]

Greatly aiding the German cavalry in 1870 was the detailed information they possessed on the French transportation infrastructure as the campaign began. German commanders were said to have had better maps of France than the French armies' own staffs.[47] German long-range cavalry reconnaissance and pursuit displayed persistence after the initial battles on the frontiers, even if it was not always completely effective. The French cavalry, on the other hand, were criticized by a contemporary not only for continued massing of formations when such mass was unnecessary but also for "never send[ing] out a single scout or vedette" in the long retreat westward from the Franco-German frontier. Such tactical ineffectiveness only worsened the logistical nightmares often accompanying French troops during their mobilization and initial deployments. At Metz on 1 August, for example, some two thousand wagons loaded with hay, straw, and oats clogged the city's streets with no other apparent destination in mind. Similarly, French cavalry at Metz had to be employed "day and night as laborers," using their mounts' saddlebags to transport matériel from stalled supply-trains to the city's depots.[48] Not until 23 July did Napoleon III demand the attention of his Minister of War, General Edmond Leboeuf, to the matter of the "establishment of a [national] requisition and remount service" in order to supplement or replace the French cavalry's extant system of regimental depot squadrons.[49] It seems incredible that such a matter wasn't undertaken *before* the French declaration of war, especially in light of the fact that such a service, among others, would normally "require months if not years of preparation."[50] By that date, the destruction of a goodly portion of the French cavalry at Wissembourg and Froeschwiller was barely two weeks off.

After all, it was not as though the French had no experience in long-range cavalry operations and the remount services necessary to support them. After Jena in 1806, for example, Napoleon I "unleashed his cavalry in a pursuit designed to complete the destruction of the enemy and the enemy state; a deep penetration to spread panic among the enemy population and destroy all hope of recovery."[51] Even so, he had seen in his cavalry not only "an exploitation force or reconnaissance asset" but also a "true shock force that could have effects disproportional to its numerical size" as at Eylau in 1807.[52] If the latter were true, if the massed attack were still to be the French cavalry's main reason for being, then massing them in the rear and holding them in place until the critical moment, though frequently condemned, would be a logical tactical disposition. In fact, the French cavalry had done as much even earlier, as before the revolutionary wars of the 1790s,[53] and one could argue that the idea in fact came from the example of the armies of Frederick the Great at Rossbach in 1757 and Zorndorf in 1758. Unfortunately, between 1807 and 1870, French commanders had apparently forgotten the former examples and remembered only the latter ones. As a matter of common sense, for French commanders—and implicitly for German ones—holding the cavalry in reserve until the decisive moment always brought with it the danger of having the mounted forces sitting useless altogether or being committed too late to make a difference. And despite the greatly increased firepower on the part of the infantry, dismounted combat for the European cavalry was still considered the exception. In any case it could only be undertaken by horsemen armed with the cavalry carbine such as dragoons and hussars in Prussia or *chevaulegers* in Bavaria. In the event, French dragoons in 1870 often dismounted to volley-fire their carbines on advancing German cavalry. Evidently, however, these defensive tactics were insufficiently tenacious and the dragoons' marksmanship was insufficiently accurate.[54] Consequently, except for this sort of occurrence, only the German cavalry in 1870 managed to be not only consistently wide-ranging in reconnaissance and screening but also able to deliver massed attacks when called upon to do so.

The cavalry's role as envisioned by Moltke in 1868 was certainly not limited to him alone. Cavalry's employment had been studied with renewed interest by Prussian cavalry officers and theorists from about 1863 onward. That does not mean, however, that there existed uniformity of view among them. Colonel Albrecht von Stosch, an officer of the Prussian General Staff who fought in 1866 and 1870 and eventually (and somewhat curiously) became Chief of the Admiralty, wrote that American cavalry in the Civil War had been essentially mounted infantry. Their reliance more on firepower than cold steel for battlefield effectiveness ran counter, he said, to the cavalry's putatively true value as a shock force, a "typically conventional" European view.[55] Other Prussian officers, however, noted in their work that the American use of cavalry as long-range interdiction forces against strategic lines of telegraphic and railroad communications constituted what later generations would call a wave of the future.[56] Nevertheless, and "almost without exception," Prussian students of the cavalry still maintained in 1866 and 1870 that the mounted arm's first duty was to stay mounted, avoid dismounted combat unless absolutely necessary, and attack with cold steel. The prevailing view remained that dismounted cavalry's role in the American Civil War arose from the uneven and overgrown nature of North American battlefields, not from significant changes in firearms' evolution. The dismounted role, it was felt, did not apply in Europe. Nor was the strategic raid viewed as of great military value. As late as 1900, therefore, the German cavalry—like other mounted forces in Europe—would still count the sword and the lance among its principal weapons,[57] and apart from the reconnaissance and screening missions so much emphasized by Moltke, German horsemen would generally be held in reserve for the breakthrough battle that, at least on World War I's Western Front, never came. Therefore, despite Moltke's admonitions and their own successes up to the Battle of Sedan, German cavalry officers preferred to "trust to their own experience" and a recollection of the smashing successes of Frederick the Great.[58] Fundamentally altering the role of the cavalry to follow any other model, particularly an American one, was still alien to German and the larger European traditions in 1870. Both German and

French cavalry officers remained "fatally fascinated" by the shock-effect of massed formations of horsemen.[59]

Of the two nations' mounted arms, it is ironic that the French did not more readily adopt another cavalry doctrine, particularly one emphasizing more long-range patrolling. After all, French cavalrymen had been active throughout the 1830s and 1840s in Algeria, where they had responded to the guerrilla war against French colonial rule with the creation of light, wide-ranging mounted units. These included the Ottoman-inspired light cavalry known by their Turkish designation as *sipahis* and the so-called *Chassuers d'Afrique*. Eventually, three regiments of the latter were also posted to Mexico in the 1860s to bolster the short-lived regime of the French-supported Habsburg emperor Maximilian. Among the noteworthy features of these particular units was the adoption of the Iberian-influenced Barb as the mount of choice, incomparable in its ability to thrive in the arid environments of both North Africa and the high plains and mountains of central and northern Mexico. These were the "little grey Arab horses" whose dead bodies, along with those of their riders, would soon carpet the hillsides above Sedan.[60]

It was toward that city that the German armies marched in the wake of the French defeat at Mars-la-Tour and the following battle at Gravelotte-St.-Privat. In advancing generally west-northwest, the Germans aimed to disrupt the French Government's attempt to raise a relief force for Marshal Bazaine's army now trapped at Metz. This period witnessed the French relief armies' movement and their pursuit by the German from Chalons to Rheims to Sedan from 20 to 28 August. During these days, the German cavalry once again ranged far ahead of the advancing infantry, often by as much as forty or fifty miles (up to 80 km).[61] As they had after the battles on the frontier at the war's beginning, the German horsemen hounded the French and provided vital intelligence. Even so, the riders sometimes lost contact through no fault of their own; the French armies were subjected to what historian Michael Howard called "lunatic change[s] in direction" in their line of march as they tried to maintain contact with faulty supply lines. Once the German cavalry found their quarry, however, they helped delay and harass French forces sufficiently to deflect them ever farther northward toward the borders of Belgium and the fortress of Sedan. All the while the German infantry came up remorselessly from the east and southeast.[62]

At Sedan one sees perhaps the most pointless waste of cavalry in the whole of the war. This occurred in the attempt by the French horsemen, under the command of General Margueritte, to pierce the German lines above the village of Floing to allow for a French breakout to the west. Shot through the face while reconnoitering the German lines, Margueritte could not ride with his troopers. They nevertheless went in gallantly according to observers, including King William of Prussia who witnessed the charge from across the Meuse. As had happened several times since the war's beginning, the result was "a useless and terrible sacrifice . . . a fearful loss of life with no result whatever."[63] The two brigades of the cavalry reserve making the repeated charges not only didn't effect a breakout; "they did not delay the German infantry five minutes." With the exception of a number of German skirmishers cut down in the initial French charge, the German infantry simply waited and "mowed [the French horsemen] down with volleys." As at Morsbronn near Froeschwiller in the war's opening days, the French cavalry "were shot down before they could get within fifty yards. It was a useless, purposeless slaughter." The five regiments involved suffered some 350 men killed, not counting the wounded and those taken prisoner. One unit of two squadrons had only 58 survivors from the 216 who made the charges. The entire time that the French had been under fire was said to have been perhaps one-quarter of an hour.[64] Rallying twice, the French horsemen came on three times in total. By the third attempt, the cavalry horses were not so much charging as picking their way gingerly over the corpses of the fallen.[65]

Even for those managing to survive the destruction of Margueritte's cavalry, the losses suffered by French mounted and horse-drawn units at Sedan were terrible. At least ten thousand horses were captured in the French surrender. Of those, the Germans killed huge numbers deemed too broken down to keep. One Bavarian battalion alone killed three thousand after being ordered to destroy "any that looked sickly."[66] At distant Metz, too, horses of the French cavalry, artillery, and transport units found themselves not only hated for eating up scarce supplies of grain intended for the nearly starving garrison but slaughtered for food themselves. These units were ordered to cull forty horses each for slaughter, and by 20 September fifty percent of the garrison's cavalry mounts had been butchered.[67] Similar fates also befell large numbers of military horses in the French capital. Once the city was invested, the Parisian diet deteriorated largely to "scraps of bread, red wine, and horse meat."[68]

With the strangulating encirclement of Paris and the subsequent occupation of most of northern France after Sedan, the German cavalry's role became one very familiar to German horsemen in Russia seventy years later: anti-partisan duty. In late 1870 and early 1871, the partisans were the *francs-tireurs*. Sometimes actual guerrillas, sometimes remnants of former French army units, sometimes newly raised formations, the *francs-tireurs* often provided more effective intelligence to French commanders than had the French cavalry whose traditional role it was.[69] The *francs-tireurs* also harassed German patrols and attempted to sabotage the Germans' supply lines still stretching back to the Rhine. In this second phase of the war, German cavalry routinely undertook far-ranging patrols to the south and west of Paris in order to alert Moltke to the possibility of a French attempt to relieve the capital. Those same cavalry units carried out missions to extend the system of requisitions ever deeper into the French countryside to supplement their own armies' logistics. Ultimately, they were ordered to "sweep the country clean of *francs-tireurs*."[70]

In the process, the war assumed ever-deeper levels of brutality as a heavy winter arrived. The siege of Paris dragged on, and the French continued stubbornly to resist (even while eventually fighting among themselves during the Commune). Prussian chancellor Otto von Bismarck raged that all *francs-tireurs* should be summarily shot or hanged. Villages sheltering them, he said, should be burned to the ground. Indeed, reprisals against real or suspected partisans were savage, what one historian of the war called "a wholesale Americanization" of the conflict reminiscent of William T. Sherman's intention to make his Southern enemies in Georgia "howl" during the Civil War.[71] Fortunately for France, the German cavalrymen and their commanders couldn't or wouldn't fulfill all Bismarck's wishes.

In that winter of 1870, the German cavalry's own difficulties made punitive expeditions questionable if not actually impossible. Supplies and remounts became relatively scarce and roads often so badly covered in ice and snow that troopers had to lead their horses instead of riding them.[72] The horsemen were nevertheless forced to keep to the roads because the countryside was sometimes impassable with deep snow. To add insult to injury, German cavalry now also frequently had to be accompanied by infantry. Precisely because of the threat posed by the *francs-tireurs* in ambushes of slow-moving, road-bound mounted columns, German commanders had to ensure they had infantry support. Of course, tying the cavalry to the speed of the infantry deprived the horsemen of their principal advantage. The long-range capability of the cavalry disappeared "the moment it had to march under the protection of the infantry."[73] The German cavalry's war of movement became a sort of snail-paced war of attrition until the spring thaw arrived. And when the spring did come, so too did France's surrender. The Treaty of Frankfurt of May 1871 recognized not only the humbling of France but the arising of a new Great Power in Europe, a once and future German *Reich*.

* * *

At Froeschwiller, Wörth, Mars-la-Tour, and Sedan the massed cavalry charges of both the Germans and the French were not typically intended to shatter fixed infantry formations, though that could sometimes be a fortunate result, as in Bredow's "Death Ride." Rather, in all cases, massed cavalry attacks were launched to retrieve situations in which one's own infantry had been driven from the field or were threatened with that fate, as had also been the case with the Austrian cavalry charge late in the day at Königgrätz in 1866. The objective was to give the infantry sufficient time to retreat and/or re-form. The massed charge therefore became the means not so much to crown the victory as to stave off a defeat. Occasionally, of course, cavalry were ordered to attack under the false impression that the enemy was actually broken and could be pursued. The most egregious example of such a mistake shows in Prussian general Karl Friedrich von Steinmetz's ordering of a mounted attack against the French lines at Gravelotte through a ravine on a raised causeway already choked with the bodies and debris of earlier, failed Prussian infantry assaults. The predictable result was the "slaughter by the hundreds" of the units in question. A "dreadful" French rifle-, automatic-weapons-, and artillery fire hit the cavalry full in the face without the horsemen's "having the least chance of returning it."[74] Naturally, the fault in this case lay not with the cavalry itself but in Steinmetz's gross misjudgment of the tactical situation.

At the same time the cavalry's real worth re-emerged in missions that only horsemen could execute in the nineteenth century: long-range reconnaissance, flanking movements, and the interdiction of the enemy's rail lines and communications. German cavalry proved consistently more adept at these tasks than did the French. After Sedan, however, the German cavalry's operations against the *francs-tireurs*; the guarding of lines of supply and communication stretching back to the German States; and foraging for the occupation forces assumed precedence. And while these important missions could still be effectively executed by the Germans' mounted troops, these nevertheless found themselves increasingly tied to the infantry for protection against roving columns of French partisans. Thus the German cavalry ran the risk of losing their most significant operational assets—speed and mobility.

As effective as the German horsemen tended to be, one question remains: why did they not emulate the American example of the strategic "ride" so much in evidence in the Civil War? It turns out they did, after a fashion, and somewhat unintentionally. To the extent that German horsemen routinely rode far in advance of marching infantry columns, one sees a long-range, mounted reconnaissance capability similar to that seen in the Civil War. This capability is most evident in the form of wide-ranging German patrols, though not very large ones. They often occurred only in squadron-strength or less. One of the most striking examples of their success showed in their cutting the rail lines at Pont-a-Mousson south of Metz in the follow-up phase after the battles at Spicheren and Froeschwiller. At times in this particular pursuit, the German troopers rode as much as forty miles ahead of their infantry, a figure corresponding closely to the distances covered daily by John Hunt Morgan's cavalry in Kentucky in 1862. German cavalry played an even more important role in helping find and fix the French army in its attempted retreat from Metz to Verdun. The mounted units thus significantly contributed to setting the stage for—and, of course, fighting in—the resulting battles at Mars-la-Tour, Vionville, and Gravelotte-St.-Privat, and, ultimately, the bottling up of the French back in Metz where they'd started. German cavalry also materially helped extend the invaders' reach in the encirclement of Paris after Sedan and in long-distance foraging during the subsequent siege of the French capital. Perhaps most important, throughout the war German cavalry enjoyed what earlier generations called moral superiority over their French opponents. That confidence, despite occasionally very heavy losses, contributed in turn to their ultimate tactical and operational superiority.

One does not, however, see German cavalry engaged in the long-range strategic raiding as conducted by both Confederate and Union horsemen between 1862 and 1865. As often as not, those earlier forays aimed at capturing entire towns, operational theaters' supply dumps, or thoroughly wrecking vast stretches of railroad. The absence of this kind of raiding in 1870–1871 is all the more interesting given the evident Prussian attention paid to the technical aspects of Civil War–era use of railroads for theater-wide deployment of forces, not to mention the importance of railroads in Prussia's victory in 1866 as well as in keeping German armies supplied in 1870.[75] German interest in the Union's and Confederacy's use of railroads did not appear to translate into a changed attitude toward the cavalry's tactics or strategy based upon the American example, at any rate certainly not before 1870. Many German students of the Civil War dismissed both Union and Confederate cavalry as merely mounted infantry, a new type of dragoon, who (somewhat ironically) relied too much on firearms for their effectiveness, rather than on "the 'vehemence and force' of shock tactics," as was evidently still preferred in Continental Europe.[76] This attitude persisted despite the particular admiration for the Confederate cavalry in Prussia by as prominent and successful a Prussian cavalry officer as Prince Friedrich Karl von Hohenzollern.[77]

On the other side, why did the French cavalry not emulate the American example set during the Civil War? Several possible explanations suggest themselves. In the first instance, no prominent French soldiers wrote about the Civil War before 1870, a period in which French armies were often already at war in North Africa or Mexico. Their own lessons learned in mounted operations would presumably have sufficed. Secondly, the American Civil War had occurred "at a distance [greatly removed from France] and in the midst of special circumstances." Not the least of these circumstances was the perceived amateurishness of American armies, Union and Confederate. Consequently their experiences' applicability to the French army was judged to be of limited value at best, though surely the French cavalry school at Saumur recognized that the distance from France to Mexico was not less than that from France to the borders of the Union or the Confederacy. Finally, it was maintained that the heavily "populated, cultivated, and civilized" nature of Western Europe made a French replication of strategic raiding as undertaken by Grierson or

Morgan unlikely, if not impossible, despite the fact that more obscure French observers noted the strategic-raiding role that cavalry might still play. Indeed, one might argue that precisely the thickly woven nature of Western Europe's transportation infrastructure would have made strategic raiding even more valuable in offering many more targets than had been the case earlier in the still relatively sparsely settled reaches of Kentucky or Mississippi. As noted at the outset in reference to the French cavalry's lackadaisical reconnaissance and interdiction in the war's opening days, there existed in Paris an "imperturbable complacency" until 1866; and despite rousing itself after Königgrätz to adopt the *chassepot* and new siege artillery and enact, in 1868, a plan for a thoroughgoing reorganization, the French army in 1870 was frequently simply outfought. And when not outfought, it suffered catastrophically bad leadership.[78] In the forty-three years following the Treaty of Frankfurt, as the new German Reich and the French Republic girded themselves for the next round in their centuries-old rivalry, the cavalry of both countries remained integral to their respective armed forces, as did horsemen in all other European armies. For the victorious Germans of 1871, the question was not so much would there be cavalry in the next war, but rather to what great victories would they ride?

CHAPTER 3

Not Quite Sunset

THE CAVALRY IN WORLD WAR I

By the end of the nineteenth century cavalry operations in European armies had become a matter of some doctrinal uncertainty. More powerful weapons, firing more accurately and at longer ranges, raised the question of the suitability, indeed the survivability, of the cavalry. This was no less the case in Germany than elsewhere. While the Franco-Prussian War had seemed to show that cavalry could still win a battle by means of the massed charge with cold steel, the true value of the German cavalry during that conflict had demonstrated itself in armed reconnaissance with a view to finding and fixing the enemy; screening and securing German forces; interdicting the enemy's communications; and, at war's end, foraging and anti-partisan operations. None of these missions, particularly neither of the first two, had changed by 1900, though some soon would as a result of the widespread application of internal-combustion technology.

At the dawn of the twentieth century, cavalry still possessed the unique ability to move almost at will, though not always rapidly, over the most varied terrain and in nearly all types of weather. Cavalrymen could leave the largely road- and rail-bound infantry literally in the dust. In

Western Europe, however, mounted forces faced an interesting potential problem, one that had been noted as early as the late 1860s, namely the congested physical nature of the landscape over which armies might move in future. That portion of the North European Plain stretching from Normandy through France, Belgium, and the Netherlands and into northwestern Germany had a very high population-density by the last quarter of the nineteenth century. With it came a significant degree of industrial urbanization and attendant infrastructure. This infrastructure constituted a set of major obstacles to the free movement of mounted troops: intensively cultivated, and therefore very soft and wet, footing; numerous canals and railway lines; mine-pits and slag heaps; and innumerable fences and garden walls, the latter a delight to fox hunters but a real hindrance for heavily laden cavalrymen and their horses. Making these obstacles even more troublesome were the increasingly vast and complex fortifications strewn right across northwestern Europe from Liège and Namur past Luxemburg to Verdun. It was the latter's job specifically to complicate the movement of armies and thereby hinder invasions or block them altogether.[1]

As the Franco-Prussian War had so amply demonstrated, modern war had become terribly consumptive not only of cavalrymen but also of horseflesh. Despite advances in breeding and veterinary services, loss-rates rose still further as the twentieth century dawned. Nevertheless, German and other cavalrymen assumed that horsed regiments would continue to have their place in the order of battle, even in the congested regions of northwestern Europe. The Germans' experience in 1870–1871 had done little to convince them otherwise. On the contrary, German observers felt that the cavalry should be strengthened and modernized, not reduced or—worse—eliminated. For example, one of Germany's most noted military authors of the era, General Friedrich von Bernhardi, called the early-twentieth-century strength of the German cavalry lamentably weak when compared to the mounted forces of France or Great Britain. The Boer War, he wrote, had shown what highly mobile and hard-hitting cavalry columns could still do, even in an age of high-powered infantry weapons. The key, he insisted, lay in ensuring that the German cavalry possessed its own accompanying bicycle-mounted infantry and more effective artillery, as well as training cavalrymen better as marksmen. Such additions would ensure that the horsemen could, if necessary, operate independently and with sufficient firepower to cause the enemy real damage. All the while they would retain their vaunted mobility, even though he never really explained what bicyclists would do once they ran out of road. He also cautioned, however, that every new war would create new conditions and totally unforeseen circumstances to which the cavalry, as all arms, would have to be ready to adapt.[2]

Across the English Channel, Sir John French, who had "established his military reputation by his performance as a cavalryman in the Boer War"[3] and who would later become the first commander of the British Expeditionary Force in France, shared this view. Though speaking for the British, his comments were ones that would have been widely shared in Germany. French wrote that cavalry circa 1900 were being taught to shirk exposure on the battlefield as a result of what he considered undue respect for infantry fire. "We ought," he wrote to the contrary, "to be on our guard against false teachings of this nature . . . [and the] consequences of placing the weapon above the man" and, implicitly, above the horse.[4] Of course, his own experiences in the Boer War might have taught him otherwise. Between 1899 and 1902, the British cavalry in South Africa "lost 347,000 of the 518,000 [horses] that took part, though the country abounded in good grazing" and possessed a "benign climate." Of those lost, "no more than two per cent were lost in battle. The rest died of overwork, disease, or malnutrition, at a rate of 336 for each day of the campaign."[5]

In the absence of motorized vehicles, however, horses remained critical for mobility in that conflict. This fact represented the only real hope for the cavalry's survival in European armies. Reinforcing the mobile importance of horse-mounted and horse-drawn forces, another feature of the Boer War stood out: among the Trek Boers, "every man was a mounted shot."[6] Like their earlier American counterparts in the Civil War and in the wars with the Plains Indians from 1850 to 1890, Boer horsemen were the quintessential mounted infantry. Though some of them might yet be armed with sabers, their primary weapon remained the rifle, and the horse served principally as a means of effective cross-country transport. If there were to be a place for mounted formations at the dawn of the twentieth century, would it not have to be that of mounted infantry who would nevertheless fight dismounted? British cavalrymen increasingly thought so after 1902. Accordingly they were equipped and trained with rifles rather than carbines and achieved a level of firepower and accuracy approaching that of the British infantry.[7] They were becoming essentially what in British and British imperial terminology were designated mounted rifles: skilled "horsemen trained to fight on foot, men who are mounted and intend to perform all the duties of cavalry, except that which may best be described as 'the shock.' It is expected of them that they should perform all the outpost [sic], reconnoitering, and patrolling of an army in a manner similar to cavalry; the only difference being that they must rely solely upon their fire power for defensive and offensive action."[8]

Commenting on the lessons to be drawn from another war of the period, the Russo-Japanese War of 1904–1905, German and Austrian officers came to a rather different set of conclusions. Under the pseudonym "Asiaticus," a German officer wrote that Russian cavalrymen were too ready to go to ground with their firearms. In doing so, he said, they repeatedly sacrificed the cavalry's greatest asset, namely its mobility. Similarly, Austrian count Gustav Wrangel observed that the Russian horsemen's experience demonstrated that troopers could not serve both firearms and the saber equally well and be skilled riders at the same time. In any case, Wrangel noted, too great a reliance on firearms robbed the cavalryman of his desire to charge the enemy and implicitly deprived him of his real weapons, the sword and the lance.[9]

Such arguments continued unabated, even as rapid technological change continued to force the cavalry to adapt. Combining horse-soldiers with the technology that did exist culminated in the following calculation: railways would be used for initial operational deployment, as they had been for German armies ever since 1866. Increasingly heavy artillery would be the primary offensive preparation against field positions. The latter would then be taken by infantry assault. For its part, the cavalry would still be used for reconnaissance, screening, security, encirclement, and pursuit, if no longer for the battle-winning charge with swords drawn.[10] One may argue, however, there's not much terribly novel in this approach. Cavalry had often been used for precisely these tasks in the Western military tradition ever since Hannibal's charging

horsemen cut off the legions' retreat at Cannae and rode down the survivors (a favor the Romans returned at Zama).[11] The mounted warrior's
ethos and the tradition of the cavalry's shock value nevertheless lingered
up to the outbreak of war in 1914. Even then, however, missions such as
long-range screening and reconnaissance or interdiction of the enemy's
lines of supply had not fully displaced the assumption that at least some
future battles might still be decided by the massed cavalry attack.[12] In a
view no doubt shared among more than a few German cavalrymen, the
British Army's *Cavalry Training Manual* of 1907 still pronounced as a matter of principle that rifle fire, however effective it might be, "cannot
replace the effect produced by the speed of the horse, the magnetism of
the charge, and the terror of cold steel."[13]

One prominent British officer, Colonel G. F. R. Henderson, deduced
from the campaigns of the Boer War that the sentiment as expressed in
the *Cavalry Manual* meant that the cavalry at the turn of the century was
"as obsolete as the crusaders."[14] If, however, the matter of the infantry's
use of the bayonet is considered, then the cavalry's retention of the
sword, and even the lance, may not seem so far-fetched, whether in Germany or Great Britain. The same officer had earlier been pleased that the
British *Infantry Regulations* of 1880 had reiterated the psychological and
tactical importance of the bayonet at close quarters, despite the by-then-
widespread use of smokeless powder, magazine-fed rifles, and rapid-
firing field artillery. Admittedly, Henderson modified his opinion about
the bayonet's efficacy as a result of the Boer War, just as he did for the
sword-armed cavalry. As the events of 1914–1918 repeatedly showed,
however, German, British, and other infantry routinely went over the top
with bayonets fixed long after the cavalry on the Western Front was
deemed utterly useless. Indeed, the success of the Japanese infantry in
their costly assaults against prepared Russian positions at Mukden and
Port Arthur during the Russo-Japanese War seemed to show that the foot
soldier's cold steel could still be employed with decisive effect provided
that the attacking infantry had sufficient preparatory artillery support
and a sufficient reserve of raw courage while covering the fire-swept zone
between the opposing trench lines. Bernhardi, as well as another influen-
tial German military writer of the period, Colonel Wilhelm Balck, shared
this assessment. Both stressed the "moral factor" (i.e., morale) as much as

they stressed the material factor as a determinant of victory.[15] They also applied it equally to the individual soldier and the nation in whose army he served. If, therefore, prominent military thinkers still posited a useful role for the bayonet, and if cold steel really could still frighten an enemy soldier—he need only imagine a foot or more of it being plunged into his gut—then the cavalry's retention of edged weapons and even lances does not seem so odd.

Ironically, however, the massed cavalry attack was in part made more unlikely by the very masses of infantry that some cavalrymen still confidently intended to drive from the field. Railways proved to be just as efficient as prewar planners had hoped in delivering unprecedented numbers of men and equipment for battle. For example, in approximately one month's time after the outbreak of hostilities in 1914, some 312 divisions of French, German, Austrian, and Russian troops had been brought by rail to the battlefronts, a number excluding hundreds of thousands of cavalry mounts and draft horses. Having reached the enemy's territory, however, those same masses of troops in a certain sense became a liability. From the railhead onward, those surging tides of men continued to have to move largely on foot even while officers, cavalry troopers, and artillerymen rode. Furthermore, such huge numbers of troops, regardless of branch of service, had to be supplied by logistics trains still relying primarily on the power of horseflesh. Therefore, horses (and mules) remained a critical element of all the European armies at war's outbreak and not merely in the putatively outmoded cavalry regiments. An indication of horses' continued necessity reveals itself in the following statistic: the single largest category of cargo unloaded in the French ports for the British army throughout the entire period of 1914–1918 was horse fodder.[16] Similarly, the Director of Military Operations in the War Office from 1910 to 1914, Major-General Henry Wilson, ensured that the BEF's mobilization plan included such apparently minor, but nonetheless crucial, details as "the provision of horse-stall fittings and gangways at the French ports" for the hundreds of thousands of horses (and mules) that the British armies in France would need from the start.[17] From the war's earliest days, similar numbers of horses were being mobilized all across Europe for the cavalry, artillery, and transport services: 165,000 in Britain; 600,000 in Austria; more than a million in Russia. The European-wide ratio of horses to men generally was estimated to be 1:3.[18]

In Germany, as in all other combatant nations in 1914, horses were called up in unprecedented numbers from their civil tasks on farms, in businesses, and field sports. On 31 July the upper house of Germany's parliament, the Imperial Federal Council (*Bundesrat*), issued decrees prohibiting the exportation of fodder, provisions, and livestock. Making Germany's equine mobilization even more efficient was the fact that German horses, like their human counterparts, had to be registered in peacetime; thus the military authorities knew where the horses were "at all times."[19] Inaugurated in 1900, this system "involved a regular census and inspection of all horses in the country. Beasts were graded and a picture was built up of the nation's horse stock. A horse muster commission was established in each corps [area] to draw up detailed orders for the impressment of animals. These orders would be carried out prior to the full implementation of Germany's mobilization plan."[20] Augmenting civilian registration and subsequent mobilization were the various State studs. The Hanoverian State Stud based at Celle, for example, alone provided annual deliveries of some 2,500 remounts to the German army by 1914, while the East Prussian State Stud at Trakehnen shipped out fully 7,000 per annum.[21] In addition to these private and State-sponsored resources at home, the German government also continued to look abroad for horseflesh. The U.S. Consul General in Berlin, Robert P. Skinner, was cited in the *New York Times Magazine* of 3 May 1914 as reporting that the German government was advertising "in certain American newspapers for 500 American thoroughbreds, 1,000 more or less pedigreed horses, and 1,000 draught horses for artillery use."[22] German purchasing agents were also reportedly active in Ireland, having evidently "contracted for every horse on the Irish landscape . . . up to 1916." Other agents had even "invaded France and bought up 18,000 first-class cavalry and artillery mounts."[23]

Though the war would necessarily nullify such prewar contracts, the Germans' need for such numbers of horses remained clear. A combat-ready corps of the regular German army in 1914 required no fewer than 280 trains comprising more than 12,000 railway cars in order to move from its depot to its deployment area. Those cars included 2,960 specially outfitted to transport only horses. Similarly, the need for provender was enormous, as already indicated. Given 1914's standard daily horse ration of approximately twenty-two pounds (10 kg) of feed and fodder, the German First Army alone required approximately 840 tons of feed and fodder each day for its establishment strength of 84,000 horses of all types. That requirement compares with approximately 555 tons of daily rations for the same army's 260,000 men.[24] "To put it another way, the First Army needed 50% more food for horses than for men, though it had over three times as many men as horses."[25] In all, the German army of 1914 intended to move not only three million men but also fully 600,000 horses merely for the initial campaign in northwestern Europe. These staggering totals required an equally breathtaking commitment of rolling stock to get the troops, their horses, and their equipment to the frontiers. No fewer than 11,000 trains were scheduled in the mobilization plan.[26]

Of course, from the war's opening days on the Western Front, the German army also attempted to requisition horses in occupied territory, precisely because anticipated losses of horseflesh demanded it. In southern Alsace around Belfort, not far from the battlefields of 1870, enforced requisitioning began as early as 2 August, according to reports in the British press. Naturally, such attempts did not go uncontested. One German officer, apparently acting alone, reportedly entered one locale only to be "forced hurriedly to retreat" by enraged civilians. Similarly, in other villages German troops on the same mission were said to have been driven off by pitchfork-wielding Frenchmen. Such searches could quickly escalate to skirmishing. German dragoons attempting to enter Villers-la-Montagne, for example, found themselves forced to retreat by French *chasseurs*, while a full German mounted regiment's attack at Montfortane failed in the face of French infantry fire.[27]

Nevertheless, at least on the Western Front, the cavalry's tactical and operational importance diminished rapidly as the lines stabilized after the First Battle of the Marne. Well aimed rifle-fire, particularly of the British "Old Contemptibles" of 1914, machine guns, and artillery quickly showed themselves capable of bringing effective gridlock to battlefields eventually made completely inert by the construction of the trenches. Furthermore, one of the cavalry's by-now-classic functions—turning the enemy's flank—proved itself increasingly difficult given the soon-to-be static nature of the lines in France. The force-to-space ratio was so high that infantrymen were finding maneuver ever more problematic absent effective and widespread motorization. It therefore became impossible for cavalry, whether German, French, or British, to envelop flanks that were never sufficiently "in the air" after September 1914. Such a conundrum was particularly troublesome for the German army. As already noted, the army's doctrine since the late 1860s had envisioned the cavalry's playing precisely that flanking role, as it had done in 1870. Once the enemy's flanks had been overlapped and his frontal defenses smashed by fire, but only then, would his positions be taken by assault.[28] If, however, flanks could not be turned, then the cavalry on the Western Front would either have to wait for the increasingly improbable great breakthrough or—the worst of fates for the cavalryman's ethos—fight permanently dismounted.

As the German cavalry rode to war in 1914, their expectations were matched by their counterparts on the Allied side. Since at least the summer of 1911, the French army's General Staff expected that in a war against Germany, the British would dispatch a force of some 150,000 men and 67,000 horses, the latter including mounts for a full cavalry division and two separate mounted brigades.[29] The French and British staffs also fully expected to meet German cavalry in force. Indeed, as early as 1908 the French Superior Council of War had received an analysis of likely German wartime action. That analysis predicted a German drive through at least eastern Belgium around the northern flank of France's frontier defenses. This prediction recognized the Germans' "tradition of enveloping their opponent's flanks,"[30] a mission almost impossible in 1914 without the employment of strong mounted forces capable of rapid, wide-ranging movement. As a consequence, no fewer than nine of the German army's eleven cavalry divisions found themselves on the Western Front in 1914. That fact alone indicated the expected importance devolving upon mounted forces in a campaign designed to defeat France before Russia could mobilize effectively.

Each of these German cavalry divisions had an establishment-strength between 4,500 and 5,200 men and some 5,600 horses, including remounts. A typical mounted division included between 3,500 and 3,600 troopers armed with carbines, sabers, and, in many cases lances, to fight specifically as cavalry. In addition, each division had an organic infantry battalion (*Jäger zu Pferde*, literally "hunters on horseback") of as many as 1,000 men. Presaging future motorization, the *Jäger* were typically bicycle- or truck-mounted, though as their name actually indicates, they often rode as well. Frequently, however, they slogged along on the boot-leather express, just as the infantry has done since time immemorial. Interestingly enough, though no one could know it in 1914, this relationship between mounted and dismounted German troops would be exactly reversed in 1939. In World War II it would be the infantry divisions that would have a cavalry squadron in their organic reconnaissance battalions.

In 1914 the standard primary weapon for both the *Jäger* and mounted troopers alike was the Mauser M1898, 7.92-mm carbine. Nevertheless, some cavalrymen also still carried straight-edged swords. In the heavy cavalry regiments the sword was a thrusting, rather than a cutting, weapon having a 36-inch (91-cm) blade and known as a *Pallasch*. The *Pallasch* weighed just a few ounces less than three pounds (1.36 kg). Uhlans and other light cavalry carried a similar weapon but one slightly lighter in weight and implicitly intended more for slashing. Still others were armed with sabers as such. As for offensive heavy weapons, German cavalry divisions also possessed—in a manner similar to other European cavalry forces—their own horse-artillery detachment of twelve guns in three batteries per division. According to the German timetable at the start of the campaign in the west, the entirety of such a division was supposed to cover between twelve and twenty miles (up to 32 km) per day. The cavalry expected to cover these miles in one of four recognized gaits: the walk, trot, gallop, and "extended gallop." The canter appears to have been used only for march-pasts. Using these gaits, German horsemen could cover between 125 (walk) and 700 ("extended gallop") paces per minute, a "pace" being about 31 inches (78 cm). In other words, cavalry at the walk—the most frequent marching gait—would cover just over one hundred yards (91 m) per minute or about three-and-a-half miles per hour. While that is about the speed of fast-moving infantry, it must be remembered that horses could keep going for longer periods of time, particularly if the infantryman was carrying his full load of equipment. At the trot, a good ground-covering gait that spares the horse if the trooper posts, the cavalry could cover 275 paces per minute or approximately 8 miles per hour (not quite 13 km/h). In point of fact, the distance covered daily by the cavalry would almost certainly be greater. Given the constant need for reconnaissance forays and screening operations, the horsemen would of necessity have to ride many more miles than that. Thus equipped and ready to move, the German cavalry in 1914, particularly the eight divisions eventually grouped in two corps during the so-called Race to the Sea after the First Battle of the Marne, constituted "the largest body of horsemen ever to be collected in Western Europe before or since."[31] In light of their numbers and their theoretical mobility, they had at least the potential to be everywhere.

Riding West

In the opening campaigns following Germany's declaration of war, the German army's cavalry units on the Western Front played the centuries-old role envisaged for European horsemen, a role reemphasized in the Prussian army in the late 1860s by Helmuth von Moltke the Elder. No one could know it with certainty at the time, but by the end of the First Battle of Ypres in November 1914 the German cavalry would find themselves essentially out of a job as mounted warriors. The entrenchment of the front from the sea to Switzerland, a distance of some 450 miles (724 km), would make traditional cavalry operations impossible. Nevertheless, at the campaign's beginning, the German horsemen were almost always in the van and often well in advance of it. For example, General Otto von Emmich's task group, sometimes referred to as the Army of the Meuse, included General Johannes Georg von der Marwitz's II Cavalry Corps (2nd, 4th, and 9th Cavalry Divisions including the Prussian Guard Cavalry). These forces crossed the Belgian frontier on 4 August 1914 and set out straight for Liège some twenty miles to the west, with mounted "outriders distributing leaflets disclaiming aggressive intent."[32] On 5 August 1914, French general Joseph Joffre responded by authorizing French cavalry to move into Belgium, that country's neutrality now having been violated by advancing German columns. The German cavalry's movements, however, helped alert French commanders to the latter's intention of driving much farther west into Belgium than Paris had earlier anticipated. On 14 August, just before the opening of the planned French march into Belgium, Joffre learned that German mounted patrols had attempted to seize bridges over the Meuse south of Namur. For their own part, French horsemen helped discover that the German armies were in fact moving deeper into Belgium than Joffre had likely expected.[33] When the French Third and Fourth Armies advanced into Belgium, they included a full cavalry corps and a separate cavalry division, along with nine infantry corps. Unfortunately, the German Fourth and Fifth Armies marching to meet them comprised not only ten infantry corps but also two cavalry divisions, as well as six reserve brigades and the garrison forces at Metz. Equally unfortunately, the French cavalry of General J. F. A. Sordet's corps failed, as the French cavalry had often failed in 1870, to find and fix the invaders. The Ardennes country into which the French horsemen advanced admittedly did not lend itself to mounted operations. This southeastern corner of Belgium is fairly rough terrain, covered as it still was at that time by heavily forested hills. Furthermore, the River Semois and its tributaries cut across the French axis of advance. Coincidentally, these same conditions would confront invading German armored forces coming from the other direction thirty-six years later. As it was, despite nine days' riding from 6 to 15 August, the French horsemen never did locate the German columns and only succeeded in breaking down their mounts.[34]

Somewhat to the surprise of the German invaders, the Belgian army fought more tenaciously at Liège than expected. In the fighting around that important fortress-city, Belgian commanders credited the German cavalry with helping prevent a successful Belgian counterattack from Ft. Embourg, one of twelve fortresses enclosing the city, in this case on the River Ourthe southeast of that stream's confluence with the Meuse. Despite having shot down large numbers of German infantry unwisely advancing across open ground around the fort, the Belgian defenders could not follow up their success. Apparently they feared operating in the open in the face of large numbers of German horsemen hovering in the vicinity. The Germans turned this hesitation to their advantage when a detachment of hussars subsequently launched a small-scale raid of their own into a gap between several of the forts in an effort to capture the Belgian commander, General Gérard Leman. In the confusion, and no doubt to their surprise, the Germans reached Leman's headquarters but were overpowered by an enraged crowd of Belgian civilians and

Civic Guards who rushed to the scene. The latter killed one German officer, two troopers, and took the rest prisoner.[35]

Despite this setback, German cavalry did contribute materially to Liège's fall. Striking out from Visé, hard by the border with the Maastricht Appendix of Holland, they broke into open country west of the Meuse. Leman responded by ordering detachments of his mobile troops—in this case a division and a separate brigade that had come to Liège's defense—to block the German horsemen wheeling to the southwest beyond the river. Unfortunately, Leman's action removed forces intended to hold the gaps between Liège's fortresses and left their garrisons essentially trapped inside. Laboriously, German artillery, including the massive 420-mm Krupp howitzer, came up to batter the works and their unfortunate defenders into submission.[36]

As the German advance gathered force after the fall of Liège, in fact before the city's final submission, the cavalry continued to ride hard ahead. As early as 9 August papers were reporting the presence of mounted reconnaissance patrols, the dreaded and ubiquitous "uhlans" of 1870s vintage, as far south as Dinant. There even appears to have been apprehension that the Germans were poised to launch an all-out cavalry assault on Brussels itself. More concretely, on 12–13 August German cavalry clashed with Belgian troops as the horsemen attempted to seize bridges over the Rivers Demer and Gette at Haelen and the Velpe at Cortenachen. At Haelen, the fighting was particularly intense. There the German cavalry launched mounted attacks against entrenched Belgian infantry supported by machine guns and artillery. The attackers, the 17th (Mecklenburg) Cavalry Brigade, "fell in heaps" with their horses as they stormed the village. Precisely as had happened to the French cavalry in their attack on Morsbronn in Lorraine in 1870, the Mecklenburgers and their mounts were shot down in such numbers that they literally walled up the streets of the village and made further attacks impossible. Around the nearby village of Donck, a similar fate befell the horsemen of the German 3rd Cavalry Brigade's 9th Uhlans and the Cuirassier Regiment *Königin*. In the case of the 9th Uhlans, the attackers charged with couched lances against what the regimental adjutant described as "murderous" small-arms, machine-gun, and artillery fire. Though the lancers rode down several lines of Belgian infantry, continued rifle-fire eventually drove them off. As they retreated via the intervening swale through which they'd attacked, they found it filled with dead comrades and their horses. In the time it took to charge and withdraw, the regiment lost perhaps half its strength: more than 100 men and 250 horses. Among the *Königin* Cuirassiers only 76 officers and men were lost but fully 270 horses. Meanwhile, to the southwest at Tirlemont (modern Tienen), fully two thousand German horsemen attempted to capture the entire town but were driven off by the defenders. At Èghezèe, on the Belgian right wing near the great fortress-city of Namur on the upper Meuse, the German cavalry fared worse, at least temporarily. Here Belgian horsemen caught German cavalry bivouacked in the town. The latter retreated after a series of sharp, dismounted street fights. In all of these engagements, German cavalry were not always able to accomplish their stated missions. Even where they failed, however, they continued to play the European cavalry's traditional modern role: screening the advance of one's own forces, reconnaissance, and finding and fixing the enemy. The realization slowly dawned that despite great bravery in the attack, such missions as these were all they would very likely be able to do. How far into the future they could carry on doing them remained another question entirely. Nevertheless, in these specific cases, so well did the German cavalry perform in the war's opening days that the Belgian General Staff evidently remained "in total ignorance" of the lumbering approach of the monstrous guns that had demolished the forts of Liège and would soon do the same at Namur.[37]

By 20 August 1914, newspapers reported German cavalry occupying a line running from Diest to Tirlemont. They were said to be pushing out in all directions over the open country of Brabant, terrain that seemed to have been "designed for them."[38] It was at this moment that German horsemen fought an interesting engagement, given what the German army's doctrine would say about cavalry in the interwar period. On 25 August near Ostend, a force of some 150 Belgian gendarmes attacked a superior force of German cavalry approaching down the Bruges road. The German riders were preceded by bicyclists acting as scouts, certainly something of a twist for the normally far-ranging troopers. When the bicycle troops were halted by Belgian rifle-fire, the cavalry dismounted in true dragoon fashion to fight on foot. Then, still more interestingly, they brought up machine guns mounted on automobiles, though reports did not indicate whether these were purpose-built or lash-ups. After about an hour's fighting, a second cavalry detachment managed to arrive and threaten to outflank the Belgians in the old style. Faced with being cut off, the Belgians withdrew into Ostend. While the Germans themselves subsequently failed to break into the town, their employment of what a later generation would call combined arms presaged the post-1918 *Reichswehr*'s doctrine for mounted forces' organization.[39]

As August wore to a close, the French and British armies continued to retreat. Placed in the Allied line between the French Sixth Army to the west and Fifth Army to the east, the British Expeditionary Force (BEF) withdrew in good order after the Battle of Mons and managed to break contact with the pursuing Germans. Attacked but not disabled, the BEF simply "disappeared into the countryside," often leaving the Germans at a loss as to its whereabouts, despite occasional chance collisions such as the one on 22 August when British horsemen of the 2nd Dragoon Guards met a German patrol of the 9th Cavalry Division's 4th Cuirassier Regiment northeast of Mons.[40] Occasionally, the BEF's withdrawal was also helped by the "self-sacrificing" attacks of its own horsemen against the pursuing German First Army. For example, on 24 August at Thulin to the southeast of Condé, the British 2nd Cavalry Brigade under General H. B. de Lisle charged advancing German troops armed with machine guns. Like the *Königin* Cuirassiers and 9th Uhlans at Haelen earlier that same month, the British horsemen were shot down in large numbers. But in a manner reminiscent of the French cavalry in 1870, they managed to buy a bit of time for the rest of the BEF to continue its withdrawal.[41] Thus, in the pursuit of the BEF, the German cavalry failed in one of its primary missions: maintaining contact with and providing information about the enemy.

The German horsemen made good the failure, however, on 4–5 September. As the Allied armies had retreated and the German armies had advanced, the right flank of General Alexander von Kluck's First Army, itself on the extreme right of the advance, became threatened with being turned by a French counterattack. Here German cavalry served von Kluck and the German cause well. The local German commander, General Hans von Gronau of the IV Reserve Corps, discovered the French threat as a result of his Corps' attached cavalry division. Doing precisely what mounted troops were supposed to do in this sort of situation, namely reconnoitering and screening the advance, Gronau's cavalry alerted him to the impending French attempt to roll up the entire German First Army. Acting decisively on the information, Gronau attacked the French, halted their flanking maneuver, and in the process alerted First Army's commander and the *Oberste Heeresleitung* (OHL) to the stand being prepared by the Allied armies on the Marne.[42] As Kluck moved forces to counter the French, a gap opened between his First Army and General Karl von Bülow's Second Army immediately to the east-southeast. Into the gap marched the BEF and elements of the adjoining French Fifth Army. The advancing Allied troops collided with two German cavalry corps whose units were screening the German First and Second Armies' fronts.[43] Once again, the German cavalry were performing precisely the sort of job that Moltke the Elder had laid out for Prussian horsemen in the previous century. An admittedly already slow British advance into a vulnerable opening in the German lines was halted by the defensive firepower of the German cavalrymen, firepower made more effective by the German cavalry divisions' own integral *Jäger* battalions.

Clearly, however, the German horsemen had not had everything their own way. They'd had only two days for rest, farriery, and the refurbishment of weapons before what was soon to be called the Battle of the Marne began. Their horses, worn down by the month-long, fighting advance through Belgium, now also showed the cumulative effects of a lack of ready fodder.[44] Their British and French counterparts, though numerous, did not exploit this situation. The BEF's two cavalry divisions were under orders to maintain contact with the French armies on the British flanks and not go riding off in any putative pursuit of the Germans. For their part, the French cavalry, still commanded by Sordet, had not only used their horses but, in certain respects, had abused them. No watering of mounts, for example, had been permitted in rest halts during the long retreat from Belgium, ostensibly to prevent the columns' being strung out. Furthermore, French troopers evidently saw no need occasionally to dismount and spare their horses, unlike German and British horsemen. As one British second lieutenant caustically noted, and as many a German trooper would doubtless have agreed, "The French cavalrymen was [sic] rarely seen off his horse. He had a rooted objection to dismounting." Consequently, 90 percent of French equine losses in 1914 resulted from sickness, and fully 25 percent of all of France's mobilized horses were dead by year's end. The French army's remount system, already skewed by prewar requirements in favor of Anglo-Norman draft horses rather than true cavalry mounts, could not readily make good such losses; and tactical bright spots—such as Sordet's troopers almost capturing von Kluck in his own headquarters on 8 September—could not overcome the French horsemen's deficiencies in the war's opening campaign.[45]

Between the Battle of the Marne and the end of 1914, the Western Front gradually extended itself to the northwest. This was the famous and somewhat erroneously named "Race to the Sea." During these almost three months, both sides attempted to gain room for maneuver by finding and turning the flank of their opponents. Contrary to popular opinion, they did not wish to terminate the lines at the coast of the North Sea, for then maneuver would come to an effective end, as in fact it did by the end of November. "Each [side] became very much aware of the defensive strength the opponent would gain when its northern flank could be anchored against the seacoast, and not [be] subject to the fluctuations of cavalry maneuvers."[46] During this period, cavalry actions occurred as both sides strove to turn the other's flank. On 19 September, for example, German cavalrymen of the 4th Cavalry Division acting as the corps cavalry for the IX Corps maneuvered over what two years later would be the battlefield of the Somme. There they fended off, but evidently did not heavily engage, British cavalry (including attached machine-gunners and bicyclists) advancing from the vicinity of Péronne against the Germans' lines of communication stretching from St. Quentin to Le Cateau.[47] Each of these actions, followed up or accompanied by advancing infantry, extended the lines farther to the northwest. But as the two sides approached the sea, conditions on the ground became ever more congested by the huge masses of troops operating in the semi-urban industrial landscape. In early October near Arras elements of at least four German cavalry divisions jostled for passage on the narrow roads of French Flanders. Due north of Arras, around the industrial and coal-mining town of Lens, the cavalry were ordered to fight dismounted. In "bitter street fighting" against Moroccan troops of the French Tenth Army and even against armed civilian miners, cavalrymen of the 4th, 7th, and 9th Cavalry Divisions held those districts until German infantry came up.[48] Of this fighting in Flanders, the later Inspector of Cavalry of the German army wrote:

> The opinion of the General Staff . . . that the army cavalry might be employed in a swift crushing of all resistance to the north of Lens with its full force, for the purpose of taking the enemy wing in rear, was proven impracticable. In the first place, the enemy had extended his northern wing still farther in the direction of La Bassée; also, a speedy passage was impossible over this country, with its railroad embankments, field tramways [and] mine pits, coal shafts, [slag] heaps and rows of workmen's houses, so characteristic of an industrial center, all of which had been merely approximately indicated on the maps. Mounted warfare, such as the army and higher command especially required this day, was simply out of the question. Step by step, the jaegers [sic] and cavalry troopers fought their way with carbines for possession of the locality, against an enemy defending from houses and pits; lacking bayonets, no headway could be won against massive factory walls without employment of heavier ammunition.[49]

As a consequence of the front's resulting stabilization in Flanders, the German cavalrymen who'd ridden the entirety of the campaign were gradually converted into infantryman.

Throughout the second half of October and the whole of November 1914, they effectively surrendered their former status and slowly became indistinguishable from the other trench-dwellers populating the lines from Ostend to the borders of Switzerland. The addition of these eight divisions' worth of troops to the trenches was, of course, advantageous for the Germans, even though abandoning their horses often meant that the troopers went into the line without greatcoats, entrenching tools, and other mundane but essential equipment. Many of them, however, evidently insisted on keeping their spurs. As for the matter of what to do with eight cavalry divisions' worth of horses, that remained "a problem well-nigh beyond conception."[50]

Whether they fought mounted or not, German cavalry made a material contribution on the Western Front in 1914, a fact recognized by friend and foe alike. The commander of the German Sixth Army, Bavarian Crown Prince Rupprecht, paid tribute to the horsemen's valor in the trench fighting around Lille in an order of the day late in October. The cavalry, he wrote, "has proven that it could successfully use the carbine against fortified trenches without being driven away and, from the very nature of its organization has been able to cover a wide area of conflict in a series of victories. It has thereby performed a highly meritorious service on a portion of the battlefield. I wish to express warmest thanks and deepest acknowledgment to the troops for their wonderful behavior and exceptional endurance."[51] Of course, one can argue that Rupprecht merely acknowledged the truism that necessity is the mother of invention. Nevertheless, his order took account of the cavalry's real remaining strength: its potential for mobility. On a fluid front, the horsemen could still move in a way that the infantry simply could not.

Nevertheless, from the end of 1914 those German cavalrymen on the Western Front remained essentially what they'd by then become: infantry. That didn't mean, however, that the cavalry disappeared. Instead, from here on out, it was the Allied cavalry that featured prominently, if only by virtue of its relative inactivity. Despite the front's immobility in 1915 and 1916, as well as the tactical dominance of artillery and machine guns, the overall British commander, Sir Douglas Haig, still thought combat horses necessary. A former cavalryman and polo player, his attachment might have appeared merely sentimental. A more practical consideration nevertheless influenced him.

An Allied victory ultimately required driving German forces out of France and Belgium. By contrast, in midsummer 1916 the Germans had less imperative reasons to advance, especially in northwestern France. Given the fighting then still raging at Verdun, as well as Austro-German defensive efforts against the Russians' "Brusilov Offensive" on the Eastern Front, German troops on the Rivers Ancre and Somme could remain precisely where they were. Unlike 1914, the Germans no longer had a real need for mounted troops. If the Allies wanted to come on, let them come. In Haig's calculation, such an offensive stood to accomplish a number of goals. The "Big Push" on the Somme, as it came to be known colloquially, would help relieve pressure on the French at Verdun; it would complicate the Germans' efforts to contain the Russians; and—Haig confidently believed—it would provide the long-awaited opportunity to break the deadlock in the west by shattering the German lines. When that breakthrough occurred, the British cavalry would be waiting to pour through the breach and raise havoc in the German rear all the way to the Belgian border and beyond.

Consequently, as British preparations entered their final stages in the late spring 1916, fully 100,000 horses crowded behind the British front lines. All of them had to be provided with shelter, feed, and fodder, an enormous undertaking; and this number did not include the additional requirements of some 400,000 men. Equally critically, water had to be plentiful as well. To that end, pumping sets were brought in from England, water pipelines were laid, more than three hundred tanker-trucks found work hauling water to the billets, and a number of two thousand-gallon canvas water tanks were set up along the front.[52] In addition to artillery and draft horses, vast numbers were contained in the three British and two Indian cavalry divisions that Haig envisioned sweeping northward through the enemy's rear areas once the German lines had been broken by the British assault. Then, as one noted historian of the battle put it, "the hunt would be on." Haig's critics in the British government would be silenced. The German army would be run to ground and defeated. Northern France and the whole of Belgium would be liberated. The Allies would be crowned with victory.[53]

As is only too well known, the battles on the Somme did not turn out as expected. Losses were unprecedented, little was gained, and the British cavalry never made their sweeping ride. That is not to say, however, that the mounted forces escaped unscathed. They didn't. But their collective fate exemplified what many European detractors of the cavalry—anyone's cavalry—had maintained since 1870. On the modern European battlefield there was no place for a horse, or at least for a horse carrying a combat soldier. No less a critic than then–prime minister Herbert Asquith bluntly told Haig in May 1916 that the British cavalry horses in France were "of no use" and that the British government maintained huge stocks of war horses in France for no purpose. Haig, for his part, dismissed such criticism as the mere carping of ill-informed civilians.[54]

Consequently, when the British offensive opened on 1 July 1916, the British cavalry stood by expectantly. They went on waiting for the next two weeks. In the afternoon of 14 July, however, Haig launched the 7th Dragoon Guards in what he thought might be the beginning of the long anticipated mounted dash through the breach in the German lines. Carrying lances, the cavalrymen charged across open ground near the village of Bazentin-le-Petit on the southeastern end of the British line not far from the boundary with the adjoining French sector of the front. They killed sixteen Germans and captured more than thirty others, only to be withdrawn to the British lines again before dawn the next day. No mounted breakthrough followed because no real breach in the German lines had been opened.[55]

But, like their fathers in 1870, the cavalrymen and artillerymen on the Somme—on both sides of the lines—saw what modern warfare would do to horseflesh; and though the mounted forces didn't suffer the way the French horsemen had at Sedan forty-six years before, the carnage was every bit as sad. A new horror, beyond even poison gas, now confronted the cavalry and other horse-dependent arms: aerial attack. Though still in its infancy, the threat posed by strafing was nonetheless real whether the horses in question were cavalry mounts or ones pulling artillery and wagons. To cite but one example, two British aviators flying a reconnaissance mission over the Somme battlefield attacked German horsemen galloping forward with ammunition caissons in tow. The results were predictable. The lead mount "crumpled up, and the others, with their tremendous momentum, overran him, and whole lot piled up in the ditch, a frenzied tangle of kicking horses, wagons, and men. The second limber, following close behind . . . could not avoid its leader; its wagons overturned, wheels spinning, and split. Shells rolled over the road. We returned elated [to our airfield]." Not far away, on the same day that the 7th Dragoon Guards rode for Bazentin-le-Petit only a bit over a mile and a half to the west, a squadron of British horsemen was caught in the open by German artillery fire on the road leading to a contested village. "Dead and dying horses, split by shellfire with bursting entrails and torn limbs, lay astride the road that led to battle. Their fallen riders stared into the weeping skies. In front, steady bursts of machine-gun fire vibrated on the air. Caught by a barrage, these brave men and fine horses had been literally swept from the Longueval road."[56] Thus the situation remained for the British cavalry on the Somme for the rest of that months-long battle. They would eventually be withdrawn in early November 1916. As Haig told the commander of the Cavalry Corps, Lieutenant General T. C. McM. Kavanagh, on 5 November, the horsemen no longer had any real hope of a breakthrough "owing to the state of the ground," sodden as it was with early winter rains. Consequently, the mounted forces "might now be withdrawn to more comfortable billets."[57]

In that same year, on the French end of the front at Verdun, not only men but horses too succumbed to the war's carnage in unbelievable numbers. It was noted that on one day of the fighting there fully seven thousand horses were killed by long-range artillery fire, ninety-seven alone by the detonation of a single shell fired by a French naval gun.[58] Still others were caught and killed in agony by the "terrible fumes" of a German barrage using phosgene-filled artillery shells on 22 June in the last major German attempt to capture the town. On the Western Front, as to a certain extent on the Eastern Front, the German army is generally recognized to have fought the war more effectively from a technical point of view, only to lose the *Materialschlacht*.[59] In such a circumstance, cavalry forces, however useful they may still have been in theory, and however effectively they were employed in the war's opening campaigns, could not affect the outcome.

Cavalry on the Eastern Front

Throughout the war on the Eastern Front, the German cavalry played a more active and traditional role than in France. With localized exceptions, World War I from the Baltic coast to Rumania remained a war of movement. It could not be otherwise. Between Riga and the mouth of the Danube lay an airline distance of more than eight hundred miles (nearly 1,300 km), but the front could never be measured in airline distances because it included many hundreds of miles more in twists and turns. One theater of operations that was of central importance to Germany, Austria-Hungary, and Russia alike, namely Russian Poland, by itself measured more than 200 by 250 miles (320 by 400 km). Completely entrenching such vast distances was simply impossible. The front would always be "in the air" somewhere. Consequently, "both sides attempt[ed] vast and daring maneuvers against the enemy's flank and rear, just as they would in a later war from 1941–1945."[60] For the success of any such maneuvers, the cavalry's mobility remained critically important.

At the war's beginning, the Russian army mobilized no fewer than thirty-seven cavalry divisions.[61] On the German side, by dramatic contrast, there was only one, at least in East Prussia. This was the venerable 1st Cavalry Division, whose regiments were based at Königsberg, Insterburg, and Deutsch-Eylau. This division, along with eleven neighboring infantry divisions, comprised about one-tenth of Germany's mobilized strength in 1914. Though the numbers of German cavalry would grow enormously during the war on the Eastern Front, the initial disparity was owing not only to Russia's having to fight both Germany and Austria-Hungary and therefore needing more cavalry but also to the German General Staff's assigning East Prussia a secondary status in prewar planning. Primary attention and the accompanying resources went to the massive attack against France and Belgium in the West.[62] This particular German cavalry division, however, not only comprised storied Prussian regiments; it would also subsequently be maintained as part of the *Reichsheer* during the interwar period and go to war again on horseback in 1939.

One of the very earliest events on the Eastern Front also involved cavalrymen, though in this case they weren't German. On 6 August 1914, several hundred men of a formation known as Pilsudski's Legion—carrying their saddles—marched across the frontier of Russian Poland from Austrian Galicia near Cracow in the hopes of finding mounts. Wisely, they retreated when they were approached by Cossacks and eventually found their way into the Austrian army.[63] The incident is revealing, for the Cossacks' presence on the Eastern Front from the war's outbreak reinforced the conflict's likely intensity over the whole of that almost immeasurably vast area. From its beginning, the fighting in the east, unlike that in the west, carried overtones of "race war," a feature reaching its gruesome extreme in the Nazis' campaigns between 1941 and

1945. The prejudices between supposedly cultured Germans and supposedly barbarous Russians, with the Poles caught in the middle, were manifested from the beginning of the war of 1914. As early as 11 August, no less an authority than the director of the Prussian Royal Library in Berlin, Adolf von Harnack, pronounced that "Mongolian Muscovite civilization" once again loomed over the eastern horizon to threaten German lands just as had happened in the eighteenth and nineteenth centuries.[64]

This conjuring of the ancestral Western European fear of the horsemen of the steppe could not have been clearer. As it turned out, the very next day Cossacks of Russian general Pavel Rennenkampf's First Army crossed the East Prussian border, sacked the village of Markgrabovo, and ignited precisely the sort of panic that Harnack's "Mongolian Muscovite" hordes had created in generations past. Intensifying the German reaction was the quasi-melding of Prussia's identity with that of Germany as a whole, a process that had begun with Germany's unification under the direction of Otto von Bismarck in 1870–1871. Though certainly not universal, this identification of Prussia with Germany made East Prussia's violation by "asiatics" a national concern, not one limited to East Prussia itself. For a traditionalist unit such as the 1st Cavalry Division, Russian troops' presence on German, and especially East Prussian, soil would pose a grave emotional threat. A prominent later commander in the post-1918 Red Army (and eventual Marshal of the Soviet Union) only reinforced the apprehension accompanying such a threat by evoking the memory of Mongols' style of warfare. "The Russian Army," boasted Mikhail Tukhachevsky, "is a horde, and its strength lies in its being a horde." This image of rampaging barbarians who "would sweep into *deutsches Kulturland*" was hardly one to reassure East Prussians or other Germans either during World War I, the chaotic later days of the 1920s, or even in the 1930s or 1940s. As it was, the commander of the German I Corps in East Prussia in 1914, General Hermann von François, lamented the sorry plight of the "mad rush" of thousands of civilians away from the Russian horsemen and fretted that the refugees would impede his own armies' efforts to contain the invaders.[65] A senior staff officer who witnessed the invasion and who planned the defenders' operations, Colonel (later General) Max Hoffmann, subsequently noted in his diary that never before had war been waged with such "bestial fury." The Russians, he wrote with brutal succinctness, "are burning everything down." Buildings not burned were plundered. One eyewitness, a captain in the Russian 1st Cavalry Division's *Sumsky* Hussars, noted that in the campaign's opening days around Markgrabovo, "[the] scene on the German side of the border was quite frightening. For miles, farms, haystacks, and barns were burning. Later on, some apologists . . . tried to explain these fires by attributing them to the Germans, who were supposed to have started them as signals to indicate the advance of our troops. I doubt this, but even if it were so in some cases, I personally know of many others where fires were started by us." Not surprisingly, Russian cavalrymen, including the captain quoted here, helped themselves to the fine horses of East Prussia when in need of a quick replacement for blown, wounded, lame, or dead Russian mounts. Not a few of these horses came from the Prussian State Stud at Trakehnen, which lay almost directly in the path of the invaders. Some Cossacks also took human hostages from the civilian population, many of whom were deported to the east.[66]

In resisting the Russian invasion, the German armies in East Prussia fought a successful series of battles between 17 and 23 August near Stallupönen and Gumbinnen. These towns lay due east of the provincial capital of Königsberg with Stallupönen being almost literally on the Russian border. Later, around Tannenberg and the Masurian Lakes to the south and southwest, another string of even larger defeats would be inflicted on the Russians. In the fighting near Gumbinnen, the 1st Cavalry Division made a measurable contribution. Though they had sometimes failed to provide accurate intelligence of the Russian advance and been dismissed by the infantry as "frog stickers" because of the lances they still carried, the cavalrymen redeemed themselves. Flanking the Russians in good cavalry fashion, the German horsemen broke clear and played havoc with the Russians' logistics and lines of communication.[67] Having already served with the frontier defense (*Grenzschutz*) before its parent Eighth Army was activated, the 1st Cavalry Division had earlier fought at Stallupönen. Now, near Gumbinnen, it was in its element against a large but lumbering opponent advancing into the acute angle formed by the Gumbinnen-Stallupönen railway line and the River Inster. This opponent was the Russian Imperial Guard Cavalry Corps under the command of the Khan of Nakhitchevan. It had the mission of securing the Russian right wing. Fought to a standstill by German infantry and artillery around the village of Kaushen, the Russian cavalry faltered, and a gap opened in their front. Into that gap plunged the 1st Cavalry Division. The German horsemen broke through, and the ride was on—fully 120 miles (190 km) behind the Russian lines in barely three days' time.[68] It was a cavalryman's waking dream for the division's older officers. The division's commander, General Brecht, had entered the Prussian army in 1867, and two of his brigadiers were well into their fifties.[69] Still, the advance occurred in a fashion never duplicated on the Western Front after the first Battle of the Marne. It also created panic in General Rennenkampf's headquarters. Proving themselves generally better horsemen than their Russian counterparts, the division's troopers moved so far so fast into the Russian rear that they lost contact with their own forces. Consequently, the cavalrymen initially failed to get the subsequent orders for the great redeployment southwestward toward Tannenberg. As that redeployment got underway, however, the division was eventually given the cavalry's other great task: to screen and protect the German movement and prevent the Russians' taking advantage. Despite exhausted mounts, insufficient water, and reduced fighting strength, the horsemen had to harass and confound the Russians to keep Rennenkampf's army from coordinating with General Alexander Samsonov's to the southwest while the Germans pounced on the latter. Even though Rennenkampf continued to advance slowly but successfully toward Königsberg, the 1st Cavalry Division nevertheless managed repeatedly to put itself in the Russians' way. Most importantly, this one cavalry division succeeded in frustrating the larger objectives of an entire enemy field army.[70]

By stunning contrast, the Russian cavalry, three divisions strong between Gumbinnen and Tannenberg, not only failed to take any effective part in the former battle but also failed to exploit the real advantage of its own larger numbers in the latter. Nevertheless, and not a little unusually, it was the Russian 1st Cavalry Division that remained in constant reconnaissance-contact with the German 1st Cavalry Division's horsemen and accompanying bicycle-mounted infantry, and that over a frontage of thirty-five miles.[71] Thus the battles in East Prussia in August and September 1914 not only served to maintain the apparent viability of the German cavalry. They also had a much greater resonance, for they helped propel General Paul von Hindenburg and General Erich Ludendorff to the eventual supreme command of the German armed forces. These victories were ones that, according to one subsequent newspaper account, would for years haunt the children and the grandchildren of the Russian soldiers who'd been so thoroughly defeated there.[72]

Somewhat later, in November 1914, several German cavalry divisions also played prominent roles in the German Ninth Army's offensive into Russian Poland along a line stretching roughly northeast from Posen to Thorn. Aimed at the juncture between the Russian First Army and its neighbor to the southwest, the Second Army, the German offensive intended to relieve pressure on Austro-Hungarian forces to the south and simultaneously to forestall an impending Russian campaign aimed at the rich industrial region of German Silesia. While the Germans' III Cavalry Corps stood in reserve and helped screen the southern end of Ninth Army's line, the I Cavalry Corps comprising the 6th and 9th Cavalry Divisions had been assigned a more active role. Along with the accompanying 3rd Guards Infantry Division, the I Cavalry Corps had the mission of supporting Ninth Army's broad southeasterly advance through the central lowlands along the left bank of the Vistula toward the Polish city of Lodz.[73] Between 11 and 16 November, the Ninth Army, supporting the XXV Reserve Infantry Corps on the right wing of the German advance, covered more than fifty miles (80 km). On 17 November cavalry and reserve infantry were ordered to completely envelop Lodz to the south and west with attacks toward Pabianice. In doing so, they threatened the entire Russian Second Army at Lodz with encirclement and destruction. Unfortunately for the Germans, the Russian Fifth Army executed a heroic march northward to Lodz's relief—two of the Russian infantry corps marched more than seventy miles (112 km) in forty-eight hours—and forced the German cavalry and reserve infantry to fight their way out the way they'd come. While the Russians could claim a victory in saving Second Army from destruction, the Germans could equally claim that Silesia had been preserved from invasion.[74] In that strategic victory the horsemen of the I Cavalry Corps had played no mean part.

In 1915 the cavalry again played a significant role in a major German victory, this time in Lithuania. Having driven the Russians out of East

Prussia at the beginning of the year in the Winter Battle of the Masurian Lakes, German armies joined with their Austro-Hungarian allies to expel Russian forces from almost the whole of Poland in a gargantuan offensive during the spring and summer. These offensives included the dispatching of a strong cavalry force into Courland (Latvia) toward Riga in April and May as part of Army Group Lauenstein (later redesignated the Niemen Army after the river of the same name). The cavalry moved ahead with orders to destroy the Russian railways wherever the horsemen found them. Near the town of Mitau (Jelgava), the German riders captured a baggage train, ammunition wagons, and machine guns. To the south, they also cut the Russian railway on both sides of the junction at Shavli (Siauliai) before falling back temporarily. This ride was followed up in early September with a drive farther to the southeast toward Kaunas (Kovno) and Vilnius (Vilna). Three German cavalry divisions participated in this attack on Lithuania's two largest cities. In this offensive, begun on 8–9 September, the German horsemen supported the advance on Grodno, cut the Russian railway linking Vilnius and Riga at Sventsiany, and raided into the Russian rear areas as far as Molodechno and Smorgon, though the Russians subsequently managed to drive them and other German forces back and thus avoid encirclement. Indeed, the first German troops to enter Vilnius were the troopers of the *Death's Head* Hussars who reminded one native of the Teutonic Knights of five hundred years before, but without the cross.[75]

Similarly, in Rumania in 1916 German and German-led cavalry again had a prominent part to play in a significant victory. In the immediate aftermath of Rumania's declaration of war on the Central Powers in August 1916, Rumanian offensives had not only gained the passes of the Transylvanian Alps but also the easternmost portion of the Great Hungarian Plain. Anticipating such a Rumanian invasion, however, the German and Austro-Hungarian governments, supported by a willing Bulgaria, had already planned an invasion of their own. This took the form of a combined counteroffensive starting on 18 September to drive the Rumanians out of eastern Hungary. That successful effort was followed by a push across the Transylvanian Alps into both Moldavia and Wallachia by German and Austro-Hungarian forces, as well as an invasion across the Danube by German and Bulgarian troops into the southern

Dobrudja.[76] Pushing the Rumanians back through the Vulcan, Red Tower, and Predeal Passes, the flank of the descending left hook of German general Erich von Falkenhayn's Ninth Army was covered in part by a mounted corps. On 10 November the force began its advance down the Jiu Valley and into the lowlands of Wallachia north of the Danube. This region of Rumania constitutes the southwestern extension of the Black Sea or Pontic Steppe, a vast, undulating grassland interspersed with trees and stretching all the way to the Volga.[77] In many respects, it was ideal horse country for the cavalry, at least as good as the Polish plains around Lodz. By 21 November the advancing German horsemen and infantry had covered the more than sixty-two miles (100 km) to the important rail junction of Craiova, which quickly fell to the Germans. By 26 November, the German horsemen and infantry had advanced another thirty miles (48 km) and captured the one remaining bridge over the Aluta River (at Stoenesti) not destroyed by the retreating Rumanians. They thereby helped open the way for the drive on Bucharest. They also once again demonstrated the cavalry's utility on the Eastern Front in a fashion impossible in France.

In spite of these successes, however, the Rumanian forces in Wallachia southwest of the capital managed to launch a fairly strong counterattack on 1 December against Falkenhayn's forces and those of General (and *Death's Head* Hussar) August von Mackensen attacking from below the Danube. Here, too, however, the German cavalry made a signal contribution. To help stem this Rumanian counterattack, Falkenhayn dispatched a combined cavalry-infantry force against the right wing of the Rumanians. The horsemen and their accompanying infantry struck the right flank of the Rumanians, broke through, and got into their rear areas. In true cavalry fashion the German horsemen set about sowing confusion and inflicting heavy casualties on the Rumanians. As a consequence, they created a sense of panic that forced a Rumanian withdrawal. Bucharest fell shortly thereafter, and the Rumanians evacuated the whole of the Dobrudja. Those Rumanian forces still holding the lines in the great bend of the Transylvanian Alps were thus threatened with being cut off from the south. As a result, their position became untenable, and they too were forced to retreat into Moldavia. The setting in of heavy winter rains and snow, however, prevented the Germans from pursuing their defeated enemies. The year 1916 ended with the Rumanians hold-ing a rump territory in Moldavia adjoining the Russian frontier along the River Pruth. Nevertheless, the strategic victory to which the cavalry had contributed its fair share was enormous: Rumania was effectively knocked out of the war; German and Austro-Hungarian forces were released for service on other fronts; and, as in another war one-quarter century later, Germany now enjoyed unfettered access to large reserves of foodstuffs, oil, and other war matériel, including much needed horseflesh.

The enormous haul of goods resulting from the eastern victories of the years 1915 to 1917 was only reinforced in early 1918 by the Treaty of Brest-Litovsk, which the Central Powers (read, Germany) imposed on a Russia already undone by revolution. Whatever else it did, the treaty brought to Germany a seemingly immeasurable area of conquest stretch-ing away to the east and southeast. Included was the bulk of the Black Sea Steppe, while from the newly occupied Ukraine alone "Germany . . . obtained 140,000 horses during the war."[78] Bearing in mind that the Ukraine really only fell under German occupation as of March 1918, and that the armistice in France brought the fighting officially to a halt in November, the Germans' requisition-process was harsh indeed but necessary in any case. General Erich Ludendorff evidently thought so. Remarking on the acquisition of horses in the newly occupied eastern lands and the protection of that resource by German troops, he said pointedly that Germany could not carry on the war on the Western Front without the horses from the Ukraine.[79] Be that as it may, Germa-ny's armies were nonetheless defeated. However unwillingly, Germany was eventually forced to relinquish all of her conquests and a great deal more once the Allies delivered their own punitive settlement, the Treaty of Versailles.

*   *   *

As regards what was still then called the Great War, one may make sev-eral observations about the German cavalry between 1914 and 1918. First of all, by 1914 the German army had more or less taken to heart the elder Moltke's admonition about the cavalry's real mission in an age of increasingly deadly infantry and artillery weapons. That is, the German cavalry had finally come to rely primarily on its own firepower, combined with its inherent mobility, rather than hard-charging speed for battlefield success. At the war's beginning, German horsemen still trained with and carried swords and lances, just as did many of their European counterparts. Nevertheless, they also trained with firearms and used them effectively.[80] Consequently, German cavalrymen could realistically be used as infantry, even if they were only lightly armed. This was precisely the role they played on the Western Front. Against British and French troops in Flanders, the horsemen of Marwitz's cavalry corps found themselves in the trenches alongside their infantry brethren for various lengths of time; and, as noted above, it was precisely that service which was publicly recognized by the Bavarian Crown Prince in October 1914. This fact was perhaps indicative of their future role. That is to say, they would not be full-fledged infantry but neither would they be solely blade-wielding riders. In 1915 or 1916, particularly on the Eastern Front, they still looked quite a lot like their forebears of 1870. Nevertheless, they were already anticipating their descendants of the 1920s and 1930s.

This doctrinal and organizational evolution already showed itself in the German cavalry's organization going into the war of 1914. German (and British) cavalry regiments, for example, were routinely attached to infantry divisions and provided close reconnaissance and communications. Independent cavalry divisions could be attached to infantry corps for the same purposes at that level, and entire cavalry corps of two or three divisions each could be assigned to an army's commander in chief for the vital mission of "deep" reconnaissance and operational exploitation of the enemy's flanks and/or lines of communication.[81] One sees the successful execution of the latter types of missions at Lodz in late 1914 or in Rumania in 1916. Of course, the classic screening function of the cavalry did not disappear. Arguably the best example on the German side was the 1st Cavalry Division's efforts in East Prussia between the battles of Gumbinnen and Tannenberg in late summer 1914.

Enhancing these missions' effectiveness was the fact that the German cavalry divisions between 1914 and 1918 were actually combined-arms units of a sort that would be resurrected after 1919. Each division included at least one *Jäger* battalion, and sometimes as many as three, providing infantry firepower and a crucial maneuver element. A typical cavalry division also included horse-drawn automatic weapons, three horse-artillery batteries of four guns each, pioneers (i.e., combat engineers), a signals detachment, and a truck column.[82] Provided that all elements were up to establishment—always a crucial consideration—the German cavalry of the war of 1914–1918 was already a far cry from that of the Franco-Prussian War. While certainly not as strong in manpower or firepower as the infantry divisions of the era, the German cavalry showed that they could hold their own when pressed in an infantry fight and, when able to operate in the open on the Eastern Front, could still make a considerable contribution to victory and more than justify their existence. What, then, of swords and lances? Many small engagements occurred on both fronts, especially in the early days of the war, when edged weapons and couched lances were employed, and not only by German horsemen.[83] Nevertheless, the storied steel-on-steel, horse-on-horse collision of cavalry formations was almost entirely a thing of the past. But even in this respect there were exceptions, the most notable of which didn't involve German cavalry at all. In August 1914 more than two thousand Austrian and Russian cavalry fought an old-style cavalry battle near Jaroslawice in the borderlands of Austria's province of eastern Galicia. This was a day-long slugging match whose participants witnessed charges and counter-charges at the gallop, saber-swinging melees, and attacks with couched lances not only against other cavalry but also against machine guns and artillery.[84] The fighting at Jaroslawice did not notably affect the course of the war on the Eastern Front and was, by its very nature, something of an anachronism. Indeed, it was not noticeably different in spirit from the cavalry battles between the Germans and the French around Mars-la-Tour and Vionville in 1870. Anachronism or not, however, it long remained in the memories of those who fought it and managed to survive.

The German cavalry's fate, like that of German army as a whole, was sealed as the war became a *Materialschlacht*. Buttressed after April 1917 by the enormous and untapped resources of the United States, Germany's European enemies were assured of material reinforcement that the Central Powers could not hope to match. Not even Russia's coincidental revolutionary collapse that same spring affected this calculation. The only real hope for the Germans was to win the war in the west, the decisive front, before the Americans really began to arrive in overwhelming numbers. The result was Operation Michael, the great German spring offensive of 1918. Unlike the Germans' opening campaign four years before, the so-called *Kaiserschlacht* was an affair for the infantry and artillery only. The cavalry had no real role at all, even though the cavalry corps' original commander on the Western Front, General Georg von der Marwitz, commanded the Second Army. But even if the German cavalry played no great part, neither did their eventual successor, the armored forces. The Germans had only ten A7V medium tanks assigned to the battle as against the Allies' eight hundred machines. Despite this almost total lack of horse- or track-mounted units, the spring offensive initially made good ground. Between the offensive's start in March and the end of June, German forces at various points from Flanders to the Marne had once again reached many of the battlefields of September 1914. As in that year, Paris was once again taken under fire by modified German naval guns.[85] After four years of supreme effort, however, the German army simply no longer possessed the reserves of manpower, material, and morale to seal the victory. By the middle of August 1918, the tide on the Western Front had turned irreversibly in the Allies' favor. By November the German forces were in full but orderly retreat. Ominously for the army's fate, however, the government in Berlin had fallen, and a revolution of sorts was under way. A new, republican Germany would have to make whatever peace it could and save whatever could be saved.

How those matters would turn out, no one could really tell as the German forces marched back across the Rhine that autumn. Still, there were indications in the armistice that any eventual peace treaty between Germany and the Allies might well be harsh.[86] Regardless of whether and in what strength the cavalry might still be found in the postwar German army, the mounted units returned to their peacetime quarters with their pride largely intact. They had on the whole conducted themselves honorably and well, if not always with distinction. As winter 1918 came on, there seemed no immediate reason for them to assume that the German horse-mounted soldier would disappear, though he might well soon serve in fewer numbers.

The tributes paid to the returning soldiers were many and fulsome. In Germany that was to be expected, despite, or perhaps because of, the quasi-revolutionary turmoil in Berlin and elsewhere. More interesting was an equally laudatory tribute paid to the German cavalry by a man who was not merely one of Germany's enemies but a Marshal of France, Henri-Philippe Pétain. In an order of the day dated 1 January 1919 on the occasion of the disbanding of the Cavalry Corps of the German army, he credited his erstwhile enemy's horsemen with having made a significant contribution to the Germans' striking success on the Western Front in 1914. "Thrown in again and again on our left wing," he noted, "they successfully lengthened [the front] from the Aisne to the dunes [of the North Sea], during which they anticipated the adversary and permitted the timely deployment of their own infantry."[87] Such an endorsement from such a committed enemy of Germany said much about what Pétain thought of the German cavalry's wartime performance. Regardless of the static situation into which the Western Front eventually devolved, the German mounted formations had continued to bolster the German war effort, particularly on the Eastern Front. Cavalry traditionalists might well bemoan the absence of regular opportunities for the massed charge by war's end; and they did. Nevertheless, when undertaking missions within the cavalry's capabilities, German horsemen (and sometimes British and French, frequently Austrian and Russian) demonstrated that they could still be effective. They showed as much before and after Gumbinnen, in the invasion of Courland, in the campaign against Kaunas and Vilnius, and in the conquest of Rumania. In all of these operations they showed much of the same skill and tenacity as their ancestors of 1870–1871. Notwithstanding the technological changes on the battlefields of World War I, the assumption, albeit fading fast, lingered among some officers that the massed charge with cold steel might just still be possible and necessary under certain circumstances, however unlikely those circumstances might be. Such an attitude did not constitute mere intellectual blindness and doctrinal pig-headedness. Survival in combat, any combat, could sometimes be ascribed to an act of faith. For infantrymen and artillerists, or, later, airmen and tankers, believing that they would not only survive but win sometimes produced precisely that result in the face of apparently certain destruction. It was no different for cavalrymen. Particularly when, as in 1918, the technology did not yet exist that could definitively relegate them to the status of museum-pieces, the horsemen could still envision for themselves a place on future battlefields. Ultimately, the key to the German cavalry's—to any cavalry's—survival going into the post-1918 period lay in such an act of faith. It lay, in other words, "in combining the mental attitude which would encourage horsemen to take advantage of fleeting opportunities with the recognition that fire kills."[88]

CHAPTER 4

_____

ɟAlSE DAWN

THE INTERWAR PERIOD, 1918–1933

In the wake of 1918, the horse still loomed large in European society. Despite the increasing mechanization of all European armies during World War I, horses remained important in all military establishments, and of course in civilian society as well. Clear indications of that importance manifested themselves in the treaty of peace presented to Germany at the end of the Paris Peace Conference in June 1919. Annex IV of the Treaty of Versailles dealt, among other things, with specific numbers, and in some cases specific types, of horses and other livestock that Germany would have to surrender and to whom. The French Government, for example, stood to receive 500 stallions of unspecified breed aged three to seven years, along with 30,000 fillies and mares. In contrast to the stallions (though presumably they would be similar), the fillies and mares had to be specifically of Ardennais, Boulonnais, or Belgian stock, all three types being very large draft-horse breeds weighing up to 2,200 pounds (1,000 kg) and standing between sixteen and seventeen hands. Similarly, the Annex called for Germany to surrender to Belgium 200 stallions aged three to seven years and 10,000 fillies and mares aged eighteen months to three years. In the case of Belgium's haul, all of the horses were to be of "large Belgian type." All animals were to be "of average health and condition." In both the French and Belgian cases, these animals were presumably ones that had been confiscated by the German army during the war. However, "to the extent that animals so delivered cannot be identified as animals taken away or seized [during hostilities], the value of such animals [i.e., those delivered by Germany] shall be credited against the reparation obligations of Germany" as detailed elsewhere in the Treaty.[1]

This clear recognition of the horse's continued value to the civilian economy also found a certain parallel in military circles. The assumption that the horse might still play a part in future wars was not uncommon in Europe and elsewhere after World War I. As late as 1926, British general Sir Douglas Haig wrote that he "believ[ed] that the value of the horse and the opportunity for the horse in the future are likely to be as great as ever. Aeroplanes and tanks . . . are only accessories to the man and the horse, and I feel sure that as time goes on you will find just as much use for the horse—the well-bred horse—as you have ever done in the past."[2] In the post-1918 U.S. Army, too, occasional voices were raised in favor of the horse cavalry. No less keen an observer of the incipient armored idea than George Patton continued his informed speculation after the Armistice that mounted forces still had a role. In the January 1924 issue of the *Cavalry Journal* he acknowledged the importance of motorization for the future of warfare; but he also continued—as did his German counterparts—to envision a place on the battlefield for mounted forces. Thus he wrote that armored cars should be equipped to operate alongside, but not to replace, horse-mounted troops. "It is the duty of [the horse] cavalry," he said in a speech of the same year to the 11th Cavalry Regiment in Boston, "and should be its pride to be bold and dashing." Not only was such sentiment inherent in Patton's character, but it had also been reinforced by his two earlier stints at the French Cavalry School in 1912 and 1913. Furthermore, like many of his counterparts in Germany and Great Britain, Patton went into the postwar period still advocating the retention of edged weapons for the cavalry, in his case the colloquially named "Patton sword" (U.S. Saber M-1913).[3] Indeed, as late as 1941, Patton responded affirmatively to the Cavalry Board's enquiry as to whether the saber should be retained. "A cold steel weapon," he maintained, "is not only desirable but vitally necessary."[4] Nevertheless,

Patton did not advocate retention of the horse to the exclusion of the U.S. Cavalry's mechanization, as did some others. His equine advocacy was driven by practical considerations such as the limits of technology, as well as a by a certain military romanticism.[5]

Beyond such advocacy, and in terms of actual European military operations, cavalry played a prominent role in the brief but large-scale Russo-Polish War of 1919–1920. Hostilities, in fact, began with a Polish cavalry patrol stumbling upon a Russian camp in Byelorussia early on the morning of 14 February 1919. This conflict, which the Germans no doubt watched intently, was a "vast war of movement" with upwards of two million men sweeping back and forth across the plains of east-central Europe in 1920. One Polish cavalry division in the drive on Kiev in April 1920 covered more than 125 miles (200 km) in thirty-six hours. At Koziatyn on the road linking Kiev and Vinnitsa, later the site of one of Hitler's command posts during World War II, Polish cavalrymen captured, among other things, eight thousand prisoners, three thousand railway cars, five hundred horses, twenty-seven artillery pieces, and—oddly—three airplanes. On 5–6 May, other Polish cavalry actually occupied Kiev itself, admittedly in the absence of effective resistance.[6] Despite these serious setbacks at the Poles' hands, the Red Army's cavalry spearheaded a counteroffensive that drove the Poles out of the whole of the Ukraine in May and June, the Bolshevik commander boasting that his horses would be riding through the streets of Paris before summer's end. In this case the cavalry in question constituted the First Cavalry Army (*Pervaya Konnaya Armia* or *Konarmia I*), a massive force of four full cavalry divisions including some 18,000 mounted troopers, 52 field guns, 5 armored trains, 8 armored cars, and even a squadron of 15 aircraft. Possessing a fearsome reputation born of its Cossack regiments and its service against the Whites in the Russian Civil War, *Konarmia I* operated under the command of General (later Marshal) Semyon Budenney. It considered itself the elite of the Red Army and produced a generation of Red Army officers believing fiercely in the idea of mobile warfare.[7] In the fighting around Kiev in late May and early June 1920, *Konarmia I* broke through the Polish defenses and raised havoc in raids on Koziatyn, Berdichev, and Zhitomir. Budenney's horsemen wore down the fiercely resisting Polish Cavalry Division reserve in a number of classic cavalry engagements but also fought dismounted in cooperation with artillery and armored cars. Kiev subsequently fell to the Red Army's infantry, and a general Polish withdrawal from the Ukraine followed. By mid-August, Soviet cavalry had reached the bend on the Vistula at Thorn, only some five days' foot-march—and a much shorter ride—from Berlin itself. There followed, however, the storied "Miracle of the Vistula." Beginning on 15–16 August, a Polish counterattack annihilated three entire Russian armies. It also saw what one writer has called the "last great cavalry battle of European history" in the "Zamosc Ring," also known to history as the Battle of Komarow, on 31 August. Some 20,000 horsemen fought here as the retreating *Konarmia I* attempted to break free of encircling Polish infantry and cavalry in the stretch of forested hill country between the Rivers Wieprz and Bug. Charging and countercharging, the two cavalry forces clashed in Napoleonic style until the Polish uhlans and lancers carried the day and forced the Russians to withdraw. Moving faster than the Poles could pursue, however, large portions of Budenney's army managed to escape destruction and cross the Bug, thus reaching the safety of Soviet-controlled territory.[8]

With such a conflict raging just to the east of post-1918 Germany's frontiers, officers in Berlin could not help but ponder the matter of what military role the horse might yet play. Not surprisingly, in the German army, too, commanders assumed that the horse would still have a place and not merely as a draft animal. The army (*das Reichsheer*; after 1935 *das Heer*) constituted the largest element of the now famous "100,000-man *Reichswehr*" mandated by the Treaty of Versailles. Article 160 of the treaty specifically directed that the army possess no more than seven divisions of infantry and three of cavalry. Such a number constituted a tremendous decline in force-structure for an army that had been one of the world's largest between 1914 and 1918. From an already imposing figure of some 840,000 in 1914, the army in 1917–1918 had numbered some six million, a force of 241 divisions deployed across Europe from the Channel Coast to Courland and the Black Sea.[9] However, the treaty not only specified absolute numbers for the post-1918 army. It also implicitly determined what relative place in the army the various arms would have by prescribing that the army "be devoted exclusively to the maintenance of order within the [national] territory and to the control of the frontiers."[10] General Hans von Seeckt, effectively the army's chief of staff in 1919–1920 and its operational commander in chief as head of the General Troop Office (*Allgemeines Truppenamt*) from 1920 to 1926, played a pivotal role in shaping what post-1945 generations of planners would call the army's "vision." In such a capacity, he and his immediate subordinates necessarily confronted the vexing question of whether and to what extent horse-mounted forces could be retained.

Unsurprisingly, the cavalry divisions under Seeckt's overall command did not initially exhibit tremendous capability. As with the army as a whole, the former Allied Powers wouldn't permit that. On the table of organization and equipment (TOE), each cavalry division of 1919 numbered six mounted regiments. Each regiment included four squadrons, a machine gun section, and a signals platoon.[11] In addition to the mounted regiments, the German cavalry's divisional TOE of 1919 also included a pioneer battalion, a signals battalion, and an artillery battalion of three light horse-drawn batteries. Total divisional establishment was 5,300 men. Still, the question remained: what would the cavalry do? In defining the cavalry's mission, Seeckt drew upon not only his considerable intellect but also his own experiences during World War I, and his observations of the immediate post-1918 period. Having served on the immense Eastern Front, largely devoid of the fixed entrenchments so characteristic of the war in France and Belgium, he appreciated firsthand the continuing, crucial importance of an army's mobility. Whereas the fighting in the west had become largely immobile after September 1914 and was destined to remain so until at least the Battle of Cambrai in November and December 1917, campaigns in the east throughout the war had regularly ranged over scores and hundreds of miles. Generals on the Western Front, particularly Allied generals, had simply not been able to make use of the cavalry forces at their disposal. In the east, generals on both sides never suffered such a restriction. Seeckt therefore retained not only a keen interest in the mobile operations arising from such physical circumstances but also how to execute those operations in a German army functioning under the limitations imposed by Versailles. The upshot of his considerations was that, after 1918, he brought to his new responsibilities a continuing interest in maintaining a strong cavalry component in the army.[12]

Seeckt thought that the cavalry's equine horsepower might still have a place in a world of internal-combustion engines. He reasoned, quite naturally, that the massed charge with cold steel had in all likelihood become irretrievably a thing of the past. In this he shared the presumption of certain other Prussian and German military leaders going back at various points to Helmut von Moltke the Elder and his assessment of the Austro-Prussian War. Even before the war with France in 1870, Moltke had concluded that the cavalry's primary (and perhaps only) real functions would be reconnaissance, screening, security, and pursuit, but always ideally as part of a combined-arms force. As we've seen, those were precisely the German cavalry's roles in 1870–1871, notwithstanding the "Death Ride" at Mars-la-Tour. Again, in 1914–1918 the German cavalry had assumed largely the same missions and, when actual combat occurred, often fought dismounted.

Since 1914, however, European armies had experienced dramatic technological and, in some quarters, organizational changes. Motor vehicles were crucial to these changes but so were weapons possessed of ever-longer ranges and ever-greater lethality. Seeckt nevertheless thought that horse-mounted cavalry, as part of a combined-arms light division, were still capable of executing independent operations. They could play a useful part, he thought, at the level of the military art above the tactical engagement but below the strategic outcome in missions as specified by Moltke. Presuming their own incorporation of newer weaponry and vehicles, horse-mounted troops could even still be a force capable of tactical success at the small-unit level. When they fought, they would do so as infantry, but they would require more infantry combat power to be truly effective. In such light divisions, sometimes also referred to as mixed divisions, cavalry would therefore require the added firepower of organic infantry assets, notably absent from the cavalry's TOE of 1919. That infantry, in turn, would require bicycles, motorcycles, and/or motorized transport in order to keep pace with the horsemen. Trucks and bicycles, however, would have only limited cross-country capability. They were bound to the roads, whether paved or not. Further, since the proposed divisions' objectives would be varied and reached only over long distances, the cavalry would also need mobile artillery, whether horse-drawn or motorized; effective wireless communications; wheeled armored cars; and, perhaps, tanks. Foreseeing things to come, Seeckt also considered cooperation with the air arm to be of particular importance to the cavalry's effectiveness. Therefore, he even advocated placing aerial units under a cavalry division's command. The airplane's primary value to the cavalry lay in its function as a reconnaissance platform. It could extend the cavalry's line of sight by flying over the battlefront well beyond the cavalry troopers' reach. Significantly, however, neither Seeckt nor his Inspector of Cavalry, Lieutenant-General Maximilian von Poseck, saw the airplane replacing the horsemen. On the contrary, Seeckt, Poseck, and others envisioned aircraft as supplementing the cavalry by providing a true over-the-horizon reconnaissance capability. Absent effective air-to-ground radios, however, and in light of the airplane's relative frailty and limited endurance even in the early 1920s, not to mention the vagaries of the weather aloft, the cavalry's champions refused to see aerial observation as inevitably relieving the horseman of the important reconnaissance role.[13]

Indeed, as late as 1930, Seeckt would write that neither aircraft nor motorization had made the cavalry irrelevant. "The solution to the problem [of the cavalry's role]," he wrote, "lies . . . in making full use of the products of technical science to extend and modernize what already exists, but not by substituting something dead for something alive. The living arm, i.e., our cavalry, should be developed to its fullest perfection on modern lines without loss of its characteristics." Of the latter, the essential one was the cavalry's inherent mobility.[14] That mobility, when combined with newly mobile artillery and motorized infantry, he maintained, still permitted the "modern Seydlitz" not only rapidly to outflank the enemy but now materially to contribute to the "annihilating victory which is the aim of all military thinking."[15]

Notwithstanding becoming proficient with new weapons and vehicles, the cavalryman's real training lay in military equitation and daily horse-care. Otherwise, said Seeckt, all one ended up with was a "mounted yeomanry." Poseck emphatically agreed. He wrote that mounted infantry were nothing more than riflemen riding badly. Their inability at horsemanship would only nullify their mounts' most important advantage: mobility in pursuit, retreat, and surprise attacks on the enemy's flanks and rear. On the contrary, the post-1918 cavalry had to ensure that the trooper always remained not only a good marksman but also a well-schooled rider. Interestingly, Poseck drew upon the post-1918 French cavalry regulations when he affirmed, as they did, that the modern cavalryman had to have all of his military ancestors' skills in equitation while remaining the equal of the infantryman in dismounted combat. The ideal result would be to exploit the horse's natural strengths in effectively bringing modern weapons to bear without the trooper's running the creature into the ground. That could only come from combining firearms training as good as the infantry's with proper equitation, stabling, and regular and competent veterinary care.[16] Thus properly trained, equipped, and mounted, the cavalry's roles would include frontier defense; screening the advance; intelligence-gathering; reconnaissance; dislocation of the enemy's lines of communication and supply; and constant probing for a weak flank to turn or attack.[17]

Certain specific elements of the cavalryman's training aimed at enabling him to accomplish these varied missions. Before 1935, for example, horsemen of the German army were expected to receive as many as three thousand hours of equitation over the course of the twelve-year enlistment specified for common soldiers in the Treaty of Versailles.[18] River crossings also played a major role in the cavalry's training both with and without the support of combat engineers. Consequently, all mounted regiments were expected to conduct at least one large-scale river-crossing exercise per year.[19] Despite such rigorous requirements, and somewhat surprisingly, most personnel in the cavalry and artillery evidently did not earn the badge constituting the outward recognition of the horseman's skill. The Horseman's Badge, depicting a horse and rider performing a classical *levade* facing the viewer's left and wreathed in oak leaves, was presented by the National Association of Breeding and Testing of German Warm Bloods and worn on the left breast pocket of the uniform blouse. Awarded in bronze, silver, and gold, the Horseman's Badge recognized the recipient's relative level of riding skill and theoretical knowledge on the basis of civilian and military tests. Cavalry and artillery officers holding the rank of captain (*Rittmeister* in the mounted regiments and horse-artillery; *Hauptmann* in the horse-drawn field artillery) were expected to pass the required examinations. Many serving officers in these groups, however, tended not to wear the award even if they'd earned it. Apparently, they considered proper equitation and theoretical knowledge of their horses to be a given in their profession of arms and consequently didn't feel it necessary to wear an outward civilian expression of the fact.[20]

Supported thus by Poseck and others, with a suitable training syllabus in hand, and with a clearly self-confident officer corps at his disposal, Seeckt's considerations resulted in a revised TOE for a cavalry division. The revision appeared in the Army Service Regulation (*Heeresdienstvorschrift*) of 1923 and proposed a significantly different organization from that of four years before. As in 1919, the number of mounted regiments remained at six, but they were now to be grouped in three brigades of two regiments each. Internally, each regiment also now possessed a machine gun company instead of the earlier, smaller machine gun section. To increase each regiment's long-range hitting power, a section of two horse-drawn guns was added. It was other additions to the cavalry division, however, that transformed it in keeping with Seeckt's and his supporters' ideas. The division now also included a separate infantry battalion, a bicycle battalion (of three bicycle companies and two motorized anti-tank batteries of three guns each), and a machine gun battalion. This was the equivalent of adding a full regiment of infantry. Poseck called this addition of "chasseur" or infantry battalions to the cavalry "exceptionally useful." This usefulness, he maintained, had been amply demonstrated between 1914 and 1918, particularly when the infantry was truck-mounted so as to be able to intervene early in an encounter battle. He felt the same could be said of the bicycle-mounted infantry, though he admitted that such had not been the case on the Eastern Front with its paucity of paved roads. The divisional artillery was also augmented to the level of a regiment through the addition of a second, fully motorized battalion of twelve guns. To provide protection against aerial attack, a motorized flak battalion of four batteries was also added. Here again, Poseck's views supported Seeckt's. Poseck maintained that the war of 1914–1918 had clearly shown the importance of the "loyal fraternity of arms" existing between cavalry troopers and the horse-artillery, which had fulfilled all the demands made upon it. He wrote that increasing the number and weight of the cavalry's field pieces and adding anti-aircraft guns would only deepen this fraternity. Similarly, he believed that continuing technical improvements to the cavalry's carbines, machine guns, and artillery, when combined with better "fire training," would steadily increase the cavalry's fighting power just as had been the case in other arms. This fighting power, in turn, would "more surely enable the cavalry divisions to overcome enemy resistance and thus take full advantage of their horses' legs."[21] A battalion of twelve armored cars also found its way into the new TOE, and even a squadron of twelve observation aircraft and a motorcycle platoon were attached to the divisional headquarters. Rounding out the division's strength were the less glamorous but nonetheless critical support elements: a pioneer battalion, a signals battalion, a truck-transport battalion, a horse-drawn wagon battalion, a medical battalion, and a veterinary detail. To the extent that trucks and wagons maintained the cavalry divisions' logistical independence, Poseck deemed them "absolutely indispensable" based upon the lessons learned from World War I.[22]

This organization reflected the experience gained from the occasional attachment of infantry and armored cars to cavalry units in the German Army on the Eastern Front during World War I, a practice Seeckt would have seen firsthand. Interestingly, the Rumanian army had effectively employed cavalry and armored cars together against the Germans in 1916. For their part, the Germans in Rumania had also used armored cars in independent units in the same theater. Meanwhile, in the Baltic States in spring 1919, several *Freikorps* formations using trains, armored cars, and truck-mounted infantry had executed wide-ranging movements to good effect against the Bolsheviks. While the addition of such motorized units would increase the cavalry's mobility, the doubling of divisional artillery and the addition of large combat-support and logistics elements theoretically permitted the cavalry divisions to execute truly independent operations. The doctrinal development of this new organization would be under the aegis of the Cavalry School in the city of Hannover. Eventually, in 1937, the school would be transferred to Krampnitz just outside of Berlin as the army expanded rapidly under the Nazi regime.[23] The relocation would put the Cavalry School not very far from one of the most famous battlefields and one of the most famous homes in Prussian military history. To the northeast of Krampnitz lay the neighboring towns of Fehrbellin and Wustrau. In June 1675 Fehrbellin had been the site of a victorious battle against the Swedes, an event sometimes regarded as the birthplace of the Prussian army. Interestingly enough, that victory under Elector Friedrich Wilhelm was fought and won almost entirely by the cavalry. For its part, Wustrau was the ancestral home of the Ziethens. Field Marshal Hans Joachim von Ziethen, "Papa" to his men and "ancestor of all hussars," had been one of the most famous cavalrymen in German military history and had commanded the Prussian Life Guard Hussars during the Seven Years' War. No German cavalryman worth his salt could overlook these associations. Be that as it may, even while the Cavalry School was still located at Hannover, the academy's location was not accidental. The Hannoverian State Stud at Celle and its branches in the adjoining regions had been producing high-quality horses for the army and for German agriculture for many generations. Indeed, one of the great European breeds, the Hanoverian, takes its name from that very locale. Therefore, in terms of both personnel and horses, the needs of the army's new-style cavalry divisions would be enormous, given that each mounted regiment alone required more than a thousand mounts, not counting the parent division's needs for horse-drawn transport.[24]

The Cavalry's Role before 1933

Prior to 1933, the cavalry's training was predicated on Seeckt's original idea that the army should be a relatively small, professional force armed with the most modern weapons available to Germany under the restrictions imposed by the settlement of Versailles. While Seeckt initially envisioned an army of 200,000 to 300,000 men, the post-1918 terms limited the force to the ten divisions noted above. The manpower total of some 100,000 officers and men was well below the numbers Seeckt and others deemed useful. Consequently, the army's role had to be altered. By about 1921, Seeckt came to view the army as a sort of cadre serving a dual function. Its primary mission would be to defend the Reich and act as a military striking force. Its secondary but not unimportant function would be to serve as a foundational element for a rapid expansion to a force of twenty-one divisions. Seeckt viewed the latter strength as the minimum necessary to protect Germany from her putative continental enemies.[25]

At the time of Seeckt's command of the army and for years thereafter, those assumed enemies did not include the Soviet Union or Great Britain. Instead, they were limited to Poland and France and perhaps Belgium and Czechoslovakia. German animosity toward Poland throughout the 1920s remained visceral. Arising in the aftermath of Germany's defeat in 1918, Poland had been re-created by the victorious Allies at the Paris Peace Conference. Large swathes of Germany's eastern territories had been ceded under pressure to help constitute the new Polish State, with Poland's eastern provinces coming from Russia. The surrendered German territories included West Prussia, Posen, and portions of Upper Silesia. The city and immediate hinterland of Danzig were also lost. Though not given to Poland, they were administered as a "Free City" under the aegis of the League of Nations. Furthermore, as a result of these cessions, East Prussia was cut adrift from the rest of the Reich and was now separated from it by the so-called Polish Corridor. On Germany's western frontiers, the Saarland, like Danzig, had been placed under the supervision of the League, and the French had been given treaty-based rights of extraction of the region's mineral resources. To the northwest of the Saarland, beyond Luxemburg, the districts of Eupen and Malmedy had gone to Belgium. Adding insult to injury, French, British, Belgian, and American troops had occupied the whole of the region west of the Rhine from Karlsruhe to the borders of the Netherlands. In these Rhenish territories, though they remained integral to the Reich, Germany was forbidden to maintain military forces or build fortifications. To cement these various changes and restrain Germany further, the French Government entered into a number of diplomatic and military alliances after 1919. Of greatest concern to someone in Seeckt's position, as well as to those who commanded the army after 1926, were alliances between France and Belgium in 1920 and between France and Poland in 1921. These, then, were the geostrategic facts confronting the army as it rebuilt under Seeckt's leadership. These, too, were the conditions for which the cavalry trained.

That training centered, of course, on the cavalry's ability to move. As has been noted, Seeckt and others recognized that mobility would be the key to the cavalry's future military viability, provided that motorization and mechanization did not make horsemen superfluous in the interim. Seeckt maintained that the future of armies, of warfare itself, lay in the employment of relatively small, highly mobile, high-quality forces capable of simultaneous mobilization of the whole for either offensive or defensive action. In other words, both tactical and operational mobility were necessary for Germany's military, and therefore political, survival. The high degree of mobility he demanded would be achieved through "numerous and highly efficient cavalry, the fullest possible use of motor transport, and the marching capacity of the infantry." Of course, Seeckt also demanded that the most effective arms be provided and that replacements of men and matériel be continuous.[26] Herein, however, resided what would turn out to be an acute problem for Germany's war-making potential, though the issue was moot in the 1920s. Given modern training, equipment, and leadership, Seeckt saw no reason why the cavalry's days in the army should necessarily be numbered.[27] Any war against the Polish enemy would necessarily be a war of movement. Conversely, a simultaneous or near-simultaneous war with France would be more static and defensive in Seeckt's estimation, at least until the outcome in the east became clear.[28] Thus, the mobility provided by horse-soldiers was still an important element in a planning and training formula that by the mid-1920s regularly included bicyclists, motorcyclists, armored cars, trucks, and early types of tracked vehicles.

To a certain extent, this thinking embodied what might be called the lessons learned from the already-mentioned war of 1920 between Poland and Russia. Though brief, that conflict saw not only the widespread employment of massed cavalry formations but also extensive use of armored cars of varying types. They included proper armored cars made by Austin, Ford, and Renault, but also mere lash-ups constructed by putting plate-armor on converted Fiats (on the Polish side) and Putilovs (on the Russian). In fact, Poseck himself noted the effectiveness armored cars had already shown in sometimes hampering the German cavalry's reconnaissance during World War I. "They [armored cars] proved," he wrote, "that their adoption by us would be very much worthwhile." To the extent that the Poles' and Russians' experiences with armored cars in 1920 became widely known, they would naturally have reinforced his assessment. By contrast with armored cars, however, the tanks used occasionally by the Poles in 1920 were mechanically unreliable, prone to breakdown, and on more than one occasion actually had to be rescued by horse-mounted troopers.[29]

It was with these strictures in mind that the army's cavalry trained throughout the 1920s. Firearms had been part of the cavalry trooper's standard equipment since before World War I, and fighting dismounted had been included in the cavalry's training since the same period. Nevertheless, the army still issued sabers to cavalrymen in the 1920s and even lances until 1927. Notwithstanding Seeckt's thoughts about the massed charge's being a thing of the past, the attraction to cold steel remained strong among the cavalry's senior regimental commanders. According to one authority on the interwar army, all of the latter insisted on the lance's retention despite many junior officers' openly expressed doubts about its usefulness.[30] Similarly, equitation continued to be stressed in troopers' training, both in close formation and in open order. Such formal riding instruction constituted the equivalent of the infantryman's regular drill and ceremony and remained natural to the cavalry for routine movement, despite the recognition that massed mounted attack in formation would likely not recur. Indeed, as early as 1914, brigade and regimental columns had been replaced by the column-of-twos as the cavalry's preferred formation on the move. Also known as the double column, it remained the standard formation throughout the period from 1919 to 1939, although regimental columns were still used in field-parades and reviews. The principal advantage of the double column and its even narrower variant, the platoon column, was that it reduced a cavalry unit's front while on the march. In the case of the platoon column, for example, the column's front was ideally only about fifteen feet (5 m). In turn, the reduced front allowed the marching cavalry column to make better use of topographical features such as defiles, swales, or forested paths for cover from hostile fire and aerial observation. The double column would continue in use during World War II. The relative traditionalism of the cavalry's training in equitation might in part be explained by the fact that the training manual in use before the middle of the decade had been issued in 1912. That manual was not replaced by a new edition until 1926.[31] Formation riding continued in the training syllabus thereafter for the very simple reason that cavalrymen aren't cavalrymen if they can't ride tolerably well for prolonged periods. Even if they were now almost always to fight dismounted, they'd still have to use their mounts as the means to get to the battle. New training manuals would not change that fact. As a concession to modernization's inevitability, however, Seeckt's replacement as the army's commander in 1927, General Wilhelm Heye—an infantryman—ordered the lance's retirement.[32] The saber, however, remained standard issue as late as 1941.

Cavalry units took full part in the army's major exercises of the mid-1920s, as commanders wrestled with how to include horse-mounted troops. In 1926, for example, elements from all three of the army's cavalry divisions—including a full-mounted brigade—participated in the maneuvers in Group 1, which encompassed East Prussia. In the Group 2 exercises in September of the same year in southern and western areas of the Reich, cavalry again took part. In both sets of exercises, "tactical maneuver and movement were stressed [and] combinations of highly mobile units were tried."[33] Mounted troops were assigned mock tanks in addition to the mobile artillery and reinforced machine-gun elements now carried on the cavalry's TOE. They thus field-tested Seeckt's earlier efforts to maintain the mounted force's mobility while increasing its combat-power. Hearkening back to some of the early advances in the wars of 1870 and 1914, however, cavalrymen did not always ride in mass formations. Instead, they rode in small detachments as screening and reconnaissance assets to the infantry. It cannot be overlooked that this was precisely the function of the German uhlans who had gained such a fearsome reputation over the two preceding generations.

In general terms, the army seems to have been satisfied with the cavalry's performance in the various large-scale maneuvers of the mid-1920s. Tactical adjustments nevertheless occurred as a result of those maneuvers' analysis. Following the exercises of 1927, for example, the Third Cavalry Division's report to Army Headquarters stated bluntly that cavalry combat without tanks was "obsolete." Significantly, however, the same report noted that the cross-country capability of the mock tanks available for the exercises was inadequate to the cavalry's mission. As a result, the vehicles tended to be held back. To remedy the deficiency, Third Division urged the acquisition of sturdier, more capable vehicles for use as mock-tank chassis, in this particular case a machine then being produced by the firm Hanomag. At the time, "these were the only vehicles available with the cross-country capability suitable for cavalry maneuvers."[34] The mid-1920s maneuvers also demonstrated the continuing development of the army's more generalized efforts toward greater motorization and mechanization,[35] a development aimed at least at this stage not so much at abolishing the cavalry as adapting it to new technological conditions. Once again, this evolution reflected Seeckt's earlier efforts.

At this juncture the cavalry appeared briefly on the verge of significant expansion. In 1927 the Interallied Military Control Commission was withdrawn from Germany. This body had been established at the end of World War I for the purpose of ensuring that Germany did not violate Versailles' disarmament clauses. Though never entirely successful in that regard, the inspectors' presence did have the effect of making the army's post-1918 efforts to rebuild more onerous. With the Commission's withdrawal, plans immediately arose to expand the *Reichswehr* beyond the treaty's limits. An "emergency army" (also called the "A-Army") of sixteen divisions was designated as a sort of way station on the path to an eventual strength of twenty-one divisions. For the A-Army, the Weapons Office, which oversaw arms procurement, recommended increasing the number of cavalry divisions from three to five.[36] This was merely a part of the larger effort as of 1927–1928 to expand not only the army's numbers, but to increase national stockpiles of arms and ammunition for both the army and the navy; increase budgetary authority through greater cabinet-level support; and provide planning guidance for industrial mobilization.[37] Coming as it did from a procurement office known for its innovative approach to technology, such a proposed expansion of the mounted arm can hardly have been an expression of the cavalry's putative obsolescence. Evidently, however, the *Truppenamt* was not persuaded. It rejected the cavalry's expansion.

Instead, the various cavalry regiments from 1928 to 1933 began to be thought of as adjuncts to the infantry, even if they were not yet actually assigned as such. This process would be both formalized and completed during the army's breakneck expansion after 1933. In the role as it was eventually implemented, the cavalry regiments would no longer be brigaded and then combined into divisions. Instead, with one major exception to be discussed later, they would second ("chop" one would say today) squadron-sized units to the army's infantry divisions. There the horsemen would function as part of the infantry divisions' reconnaissance elements and serve alongside the other arms they'd operated with since 1919 and in some cases before: armored cars, bicycle- and motorcycle-mounted infantry, and combat engineers. Until the early 1930s, the army also envisioned attaching tanks to the cavalry when the latter needed extra firepower to hold positions for follow-on infantry forces. Indeed, from about the time of the maneuvers of 1927–1928, some cavalry officers themselves began to become more enthusiastic advocates for a progressive motorization and mechanization of the mounted arm, a position in step with the views of the then–minister of defense, General Wilhelm Groener, whose term of office had begun in January 1928 and ended in early 1932.[38] Nevertheless, significant opinion still saw a useful place for the military horse in an internal-combustion German army. In the same year that Groener's term of office ended, retired lieutenant general Ernst Kabisch, a military correspondent for the *Kölnische Zeitung*, wrote to Groener about the cavalry's new capabilities. Citing the military exercises of the autumn of that year, Kabisch maintained that the cavalry had undergone great changes and was no longer what it had been in 1919. It had now, he wrote, become popular among cavalry officers to envision their arm as constituting a force of light divisions. They would retain their horses and the Seeckt-era armored cars and other motorized elements, but they would also now add tank formations.[39] Popular though armored forces were becoming on the eve of the Nazi regime's accession, the tank and the armored car had not yet fully replaced the horse in the cavalry's mind.

CHAPTER 5

The Field of Mars

CAVALRY EQUIPMENT, HORSES, AND
DOCTRINE IN THE 1930s

The characteristic weapon of the German cavalry in the interwar period was the same one with which cavalrymen had been armed for centuries: the saber. The blade was thirty inches (76 cm) long and had a chord or width of one-and-a-quarter inches (3 cm). Normally sheathed in a steel scabbard, the M1916 saber's design very closely adhered to that of the truly fearsome light cavalry saber adopted in Prussia as early as 1796. It had an overall length of just under thirty-seven inches (93.9 cm). Issued to both officers and men until 1941, the saber was slung, edged curve to the rear, in a buckled frog attached to the saddle behind the rider's leg on the off side (the right) for enlisted men and the near side (the left) for officers. At the hilt the saber carried a fist strap tied in a colored knot denoting the trooper's regimental squadron.[1] In addition to the saber, cavalrymen also carried another edged weapon in the form of a fifteen-and-one-quarter-inch-long (38.7 cm) bayonet. The same as that issued to infantrymen, the mounted trooper's bayonet differed only in having a small leather strap and buckle attached to the frog. This addition kept the bayonet from moving excessively when the trooper was in the saddle. The saber's and bayonet's object, of course, was what it had always been among mounted troops: to instill the fear of cold steel. For the same purpose, as already noted, the cavalry also still carried lances, complete with pennants, until 1927. The lance was intended to be at least as psychologically intimidating as the saber and consisted of a piece of tubular steel ten-and-one-half-feet (3.2-m) long. When riding in column, a trooper gripped the lance at its midpoint with his right hand, arm bent, and carried the weapon at an upward diagonal extending over the horse's withers to the near side.[2] Despite their retention of edged weapons, and unlike in some of their grandfathers' experiences in 1870, German cavalrymen of the interwar period wore no armor other than a steel helmet, and their uniforms remained essentially the same as the infantry's. Modeled on the M1918 headgear of World War I, the cavalryman's helmet before the 1930s differed only in having shallow ear cutouts along the bottom edge, supposedly so that bugle calls could be better heard. Possessing a singular, wavy appearance when viewed from the side, this colloquially named "cavalry helmet" was eventually replaced by the standard M1935 helmet familiar to post-1945 generations as the *Stahlhelm* (even though the term applied also to earlier versions). As for the cavalry's service uniforms, the principal differences from the infantry's dress lay in the cavalrymen's wearing breeches with a full-seat leather addition, the leather overlay helping to keep the rider in the saddle while mounted. Proper riding boots were issued to all ranks. These differed from the infantry's in having a taller leg reaching to just below the knee; additionally, they lacked a hob-nailed sole. This feature allowed for easier use of stirrups. Naturally, mounted troopers also wore spurs. For the cavalry's dress uniform, some small traces of the traditional rider's flair were retained. The dress tunic or blouse, introduced in 1936, somewhat curiously had no pockets, but it did have the addition of decorative, turned-back "Brandenburg cuffs," the whole being trimmed in traditional cavalry-gold piping.

As for firearms, the cavalry trooper's principal individual weapon throughout the 1930s and into the first years of World War II was the Mauser 98k (for *kurz*, i.e., "short") carbine. This was a 7.92-mm, bolt-action weapon. It carried a five-round clip and weighed between eight-and-a-half and just over nine pounds (4 kg), depending upon the wood used for the stock. Based on an older version of the same rifle from World War I, the 98k was just over three feet (1 m) long. Originally designed for horse-mounted and horse-drawn troops, it was eventually adopted by the entire army owing to its ease of operation and "excellent ballistic characteristics."[3] The carbine originally rode, butt-down, in a boot or scabbard on the near side behind the rider's leg and was attached to the back of his belt by a strap. As happened with the German cavalry in World War I, however, the 98k eventually came to be routinely slung diagonally across the trooper's back in what was called the "Russian style." After 1940, cavalry troopers would see ever more types of semiautomatic weapons and machine-pistols entering service to replace the 98k.

Supplementing the cavalrymen's individual weapons, several types of machine guns supplied heavier firepower between the mid-1920s and 1936. The principal heavy machine gun in service before the 1930s was the "heavy machine gun Model 1908" (sMG 08 or MG 08). As the name indicated, the army had adopted the gun in that year. In its earlier variants, this weapon dated all the way back to Hiram Maxim's original of 1885. It had been used extensively, and to murderous effect, by the German army in World War I, particularly in defense of fixed entrenchments and fortifications. However, the weapon's weight of more than forty pounds (its immediate predecessor, the MG 01, had weighed more than fifty; 18–22.6 kg), not including ammunition and the gallon of water necessary for coolant, dictated that infantrymen simply would not be able to maneuver with it. In 1915 a somewhat lighter variant, the MG 08/15, entered service and was, in its turn, beginning to be replaced by the air-cooled and still lighter MG 08/18 when World War I ended. Despite the weight of all three versions, the cavalry's horsepower eliminated the problem of the MG 08's cumbersomeness, at least until the weapon was dismounted. Therefore the cavalry continued to use it after 1918. The gun had proven itself in mobile combat operations with mounted units as recently as 1920 in the Polish-Russian War. There the Red Army's cavalry had widely used a Russian-built version in the form of the *tachanka*, consisting of a Maxim gun mounted on a light, horse-drawn buggy or carriage. With the gun aimed to the rear, the Red Army cavalrymen would gallop up, turn and fire, and then, if necessary, gallop away again, firing all the while in a sort of modern-day Parthian shot. Though German cavalry did not employ the MG 08 in this fashion, the Russian experience did show the continuing usefulness of an older technology. When on the march in a German cavalry column, the gun, its ammunition, and its crew all rode on a limbered wagon pulled by a team of six horses.[4]

To overcome the earlier weapon's limitations, the army issued a new set of requirements in the 1920s, and the Dreyse model MG 13 was adopted. The MG 13 accorded with Seeckt's doctrinal emphasis on putting as much firepower as possible in forward units such as the mounted arm. Consequently, he followed the MG 13's development with some attention. At about twenty pounds (9 kg), it not only weighed much less than the MG 08 but also had a higher rate of fire.[5] By 1936, both the remaining MG 08s and the MG 13s were beginning to be replaced, along with the automatic weapons in other arms, by the justly famous MG 34 and, after about 1943, by the even more famous MG 42. Considered perhaps the first "universal" or true multipurpose machine gun, the air-cooled MG 34 was first tested in late 1933 by Mauser and constructed on the basis of an earlier, Danish design.[6] Weighing just over twenty-two pounds (9.9 kg) and measuring slightly more than four feet in length (1.2 m), the MG 34 fired 7.92-mm rounds of drum- or belt-fed ammunition to an effective range of approximately 2,200 yards (2,000 m). With a bipod stabilized cyclic rate of 300–400 rounds per minute, the MG 34 delivered very effective fire support for mounted and other troops not least owing to its rapidly interchangeable barrels. Made as it was, however, from finely machined components and requiring producer-specific ammunition for optimum performance, the MG 34 was relatively expensive and slow of manufacture. Its successor, the MG 42, possessed all of the same basic features and ballistic characteristics but with the advantages that it had a higher standard cyclic rate of 800–900 rounds per minute, was made of stamped metal parts, weighed slightly less, and could be produced somewhat more rapidly and cheaply. Given the larger demands of the *Heer* after 1943, however, the MG 42 was never as widely used among horse-troopers as the MG 34. In either case, the mounted arm now possessed an easily transportable and deadly automatic weapon. The MG 42 also enjoyed a considerable psychological advantage in the "tearing-silk, buzz-saw sound" it made when fired, a sound that made it impossible to separate the sounds of individual rounds being fired.[7] The MG 42 would go on to acquire a fearsome reputation among Allied troops on both the Western and Eastern Fronts, Russian soldiers even referring to it as the "mincemeat machine." When the cavalry was on the march, the weapon was carried barrel-down in a scabbard on the near side behind the gunner's saddle. The rest of the two- or three-horse load included the other members of the gun crew, extra ammunition, cleaning gear, and a tripod. Some indication of these weapons' success is revealed by the fact that a combined total of perhaps 526,000 MG 34s and MG 42s were produced by 1945.

The heavy weapons of the cavalry throughout the 1930s and at the outbreak of war in 1939 consisted of three main types. The most potent was the 75-mm "light infantry gun" (leichtes Infanterie-Geschütz 18; le.I.G. 18) developed by the firm Rheinmetall in 1927.[8] Actually a howitzer in American military terms, it carried the designation "cavalry gun" in the German mounted regiments. The le.I.G. 18 was specifically designed to be horse-drawn. Its caisson, originally rolling on two spoked, wooden wheels, gave the cavalry gun units the nickname "gypsy artillery." Later models of the cavalry gun replaced the spoked wheels with steel ones mounting rubber tires. This weapon was well suited to use in mounted units. Its high-trajectory fire could take good advantage of concealment, and its plunging shot was effective against reverse-slope targets. Further-more, the weapon's typical placement simultaneously offered protection from direct counter-battery fire. Specifically for these reasons, however, the le.I.G. 18 required good spotting of the fall of shot in order to ensure accurate fire. Depending upon a given regiment's designation following the mounted arm's eventual reorganization in 1935–1936, either four or six of these highly accurate weapons appeared on the unit's TOE. Fur-thermore, and again depending upon the regiment's designation and mission, the le.I.G. 18 would be towed either by a six-horse team or by motorized prime mover.[9] In the latter case, the vehicle in question was the much liked "motor vehicle 69" (Kraftfahrzeug 69; Kfz 69) built by Krupp. This was the so-called Krupp-Protze (Krupp limber), a six-wheeled, 1.5-ton truck with double rear axles.[10] In addition to the 75-mm howit-zer, the cavalry regiments also included a battery of three, towed 37-mm anti-tank guns in the headquarters troop and, at least notionally, a crew-served 50-mm mortar in each bicycle platoon.[11] The bicycle platoon was often equipped with the M1939 *Patria WKC* bicycle, a simple and rugged machine. It was unadorned except for an occasional headlight and the canvas cyclist's cape carried in a roll slung from the crossbar or handlebars. The *Patria* took its place in the cavalry's columns along with horse-drawn wagons. Of the latter, the most common was the ubiquitous Army Field Wagon 1 (*Heeresfeldwagen* 1; Hf1). Pulled by a team of two horses, the Hf1 weighed 1,430 pounds (650 kg) empty and could transport a useful load of 1,650 pounds (750 kg). The Hf1 also served throughout the rest of the army's non-mechanized formations.[12]

The Cavalry's Horses

In the 1930s, "cavalry" still meant horses. The concept of armored cavalry hadn't yet taken hold, though it loomed on the military horizon. Because the German army couldn't have cavalry (or horse-drawn logistics trains and artillery for that matter) without horses, several major breeding sources assumed particular importance. Given the varying requirements for cavalry mounts and draft horses, as well as mounts for officers in other arms, breeds' different characteristics influenced which horses went to which arm-of-service and in what numbers. Ensuring the supply of sufficient numbers also became critical. The losses of horses in World War I had been enormous, and not only in Germany. In the interwar period, breed-stock and the overall equine population nevertheless recovered substantially, and between 1929 and 1937 the number of horses in Germany fluctuated only slightly. In the former year statistical estimates indicated that 3,617,000 horses of all breeds were to be found in the country; in the latter year 3,434,000. By 1939 the number had risen to approximately 3,800,000, presumably under the pressure of the army's increased requirements as it expanded.[13] Though several different breeds were native to Germany, certain types, and the regions producing them, excelled in their service to the army both during the interwar period and World War II.

Certainly one of the most famous points of supply for both military and civilian horses in all of Germany was the East Prussian Central State

Stud at Trakehnen. Located just off the rail line linking Eydtkuhnen on the Polish border with the World War I battlefields of Gumbinnen and Stallupönen, Trakehnen had been established as a stud between 1726 and 1732 by King Frederick William I, the "Soldier King."[14] Originally a large stretch of low-lying, open, and wet moorland ("Trakehnen" means "great moor") adjoining the Rominten Heath, the Stud eventually encompassed some three thousand hectares of pasture and meadow and an additional three thousand hectares of rich farmland. The processes of canalizing and converting Trakehnen's moors to pasture and farmland were perennial interests of the Hohenzollern princes, as were the horses themselves, 30,000 of which were said to have been required to carry the first Hohenzollern king and his retinue from Berlin to Königsberg for his coronation in 1701. Frederick William I's son, the eventual Frederick the Great, would go on to drain more swamps than any other ruler of the age. In these efforts, pasturage for Prussian horse breeding would have remained important among the latter's concerns, as it had for Frederick William I. Land reclaimed from water-logged moors provided sustenance for horses as well as people, and horses were critical not only for farming but also for the Prussian cavalry.[15] After 1918, the army established a remount depot on the northern side of the railway adjoining the Stud. The depot also encompassed the adjacent village of Kattenau and its surrounding moorland. It was in the remount depot that the army collected and temporarily stabled horses purchased from the Central State Stud and the outlying regional State Studs elsewhere in East Prussia before shipping them to their various units.[16] The army prized these horses, and by 1912 East Prussia produced more than seven thousand remounts per year. By the 1930s, remounts were being purchased at three to four years of age, and all underwent a year of general conditioning at remount parks to bring them up to roughly the same standard of fitness. There followed a year's assignment to their units for a period of initial introduction to the saddle or the harness and a second year's more rigorous training for the horses' respective duties. Only at about six or seven would remounts actually begin an active-duty career generally envisioned to last for about ten years barring permanent injury, incapacitating wounds, and/or premature death. Though the army's demands fell immediately after 1918, by the 1920s the Central State Stud and its satellites were once again producing fine horses. These, however, exhibited a somewhat stockier build than those so heavily influenced by cross-breeding with English and Irish Thoroughbreds before World War I. The post-1918 horses consequently had a greater bone mass and a truer warmblood's disposition but still possessed elegant proportions. The Trakehner thus became the standard riding horse of the interwar German army, as it already had been of the Prussian army before 1914 and as it would remain later for the *Wehrmacht*. The official breeding goals as specified by the army for what it called the East Prussian Horse included, *inter alia*: "flexibility, toughness, a great galloping ability . . . endurance, a noble head, a strong elastic back with good saddle positioning, a deep and capacious chest cavity, [and] a high degree of impulsion (*Schwung*)."[17] By 1939 standard expectations for a good Trakehner stallion or gelding included heights measuring between 15.3 and 16.2 hands. Suitable girths measured between 75 and 79 inches (190–200 cm). The same measurements for Trakehner mares were 15.2 to 16 hands and 70 to 79 inches (177–200 cm) in girth.[18]

A second major source of horseflesh for the army's needs lay in another traditional region of German horse breeding. This was in Hannover, in what is today Lower Saxony. Centered on Celle—the aforementioned location of the army's Cavalry School—this area stretched northward from the River Aller into the Lüneberg Heath. Downriver it ran northwestward beyond Verden to Bremen and encompassed the flatlands of East Friesia and Emsland. In these fertile, windswept plains and low, rolling hills originated the renowned Hanoverian horse and its close cousin the Oldenburger.[19] Horses bred in the region were well known as early as the seventeenth century. They had served in the armies of the Swedish kings Gustavus Adolphus and Charles XII. In the 1690s, the English had also acquired cavalry remounts from this source. About 1675, the governor of the Spanish Netherlands wrote that he had never seen finer cavalry horses than those later called Hanoverians.[20] It was only in the 1730s, however, that the breed began to assume its modern characteristics. In 1735 King George II of Great Britain, in his capacity as Elector of Hannover, decreed the establishment of a centralized effort there to "promote horse breeding in our German lands, especially in the duchy of Bremen and the county of Hoya [southeast of Bremen on the

River Weser] . . . until such time as it has been seen what good comes of it for the land as a whole."[21]

After 1815, the establishment of the Kingdom of Hannover in the wake of the Congress of Vienna accelerated the development of a distinct horse-breeding economy in the region. In the second half of the nineteenth century, the Hanoverian finally became a valuable, multipurpose military and civilian horse. Indeed, the breed's military priority was stated explicitly in 1900 by the president of the Central Stud at Celle, who also happened to be a general officer in the army of what by then had become part of Prussia: "A horse suitable for use as a troop horse, heavy cavalry horse, artillery horse, or middle-weight carriage horse."[22] As to the breed's size, the Hanoverian's standard measurements before 1945 tended to be close to those of the Trakehner, though somewhat deeper from the point of withers to the chest and of a slightly heftier overall proportion owing to the lingering influence of the latter's eighteenth-century oriental crosses. As with most horses of predominantly German origin, the Hanoverian's overall standard height would increase somewhat after World War II, while the standard bone mass would drop a bit. The leaner, purpose-bred sporting horse of the postwar era was not the norm in the period from 1920 to 1945 for either the Hanoverian or the Trakehner. Of course, the indicated specifications of the German army's cavalry mounts did not necessarily coincide with those needed for the draft-horse labor of pulling artillery caissons or supply wagons, though cavalry horses were later routinely pressed into draft-horse service. Just as 1920s-era engineers of tanks or armored cars confronted difficult tradeoffs among vehicles' weight, weaponry, armor, and range, so too did horse breeders have to balance size, stamina, brute strength, soundness, and the nonquantifiable but critical factor of "heart" in horses intended for military use.

By 1914, 2,500 Hanoverians were being sold to the army annually. While fewer than the numbers of horses coming from East Prussia, the Hanoverians were at least as high in quality. Such sales were critical to the Central Stud's economic viability. As with the Trakehners of East Prussia, however, sales to the army fell dramatically in the years immediately after 1918 as Versailles' restrictions hit home. Nevertheless, and again like the Trakehners, but also as with the Hanoverians' close relative, the Oldenburger (as well as the somewhat smaller Haflinger of southern Germany and Austria), the currency collapse of 1923–1924 ironically helped stabilize breed-stock as persons still possessing cash looked for investments in property that might hold its value over time, despite the impending age of the automobile. This development stood the breed in good stead, as did the army's gradual and initially surreptitious expansion after the mid-1920s. The breeding goals specified by the army for the Hanoverian included a conformation similar to the Trakehner but with a slightly heavier head. Given the breed's intended military mission, its then heavier bone mass won the army's favor, as did its "outstanding jumping talent [and its] much calmer and more agreeable temperament." While the mass of the army's riding horses continued to come from East Prussia, the Hanoverian was only slightly less prized in both riding and draft roles. Somewhat by contrast, other refined breeds such as Oldenburgers, Holsteiners, and East Friesians served primarily as light draft horses for the army's field artillery as well as for the infantry's service support units such as logistics trains. Other German horse-breeding areas provided the bulk of the army's heavy draft horses. Interestingly, an indication of the army's view of the horse's future may be seen in its willingness to pay more for "coarse" artillery horses than for pure cavalry mounts, the former possessing greater bone-mass and pulling strength than the latter.[23] Whatever the breed of horse, the essence of cavalry warfare at the time lay in the transition from steady, sometimes fast, and often far-ranging riding in any weather and over varied terrain to dismounted infantry fighting. The German cavalryman having essentially become what earlier generations had called the dragoon, the horses selected for service in the mounted arm had to be able to endure routine marches of several days' duration over distances of 30 to 60 miles (48–95 km) per day all the while carrying between 200 and 250 pounds (90–113 kg) of rider and equipment.[24] Throughout the 1920s and 1930s, then, the army still had superb sources for the vast numbers of horses it required, even though it already envisioned a future of increasing motorization and mechanization. Whether cavalry or not, all divisions would include ever larger numbers of vehicles of all kinds (even though the vast majority of units outside the panzer arm never possessed adequate numbers of adequate machines). But until the sometimes facile prewar assumptions about vehicles bore themselves out, horses—Trakehners, Hanoverians, Oldenburgers, Haflingers, and other breeds—would still be needed in extraordinarily large numbers.

Veterinary and Remount Services

By 1939, caring for the hundreds of thousands of horses in the army on the eve of war consumed enormous resources of men and matériel, resources that would be expended in ever-greater amounts as the inevitable attrition of the animals occurred once the shooting started. Hence a sketch of the veterinary and remount services becomes important for a better understanding of the task confronting all mounted units as Hitler unleashed his war. The commander of the Army Veterinary Service was the Veterinarian Inspector General (*Generaloberstabsveterinär*), a post held from 1938 to 1945 by General Curt Schulze. Schulze's command, the *Veterinärinspektion*, was an Inspectorate of the Armed Forces High Command (*Oberkommando der Wehrmacht*; OKW). Thus he served as the commanding technical director in all matters of veterinary medicine and farriery for the entire army, not merely for the cavalry.[25] "During the war, he was responsible for [a nominal strength of] 1,250,000 horses, 37,000 blacksmiths and 125,000 soldiers. The veterinary service was divided into 236 veterinary companies, 48 veterinary hospitals, and 68 horse transport [units]."[26] The hospitals of the veterinary service treated approximately 100,000 horses daily for ailments ranging from general lameness and communicable disease to wounds from bullets and shrapnel after 1939. An indication of the service's success can be seen in a return-to-active-duty rate of approximately 75 percent of all horses treated.[27]

Each cavalry division was assigned two veterinary companies. Infantry, alpine, and *Luftwaffe* field divisions each were assigned one. Each veterinary company's hospital section provided care to wounded, injured, or sick horses brought in from the company's two collection stations. The latter could also provide the animals first aid. The collection stations were usually located five or six miles (8–10 km) behind the divisional front lines. Recuperating horses were shuttled from the hospital section to the veterinary company's supply section. Following recovery, the horses were first moved back to the collection stations and then out to the division. Horses in need of longer-term care were instead passed back to army-level hospitals and, if necessary, to the level of the appropriate army group. If necessary, they could be sent still further back to the "zone of the interior." Conversely, newly assigned or recovered horses coming from veterinary parks and remount depots at the army and army-group echelon flowed down the same chain. Eventually they reached the company-level supply section and moved through the company's collection stations to the division.[28]

Closely supporting and reinforcing the divisional veterinary service, army-level facilities played a major role. Each army was assigned a hospital for wounded and injured horses. A second hospital treated any horses suffering from infectious diseases, especially captured horses. The hospitals had a rated capacity of 550 horses, but subsequent conditions in Russia drove the numbers into the thousands. Supplementing the army-level hospitals were two motorized veterinary clinics, as well as a motorized veterinary test station capable of executing bacteriological, serological, and chemical examinations. The army-level remount depot, like the hospitals, carried a rated capacity of about five hundred horses but often stabled many more. An interesting feature at this level of command was the motorized veterinary park where horses might recuperate. The veterinary park, however, needed ready access to railway transport owing to its very heavy complement of equipment and, of course, for shipping horses to and receiving them from the zone of the interior. Hospitals could also be located at an intervening army-group echelon, but the principal connections remained those directly linking the zone of the interior and the army-level facilities.[29] As of 1935, the army's veterinarians were trained at the Army Veterinary Academy in Hannover in conjunction with the civilian Veterinary University (*Hochschule*) in the same city. There were also three principal military farriery schools in Hannover, Munich, and Berlin.[30] Given the huge numbers of horses in question, the demands on the skills and physical endurance of the army's veterinarians and farriers may be easily imagined.

Keeping the cavalry and the rest of the army supplied with riding and draft horses was an enormous undertaking. Remounts came from two sources: the army's own remount service and requisitions. Working in the Inspectorate of Riding and Driving of the Army High Command, the remount service's purchasing commissions bought horses both from state establishments such as those at Trakehnen and Celle and from private owners.[31] As before World War I, horses in the Reich were registered as to their potential military suitability and availability. Before 1933, registration took place under the auspices of various civilian agricultural organizations supervised by the army's Inspectorate of Conscription and Recruiting. Horses could thereby be declared militarily indispensable just as could civilians in critical occupations. Ideally aged three or four at the time of purchase, horses initially spent a year in one of fourteen regional remount depots before entering formal training at the Riding and Driving Schools located in the various Military Districts (*Wehrkreise*) of the Reich. In the remount depots, horses were brought to a uniform standard of maintenance. After 1939, the one-year conditioning period was often omitted with horses going directly into training. Even before the war's outbreak, the army's demands grew faster than the Reich's equine population. These demands forced the army to purchase horses abroad as early as 1936. Obviously, by 1939 demands for horseflesh had become voracious. In that year the number of required horses rose at a stroke from some 120,000 to almost 600,000. Domestic and foreign purchase, as well as requisition (whether compensated or not), rose even more dramatically once the war began: 148,000 in 1940; 282,000 in 1941; 400,000 in 1942; and 380,000 in 1943. As far as actual purchases were concerned, Hungary constituted a favored prewar source. That country alone supplied 25,000 horses for the *Heer* in the year 1934–1935, that is before the expansion of the *Wehrmacht* even really gathered speed. Rumania, Czechoslovakia, and, until 1939, Ireland also supplied stocks of horses. Eventually, between 1939 and the beginning of 1942, the German armed forces would also acquire 435,000 captured horses from the armies of Poland, France, and the Soviet Union.

In the latter case, the horses in question were the soon to be famous *panye* or *panje* horses. Known to the Germans by the same name as the small, two-wheeled wagons and wintertime sledges they pulled, these horses were often colloquially called "steppe ponies." In fact, they were seldom ponies at all in the zoological sense. Of indiscriminate breed, they nevertheless frequently reflected the physiological influence of the horses of the Black Sea and Kazakh Steppe, though one should be cautious in ascribing too much influence here to the taller and more elegant oriental breeds such as the Russian Orlov Trotter, the specifically Turkmen Akhal Teke, or, by extension, the Turkic Karaman. Often measuring only fourteen hands, *panje* horses tended to be smaller than their German or other Western European counterparts and therefore not as able to bear or pull extremely heavy loads. What they lacked in stature and finesse, however, they more than made up in hardiness. Capable of enormous feats of endurance, the *panje* horse could travel as much as ninety miles (150 km) in a day and sustain itself on nearly any edible vegetable matter: oats, corn (i.e., maize), barley, hay, grass, straw, weeds, and, when necessary, even roofing thatch and tree bark. Somewhat less efficient in its way of going than its larger western cousins, the *panje* horse could not easily be incorporated in marching cavalry columns without rapidly becoming exhausted owing to its shorter legs and the more rapid average pace of larger breeds. In horse-drawn logistics or artillery trains, the *panje* horse did not fit well when coupled to standard *Wehrmacht* vehicles whose traces and higher centers of gravity made it a much less effective draft animal. When pulling native Ukrainian- or Russian-style carts, wagons, or sledges, however, the *panje* horse performed well and earned a good reputation among German troops, particularly those outside cavalry and artillery units who often didn't possess good horse-handling skills. Given the smaller size of *panje* wagons and the numbers of extra personnel who would be required to man ever larger *panje* columns attempting to move the required amounts of supplies and ammunition, the German army never saw the *panje* horse as anything more than a temporary expedient, albeit a welcome one, for hard-pressed units, particularly in Russia's winters. Nevertheless, as German soldiers were to discover in the first winter in Russia in 1941–1942, *panje* horses could survive unsheltered in all but the very coldest conditions; and, as noted, they enjoyed the additional advantage of not only needing less, but also much less refined, feed and fodder than the *Wehrmacht*'s horses. In that respect, the German horses' standard daily ration in 1941 consisted of a whopping eleven pounds (5 kg) of oats for cavalry mounts and light draft horses; fourteen pounds (6.5 kg) for heavy draft horses; and nearly eighteen pounds (8 kg) for very heavy draft horses such as Belgians and Percherons. Of course, it should be borne in mind that uncooked oats in and of themselves do not have the same nutritive value for a horse as they do when rolled, steamed, or cooked as feed-mash. Rolled oats have their hulls cracked in the process, and steamed or cooked oats will tend to slough off their hulls altogether. In these cases, horses will be better able to digest the nutrients in the grain. By contrast, the hulls of the raw seeds make proper digestion more difficult. Consequently, much of the nutritive value of a given ration of raw oats would go in one end of the horse and out the other. Thus a larger amount of raw oats would be necessary to compensate for the relative loss of nutrition if the oats could not first be rolled, steamed, or fully cooked. Obviously, German cavalry, artillery, or draft horses would not always be able to be fed prepared oats in forward areas and/or locations at the far end of, much less beyond the end of, the logistics trains. This very situation would often present itself in Russia, as in the winter of 1941–1942. Greater reliance on local resources—sometimes adequate but all too often not—would necessarily result, with all that that would imply for the condition of the horses. In the mid-1930s, however, such a condition still lay in the realm of the unknown. In the meantime, peacetime rations of grain and sweet feed remained unchanged. It should be added that these rations of oats did not include an additional daily ration of hay varying from eight to eleven pounds (4–5 kg).

Of course, military horses work very hard and need generous rations of feed and fodder regardless of their arm of service. The rations-allowance nonetheless constituted a huge commitment of resources. Given the eventual exigencies of the war, such rations were not always available even when the horses themselves were. Consequently, *panje* horses not only came to provide a large proportion of remounts and draft horses after 1942, but they also drew less heavily on the army's supply chain. The latter factor assumed ever-greater significance with the increasing intensity of the Allies' strategic bombing campaign of Germany's infrastructure as of mid-1943. Coming from whatever sources they might, however, the army's cavalry remounts and draft horses still had to be found, and found they were. In the end, the total number of horses purchased or requisitioned from all private sources through 1944 reached the amazing figure of 1,645,000. Not counting further requisitions in the chaotic final year of the war, the grand total of horses (and mules) employed by the *Wehrmacht* during World War II approaches 2,500,000, and one source cites an even higher total of 2,750,000.[32]

On the Brink of War: 1935–1939

As with so many aspects of Germany's national life, the *Reichswehr* saw itself transformed by the accession of the Nazis to power on 30 January 1933. Throughout his public career before being named Reich Chancellor by President Paul von Hindenburg, Adolf Hitler had made it abundantly clear that history's verdict as handed down in 1918 possessed no validity for him or his party. That verdict would be overturned, and his would be the court to do it. As early as his first speech to assembled military officers on 3 February 1933, Hitler maintained that the prerequisite to regaining the Reich's strength, in fact the essential definition of that strength, was the expansion of the armed forces beyond the limits set by Versailles. For him, the armed forces were the most important institution in the State. No one and nothing could or would be allowed to interfere with their expansion: not the Western Powers, not any bilateral or multilateral international agreements, not general domestic constraints, not his closest associates in the party. On this score he never wavered, though initially he could not say so publicly. Until he could in fact speak publicly about the subject—that is, until rearmament had actually proceeded so far as to make international opposition less likely—his mission would be to mask the expansion process politically.[33]

An important early step in this process was Hitler's decision, supported by various elements in the army and the Foreign Ministry, to withdraw Germany from membership in the League of Nations as well as the League's Disarmament Conference. Taken in the autumn of 1934, this decision scored a huge domestic propaganda success for the Nazi regime. Furthermore, Hitler's determination helped solidify his early support within the armed forces and among the public at large.[34] Not coincidentally, it also occurred at same time as his decision, apparently made in May 1934 and announced privately on 1 October, to begin the secret expansion of the armed forces to three times the size allowed under the Treaty of Versailles.[35] With breathtaking rapidity, this secret decision was followed by Hitler's dramatic public announcement on 16 March 1935 that Germany had once more assumed her rightful sovereignty in military matters. He simultaneously announced the reintroduction of conscription with a one-year period of service effective 1 October 1935 and yet another expansion—a doubling in this case—of the army to a base figure of 600,000 men in 36 divisions. The unveiling of a not-so-secret *Luftwaffe* followed shortly thereafter.[36] Incidentally, in that same spring and summer of 1935, changes occurred in the nomenclature of the armed forces. The old, Weimar-era designations began officially to fall away. The term *Reichswehr* came to be replaced officially by *Wehrmacht*. Before 1935, the latter term had referred more or less generically to the military power of the Reich or any other State. Similarly, the post-1918 term *Reichsheer*, specifically referring to the army, also went by the boards. It was superseded by the simple *Heer*. Seeckt's old billet, the *Truppenamt*, also officially disappeared. In its place there reappeared the older "General Staff," a term and an office that had been specifically banned by the Treaty of Versailles as reflecting a putatively inherent Prussian militarism.

As much for political reasons as military ones, Hitler demanded that Germany's rearmament be driven forward at breakneck pace. In this demand he overrode or simply ignored occasional opposition from the army's leadership. He also permitted ferocious and ultimately unresolved competition for resources and manpower among the three branches of service—*Heer*, *Luftwaffe*, and *Kriegsmarine*.[37] Requirements for the same resources by many grandiose and propagandistically important public works projects only compounded administrative confusion as the Nazi satraps battled each other for prominence and perquisites. This internecine political rivalry further eroded whatever efficiency still existed in the army's expansion. This situation directly affected the cavalry in that the army's programs for motorization and mechanization, already viewed by some in the late 1920s as certain to replace the horsemen, did not proceed effectively. The *Wehrmacht*'s growth "remained a fundamentally unco-ordinated [sic] expansion of its individual services. An overall rearmament programme for the Wehrmacht did not exist." Of course, much is often made of the fact that the first three armored divisions were established as early as the autumn of 1935. Furthermore, almost exactly one year later the army had already reached, indeed exceeded, its own and Hitler's goal of a thirty-six-division force, a total that it was originally not supposed to attain until autumn 1939.[38] Nevertheless, throughout the six years of peace remaining between the Nazis' accession to power and the invasion of Poland, the army continued to operate under the guidance of a doctrinal manual still giving horse-mounted troops militarily important, if not critical, tactical and operational roles.

This manual, *Truppenführung* (Unit Command), appeared in two parts published in 1933 and 1934 as *Heeresdienstvorschrift 300* (Army Service Regulation 300). In its turn, *Truppenführung* had succeeded the important manual which had provided the basis of Germany's military doctrine throughout Seeckt's tenure as head of the *Truppenamt* and afterward. That earlier manual was entitled *Führung und Gefecht der Verbundenen Waffen* (*Command and Combat of the Combined Arms*—widely known simply as *das FuG*).[39] Important for the army as a whole and for the cavalry in particular was the latter's doctrinal restoration of the importance of mobile battle leading to the enemy's annihilation. The *FuG*'s emphasis on mobile battle resulting in the battle of annihilation (*Vernichtungsschlacht*) attempted to overcome the legacy of the positional warfare (*Stellungskrieg*) earlier waged on the Western Front between 1914 and 1918, despite that legacy's inapplicability to the campaigns on the Eastern Front. Importantly, the *FuG*'s restoration of the centrality of mobile-combat doctrine also returned to an older Prussian-German tradition of emphasizing as much mobility as possible, according to whatever the then-current technology allowed. Such a principle favored military commanders possessed of great initiative and fighting campaigns as briefly and decisively as possible. If anything could be said to constitute a true German way of war, this was it, not the great battles of attrition which had so dominated the image and conduct of the Western Front before 1918.[40]

In *Truppenführung*, the German army distilled its experiences since 1870, particularly in light of the initial victories and the eventual defeat in the war of 1914–1918. Throughout the manual, the army's doctrinal thinkers continued to envision a prominent role for the cavalry and for horses generally, notwithstanding the advent of the panzer arm. "Combat is the cavalry's principal mission."[41] A clearer statement of doctrinal intent and the cavalry's putative contribution to the army could hardly be imagined. It would be in reconnaissance and screening that most of the cavalry's combat would occur. From these two principal tasks others would derive: movements against the enemy's lines of communication; flank security; pursuit; and delaying actions (706–710). Eventually, after the invasion of the Soviet Union, anti-partisan duties would be added to the list. In clear recognition of the events of 1870 and the Western Front between 1914 and 1918, *Truppenführung* urged avoidance of mounted attacks against prepared positions. If, however, such efforts were necessary to fix the enemy in place (another classic task of the cavalry, as at Mars-la-Tour in 1870), then the horsemen were to undertake even these (707). In any case, they would normally fight dismounted, dragoon-style, and were to be supported as closely as possible by their own horse-artillery and automatic weapons (716). Mounted combat would be a rarity. If it did actually occur, *Truppenführung*'s authors wrote that such combat would usually result only from a chance engagement of two small units or from the surprising of an enemy formation. Nevertheless, the manual also stressed in very traditional fashion that a mounted attack against a demoralized enemy could have great psychological effect (718). When engaged, the cavalry divisions' own motorized infantry and artillery, as well as their bicycle- and motorcycle-mounted troops, would augment the horsemen's firepower. *Truppenführung* acknowledged, however, that these units would largely be limited to the roads and be dependent on "other arms" (i.e., horsemen, armored cars, and aircraft) for their reconnaissance and march-security (720–722). In spite of any such limitation, the cavalry divisions were deemed fully capable, along with their infantry counterparts, of independent operations and self-support precisely because of their organic composition (22). Their reconnaissance and screening value was highly regarded because of their all-weather, cross-country capability, a capability not yet matched by motorized vehicles (133). Conversely, horses' marching speeds of perhaps five miles per hour (7 km/h) at the walk and seven (10 km/h) at the trot compared very unfavorably with the eighteen to twenty-five miles per hour (30–40 km/h) of motorized vehicles (292 and footnote there), not to mention the critically important equine requirements of regular rest and watering halts (272–273, 303).

For all that the *Truppenführung* retained a major role for the cavalry, the writing appeared to be on the wall, or at least it would have been had peace lasted long enough for the army to acquire sufficient numbers of motorized and mechanized vehicles. A second part of the manual, published in 1934, covered the matter of armored combat vehicles (*gepanzerte Kampffahrzeuge*). At the time, this designation included both wheeled armored cars and the tracked progenitors of proper tanks (725–758). While the first panzer divisions would only be established in 1935, the manual clearly foresaw the horse cavalry's replacement. Furthermore, armored cars were explicitly envisioned as assuming the cavalry's reconnaissance functions despite armored cars' then-still-poor, off-road capability (727). For its part, the tank possessed much better cross-country capability but was still hampered by short range and relatively low road speed compared to its wheeled counterpart. Consequently, the gaps in the various vehicles' characteristics still left a place for horse-mounted troops to occupy in the years between 1935 and 1939, even if the evident tendency was toward the horse's retirement from the combat role.

Even if the *Truppenführung* seemed to herald the end for the German cavalry, nothing was yet a done deal, even in 1935. Similar arguments over the mounted arm's viability occurred at roughly the same time in other European armies as well as in the U.S. Army. To maintain that in 1920, 1930, or even 1935 all officers in every army stood convinced of mechanization's inevitability badly misrepresents the then-prevailing situation. Four of the five cavalry divisions in the French army, for example, were modified into mixed divisions between 1932 and 1939, and three still were still in service when war came. Each of these divisions required more than five thousand horses for its two horse-mounted brigades.[42] Similarly, in the British army, only two of twenty cavalry regiments had been converted from horses to armored cars, much less tanks, by 1933, and major armored experimental exercises had largely ended in 1931.[43] Of course, it remains true that the British army is the only major European army to go to war in 1939 without significant numbers of horses in the active forces. Nevertheless, what was written of the British army applied at least as well to the *Heer* after 1934. There was no

> heroic but vain struggle [in the German army] of a handful of brilliant iconoclasts, who were later proved right, against a compact

majority of antediluvian cavalry-loving diehards. Closer inspection
. . . shows that the reality was more complex. The progressives or
radicals did not agree with each other on all points and in some
respects their predictions proved mistaken or inadequate. Moreover,
although diehards or reactionaries certainly existed, the majority of
officers . . . could be described as cautious or moderate progressives;
that is, they recognized that machines such as tanks would play an
increasingly important part in future war, but they tended to stress
the numerous problems and uncertainties. How, for example, would
armored forces be supplied and repaired when far from base? Would
they not soon be countered by antitank guns? And above all, what
part would armored units play in military organization as a whole,
given the shortage of funds and equipment, and traditional interser-
vice rivalries?[44]

All of these considerations applied, mutatis mutandis, to the armies
that Adolf Hitler was even then preparing to unleash against Europe.

CHAPTER 6

bucking the Trend

THE CAVALRY RIDES TO WAR, 1939–1940

"**N**o one wants to see horses go to war, but they always go just the same to do the work no machine can do, wallow around in the mud, scout through forested and hilly country and bring up supplies where nothing else can get through."[1] Though written in the United States, these words still applied to warfare in Europe in the late 1930s. Despite the experience of World War I and the interwar years, the internal-combustion engine had not yet been married with wheels or tracks sufficiently well or in sufficient numbers to supplant the horse in every circumstance. In Germany and elsewhere, horses still played an important military role, particularly as draft animals. The German army's doctrine throughout the period from 1918 to 1939 certainly envisioned their use to pull artillery, supply wagons, field kitchens, and other vehicles; and even though the *Truppenführung* still countenanced a horse-mounted cavalry, the question remained whether the latter had any real role to play on the modern battlefield.

In 1939 the head of the Transport Department of the General Staff, Colonel Rudolf Gercke, noted that "as regards transport, Germany is at the moment not ready for war."[2] Coming as it did from the General

Staff's expert in the matter, such an assessment could only reinforce the assumption that literal horsepower was going to be crucial for the army's war effort. Of course, Gercke referred only to transport and logistics. Nevertheless, his statement also implied that if motor vehicles couldn't be had in sufficient numbers for the army's logistics trains, then they might also be lacking in the combat arms. If and when a war between Germany and her neighbors became a war of attrition, as indeed it did as of 1942, the matter would only become more acute.

Gercke's concerns touched upon the crucial matter of military means and political ends. Balancing the relationship between military strategy and foreign policy in Hitler's Germany constituted a crucial gamble for the dictator and the Reich. As in any State, Nazi Germany needed sufficient armed strength to make its policy's realization by force credible, if force were required. The *Wehrmacht*, in turn, required an organizational structure suitable to accomplish whatever missions were determined by the regime's foreign policy.[3] As events developed, serious imbalances between the two elements of this calculation caused equally serious problems for the realization of Hitler's ambitions. The longer Hitler remained firmly in power, the greater his ambitions grew. Similarly, the more he consolidated his authority, the greater became his apparent certainty that he and only he could achieve the goals he set for Germany. By 1939, he would repeatedly tell his military commanders, Foreign Ministry diplomats, and Nazi Party bosses that he was literally irreplaceable: no other German, whether military commander or politician, had ever possessed or would ever again possess his competence and daring.[4] The subsequent early victories between 1939 and 1941 only dramatically increased his hubris. Ultimately, he came firmly to believe in his own infallibility. Surrounded by an inner circle of military officers and party insiders who either could not or would not stand up to him—admittedly no easy thing, wielding as he did all the corrupting and murderous power of a popular, one-party dictatorship—he ultimately plunged headlong into the abyss. With him he took Germany, the rest of Europe, and untold millions of innocents.

Notwithstanding the regime's incessant propaganda, the armed forces generally and the *Heer* specifically were not the completely modern, battle-ready forces they appeared to be. Their readiness, or the lack thereof, largely depended upon the economic policies pursued after the

Nazis' accession to power. To be sure, Hitler inherited an army that was professionally competent and highly motivated. The views of individual officers notwithstanding, the *Heer* as an institution did not suffer from monarchist longings. At the same time, however, its interwar officer corps had not generally arisen in the same milieu as the civilian leadership of the defunct Weimar Republic. Instead, as a consequence of its now famous status as a "State within the State," the interwar army had focused its professional attention on its institutional competence, especially as regarded armaments and training.[5] In this respect, the *Heer* that Hitler's government relied upon can perhaps be regarded as the first truly professional army of the modern era.[6] How this professional competence and its attendant readiness would be affected by the new government's drive to war remained to be seen.

In the six years before the invasion of Poland, the Nazi government had achieved apparently spectacular economic successes. Nevertheless, harnessing the national economy efficiently to the production of war matériel never succeeded as thoroughly as the regime asserted. At the time of the Nazis' accession to power, the party had no coherent economic program.[7] Of course, Hitler had campaigned for the chancellorship partly on the basis of his intention to reduce Germany's severe, Depression-era unemployment. He also promised to secure the country's agrarian resources and to restore Germany's military strength. These generalities he made very clear. Attaining these goals was another matter, and he had no fixed plan. To the extent that he did state his government's economic objectives, several seemed inherently contradictory. Since the early 1920s, for example, the Nazi party had stressed a sort of lower-middle-class anti-capitalism and a desire to achieve agricultural autarky. Having now come to power, however, Hitler and his regime clearly required not only the economic but also the political support of Germany's traditionally export-oriented heavy industry.[8] Absent such support, there could be no re-armament. Without re-armament, there could be no reassertion of Germany's role in Europe. Certainly there could be no avenging the loss of World War I, no reacquisition of German lands surrendered in the hated Treaty of Versailles, and no conquest of anything more. Germany would not, so Hitler believed, be able to feed herself, and unemployment (affecting some 5.6 million people by the end of 1932) would not be tamed. Therefore on land, on the sea, and in the air, the aim of re-armament under the Nazis was the alteration to Germany's advantage of the European balance of power, and that as rapidly as possible.[9]

As early as 8 February 1933, Hitler insisted in Cabinet that "every publicly sponsored measure to create employment had to be considered from the point of view of whether it was necessary . . . to rendering the German people again capable of bearing arms for military service. This had to be the dominant thought, always and everywhere."[10] "The main principal," he went on to emphasize, "was everything for the armed forces. Germany's position in the world depended decisively upon the position of the German armed forces. The position of the German economy in the world was also dependent on that."[11] Hitler flogged re-armament along at a furious pace and not without the support of the generals and admirals. As seen in the preceding chapter, the total strength of the armed forces was something over 100,000 men in January 1933, as mandated by Versailles. By spring 1935, conscription, though banned by the treaty, had been re-introduced, and the ceiling of the army alone had risen to thirty-six divisions. The well-organized police regiments of the Rhineland were incorporated into the army when the Rhineland was remilitarized one year later. Austrian units were added with that country's annexation in early 1938. By the fall of that year, fully 52 percent of the German government's expenditure and a whopping seventeen percent of the Reich's gross national product flowed into armaments. These percentages constituted sums greater than those for Great Britain, France, and the United States combined. In that same year, the German army's nominal strength had risen still further to some forty-two active and twenty-nine reserve and *Landwehr* (third-line) divisions. Yet, there was still more to come. At the time of the invasion of Poland, the army's order of battle for field divisions was an almost unbelievable 103 divisions of all types. Of course, these figures did not include the extraordinary growth of the *Luftwaffe* since 1933 or the admittedly slower but nonetheless remarkable increase in the *Kriegsmarine*.[12]

Given these staggering numbers, the retention of a single horse-mounted cavalry brigade (subsequently expanded to a division) on the eve of war would seem superficially unimportant. One must, however, also consider that the *Heer's* infantry divisions in 1939 still retained horse-mounted cavalry reconnaissance formations, one cavalry troop (essentially equivalent to a company) being assigned to each infantry regiment. Thus each division had three troops of horse-mounted cavalry, as well as a mounted squadron in the divisional reconnaissance element. Furthermore, the infantry divisions also relied on horses to pull artillery pieces, heavy machine guns, ambulances, field kitchens, and supply wagons. Consequently, each infantry division of 17,200 men would include 5,375 horses in its TOE at the time of the invasion of Poland in September 1939.[13]

Of course, as early as 1934 certain officers had noticed the inefficiencies inherent in a too-rapid expansion of the army. Colonel Georg Thomas, then-head of the Defense Economy and Weapons (*Wehrwirtschaft und Waffenwesen*) Bureau, complained directly to Hitler. In a strongly worded memorandum dated 20 June of that year, Thomas complained of the economic friction and industrial wastage caused by the often vicious rivalries among Nazi Party bosses, competing industrial firms, and "misguided interventions and opinions of individuals." The result, as he bluntly put it to the Chancellor, was that "no decisions are made."[14] Consequently, he wrote, the economy, and implicitly Germany herself, would not survive the "coming struggle" if the economic chaos continued.[15] Hitler eventually responded to these and similar concerns not through administrative efficiency but by adding another layer of bureaucracy. Nevertheless, he certainly did not slacken the pace.

If re-armament were to continue and to be more effective, so Hitler reasoned, then greater economic centralization would be necessary, though he envisioned no State ownership of property per se, as in the Soviet Union. Similarly, he came to demand the greatest possible autarky in foodstuffs and strategic raw materials. His demands, however, were driven at least as much by strategic considerations as by mere economic concerns: the Allied blockade during 1914–1918 had demonstrated how vulnerable Germany could be if foreign sources of food and vital materials were interrupted.[16] In August 1936 Hitler ordered the establishment of a new national authority to coordinate the economics of re-armament. This coordination came to be embodied in a program known as the Four-Year Plan. To direct the effort and thus head the office of the Reich Plenipotentiary for the Four-Year Plan, Hitler named one of his oldest henchmen, the commander of the *Luftwaffe*, Hermann Göring.

With Hitler's constant urging and under Göring's direction, maximum speed and breadth, but not depth, of re-armament remained the watchwords. In theory, nothing would be allowed to hinder re-armament's pace. The plan placed particular emphasis on the greatest possible domestic production of several key industrial raw materials, including synthetic oil, gasoline, and diesel fuel; synthetic rubber; non-ferrous light metals; and iron and steel. Whether the processes were cost-effective or not was irrelevant, at least to Hitler and Göring. Nor was it particularly important to them whether great stocks of surplus matériel were collected before the outbreak of war. What mattered to them was having the weapons and matériel to hand when they decided to go to war. And as Hitler said in concluding the memorandum establishing the Four-Year Plan, the German economy and the German armed forces were to be ready for war by 1940.[17] Besides, as Hitler sometimes pointedly reminded his officers, Germany would go to war more or less when he decided, where he decided, and against whom he decided. As he quite baldly put it to his commanders in chief, everything depended upon him, upon his personality, upon his authority, upon his very existence.[18]

In May 1939 Thomas, by then promoted to general, presented his assessment of the economy and the state of re-armament in a presentation to personnel of the Foreign Ministry. In general terms, he praised the regime's accomplishments regarding re-armament, though he also pointed out that the depth of the regime's re-armament program in spare parts and material reserves did not match the program's breadth. Referring to the army, he noted with evident pride the successful creation of the new armored formations. Interestingly, however, he also specifically noted the establishment of what he called "the modern battle cavalry." Like the armored formations, he said, these cavalry units were "completely new" and had been developed only in the preceding five years.[19] His statement, of course, contradicted the record of steady efforts since Seeckt's day to adapt the cavalry to Germany's post–World War I military doctrine. Nevertheless, Thomas' reference to the cavalry in such a setting constituted at least an indirect indication of horse-mounted forces' continuing operational relevance. Any Foreign Ministry staffers interested in military affairs and worth their pay would have been fully aware that the Polish army at the time fielded some eleven cavalry brigades of its own, while the French army included three full cavalry divisions.[20] Furthermore, such diplomats, like their military counterparts, would have at least assumed that Poland would be Germany's likeliest enemy in the event of war. France would probably follow. Great Britain's inclusion in such calculations remained at that point a matter of some uncertainty. Subsequently, and only fourteen days before the invasion of Poland, General Thomas briefed, among others, the chief of the OKW, General Wilhelm Keitel, on the state of Germany's war economy. Thomas stated, evidently rather bluntly, that the Reich's economic preparations for war did not suffice. Germany "could not last through a war on the grounds of its war economy."[21] Insofar as the cavalry was specifically concerned, if Germany went to war with horses still on the army's TOE, and of course they were, then it would in all likelihood still have horses soldiering on when the end came (however that might be) for the good and simple reason that there was no way to replace them with machines.

Thomas' laudatory comments and simultaneous reservations notwithstanding, and despite the Four-Year Plan's relative successes, the Reich's economic mobilization was certainly not complete when Hitler launched the invasion of Poland:

> The war that broke out in 1939 cut across all [of Germany's economic] preparations. Neither foundation nor superstructure was complete; despite the growth of state planning and control, the transformation of the German economy into the instrument of super-power status was slower than expected. If war had not started until the mid-1940s Germany might well have proved unstoppable. In 1939 the whole military-industrial complex was still in the throes of expensive and lengthy construction.[22]

This condition had immediate implications for the cavalry's continued existence not least because economic inefficiency affected the army's motorization.

Incomplete motorization on the eve of war was, in turn, a conse-quence of the *Wehrmacht*'s inefficient growth after 1933. This growth was too rapid to be effectively managed, a situation exacerbated by the inevitable competition for resources among the three services. Hermann Göring and the navy's commander, Admiral Erich Raeder, both enjoyed direct access to Hitler. Ludwig Beck, the chief of staff of the army, did not. He had to go through not only the office of the army's then–commander in chief, General Walther von Brauchitsch, but also, after early 1938, through Keitel and the OKW. By attempting to create the largest and strongest possible *Wehrmacht* in the shortest possible time, Hitler in effect forced the army to rely upon much greater numbers of horses than might otherwise have been the case had re-armament been pursued with a steadier pace and clearer intent. As it was, shortages of materials and an increasingly fierce struggle among the services for what resources were available prevented a complete motorization and mecha-nization of the army. When combined with a certain traditionalism on the part of the cavalry itself, these factors resulted in the army's reten-tion of large mounted forces not only for logistics and combat-support but also for the combat arm.[23]

The Army High Command also played a role in the horse's retention. In the period between Hitler's accession and the invasion of Poland, it did not foresee a coming war's being won on the roads of Europe. The war, when it came, "was [envisioned] to be a railway war, just as 1870 and 1914 had been railway wars."[24] Not unreasonably, the army saw rail-ways as the most efficient means of moving the most men and matériel in the least amount of time. This view persisted despite the fact that the railways themselves constituted fixed, high-value targets for long-range interdiction either by fast-moving, horse-mounted or mechanized ground forces or, increasingly, aerial bombardment.[25] Before 1939, when the army's leadership fretted about the transport sector, it was the rail-ways that those leaders had in mind, not canals, air transport, or motor-ized road-haulage, the latter of which represented an equivalent of about only 0.5 percent of potential rail-borne capacity.[26] Not even Hitler's vaunted project for the *Volkswagen*, the "People's Car," met the army's motorization requirements. A military prototype entered testing only in 1940, and the army disliked it, even though it eventually entered service known as the *Kübelwagen* owing to its tub-shaped body. The vehicle lacked sufficient all-terrain capability and was underpowered with its air-cooled engine. The armed forces were also reluctant to commit to a single machine. Instead, they continued to allow automotive manufacturers to produce too many designs of cars and trucks. By 1942 the forces employed at least twenty-nine different types of automobiles and twenty-three types of trucks. This lack of standardization had unfortunate effects in the supply of spare parts and vehicular mass-production, effects that were not even partially remedied before 1944.[27] Whether in laying out the *Autobahnen*, producing the *Volkswagen*, or constructing and running the factories to build them, the automotive industry and the army did not coordinate their efforts in any way that corresponded to the Nazi regime's propaganda. On the contrary, "for most of the period [from 1933 to 1942] motorization and rearmament give the impression of being in competition not co-operation."[28] At the same time, there were never sufficient numbers of drivers and mechanics. The regime's two principal means of such training by 1939, the motorized units of the Hitler Youth and the National Socialist Drivers Corps (*Motorisierte* HJ and NSKK), never produced enough personnel. Those who did eventually complete the sequential training of the HJ and NSKK were for the most part siphoned off by the army's armored divisions. That demand was compounded after 1940 by the *Waffen*-SS, whose well-equipped mechanized divisions sucked up even more of the organizations' graduates. Simply put, there were not enough drivers and mechanics left over to meet all of the army's requirements, not to mention those of the navy and the air force.[29]

Thus the army that went to war in 1939 suffered from a great disparity between what it wanted to do and what it could do in terms of motorization and mechanization. This discrepancy only grew between 1939 and 1944, as attested by the chief of the Organization Department of the Army General Staff, Colonel Walter Buhle.[30] In general terms even Germany's victory over Poland, one of the most lopsided campaigns of the war, saw vehicular losses of 50 percent of machines deployed. Though the breathing space preceding the invasion in the west in 1940 allowed some expansion of reserves, especially of armored vehicles, the demands on motorized vehicles of all sorts would always outrun the Reich's ability to replace them.[31]

The army's expansion after 1933, as well as the rapid growth of the air force and the navy after 1936–1937, never constituted the perfectly organized, centrally directed, bureaucratically efficient process trumpeted so loudly by the Nazi regime. Propaganda notwithstanding, the desire to expand the army as rapidly as possible both numerically and qualitatively always remained hamstrung by Nazism's chaotic organization and by Germany's relatively limited resources. These were problems the regime never resolved, particularly when one considers the fact that the expansion of the other armed services and the *Waffen*-SS, when combined with that of the *Heer*, more than doubled the raw-materials demands of the *Wehrmacht* as a whole.[32]

The cavalry's retention, therefore, might reasonably be regarded as an anachronism, though a necessary one. The necessity becomes evident when one considers that the numbers of cavalry, whether in the independent cavalry formations or in the horse-mounted squadrons organic to the infantry divisions' reconnaissance battalions, went up throughout the war. They did not go down. "The speed and almost unrestricted and unco-ordinated [*sic*] armament of the armed services along with political factors led to the complete disregard of the lessons learned from the First World War which had earlier [i.e., in the 1920s] found total acceptance." The lessons referred to here applied to the management of Germany's national economy for war. Nevertheless, the mismanagement accompanying re-armament after January 1933 necessarily affected how the army procured vehicles, what types it procured, and how they might be employed. Thus, in addition to the army's peacetime complement of horses, 14,870 more had to be conscripted for the annexation of Austria in early 1938 and a further 4,539 for the occupation of the Sudetenland later that same year.[33] Not only did the cavalry and horse-drawn transport and logistics still exist at the beginning of 1939, the army could not execute even a major *non*-combat operation without them. Under the conditions prevailing in that year, horses simply could not be eliminated, and under the eventual demands of the coming war, the need for them would only grow.

Even the later panzer commander Heinz Guderian's detractors were proven wrong by these events. Early in his career when he'd been assigned to the army's Motorized Transport Department, he'd expressed the hope that one day truck-borne troops would become part of the combat arm. His immediate superior, a Colonel von Natzmer, brought Guderian up short. "To hell with combat!" snapped Natzmer. "They're supposed to carry flour!"[34] Not only was Guderian's hope largely thwarted by events, so was Natzmer's. Instead of trucks, it would be the army's horses that would continue to haul flour and a great many other things. Very often those other things included considerable numbers of combat soldiers.

Consequently, the German army would undergo a "de-modernization" during World War II, particularly on the Eastern Front. While the causes were many, including prewar economic mismanagement, combat losses, breakdowns, and eventual disruption of replacements owing to the Allies' strategic bombing offensive, the results for the troops on the ground were profound in any case. "Armoured divisions," writes one noted author, "began the war with 328 tanks apiece; by the summer of 1943 they averaged 73; by the end of the war the figure was 54. The German army fell back on the use of horses. During 1942 German industry turned out only 59,000 trucks for an army of 8 million men, but the same year 400,000 horses were sent to the Eastern Front. The German forces concentrated their air and tank power on a few elite divisions; the rest of the army moved like those of the Great War, by rail, horse, or foot."[35]

Organizing and re-arming the *Heer* to include a relatively small number of mechanized and motorized formations has been described by another author using what he calls the "Lance Comparison" (*Lanzenvergleich*). That is, the army by May 1940 would possess a "steel point on a wooden shaft."[36] Ten armored divisions would constitute the sharp end. These would be backed up by six mechanized infantry divisions whose personnel would eventually be known as *Panzergrenadiere*. Following on the organizational table and in the field were sixty-one ground-pounding infantry divisions. These, like the armored and mechanized infantry formations, were deemed fully operations-capable (*voll einsatzfähig*) both offensively and defensively. A further twenty-nine infantry divisions were designated as only conditionally capable (*bedingt einsatzfähig*) of offensive and defensive operations, and another twenty-eight divisions were designated for defensive combat only. However, one must always bear in mind that, in addition to the dedicated cavalry brigade still in service in

1939, each infantry division had horses in its organic reconnaissance element, usually referred to as a "detachment" (*Abteilung*). The standard TOE of such a detachment included 623 men, at least 260 horses (most, about 213, for the officers and men of the mounted squadron), 5 horse-drawn vehicles, and 130 motorized vehicles. Of the latter, only 2 or 3 were armored cars. Counting only the fully operations-capable infantry divisions—but not including any of the horses in those divisions' vast logistics trains—the total number of horses reached a nominal sum of 15,860. If one includes the army's 29 conditionally operational infantry divisions' reconnaissance units (again leaving out all draft horses and all of the 1st Cavalry Brigade/Division's horses), one adds a further 7,540 horses for a grand total of at least 23,400 mounts for combat personnel.[37]

Of course, once the war began, and especially in the victorious years between September 1939 and December 1942, Germany and the rest of the world seldom saw the foot-slogging, horse-supported infantry divisions. Instead, the regime's mass-circulation propaganda organs such as the very successful "German Weekly Newsreel" (*Deutsche Wochenschau*) and the lavishly illustrated magazine *Signal*, typically and effectively depicted just the opposite. One saw seemingly endless columns of "mobile troops" (*schnelle Truppen*) of which the cavalry were a part: trotting or galloping horses and, much more frequently, tracked and wheeled vehicles. Then, too, there were beguiling images of soaring fleets of bombers and fighters, majestic warships, lurking U-boats, audacious infantrymen, and daredevil paratroopers.[38] Whenever the equine reality predominated in still photography or newsreels, it tended toward the sentimental or the militarily romantic: depictions of mounted trumpeters, officers taking victory salutes, or intrepid cavalrymen by twos and threes in the depths of Russia.[39] Notwithstanding such images, the assignment of horse-mounted reconnaissance units to each nonmechanized/motorized infantry division; the continued existence of the 1st Cavalry Brigade/Division; and the hundreds of thousands of horses assigned the mundane but absolutely crucial jobs of pulling everything from ammunition wagons to ambulances to field kitchens, meant that the army simply could not have gone to war without the horse. And in light of the economic problems already discussed, not to mention the wartime dislocation eventually caused by the Allies' strategic bombing campaign, the horse's importance to the army's war effort would only ever increase.

Poland—1939

In September 1939 the army's 1st Cavalry Brigade had a mobilized strength of some 6,700 officers and men and nearly 5,000 horses. Its principal units (as also later in the SS Cavalry Brigade) were two mounted regiments, the 1st and 2nd *Reiter* Regiments. Stationed respectively at Insterburg and Angerburg in East Prussia, they maintained the unit traditions of such storied Prussian regiments as the 1st Dragoons, 4th Uhlans, and 5th Cuirassiers. As will be seen, these two *Reiter* regiments had been allowed to remain largely unaffected by the interwar decision to parcel the cavalry regiments out among the army's infantry divisions. Instead, the 1st and 2nd *Reiter* were tasked with the mission of determining whether and to what extent horse-cavalry could still actually operate in combat as a large maneuver element. Consequently, they were brigaded and had assigned to them a bicycle-mounted infantry battalion, the latter including a motorized signals platoon. The brigade's heaviest weapons lay in a horse-artillery battalion. It comprised three horse-drawn batteries, two of which were activated for the Polish campaign. Each of the horse-artillery batteries included four 75-mm guns. Other heavy-caliber weapons could be found in the brigade's motorized anti-tank company. It consisted of twelve 37-mm guns and a motorized anti-aircraft company of twelve 20-mm guns. Neither of these companies was activated for the invasion. Supply and administration, also not fully activated for Poland, included two light motorized and two horse-drawn supply columns; one light, motorized refueling column; a motorized medical company; ambulance, workshop, and supply platoons; and the critically important veterinary company. In its inclusion of motorized anti-tank, anti-aircraft, and signals elements, cyclist infantry, and so forth, the brigade somewhat resembled certain of the army's light divisions. On the other hand, in its horse-artillery it recalled the army's infantry divisions. Of course, the great difference between the brigade and any other unit in the army was its inclusion of two full, mounted regiments.[40]

For the opening campaign of World War II in Europe, the brigade, commanded by Colonel Kurt Feldt, was assigned to the 12th Infantry Division. The horsemen had the mission of guarding the extreme left (eastern) flank of the division, and thereby the whole of General Georg von Küchler's Third Army's advance southward from East Prussia toward the Polish capital of Warsaw. Prussia—and East Prussia in particular—represented the heartland of the German cavalry tradition. This was the land of the Trakehner horse, and it was here that the German cavalry had executed the famous delaying action in 1914 by screening German forces as they retreated and regrouped in the face of the Russian advance prior to the Battle of Tannenberg. Now, in 1939, the 1st Cavalry Brigade performed the German horsemen's classic missions of screening the advance and serving as flank-guard as set down in the 1860s by the elder Moltke, missions that began on the morning of the invasion's first day, 1 September. [41]

After a preliminary artillery bombardment, 1st Brigade advanced on and seized the small Polish town of Myseinice. At that time, Myseinice lay about twenty miles (32 km) southeast of the Prussian railway junction of Ortelsburg and about five miles inside the Polish frontier. Two Polish cavalry units, the *Novogrodska* Brigade and, more immediately, the *Mazowiecka* Brigade, were operating in the German horsemen's vicinity. It was evidently the latter's uhlans whom the 1st Brigade's troopers encountered and drove off in an actual cavalry battle on 3 September near the hamlet of Frankowo. [42] In the same three-day period, the brigade executed another classic mission of the cavalry. Determined Polish forces had unexpectedly held up the advance of Third Army's right wing at Mlawa, a town about fifteen miles (24 km) down the railway running southeastward into Poland from the former Prussian Soldau (Dzialdowo). This resistance, in turn, blocked any further advance by Third Army toward the larger and more important objective of Modlin and thence to Warsaw. Küchler therefore ordered Third Army's left wing to swing southwestward through Przasnysz, take the Polish positions in flank on their (the Poles') right, and then push on to Ciechanów. The country through which the cavalry and other German forces would have to pass lay along both banks of the Omulew and Orzyc Rivers, two southward-flowing tributaries of the Narew. Characterized by scattered, large forests and marshy terrain, the land proved tough going and not merely for the cavalrymen. Nevertheless, the encirclement succeeded. It effectively pried the Polish defenders out of their positions at Mlawa and permitted Third Army's advance on Modlin to continue. Screening and guarding this entire operation, at the furthest and most exposed end of the line, was the 1st Cavalry Brigade.[43] The brigade's campaign, along with that of much of the German effort, effectively ended by mid-September with the horsemen continuing to guard the eastern flank of the corps to which the 12th Infantry Division was attached in the advance up the valley of the Vistula. During the subsequent siege of Warsaw, the cavalrymen effectively used their horses' mobility to patrol the river's eastern bank and intercept scattered Polish units attempting to break through to the southeast.[44]

In its initial action, and more particularly in the turning movement near Mlawa, the brigade itself was not the only unit executing a classic cavalry mission. The entire corps (Corps *Wodrig*, after its commander) was acting, as it were, in the manner of the cavalry: executing wide,

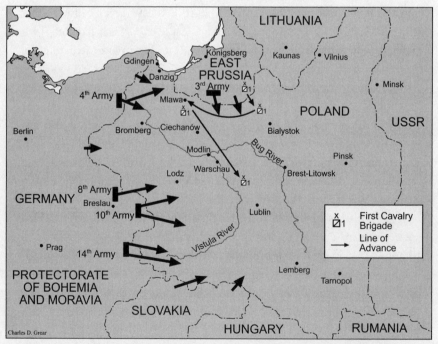

Map 2. The Invasion of Poland, September 1939

rapid, sweeping movements; outflanking the enemy's fortified positions or strongly held fronts; operating against his lines of communication; and either forcing him to withdraw or fixing him in position for the battle of annihilation. The German cavalry had done precisely this in 1870 as the French retreated from Metz. The result was Mars-la-Tour and the "Death Ride" of Bredow's horsemen. Subsequently, in 1914, the German cavalry had tried the same thing on the then-still-fluid Western Front, only to fail in the misnamed "Race to the Sea." Somewhat later, in 1916, German and Austrian mounted and motorized forces, accompanied by hard-marching infantry, had forced the passes of the Carpathians and carried out yet another such movement in the Rumanian lowlands, resulting in the conquest of an entire country in slightly more than a month. Now, in 1939, the army's post-1918 experimentation with what were then new technologies bore fruit in a sort of "cavalryzation" of warfare in Poland. The great and murderous difficulty of World War I, the recurrence of a war of fixed positions (*Stellungskrieg*), seemed finally overcome. War of movement (*Bewegungskrieg*) had apparently returned. The tradition stretching backward from Seeckt, via Alfred von Schlieffen of 1914 fame to von Moltke the Elder was restored.[45] The soon-to-be panzer armies would expand this practice to a vast scale in France in 1940 and, even more dramatically, in Russia in 1941. For the moment, the cavalry brigade seemed to be only a small part of that tradition and a superficially anachronistic one at that. Nevertheless, the cavalrymen would ride on.

Of course, both the German and the Polish armies employed horse-cavalry in 1939. One German panzer commander, F. W. von Mellenthin, recounted in a memoir of his wartime experiences that the best units in the Polish army in 1939 were "undoubtedly their cavalry brigades." These, he wrote long after, "fought with magnificent gallantry," and he went on to add, as have many others, that "on one occasion they charged our panzers with drawn sabers," a report also later noted by the commander of the 7th Armored Reconnaissance Regiment, Hans von Luck.[46] Though this oft-told story still makes the rounds in the history of the Polish campaign, it does not appear to accord with the facts on the ground in 1939. Certainly it resonates with the cavalryman's traditional sentiment. Even so, historian M. K. Dziewanowski states flatly that no such attack ever occurred, though something like it may have been the result of a meeting engagement, in other words a chance encounter between Polish cavalrymen and German armored units. Instead, Dziewanowski maintains that the story, however tragically endearing it may be for the tradition of the Polish cavalry, was the product of the Nazi propaganda ministry's efforts to convince neutral European States, as well as Great Britain and France, that further resistance to Germany's military might was futile. This version is supported by a recent history of the war that pays special attention to the Eastern Front. There the tale is of a Polish cavalry regiment hiding in a forest and subsequently attempting to escape but being encircled by German mechanized forces. Unable to break the ring, the Polish riders are decimated by German tank guns, and the account is then spun into the propaganda myth of Polish cavalry stupidly attacking German tanks. This individual incident aside, Dziewanowski nevertheless concedes the obvious: namely that the Polish army of 1939, though unfailingly brave, sorely lacked sufficient motorized transport and possessed "only two recently organized armored brigades."[47] Even so, the Polish cavalry was never so benighted as some have thought. They had, for example, experimented with the mixed divisional organization just as the Germans and French had done between the wars, and in 1939 each Polish cavalry brigade had an armored troop on its TOE.[48]

The tragic consequence of the technological disparity between the Polish army and the *Heer*, so far as cavalry was concerned, was the destruction of the *Pomorske* Cavalry Brigade, the very incident referred to by Dziewanowski. Within about three days of the invasion's beginning, the *Pomorske* Brigade and a number of other units were cut off in the corridor that had separated Germany proper from East Prussia since 1918. Whether the horsemen of this famous unit actually charged German tanks in massed assault or were ground up in a series of meeting engagements is of much less consequence than the final result, for in the general and desperate attempt to break out southward, the brigade was destroyed. Much the same end awaited other Polish cavalry formations, the "pride of the army" as the *New York Times* described them, as they retreated along with the remaining Polish forces toward the line of the Rivers Narew and Vistula.[49] One of these cavalry formations was the 18th Lancer Regiment commanded by Colonel Kazimierz Mastelarz. In an action that may well have been the genesis of the entire story of horsemen versus tanks, the 18th Lancers attacked and overran a weak German infantry position during the fighting in the Corridor. The lancers rode on, only to encounter several German armored cars whose gunners made short work of the cavalrymen. Notwithstanding such losses, the Polish horsemen during the campaign always hoped to have a better chance at least against German motorized columns and infantry, if not against mechanized formations, in the low-lying, often sodden, and frequently forested watersheds of the Vistula and Narew, precisely the sort of ground that the 1st Cavalry Brigade had successfully negotiated in its advance toward Mlawa.[50] Despite their many reverses, Polish horsemen did occasionally score successes against the invaders. On the night of 1–2 September, for example, Polish cavalry had panicked the staff of the German 2nd Motorized Division into hastily ordering a retreat from its assault into the Tuchel Heath between the Prussian towns of Firchau and Grunau. Only a direct intervention by the corps commander, General Heinz Guderian of XIX Panzer Corps, rectified the situation when he berated the divisional commander and tartly asked whether the latter had ever heard of Pomeranian Grenadiers being broken by enemy cavalry.[51]

In the final analysis, overall German superiority against Poland in 1939 meant that localized Polish successes and occasionally heroic Polish resistance could not stave off German victory, especially given the Soviet invasion of eastern Poland on 17 September under the terms of the Nazi-Soviet Non-Aggression Pact of the preceding August. Thus what the Germans unofficially called the "campaign of eighteen days" didn't really seem to give the German cavalrymen a chance to prove whether they could still fight effectively on the modern battlefield. The *Pomorske* Brigade's fate seemed to represent the fate of all mounted forces in the dawning age of truly mechanized and motorized warfare. Nevertheless, if that fate were already sealed, then it is worth noting the irony that the invasion "left half the German tanks and motorized vehicles out of action"[52] against a foe not possessing a truly effective anti-armor capability. Under the circumstances, therefore, OKW still did not yet know how the Germans' own cavalry would ultimately fare. Perhaps an expansion of the cavalry was necessary in order to provide the potential for the horsemen's true operational independence. To try to determine the answer to this question, the 1st Cavalry Brigade was reorganized after the end of the fighting in Poland. It was augmented with troopers from other mounted regiments whose personnel had been assigned to various infantry divisions' reconnaissance battalions in keeping with the army's doctrine from the late interwar years. Thus were added two new mounted regiments, eventually designated the 21st and 22nd *Reiter* Regiments. Additional elements, such as a second horse-artillery battalion, increased the brigade's strength to that of a full division.

The West—1940

Whatever disparities had existed in the Polish campaign between the capabilities of the cavalry and the mechanized and motorized units of the *Heer*, the mounted brigade's combat effectiveness seemed to warrant expansion to divisional status in the last quarter of 1939. As earlier with the Cavalry Brigade, so now in the 1st Cavalry Division, the principal maneuver elements remained the horse- and bicycle-mounted units, with the horse-artillery still delivering the heaviest offensive punch. The recognition of the cavalry's contribution through its expansion to divisional status was no doubt gratifying to its personnel. It should also be noted, however, that others also watched keenly. The cavalry's relative success to this point in the war was not lost on the Nazi Party's SS formations. Their leadership, too, had already begun deploying horse-mounted units in occupied Poland for rear-area security duties. These units' subsequent organization and mission would in certain respects ape the Cavalry Division's own, even if SS men's ethos didn't.

Be that as it may, by the spring of 1940 and with the impending campaigns in the west, and following the unprovoked invasions of both Denmark and Norway in April, the newly redesignated 1st Cavalry Division was assigned to Küchler's new command, Eighteenth Army of German Army Group B. As had been the case in Poland, the horsemen found themselves on the far end of the line, this time the extreme right (northern) flank of the army. It remains an open question whether the division was assigned there merely to keep it out of the way or so that it could once again perform the traditional mounted troops' mission of providing security and screening the flanks of an advance. Presumably its assignment there was intended further to test the operational viability of a now-division-sized, mounted maneuver-force. However that may be, the cavalrymen's assigned frontage began at the Dollard, a bay of the River Ems lying directly to the south of the German port of Emden. From the Dollard the division's area of operations stretched some sixty-two miles (100 km) to a point just southwest of the German city of Lin-gen. The horsemen's mission was to break through Dutch frontier obstacles—a zone judged to be about twelve miles (20 km) deep—and occupy the northern provinces of Groningen, Drenthe, and Friesland. The cavalrymen would then face south, be shipped across the Ijsselmeer, and break into "Fortress Holland," the quasi-official Dutch name for the core defensive area of the Netherlands.[53]

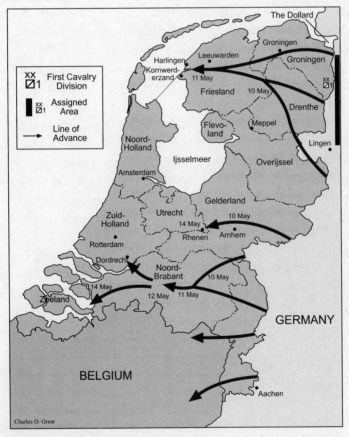

Map 3. The First Cavalry Division in the Netherlands, May 1940

The division's command assessed its assigned mission area as "the most unsuitable terrain imaginable" (*das denkbar Ungünstigste*) for mounted operations: numerous rivers, countless bridges, and virtually bottomless footing (*ungangbare tiefe Gelände*) made movement "almost impossible." The fact that the Dutch forces facing them were motorized made the cavalrymen's task of maintaining contact with the enemy even more difficult.[54] Nevertheless, the division reported that on the campaign's first day, 10 May 1940, things had gone well. In several areas the cavalrymen had outflanked Dutch pillboxes at the gallop and had penetrated enemy territory to a depth of several miles within the first twenty minutes of fighting, and this over terrain "impassable for motorized vehicles." By day's end, the initial objective, a line running southwest from the city of Groningen to Meppel and roughly bisecting the whole of northern Holland, had been reached. By the end of 11 May the horses of the division's most advanced elements were being watered on the coast at Harlingen and along the northeastern shores of the Ijsselmeer, follow-on units reaching these areas over the next five days. Remarkably, the division's *Reiter* regiments had covered some 111 miles (180 km) in two days, a feat indicating less than fanatical Dutch resistance. On the coast, however, the division's troopers ran headlong into strong fortifications along the edge of the Ijsselmeer. At the northern end of the dike separating that body of water from the sea and linking the province of Friesland with North Holland farther to the south stood a number of modern fortifications at Kornwerderzand. Ordered to storm the casemates and gain control of the dike, the division's (cyclist) infantry, dismounted horsemen, and horse-artillery nevertheless failed to overcome the Dutch defenses despite repeated assaults on 12–13 May. Even supporting attacks by *Luftwaffe* dive-bombers and shelling by a battery of 88-mm guns that appeared on the scene could not blast the defenders from their positions. The point was moot in any case. Too high a sea-state and a galling fire from three Dutch naval vessels would have prevented the division being ferried across the Ijsselmeer to fight in "Fortress Holland" even if Kornwerderzand had fallen to the invaders.[55] Ultimately, however, such reverses for the cavalrymen made no difference. The invasion's outcome was decided much farther to the south where the principal fighting had occurred. On 14 May, Dutch forces capitulated.

After a campaign of only one week, the division received orders on 17 May to return to its original main assembly area around Lingen pending further assignment. By the time the *Reiter* regiments completed their reassembly three days later, they had ridden almost 435 miles (700 km) in ten days.[56] With the exception of the fighting at Kornwerderzand, all assigned objectives had been achieved, and all of the division's vehicles had been successfully brought along. After-action analysis maintained that the division's advance would not have been possible had it been forced to rely solely on vehicles. Though difficult for horses, the sodden terrain would have been impassable for vehicles, though the same report pointedly failed to explain how the Dutch repeatedly managed to use their own vehicles to escape. On the contrary, the division's horses had made possible the initial skirting and envelopment of Dutch frontier defenses by means of tracks (*Wege*) that only horses could use. Even so, divisional staff deemed it particularly important that the (unspecified) casualties among men and horses be replaced and that all of the latter be reshod before any possible action in France. Where the horsemen had ridden hard-graveled roads (*Klinkersteinstrassen*), they found that their horses' shoes had worn badly. No one wanted worn horseshoes to interfere with the entire division's sole desire: to take part in an invasion of France. To ensure that the point was not lost on higher echelons, and perhaps to stave off army- or army group–level criticism of the division's performance, the report struck a defensive note and argued that the fighting in the Netherlands simply could not be used to determine whether a horse-mounted cavalry division was still effective.[57] Between 24 and 28 May, the 1st Cavalry Division moved by rail to the area around Aachen where it encamped and awaited its next assignment. Twice in this period, Army Group B issued orders that the division would handle the transport of POWs to Germany. The division's records dryly noted that these orders badly lowered morale (*die Stimmung in der Division [sank] erheblich*).[58] A reprieve, however, arrived on 28 May. Orders came that day for the division to move as rapidly as possible to Amiens for frontline service with Fourth Army, a movement that required a march of 310 miles (500 km) and an early-morning crossing of the Somme on 7 June.[59]

In France the division was reinforced with an additional bicycle-mounted infantry battalion, motorized howitzer and heavy artillery

detachments, and an anti-aircraft machine gun company. It now constituted a sort of reinforced division. The artillery was deemed particularly
important in making the division fully operationally independent. But as
the army group giveth, so the army group taketh away. Thus, at the
same time that the additional units came in, important brigade-level staff
elements were ordered seconded to other units, and the division's subsequent operations suffered accordingly.[60]

As in Poland and the Netherlands, the cavalrymen once again received
a classic cavalry mission: guarding the flank of an advancing unit, this
time the eastern or left flank of XXXVIII Corps. On 7 June divisional elements crossed the Somme just northwest of Amiens. Encountering no
significant French forces, the horsemen drove on in a southwesterly
direction. In the so-called Poix District, a task force formed around the
division's own 22nd *Reiter* Regiment and the temporarily assigned 21st
Kavallerie Regiment rode hard against increasingly heavy French resistance. In this instance the horsemen actually did what virtually everyone
assumed would never again be done: they charged the enemy en masse
at the gallop. The cavalrymen attacked through artillery-fire, successfully gained defilade in a streambed, and then stormed heavily defended
high ground on the other side to capture six hundred French troops.[61] By
the end of the next day, divisional elements had reached the area around
St. Omer. The following day's operation on 9 June witnessed a bitterly
contested, daylong advance of about thirty-seven miles (60 km) resulting
in the cavalry's destroying twenty-eight of about thirty French tanks
deployed to block their march.[62] Sporadic fighting continued over the
next two days, and by the end of 11 June the division had bypassed Paris
and had reached a line running roughly southwest from Pontoise to
Mantes. No French forces remained north of the Seine in the division's
area of operations.[63] At this point the 1st Cavalry Division was transferred to VIII Corps of Eighteenth Army, one of several reassignments
during this hectic advance. Simultaneously, it had to give up the motorized artillery and howitzer detachments earlier attached to it. Its flank-
guard mission, however, remained unaffected by the removal.

Meanwhile, on 1 June the division's 1st *Reiter* Regiment had attempted
a forced reconnaissance across the Seine by rubber boats, all bridges having been destroyed by retreating French forces. Surprised by concealed
enemy artillery on the south bank, the boats were shot to pieces.[64] A sec-

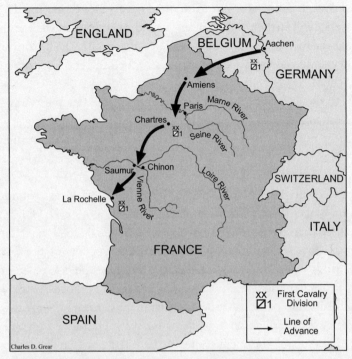

Map 4. The First Cavalry Division in France, June 1940

ond attempt the next morning to send scouting parties across the river succeeded. The French had withdrawn during the night. Nevertheless, the division reported to Eighteenth Army that it would take seventy-two hours for all personnel and horses to cross. The latter—some 12,000 of them—had to swim the river aided by floats (*die Seine an Floßsäcken durch-schwimmen*) while the motorized units crossed via a bridge built far to the northwest by German combat engineers at Vernon. Eventually, all divisional elements found themselves on the south bank of the Seine by sunset on 15 June.[65]

In the week leading to the Franco-German armistice, the Cavalry Division continued its advance to the south while bypassing Chartres on the city's western side as part of the larger German offensive. On 16 June alone, units of the division advanced nearly sixty miles (95 km), the bicycle-battalions in particular seeing occasionally hard fighting. When the next day passed uneventfully, commanders reckoned on the division's being withdrawn from the front in the face of the evident weakening of French resistance.[66] Instead, orders arrived directing the division to advance still farther to the Loire. There the cavalrymen were to throw bridgeheads across the river in the vicinity of Saumur. The historic irony, surely lost on no one, was that Saumur housed the French army's Cavalry School.

At this stage, ad hoc divisional advanced parties of bicyclists and vehicles were followed by the *Reiter* regiments. French resistance was weak, and large numbers of French prisoners streamed back along the division's line of advance.[67] After a march of nearly 125 miles (200 km) from Chartres, the cavalrymen reached the north bank of the Loire on the afternoon of 19 June. Not surprisingly, most of the bridges around Saumur no longer stood, and when one of the division's bicycle-mounted units tried to a take a remaining span by quick assault, the French blew it up as the first soldier crossed it. Nevertheless, troopers of the division managed to cross the Loire to the east of Saumur, and horsemen of the 22nd *Reiter* Regiment even seized the bridge at Le Port Boulet when French efforts to demolish it failed. Having thus crossed the great water barrier of the Loire on 20 June, the same regiment pushed on and succeeded in crossing the Vienne, one of the Loire's eastern tributaries, by seizing an intact bridge at Chinon without loss. There they also managed to completely surprise and capture a French cavalry detachment from Saumur consisting of forty officers and two hundred men.[68] In the next two days, the division broke out of the bridgeheads south of the Vienne. Advancing in the direction of La Rochelle, the horsemen repelled several occasionally fierce French counterattacks, including ones employing armored cars, and reached the coast on 23 June. On that day at La Rochelle, news of the armistice reached divisional headquarters. The 1st Cavalry Division's war in the west was over.[69]

In assessing the campaign, divisional commander Kurt Feldt, by this time a major general, maintained that his troopers' greatest successes had come in forcing the heights in the Poix District and seizing the bridges at Le Port Boulet on the Loire and those on the Vienne. By far the most notable combat victory, however, was the destruction of "an entire tank battalion" on 9 June. By temporarily stripping the division of its heavy artillery and repeatedly changing its corps assignments, however, higher commanders had constantly created disadvantages. Nonetheless, the division had "completely accomplished" (*restlos erfüllt*) every mission assigned to it.[70] As for the division's future, Feldt wrote that the cavalry should not be regarded as a "fast force" (*schnelle Truppe*) in an age of motorization, even though the cavalry had been officially regarded as such in 1939. It simply could not maintain contact in places where good roads made an enemy's motorized retreat possible. On the contrary, the cavalry's principal advantage lay in its tactical mobility on the battlefield: it was independent of roads and the limiting factor of weather, bicycles notwithstanding. "As long as technology makes the leadership dependent on weather and the season of the year [Feldt might well have added "the terrain"], the horse has not lost his role." But he also believed that the cavalry's future depended on whom Germany's next continental enemy might be. That enemy, he wrote, would always be looked for "in the East." Given Poland's already occupied status, Feldt could only mean the Soviet Union. There weather conditions and the vast, largely open, and often roadless spaces were made for horsemen. There "the motor is not yet the sole ruler." Even there, however, Feldt maintained that the cavalry made sense only if it were expanded to a corps of two or three divisions. That force-structure and nothing less, Feldt urged, would be capable of the true operational freedom and decisive combat effectiveness that would justify the horsemen's continued retention.[71]

At almost the same time that Feldt wrote these words, his French cavalry counterparts were being destroyed. In May 1940 French general Charles Huntzinger, commander of the French Second Army, had employed several large, forward-deployed cavalry units in the forested heights of the Ardennes. Though the Ardennes' highest elevation reached not much more than 2,500 feet above sea level, these often heavily wooded highlands presented to the armies of any eastern invader a rugged terrain of "deep and meandering defiles cut by myriad creeks and small rivers" that would "sharply restrict and canalize movement either along or across the grain of the land."[72] This was the region, claimed by some German nationalists as an integral part of Germany as early as 1813, where German and French cavalry patrols had hunted each other at the outbreak of World War I. In 1914, French general Charles Louis Marie Lanrezac was reputed to have described the Ardennes as a death trap from which, once entered, no one could return.[73] Whether his observation, if made, had actually typified French attitudes toward the region at that time, the Germans in 1940 had certainly intended to test the theory in a way that they hadn't done in 1914. Rather than marching the bulk of the field armies around the Ardennes as in 1914, OKW sent a massive armored force crashing straight through the hill country in the hope of cutting off and eventually destroying French and British forces marching northeastward to meet the German invaders in the Low Countries.

To some German commanders, the prospect of success, much less a rapid one, in such a daring undertaking had seemed dim. Representing that view, General (later Field Marshal) Wilhelm Ritter von Leeb, commander of German forces facing Alsace-Lorraine, noted in his diary that the French were expecting a drive through Belgium. Surprise was impossible. The invasion, he wrote, could not be waged as in Poland. The army would have to fight a drawn-out (*langwierig*) campaign against much more capable opponents and would suffer extremely heavy losses in the process. Even then, he feared, "the Frenchman would still not be able to be subdued."[74] The campaign came nonetheless.

Unlike 1914, however, French and German cavalry did not hunt each other in the tangles of the Ardennes. Instead, only the French cavalry were preyed upon, and they didn't face their German 1st Cavalry Division counterparts who were in the Netherlands at the time. Instead, they faced German tanks and mechanized infantry. Still, like their German horse-mounted cousins, their mission remained a traditional one for the cavalry arm: screening Huntzinger's main line of resistance running south of the Meuse from the town of Mézièrs, past the battlefields of 1870 at Sedan, and thence to Montmedy where his troops approached the westernmost extremity of the Maginot Line. Units under Huntzinger's overall command included the 2nd and 5th Light Cavalry Divisions (LCD) and the 1st Cavalry Brigade. The French 1st and 4th Light Cavalry Divisions and the 3rd Spahi Brigade were assigned to the adjoining Ninth Army under the command of General Andre Georges Corap. The 2nd and 5th LCDs were mixed divisions, the type with which the German army had experimented in the 1920s. The 5th LCD, for example, included an artillery regiment, a mechanized infantry brigade of two regiments, and a mounted brigade, also of two regiments: the 11th Cuirassier Regiment and the 12th Cavalry Regiment. In the Germans' passage through the Ardennes and their drive to the Meuse crossings at Sedan, these mounted troops were unceremoniously brushed aside by the advancing 1st Panzer Division of XIX Panzer Corps.[75] In all, the French cavalry screen delayed the German advance through the Ardennes by just over two days instead of the five days envisioned by French prewar planning. As General Erwin Rommel wrote, victory in the encounter battles of the Ardennes between the advancing Germans and the Franco-Belgian defenders usually went "to the side that is the first to plaster its opponent with fire. The man who lies low and awaits developments usually comes off second best."[76] Consequently, the results were about the same on both Huntziger's front and on Corap's. Rommel's 7th Panzer Division's tanks and mechanized infantry, for example, often advanced while conducting what U.S. soldiers thirty years later in Viet Nam would call reconnaissance by fire: maintaining as heavy and continuous a fire as possible into the woods on both flanks and to the front of every advancing column. "Into these woods, the French cavalry, horses and tanks mixed up with one another, scattered in disorder."[77] The typical result was poignantly captured on 12 May by Lieutenant Georges Kosak of the 4th LCD of Corap's Ninth Army as French forces retreated to Dinant on the Meuse:

> Towards midday, groups of unsaddled horses returned, followed on foot by several wounded cavalrymen who had been bandaged as well as possible; others held themselves in the saddle by a miracle for the honour of being cavalrymen. The saddles and the harnesses were all covered with blood. Most of the animals limped; others, badly wounded, just got as far as us in order to die, at the end of their strength; others had to be shot to bring an end to their sufferings.[78]

Ultimately, a lack of proper coordination between French cavalry and the Belgian light infantry in the Ardennes prevented their using that rugged terrain to best advantage in delaying the German invaders. Conversely, when proper coordination occurred, defensive planning proved too methodical or too weak for the Germans' war of movement. The French cavalrymen, whether horse-mounted, on board vehicles, or dug

in, "refrained from holding key positions as long as possible and, therefore, were never in a position to stop the German attackers for any length
of time." They "got no rest, neither during the day nor at night [and]
their delaying actions frequently degenerated into wild flight."[79] One
could scarcely imagine a greater contrast to General Feldt's triumphant
summation of the successful campaign of the German 1st Cavalry
Division.

Mounted band on parade at an equestrian tournament. Note the ornamental drum-skirts and the kettle drummers' stirrup-reins. The latter permit the rider to guide the drum horse while leaving the hands free. Close examination shows that the kettle drummers and at least one of the buglers wear the pre-1939 "cavalry helmet" with ear cut outs. (*From the private collection of the author.*)

Hitler presides at an international equestrian tournament in Berlin. Propaganda Minister Joseph Goebbels is at right. (*From the private collection of the author.*)

German cavalry on parade. The original caption of 1940 referred to the cavalry of the "Army of the Greater German Reich," thus implying a date subsequent to the annexation of the Sudetenland. The venue appears to be the annual Nazi party rally at Nuremberg. However, the Parteitag of 1939 was cancelled owing to the war's outbreak. Therefore, this picture may well date from 1938 or earlier. (*From the private collection of the author.*)

Undated photo shows the victorious equestrian team of the German army's Cavalry School. The apparently altered background hints strongly at a photomontage. Note the convex or "Roman" nose, accentuated by the white blaze, on the horse at right. (*From the private collection of the author.*)

A striking, late-1930s example of a Trakehner (East Prussian) mare. The Trakehner was prized by the officers and men of the Prussian cavalry from the days of King Frederick William I to the end of the World War II. Though the breed barely survived Germany's defeat in 1945, Trakehners thrive today as sport horses known for their athleticism. (*From the private collection of the author.*)

Horse-artillery on the march. Helmet bands, as seen here, were frequently worn on peace-time maneuvers. Note the saddle scabbards for the outriders' Mauser 98k carbines. Spoked, wooden wheels on gun carriages and caissons gave these units their nickname, "gypsy artillery." (*From the private collection of the author.*)

An SS rider takes a jump. The SS aped the equestrian manners of the army's cavalry units. (*From the private collection of the author.*)

An evocative pre-1945 depiction of horse-breeding country in the valley of the Weser River. This area, as well as the adjoining region along the Aller River, comprised the ancestral home of Hanoverian horses. The Hanoverian became justly famous as the German army's second great type of cavalry mount. (*From the private collection of the author.*)

German horsemen laying telephone communications wire. Note the M1925 cavalry saddle and standard-issue, folded, woolen saddle blanket on the horse at left. The "cavalry helmet" with ear cut outs has now been replaced by the standard infantryman's *Stahlhelm*. (*From the private collection of the author.*)

German cavalrymen, not to mention army officers more generally, were expected to ride and, if possible, to compete. Here horse and rider take a combined fence-and-water obstacle in dramatic fashion. (*From the private collection of the author.*)

A postage stamp commemorates the "Brown Ribbon of Germany," a major horse race run annually from 1934 to 1944 at Munich-Riem. Riem was the location of the SS Main Riding School. (*From the private collection of the author.*)

Reichsführer-SS Heinrich Himmler presents awards to a victorious SS equestrian team in this undated photo. Himmler put great emphasis on sporting accomplishments and physical fitness for SS men, though he himself was no athlete, possessed only a weak constitution, and suffered from poor eyesight. (*From the private collection of the author.*)

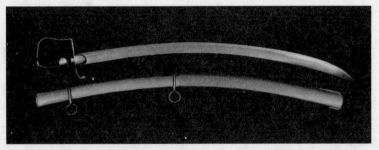

First adopted in Prussia in 1796 and modified only slightly in 1916, the Light Cavalry Saber remained standard issue for German cavalrymen until 1941. Troopers of the 1st Cavalry Brigade/Division carried this weapon in Poland in 1939 and the Netherlands and France in 1940. (*Saber courtesy of Cold Steel, Inc. Photo by the Office of Public Information, Western Carolina University.*)

CHAPTER 7

BARBAROSSA

THE 1ST CAVALRY DIVISION IN RUSSIA, 1941–1942

G eneral Kurt Feldt's assessment from summer 1940 concerning Germany's next enemy was not far from the mark. Though intervening campaigns in spring 1941 led to the conquest of the Balkans and Crete, and though German forces found themselves dispatched to North Africa as well, Hitler's real enemy always lay in the east. The non-aggression pact with Stalin would last not one minute longer than necessary. Along with several million other soldiers, the German cavalrymen would play their part in what would become by far the largest land war in history.[1]

With the invasion of the Soviet Union in June 1941, the 1st Cavalry Division initially found itself operating in the area of the Pripet Marshes. Straddling the borders of prewar Poland and Russia, the marshes stretched away eastward for more than two hundred miles (321 km) from a point near the River Bug and the city of Brest-Litovsk on the border between German- and Soviet-occupied Poland to the Berezina River and the cities of Bobruisk and Gomel. Covering, according to one estimate, a vast area of nearly 100,000 square miles (258,998 sq/km), the region called *Polessia* ("woodlands") by Poles formed the largest contiguous wetland in Europe.[2] Somewhat reminiscent of the lakes and moorland around the East Prussian State Stud at Trakehnen, though never effectively canalized, the marshes' relatively dry areas were interspersed with sand dunes, innumerable meandering streams, and, occasionally, larger rivers such as the Pripet and Horyn. Indeed, the Pripet River was the only significant stream flowing more or less west to east (i.e., roughly parallel to the path of the German invasion) in the whole of the western Soviet Union. Its and the Horyn's tributaries, and most other rivers in the western Soviet Union, flowed perpendicular to the Germans' axis of advance, thereby creating innumerable large and small riparian barriers to the invaders and requiring "an infinite number of bridges." All of the Pripet Marshes' watercourses drained a shallow basin that at its widest extent stretched some one hundred miles (160 km) north to south. Extensive forested belts included thick stands of willow, birch, and alder. In 1941 the Pripet Marshes sheltered a sparse human population living close to the land on both sides of the border in villages and small towns. Pinsk remained one of the largest of the latter and also served as an administrative center. In addition, the marshes also provided extensive habitat for wolves, wild boar, waterfowl, millions of mosquitoes,[3] and eventually Soviet partisans.

Twice a year the marshes expanded. In the spring, runoff from snow-melt raised water levels and caused rivers and streams to flood. In the fall, for a period of about four weeks, autumnal rains repeated the pro-cess until the first hard frost.[4] Cross-country movement for foot soldiers could be agonizingly slow in the marshes. For vehicles it was often liter-ally impossible. The roads that did exist were usually no more than unimproved lanes and usually so narrow that military vehicles could nei-ther detour nor turn around. German combat engineers could, and did, build bridges and corduroy roads in the marshes from readily available logs, but a motorized convoy's speed over such surfaces was limited to about five, kidney-pounding miles per hour (8 km/h).[5] By contrast, horse-mounted columns possessed real advantages. They could move at least as fast as vehicles in the marshes' terrain. They didn't need cordu-roy roads and could usually ride easily on dirt tracks, wet or dry. They didn't need much, if any, gasoline. If necessary, cavalrymen's horses could forage for their fuel, and they could usually outdistance marching infantry with ease, even at the walk. Mounted or not, however, German soldiers always had to remain watchful, for their maps did not always reveal the true nature of the ground, whether in the Pripet Marshes or in the hundreds of other large, forested wetlands they encountered. What often appeared to be, and what maps often depicted as, meadow-like flats were frequently covered with a sort of dark turf effectively floating on a glutinous, apparently bottomless substratum. The "slight-est pressure" would break the turf, and the result would be a "motor vehicle swallow[ed] to its very top" or a horse to its haunches. Such defi-ciencies in intelligence, whether on maps or in other respects, were later admitted by German veterans to have been a significant contributory factor in their underestimation of the difficulties inherent in conquering a country as immense as Soviet Russia.[6]

As in much of the Soviet Union, the expanses of the Pripet Marshes remained largely bereft of modern transportation arteries. "The entire Soviet Union had only 51,000 miles of railroad, all of a different gauge than those in Germany and eastern Europe. Of 850,000 miles of road, 700,000 were hardly more than cart tracks; 150,000 miles were allegedly all-weather roads, but only 40,000 miles of those were hard surfaced."[7] On the edges of the marshes themselves, roads and railways ran roughly northeast from Brest-Litovsk to Minsk and others almost due east from Brest-Litovsk to Gomel. Connecting the latter two cities was yet another stretch running generally southeast from Minsk via Bobruisk to Gomel. The Pripet Marshes thus found themselves enclosed in a sort of triangle with Minsk at the apex. Within that triangle, however, almost all move-ment frequently reverted to walking speed at best, particularly in the wet seasons. In the event, that very factor, combined with the marshes' unique topographical features, made the basin of the Pripet River a haven for Red Army soldiers scattered from their units in Operation Bar-barossa's initial stages. Eventually added to those stragglers came orga-nized bands of Soviet partisans and civilians fleeing the German invad-ers. All such persons thus became a major concern for the German 1st Cavalry Division in 1941 (and later for the principal cavalry unit of the *Waffen*-SS), for the marshes could not be safely bypassed. If they were, then partisans could pounce at will on the logistical columns fol-lowing in the wake of the then–steadily advancing German frontline formations.

Aggravating this situation was an even greater practical problem. The Pripet Marshes lay astride the operational boundary line dividing the Germans' Army Group Center and Army Group South. Consequently, not only the southern sectors of Army Group Center's axis of advance but also the northern sectors of Army Group South's could be attacked by Soviet partisans holed up in the marshes. Cavalry units might therefore not only be effective in combing the swamps of enemy fighters, as the Germans' situation reports often said. They might also help play the crucial role of operational liaison through the marshes between the two army groups until the German advance reached the Berezina.

This set of problems regarding German motorized and mechanized formations' lack of mobility in the Pripet Marshes casts an interesting light on an issue that had confronted German cavalry in 1914. In that earlier conflict, the great masses of horsemen advancing through Belgium were significantly hampered by the heavily built-up nature of the landscape in Flanders. Their mobility was impeded by numerous villages, walls, fences, hedges, canals, industrial plants, slag heaps, railways, and rivers. In 1941 it was German motorized and mechanized formations that found themselves in an analogous situation regarding the vast extent of the Pripet Marshes and other forested wetlands. The shoe was now on the other hoof: it was the mechanized and motorized forces that either could not move at all or, when they could, then only with difficulty. By marked contrast, the horsemen of the 1st Cavalry Division (and later, once again, the cavalry of the *Waffen*-SS) could operate more easily in this difficult country and thereby still render valuable service to the German army.

Interestingly enough, that army wasn't alone in having leaders who thought that mounted forces might still play a useful role in such country. The Red Army, too, was aware of the value of horsemen in the region of the Pripet Marshes and elsewhere. Along with partisans, the Red Army sometimes deployed its own cavalry units in what eventually became a sort of front-behind-the-front. To note merely one example, in the fall of 1941 a motorized German supply column of thirty trucks with trailers heading to Bobruisk on the eastern leg of the road-triangle enclosing the marshes ran headlong into elements of a Russian cavalry force of some 2,500 men moving into position in a forested area south of Minsk. Heavy fighting ensued with the Russian horsemen bringing up anti-tank guns. They destroyed several vehicles and the German column

managed to extricate itself only with the timely arrival of infantry reinforcements, including units of a machine gun battalion.[8] In this particular battle the Russian cavalry in question may have been a unit isolated in
the initial German invasion. Further, there would not be pitched battles
in the Pripet Marshes between German and Russian horsemen as such.
Nevertheless, whether intentional or not, the very fact of Russian cavalrymen's presence in such numbers both then and later indicated that the
Red Army thought mounted combat forces still had a role to play. Indeed,
in the summer of 1941, the Red Army undertook a massive expansion of
its cavalry arm. In July, precisely when German cavalry were beginning
operations in the Pripet River basin, orders went out from the Soviet
high command (*stavka*) establishing thirty new light cavalry divisions of
3,447 horsemen each. Later in the same year the number of such divisions rose to eighty-two.[9] Though the expansion may have been driven
by alarm as the Soviets attempted to fend off a seemingly unstoppable
onslaught, the fact remains that the Red Army high command felt that
mounted forces were still useful. As events would show, these same Russian horsemen would prove effective in the long-range, guerrilla warfare
that accompanied the immobilization of mechanized forces during the
winter of 1941–1942.[10] Furthermore, it is worth noting that in the specific instance cited here, the Russian horsemen executed a traditional
mission of the cavalry: interdicting the enemy's supply columns and creating havoc in his rear. The Red Army's cavalry were also deemed to
have an advantageous psychological effect upon German infantry. Soviet
marshal S. K. Timoshenko, commander of the Red Army's Western
Front (i.e., army group) in 1941, noted that German infantry tended to
flee before onrushing horsemen and simply go to ground.[11]

Whether in the Pripet Marshes or elsewhere, the war facing the German 1st Cavalry Division and all other German forces in 1941 and afterward in Russia was unlike any in modern European history. For sheer
savagery, nothing surpassed it. From the beginning to the end, the war
on what the Germans called the Eastern Front was a war of annihilation
sparing no one. As is now universally recognized, Hitler's intentions
were clear. The war in "the East," as the Soviet Union was so often called
in Nazi, and even non-Nazi, parlance, had as its objective not only the
conquest and colonization of that country's land but also the suppres-

sion and, if necessary, the extermination of her people. Not all German soldiers would have seen the war in that fashion, but all too many did; and while the murderous treatment of the peoples of the Soviet Union was the particular hallmark of the formations of the SS, the German army did not escape complicity.

Some senior army commanders refused to publish orders issued by Hitler via the OKW calling for the summary execution of communist party officials (the "Commissar Order") or effectively exonerating Germans in advance for whatever atrocities they might commit. Still, those same senior commanders were sometimes out of touch with junior officers and enlisted troops who had come of age politically during the Nazi years and who tended to be more ideologically committed to support the regime's heinous policies.[12] In addition, years of nationalist prejudice against Slavs, as already witnessed during the war of 1914–1918, affected how the army behaved:

> A large portion of the Wehrmacht regarded the Soviet people as bumbling and potentially treacherous subhumans. In itself this is by no means a unique psychological failing. Soldiers feel the need to dehumanize or demonize their opponents in order to overcome the natural reluctance to kill, and atrocities have all too frequently ensued. In dealing with Soviet prisoners and civilians, however, this unofficial German attitude produced widespread instances of brutality and murder. Quite apart from the moral implications of such conduct, the German behavior served to alienate potential allies and to spark widespread resistance.[13]

The same widespread resistance would greatly augment that of the Red Army and create the very front-behind-the-front whose dangers the men of the German 1st Cavalry Division would so often have to face.

They began this task when the division crossed its start line, the River Bug, on the invasion's first day, 22 June 1941. Along with the 3rd and 4th Panzer Divisions and the 255th Infantry Division, it constituted an element of XXIV Panzer Corps. Not surprisingly accompanied by some confusion, the crossing of the Bug was nevertheless successful everywhere in the division's area of operations around Slawatycze, just south of Brest-Litovsk. Of course, there arose the inevitable unanticipated difficulties. Elements of the division's 1st *Reiter* Regiment, for example, encountered unexpected resistance from a line of bunkers on the river's eastern bank. In addition, unusable fords and unfavorable riparian shorelines prevented the division's horses being swum across. Consequently, captured bridges had to be used to make the crossing, this being made easier by the fact that "every bridge on all the border rivers from the Baltic to the eastern tip of the Carpathians" was seized within several hours of sunrise.[14]

Initially the division had the mission of guarding the southern flank of XXIV Corps' 4th Panzer Division advancing toward Pinsk, the local administrative center of the western reaches of the Pripet Marshes. The route meant that the cavalrymen would be skirting through the marshes' northern region. Evidently, the mounted elements of the division adequately managed the terrain. The division's motorized vehicles, however, found the sandy soil rough going even though it was still relatively dry, the spring rains and snowmelt having gone, the autumnal rains having not yet begun. This same deep, powdery sand completely exhausted marching infantry, wherever they were found. To the clear frustration of the cavalrymen's commanders, the main paved road running eastward, the so-called *Panzerstraße* or *Panzer-Rollbahn*, was reserved for armored and motorized-infantry units. Consequently, the Cavalry Division's vehicles made slow progress and led General Feldt to report that his entire unit would not be "combat capable" (*Kampffähig*) until his vehicles could get back on the road.[15] Nevertheless, throughout the period to 30 June, the division pushed hard to the east, employing combined-arms attacks by its *Reiter* regiments, the Bicycle Battalion, and motorized reconnaissance elements to fend off sporadic Red Army counterattacks against the armored forces' flank. In this advance, the horsemen kept pace with, and sometimes got ahead of, neighboring armored units, though not without cost. On 24 June, for example, Russian air raids caused "heavy losses" among the division's horses. Nonetheless, three days later the mounted units cut loose from their motorized elements and pushed on without them. The *Reiter* regiments reached the divisional objective of Siniawka early on 29–30 June, with the motorized elements arriving in the afternoon of the latter day.[16]

As had occurred after the division's campaign in the Low Countries and France in 1940, so now in early July 1941 divisional staff prepared a lessons-learned report on the eastern campaign to that point. Not surprisingly, the report made the case for the unit's continued existence.[17] The Cavalry Division was "particularly suited for flank protection of armored units in roadless areas (*abseits der Strassen*)" and for covering gaps in the line. Furthermore, until the armored pursuit of broken enemy forces actually began, the cavalrymen had demonstrated at least as good a marching ability as the mechanized units, even over the most difficult terrain and even on the part of the Bicycle Battalion. Therefore, command concluded that the Cavalry Division should still be included in a panzer corps. Nevertheless, the same report didn't shy away from pointing out problems, and in this respect Feldt seems to have been notably forthright. He observed that the reconnaissance element possessed insufficient personnel, cross-country capability, speed, and uniformity of equipment. Comprised of a collection of horse- and bicycle-mounted troopers, motorized vehicles, and even horse-drawn vehicles, it showed itself insufficiently nimble (*wendig*) and hard to manage. Similarly, divisional artillery and logistics needed greater off-road capability and lighter overall weight. Finally, total losses to 30 June were reported as 77 officers and men killed in action, 289 wounded, and 9 missing.[18]

By 7 July the division had advanced a straight-line distance some 250 miles (402 km) and had reached Bobruisk on the Berezina River where they paused before the next stage in the armored corps' drive on Smolensk. During the rapid advance to the Berezina, threats to the Cavalry Division's horses manifested themselves beyond the combat injuries sustained in the Pripet Marshes. Directives warned, for example, against rabies and glanders, a potentially fatal bacterial disease afflicting a horse's mucous membranes. The directives stipulated that Russian military and civilian horses were not even to be touched if they showed symptoms of nasal drainage or lesions. Russian stalls were not to be used, nor were Russian saddles or tack. Healthy-appearing Russian horses, if requisitioned, were to be screened by the division's veterinary officers before use. To prevent the spread of rabies, no unauthorized dogs were allowed in the division's bivouacs. All strays were to be shot.[19] Despite such warnings about the hazards of employing *panje* or other Russian horses, particularly for logistical purposes, the necessity for it inevitably arose. As early as 5 July, General Feldt indicated that the troopers would have to "live off the land" owing to difficulties in bringing up re-supply columns.[20] Living off the land obviously implied using not only Russian supplies but also Russian horses. This necessity also reflected the lingering concerns about Barbarossa's logistics, concerns that predated the actual start of the campaign and, because they were never resolved, contributed materially to the Germans' eventual defeat.[21]

Notwithstanding these initial difficulties, normal operations continued. The first week of July saw the cavalrymen providing security in various localities around Bobruisk including, at one point, forward-airfield security for the *Luftwaffe's* famous 51st Fighter Wing *Mölders*. Reports in this period tartly observed that the division was spread out over an area of fully 463 square miles (1,200 sq/km) of dense forests and was constantly engaged in clearing actions (*Säuberungsaktionen*) against enemy-occupied villages, isolated armored columns, and Soviet paratroopers.[22] Even so, the horsemen were also tasked with helping secure the southeast flank of XXIV Panzer Corps as the latter moved east and slightly north to prepare a forced crossing of the next significant riverine barrier, the Dnepr. The corps' tanks began crossing on 11 July near the town of Novo Bykhov just downstream from the city of Mogilev, and the horsemen's fight was fierce for the next ten days on both sides of the river. While the panzers rolled away eastward from the Dnepr, the Cavalry Division fought off repeated Russian counterattacks against the crossing point from both north and south. Even bypassed Russian troops still on the river's western bank attempted to cut off the eastward-driving panzers by seizing the approaches to the crossing point from the western side of the stream. Thus the cavalrymen, out of contact with their own armor and being only slowly relieved by follow-on German infantry approaching from the west, played a major role in holding open a vital corridor—and at that moment the only bridge across the Dnepr—for General Heinz Guderian's entire 2nd Panzer Group.[23] Gradually, the German 17th and 112th IDs came up in support of the cavalrymen, and German lines on the eastern shore of the Dnepr were gradually pushed out in heavy fighting to the south and southeast.

In reviewing the month's action, divisional command reported with satisfaction that the Cavalry Division's troopers had once again proven themselves. After-action reports struck a slightly newer tone, however. Whereas in Barbarossa's opening weeks the division's principal accomplishments had been rather traditional—hard-riding, rapid advances over long distances in the partisan-infested country of the Pripet Marshes—the battles along the Dnepr seemed to show that the cavalrymen could be equally effective in defensive fighting as dismounted infantry, in a sense a throwback to the concept of the nineteenth-century dragoon. The great superiority of Russian artillery was duly noted, but this was a fact of life for a division whose "gypsy artillery" was never organized or equipped to engage in sustained gun-on-gun combat. This unavoidable disparity, however, was made worse by difficulties in maintaining supplies of ammunition for the horse-artillery batteries. In mid-July alone, for example, the division's guns had expended a number of rounds equal to fifty percent of those used in the entire campaign of 1940. That expenditure, however, was merely one of ammunition. As always, the clearest indicator of the severity of the fighting was the number of losses incurred among divisional personnel. From 22 June to 29 July, the division lost 366 officers and men killed, 1,593 wounded, and 43 missing. Individual mounted squadrons' combat strength had been reduced by as much as 85 percent. After-action summaries made clear that for the division to be once more fully combat-effective, 1,280 noncoms and men and 1,435 remounts would have to be supplied, primarily for the *Reiter* regiments. These remained the division's cutting edge, and until replacements came up, the *Reiter* regiments would have to comb divisional and brigade staffs and other sources for spare personnel and horses. In addition to men and horses, however, more prosaic equipment was also badly needed. Among other things, such equipment included 350 bicycles for the Bicycle Battalion and totally unglamorous but absolutely essential items such as bicycle tires and spare parts for automatic weapons.[24]

As for the horses themselves, the division reported a strength of 12,153 on 10 August, of which 1,685 had earlier been captured or requisitioned (*Beute- und beigetriebene Pferde*).[25] When ridden, the requisitioned horses had shown themselves incapable of keeping up with the average German-bred mount and therefore had to be constantly replaced with other captured or requisitioned horses. By contrast, "nine-tenths" of the *panje* horses taken into the division's service solely as draft animals had held up without apparent difficulty. To date, 3,365 of the Cavalry Division's horses had "fallen out." Of these, 2,551 had been sent back through the veterinary services' network: one-third as a result of wounds suffered; one-quarter owing to general lameness; the rest from various other causes such as exhaustion, colic, nervous stress, or problems with farriery. More than 550 had been killed or had died of natural causes, and 258 had bolted during artillery or aerial attacks and had not been recovered. In order to rebuild the stock of horseflesh, as well as to rest the men and re-equip, the division received orders for another much needed operational pause effective 1 to 11 August.[26]

During the same pause, the hard-hit Bicycle Battalion was reorganized from three squadrons to two owing to its reduced manpower. At this time the division also found itself transferred to Second Army's XIII Corps for a projected drive to the southeast on the city of Gomel. The division's mission would be to block a possible Soviet retreat via that city.[27] In this capacity, the horsemen prepared to participate in the great drive to the south ordered by Hitler. This meant, of course, that the movement toward the Soviet capital would have to wait. The strategic goal in the diversion was to seize the economic resources of the Ukraine before the resumption of the assault on Moscow. The operational objective was to smash the remaining Soviet armies in the Ukraine so that they might not threaten the eventual movement of Army Group Center toward Stalin's center of power.

As the drive on Gomel commenced, the Cavalry Division was ordered to hold up behind the 17th ID that had by now been brought forward. On the contrary, the cavalrymen should have been deployed ahead of the infantry. Coincidentally, this very same foul-up had occurred in the initial Prussian deployment against Austria in 1866. As one would expect, this arrangement generated evident annoyance in the division's command and necessitated a forced march by the horsemen of more than sixty miles (100 km) between midday on 12 August and dusk the following day in order to get out in front; that is before they even came into contact with Soviet forces. Consequently, both the cavalrymen and their horses went into action insufficiently rested.[28] Nevertheless, by 15 August they had cleared the important road junction of Chechersk, north of Gomel, of enemy troops. They had also fended off repeated Russian counterattacks, including ones by armored vehicles, employing the division's own armored reconnaissance and reinforced bicycle detachments. They had further bottled up Soviet troops attempting to avoid encirclement near the Dnepr River town of Rogachev in the face of a riverine assault executed there by XLIII and LIII Infantry Corps. Acidly, divisional after-action reports noted that the German infantry whom the horsemen preceded were able to "march" without fighting all the way to the last prepared Russian positions outside of Gomel.[29] On 16 and 17 August, the Cavalry Division pushed on to Vetka, immediately north of Gomel on the River Sosh. An attack by one of the division's mounted brigades succeeded in capturing the place, and the cavalrymen immediately turned bridge builders. They threw two spans across the river and built up a considerable bridgehead on the eastern bank. Along the way, they just missed capturing the entire staff of the Soviet Twenty-First Army. The horsemen subsequently noted that their action made it possible for the German infantry to avoid assaulting Gomel directly from the west and northwest. Instead, the latter could now attack the city from the northeast by way of Vetka if necessary.[30] There the Russians' defenses were weaker, and on 19 August the German XIII Corps occupied this regional capital.

This remarkable feat was followed by an equally noteworthy one. In a move reminiscent of the uhlans of 1870, the division's 21st *Reiter* Regiment lunged (*ausholen*) eastward almost sixteen miles (25 km) on the same day Gomel was occupied to reach the bridge at Dobrush on the Iputs River. Though it had to shift slightly to the north to avoid being cut off from the rest of the division, the regiment had single-handedly and considerably extended the Germans' advance in a day. The extension nevertheless forced the 1st *Reiter* Regiment and the divisional armored reconnaissance detachment to cover the 21st Regiment's northern flank and rear against Soviet counterattacks. This they did successfully. As the cavalrymen had done on the Dnepr, so now they were once more forced to fight on multiple fronts simultaneously. Still, with support from a following infantry regiment, the cavalrymen cleared Dobrush and yet again forced a river-crossing by 22 August in the face of "well positioned and stubbornly resisting enemy forces" (*geschickt eingebauten und zäh kämpfenden Feind*).[31] In the face of two full Soviet infantry divisions dug in on the Iputs' vast and swampy eastern bank, the cavalrymen could not seize their ultimate objective, an area of high ground beyond known as the Korma Heights. In this frustrated operation the troopers replayed, after a fashion but on a larger scale, their failure to seize the fortified Dutch positions at Kornwerderzand in 1940. Nevertheless, they had accomplished much. In four days, they'd materially hastened the capture of a major regional capital and numerous enemy troops between Gomel and the Dnepr. By so doing, they had forced Soviet commanders to withdraw still other formations to avoid the latter's being cut off. In the process, the horsemen had repulsed any number of Soviet counterattacks. Certainly not least, they'd significantly extended the Germans' furthest advance in an important sector of the front. Indeed, said after-action reports, had the 1st Cavalry Division been a cavalry corps instead, it would even have enjoyed the success of seizing the Korma Heights. This was because, had it been a corps, it would have possessed not only a much larger complement of artillery but also guns of heavier caliber. Further, there would have been more numerous armored reconnaissance elements, as well as combat engineers possessing heavier equipment.[32] In the event, the division's 1st and 2nd *Reiter* Brigades, their four regiments once again united, only seized the Korma Heights on 24 August and then only in the wake of the more slowly advancing infantry of XIII Corps.[33]

Without any real rest, the division subsequently continued its advance as part of XIII Corps' drive to the south toward the city of Chernigov. On 27 August the troopers were transferred once again, this time to the command of XXXXIII Corps. On the same day the cavalrymen crossed the Ukrainian frontier.[34] Throughout the period, division's troops fought a number of limited, though sometimes intense, actions in the vicinity of the small towns of Snovsk and Novi Barovichi, southeast of Gomel. As they had done earlier along the Dnepr, the *Reiter* regiments proved themselves capable of repeatedly alternating between mounted movement and dismounted combat; and, once again, the armored reconnaissance detachment and the Bicycle Battalion engaged often bitter Soviet resistance. The confusion of combat was exacerbated, however, by yet another transfer, this time to the command of the 2nd Panzer Group. In the view of the division's commanders, the resultant stream of conflicting orders materially complicated operations.[35] Nevertheless, by 2 September this phase of operations was successfully completed, and the Cavalry Division could once again lay claim not only to having hindered a Soviet retreat via Snovsk but also to having blocked reinforcement of those same forces.[36]

Looking back on the campaign since 22 June, General Feldt assessed the division's progress with an unsentimental eye. By some measures, the cavalrymen had performed extremely well. They had, for example, captured 13,872 Soviet soldiers since the start of Barbarossa. They'd also hauled in large quantities of Soviet equipment, including 48 tanks, 73 heavy guns, 230 machine guns and, somewhat improbably, 11 aircraft.[37] In the most recent fighting since 1 August, the division lost 185 officers and men killed, 816 wounded, and 11 missing. Not surprisingly, a significant majority of those losses (79 percent) had been suffered by the four *Reiter* regiments and the division's horse-artillery regiment. By contrast only 859 personnel had come up from the divisional replacement depots in East Prussia and elsewhere. As a panzer division commander put it in the face of similar losses to his own unit, the German armies in Russia were in danger of winning themselves to death.

For the division's horses Feldt had only unstinting praise and deep sympathy. They had made an immeasurable contribution (*Unendliches geleistet*) to the division's success in spite of what they'd endured. The campaign's pace and bitterness had prevented effective farriery, general care, and the regular delivery of oats. Further, the horses had all too often simply been unable to rest owing to the fighting going on around them, a lament doubtless echoing the concern of cavalry commanders since the dawn of firearms. The division's East Prussian–bred horses— the majority would almost certainly have been Trakehners and crosses bred from them—came in for specific praise. Feldt lauded what he called their "iron" constitution and their ability to keep themselves relatively well nourished even under difficult circumstances (*sich einigermaßen im Futter hält*).[38] Nevertheless, he openly recognized the fact staring him in the face in early September: the condition of the division's horses could "hardly be described as satisfactory" (*kaum noch als genügend zu bezeichnen*).

Just as he did in praising the division's horses, so the commanding general also recognized his men. Here he singled out the division's horse-mounted reconnaissance riders (*Spähtruppreiter*). Whether he intended to or not, Feldt invoked the image of the uhlans of 1870 and 1914 in describing their accomplishments. As he explained, these troopers almost always had to rely solely on themselves while on their missions. They had only poor maps, if they had any at all. Yet they still regularly managed to secure valuable information for divisional commanders. In short, they deserved more recognition. Just as infantrymen, artillerists, and panzer troops had their own specific assault badges, he said, so should the reconnaissance riders. Notwithstanding their achievements and those of the rest of the division's personnel, however, Feldt also recognized that, for the moment at least, the division was played out.

He also confronted other unsavory realities. Even while maintaining that the division had shown itself entirely capable of rendering valuable service in closing the gaps between corps and other units and staying out in front, Feldt asked rhetorically whether a panzer division of some sort might not be more effective in fulfilling the cavalry's mission. The cavalrymen had often been hampered by being assigned to follow infantry divisions rather than leading them, a condition made worse by the division's having been shunted around much too frequently among higher-echelon commands. This fact had necessitated not only a great deal of ultimately useless marching and counter-marching. It had also generated mountains of paperwork, the torment of all commanders. A much more pressing concern, however, remained the division's lack of artillery firepower, a concern dating back at least to the division's operations in the Netherlands the year before and one which had arisen again in the fighting on the Iputs River around Dobrush. Trying to get heavy guns from neighboring infantry units caused friction, Feldt opined, but in those instances where assault-gun artillery had been available to the horsemen, cooperation had been good and successes enhanced. Consequently, he urged that heavy motorized (i.e., towed) artillery and self-propelled assault guns be added to the division's establishment.

Similarly, Feldt argued that the motorized vehicles the division did possess had not been sufficiently supported by rear-area commands. There was never enough fuel or oil; there were never enough spare parts; there was never enough time for maintenance. The results were predictable: nearly 40 percent of the division's armored reconnaissance vehicles remained inoperable in early September. More galling still, even the division's bicycles had never been brought back up to strength owing to a pressing lack of spare parts. Clearly exasperated and evidently reflecting the logistical reality in Russia for most German commanders, Feldt wrote that those spare parts, as well as bicycle tires, simply could not be found in Russia.

In this brutal contest in Russia, a contest not yet won in September 1941, the Cavalry Division's mobility, if not its speed, would be crucial in justifying its continued existence. Feldt understood this. Wherever motorized or mechanized columns could operate freely on dry roads, the Cavalry Division seemed to be at a relative disadvantage, and, as already noted, road congestion had plagued the Germans' advance since the start of the invasion. Its troopers—indeed all units in Fourth Army— were therefore ordered to maintain strict march discipline.[39] And however much such an order might tell on any formation having horses, which is to say almost the entirety of Fourth Army outside the mechanized forces, it would disproportionately affect a predominantly horse-mounted unit such as the 1st Cavalry Division. The division's columns were to stick solely to the right shoulder with a ten (horse)–length interval between mounted formations. While single vehicles of other units were always to be given right of way, wheeled or tracked columns from other formations would have to wait for the ten-length gap before intersecting the horsemen's line of march. At that point, ten vehicles could pass. The following mounted unit could then carry on, then ten more vehicles, and so forth. This procedure would spare the division's horses and keep mounted columns intact while simultaneously allowing the vehicular columns to exploit their greater speed. Coincidentally, these orders went out at precisely the time when the annual autumnal rains had begun to fall in Russia, rains that would soon frequently bring much of the army's vehicular traffic to a halt. As would so many German records, an order of the day dated 13 September 1941 commented on the "continuing rain and nearly bottomless tracks (*Wege*)," conditions demanding the equally continuous employment of the Cavalry Division's combat engineers to help ensure the hoped-for regular delivery of supplies.[40]

Despite such conditions and the increasing psychological and operational intensity of the anti-partisan war being waged behind the front, the Cavalry Division's accomplishments were recognized in at least some higher-echelon commands, no doubt to Feldt's satisfaction. The XIII Corps' commander, General Hans-Gustav Felber, credited the division with making possible XIII Corps' earlier taking of Gomel. The mounted forces' "rapid exploitation of favorable opportunities" (*schnelles Erfassen günstiger Gelegenheiten*) were critical, he wrote, in the successful German advance on that city. He also commended the cavalrymen with containing (*binden*) "strong enemy forces" on the corps' flank in the subsequent advance to the southeast.[41] Securing the flanks of advancing infantry was as traditional a mission for the cavalry as ever there was, even though the troopers also received a rather firm warning about the dangers inherent in allowing their minds to fall into a "partisan psychosis." Such a mental state among the division's troopers might "undermine the pacification of the [occupied] territory" through overly harsh treatment of civilians. Unfortunately, other German units, such as the SS cavalry in Russia, had no such scruples.

Such warnings appeared justified given the horsemen's next mission. In the second half of September, the Cavalry Division was transferred once more, this time from XIII Corps to XXXXVII Panzer Corps, and assigned to relieve 18th Panzer Division. Following a brief stint as army group reserve, the cavalrymen's mission throughout late September and into October was evidently confined to a sort of security role on the front lines and immediately to the rear while the LIII Infantry Corps prepared to assault the major city of Bryansk east of the River Desna.[42] Its area of operations in this period lay east of Gomel around the town of Novgorod Severski and the bridgehead there on the Desna's eastern bank. The cavalrymen also operated southward along the Desna to Trubchevsk, a distance of about fifty miles (80 km). Though Russian cavalry—the 4th and 52nd Cavalry Divisions and the 118th Cavalry Regiment—were reported in the vicinity, there does not appear to have been mounted contact between them and the German horsemen. Just the same, the Cavalry Division's constant operations required continuous replacements of both men and horses. On 28 September divisional staff officers were requisitioning two hundred saddles from rear-area supply depots for an expected shipment of remounts, though tack and saddle blankets were evidently harder to come by.[43] Furthermore, *panje* horses had to be rounded up for distribution to troopers from the Bicycle Battalion. Because of the large number of mechanical breakdowns already noted and the ever-poorer roads as the division pushed eastward, these troopers had left their two-wheeled mounts behind at various stages in the division's march. As occurred so frequently on the Eastern Front, such troops were effectively immobile until the ubiquitous Russian

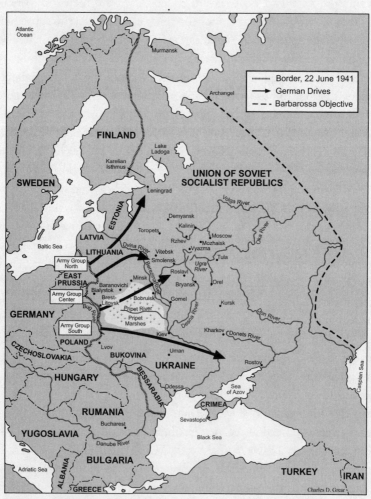

Map 5. Eastern Front, General Situation, Late September 1941

horses could be collected. Divisional headquarters ordered that this particular situation be rectified by 30 September.[44]

Despite constant references in this period to the threat posed by partisans and the emphatic order that the men should always carry loaded weapons except when in their quarters, divisional command also kept insisting that soldierly discipline be maintained. Unauthorized shooting, apparently widespread, was expressly forbidden because it wasted ammunition and revealed defensive positions. Furthermore, graffiti and stuffed animals were not to be used to decorate the division's vehicles, the stuffed animals evidently being attached to radiator-caps as hood ornaments. Furthermore, men were strictly ordered not to appear out of uniform. Decorations were to be worn and military courtesies always observed. Such observances remained the "calling card of any unit." In sum, as General Feldt wrote, the Cavalry Division was to be known as a unit in which "exemplary discipline reigned."[45] Perhaps he felt that the strain of the campaign could only be rectified by discipline and good order. Perhaps, too, he felt that he had other good grounds for urging such exemplary discipline. As it turns out, in September 1941 the division was in the process of beginning a reorganization, with all of the administrative and personal tumult that a reorganization in wartime brings with it. Fate and the OKW/OKH had decreed that the 1st Cavalry Division was to give up its horses and replace them with tanks. It was to become a panzer division.

In 1939 the ultimate fate of the then–1st Cavalry Brigade had still been uncertain. Even earlier, the German cavalry's corps and divisional structures had been ordered abolished, effective 1936; and, as has been seen, the army's cavalry regiments had been tasked at that time to provide squadrons for the infantry divisions' organic reconnaissance battalions, as well as cavalry troops (i.e., companies) for individual infantry regiments. Only the 1st Cavalry Brigade had remained as an autonomous, dedicated, horse-mounted unit. Following its expansion in the winter of 1940–1941, the Cavalry Division had been ordered, in addition to its actual operational objectives, to determine whether horse-cavalry in the eastern campaign could still execute useful missions or whether its role could be better served by armored formations. Now, in the autumn of 1941, General Feldt submitted his answer to that question.[46]

He began by noting that throughout the eastern campaign, the division had been assigned the following missions: screening the flanks of German armies and panzer groups; closing the gaps between friendly units; pursuing Soviet forces along the flanks and in front of German infantry corps; rapidly seizing and holding sections of the front until follow-on forces came up; attacking the flanks and rear of enemy formations; and executing wholly dismounted defensive infantry operations. With the exception of the last-named task, all of these were traditional functions of the cavalry. In Feldt's view, all of these missions had been completely accomplished. By itself, as he also noted, the Cavalry Division could not contribute decisive combat power, and other German formations had done quite as well with no attached cavalry at all. Nonetheless, he believed that a single cavalry division could do good work even if it was not absolutely necessary to the army's success as a whole.

By contrast, and with what seems to have been more than a touch of bitterness, General Feldt maintained that had his division been a corps instead, then the horsemen could indeed have made decisive contributions to the campaign in Russia, whether in the Pripet Marshes, around Gomel, or even in the massive operational encirclements that were at that moment occurring farther southeast in the Ukraine. Even so, Feldt still recognized that the establishment of a cavalry corps didn't seem likely, since effective cavalry forces couldn't simply be improvised on the spur of the moment. Therefore, if a cavalry corps' establishment were not in the offing, then he felt it would be better simply to disband the division despite its three successful campaigns in Poland, the west, and Russia, and despite the constant demands for its services by other formations, not to mention the troopers' genuine love for their horses.

No sentimentalist, Feldt listed the reasons for his conclusion. The ever-increasing number of motorized and mechanized divisions meant that the Cavalry Division would no longer have a useful place, even if the vast majority of the army's divisions always remained ground-pounding infantry. As he'd already noted, a single cavalry division couldn't deliver decisive, battle-winning combat power at an operational level; and a panzer division could accomplish the same results as the cavalrymen had done and do so more quickly. Evidently believing, as so many German officers still did, that the war in the Soviet Union could have only one outcome—German victory—Feldt maintained that the division would have no reasonable geographic area of operations for its employment beyond the spring of 1942 in any case.[47] More parochially, he pointed out that German youth had increasingly little interest in things equine, the automobile having become their passion. Consequently, younger officers interested in a cavalry career were harder to come by, even as their older cavalry comrades were already finding it difficult to rise to higher command.[48]

Feldt judged that not even the cavalry's vaunted cross-country capability was sufficient to save the horsemen for the simple reason that a purely horse-mounted cavalry was no longer possible. Even the Cavalry Division had ultimately required motorized vehicles for its combat engineers; some of its anti-tank and reconnaissance detachments; and, increasingly, for the all-important logistics elements. When such units had been entirely horse-drawn, they'd simply not been able to keep pace with the hard-riding *Reiter* regiments. However, when those same supporting elements converted to vehicles in the interest of speed, they lost whatever cross-country capability they'd earlier enjoyed while horse-drawn. Only appropriately outfitted, fast-moving, tracked vehicles, said Feldt, would possess the speed to keep up with the *Reiter* regiments and the off-road capability of the division's horses. Furthermore, if vehicles ran out of fuel and were idled for a prolonged period, barring mechanical failure or battle-damage, they could nevertheless resume full-speed operations once they were refueled. By contrast, when the division's horses didn't get proper feed and fodder and/or were immobile for an extended period of time, they could well require periods of muscular and cardiovascular reconditioning before they could resume their missions. Facing his own apparently unavoidable conclusions, Feldt nonetheless pleaded that there had to be found a way to keep the art of riding available and accessible to all officers. Precisely because of the army's degree of motorization, one that Feldt evidently presumed to be a matter of endlessly increasing percentages, only *Reitsport* (though he did not use this word) could provide German officers, especially panzer commanders, with the combination of self-control, daredevil risk-taking, and lightning-fast decision making so essential for modern officers' success.[49] To that end, he urged, every officer in every armored division should have his own mount, at least once the war ended.

All things considered, Feldt clearly believed that he could not avoid recommending that the Cavalry Division be converted to an armored formation. He further recommended that the transformation be quick and en masse so as to avoid disrupting the division's battle-born cohesion. Speeding the conversion would avoid missing the perceived opportunity to acquire up-to-date motorized vehicles. He also urged, however, that rapid conversion should not result in abandoning the cavalry's heritage and traditions such as the cavalry's yellow-gold piping on troopers' uniforms or the "Leaping Horseman" divisional insignia. These, said Feldt, should be transferred to whatever new panzer formation assumed the division's role. Lest they be forgotten, Feldt also addressed the matter of the mounted elements of the infantry divisions' reconnaissance battalions, at least by way of saying that the Cavalry Division did not feel competent to make recommendations for their future status. They, too, he nevertheless pointedly noted, were heirs in fact as well as in name to the German cavalry's traditions and should by no means be ignored. In completing his recommendations, General Feldt fully acknowledged the wide-ranging ramifications of his decision. However much the Cavalry Division had accomplished to that point in the war, and however much the cavalrymen genuinely loved their mounts, the practical experiences to date forced him to make the recommendations he'd made. "The cavalry," read his report's last sentence, "feels compelled to go with the times since no combat arm (*Waffe*) may be allowed to stand still."

Even as Feldt's recommendations went up the line, however, the division's operations continued unabated, especially in the period from 8 to 20 October.[50] Having received one thousand men and four hundred horses as replacements late in the previous month, the cavalrymen along the western bank of the Desna now found themselves fighting not only battles with Russian troops trying to retreat to the east but also large numbers of partisans, both soldiers and civilians, attempting to help their comrades flee. In a phrase sadly reminiscent of orders repeatedly heard elsewhere on the Eastern Front, divisional reports indicated that "this partisan monster (*Partisanenunwesen*) will be fought with the ruthless arrest of all civilian persons suspected of being fit for military service; with [the taking of] hostages; and with the shooting of the guilty." Operating alongside various infantry and panzer divisions, the horsemen also found themselves fighting the weather. On 9 October the autumnal clouds broke once again, and snow now began to mix with the frequently heavy rain that had been regularly noted in the division's war diary since early September. By the next day every dirt track had been turned to bottomless muck, every stream had become a torrent, and even the smallest blown bridge became a matter of long delays in the pursuit of retreating Soviet troops. Even so, the division's bicyclists managed to form a bridgehead across the 300-foot-(100-m)-wide Desna on 11 October and link up with the Germans' 29th ID near Sytenki as the latter attempted to encircle retreating Russians from the eastern bank. This feat the cavalrymen followed up with the construction of a five-ton capacity bridge that allowed the 1st *Reiter* Brigade to continue the advance to the southeast. As had occurred before, however, the region's horrible roads, particularly at that season, as well as persistent fuel shortages, prevented many of the division's vehicles from following the riders.[51] For the next nine days, the various *Reiter* regiments and the division's Bicycle Battalion saw almost constant, and sometimes fairly large-scale, action against retreating Russian forces. With the exception of a major battle on 17 October, however, most heavy fighting ended in the immediate aftermath of the crossing of the Desna. At a cost of 122 officers and men killed, 410 wounded, and 8 missing, the division had captured 8,132 Soviet troops by 20 October, the number killed not being indicated. The cavalrymen had also taken 3 tanks, as well as 39 guns, 91 motor vehicles of various types, and some 250 horse-drawn wagons. They'd even managed to capture an entire ammunition train and a Soviet field hospital complete with "six omnibuses." After-action reports proudly noted that the cavalry's mobility on the march and in combat had once again proven itself. "A panzer division," the reports concluded smartly, "could hardly have done better."

Nevertheless, the writing appeared to be on the wall regarding the 1st Cavalry Division's future. Orders arrived at divisional headquarters at the end of the first week of November indicating that the division would be reorganized as the 24th Panzer Division.[52] The cavalrymen were ordered to move by train and motorized columns back to their old home in East Prussia prior to their ultimate relocation for armored-forces training at Ohrdruf in Thuringia. While in East Prussia, the division's units were dispersed for preliminary billeting. Divisional elements such as the combat engineers and logistics units were assigned to Insterburg and Angerapp. The *Reiter* regiments took over camps in the large (more than 24,000 acres) prewar military training area around the small town of Stablack that lay about twenty miles south of the East Prussian capital of Königsberg. The principal changes in the division's organization saw the 2nd and 21st *Reiter* Regiments becoming panzer regiments. The 1st and 22nd *Reiter* Regiments were designated rifle regiments (*Schützenregimenter*). Analogous changes were made for the Bicycle Battalion and other subordinate commands.

Throughout the process of reorganization, however, the division's horses still required their regular attention. Veterinary care and daily maintenance thus continued throughout November and December and was duly noted in activity reports, often with the laconic marginal notation "nothing out of the ordinary" being inserted in the appropriate space on the form.[53] Nonetheless the reduction in the numbers of horses proceeded fairly rapidly. On 1 November, for example, the division's combat-strength in horses was still 8,969. The ration-strength was 10,681. By 21 November, a week before the official date of the division's redesignation, those numbers were 2,498 and 3,899, respectively.[54] Further reductions followed to the end of the year. As deemed necessary by their condition, sick or injured horses were sent back to veterinary hospitals at Potsdam and Neustettin and even as far away as Frankfurt am Main. Others were transferred to infantry and artillery units and various riding and driving schools, such as the one at Soltau in Hannover. In the three Studs under the division's command, at least 428 mares were designated as fit for breeding. Of these, it appears that 153 were sold to the Stud Book Society, the organization then maintaining official breeding standards in Germany. Given the traditional emphasis on quality in modern German horse breeding, this disposition of mares would certainly seem to demonstrate that high-quality breed stock was still to be found in mounted units. At this still successful stage of the war, such a disposition would not seem indicative of a desperate search for brood mares. In addition to those sold to the Society, an unspecified number of other mares were sold directly to the division's personnel. Interestingly, at least one presumably valuable horse from 22nd *Reiter* Regiment, Sonnengott

(Sun God), came in for particular attention. He was sent directly to an unnamed recipient serving on the General Staff of the army and stationed at Angerburg and was the only horse singled out by name in the division's daily activity reports. Finally, most of the division's staff-level veterinary officers were transferred.[55] As a tribute to the new panzer division's heritage, and in keeping with General Feldt's wish, its insignia remained the Cavalry Division's "Leaping Horseman," depicting a rider in profile jumping to the viewer's left over a fence and surrounded by a reversed "C." Whether for reasons of tactical simplicity or mere speed of application, the horse and rider were later sometimes represented by a mere diagonal bar. In whatever form, the "Leaping Horseman" would now find his way onto the hulls of tanks. Though the newly minted panzer troops could not know it at the time, those same tanks and the division's troops would in turn meet their end at Stalingrad one year later.

CHAPTER 8

Hell's Outriders

CAVALRY OF THE *WAFFEN*-SS

In the ideology of the Nazi regime, animals often featured prominently alongside blond-haired, blue-eyed exemplars of the Nordic man. Certain of these animals were considered to embody particularly "Nordic" characteristics. The horse was one such creature, as were hunting dogs, falcons, and eagles. Horses—or at least well-bred and well-groomed ones—possessed nobility and grace, martial strength and courage. In and of itself, such a view is nearly as old as humankind's connection with genus *equus*. Yet, under the Nazis, the aesthetic and practical use of the horse acquired a much more sinister purpose. Along with many other wholly innocuous symbols and objects, horses in the Nazi era came to project an increasingly ominous image, not least because they so frequently carried the paladins of the new regime in the endless parades so dear to Hitler and other Nazi functionaries. To note but one example, the parade celebrating "2000 Years of German Culture" in Munich on 18 July 1937 featured thousands of marchers and legions of horses, many of whose caparisons and armor-plated riders were suitably emblazoned with Nazi insignia. As with all other cultural expressions of the regime, the artistic mission celebrated in this particular instance demanded obeisance not only to lofty sentiment but also to fanatical devotion.[1] In more literally concrete and metallic terms, horses featured prominently in the regime's architecture as well. For example, two monumental bronze horses by Josef Thorak, called "our greatest sculptural talent" by the Nazi government's propaganda minister Joseph Goebbels, adorned the garden entrance of Hitler's new Reich Chancellery that was completed just before war's outbreak in 1939.[2]

Such symbolism was perfectly in keeping with propagandistic agitation and the consequent radicalization of the German people by the Nazi government. To a very great extent, the regime relied upon slogans, monumental architecture, and evocative symbols to express itself and its aims. Of course, the most striking symbol remained the swastika. Though in the early days of the 1920s it served as a sort of "personal totem" for Hitler, the *Hakenkreuz* (hooked cross) soon became not only the party's emblem but also Germany's national insignia.[3] Besides the swastika, however, there were other equally evocative, and often dreaded, symbols culled from both Germany's actual history and the fevered imaginations of Nazi mythmakers. To such long-established and honored symbols as the Iron Cross, later adulterated through the addition of swastikas, came many others. Neo-peasant clothing styles and domestic buildings were very often, though no less spuriously, cited by the regime as recalling the ideals of a Germanic past. There were oak leaves and eagles in profusion, all intended to evoke past imperial glories. But there was also terribly more sinister Nazi regalia, specifically intended to evoke "an older, darker Germany of forests and hunters." These included "the broad-bladed daggers worn by [the Nazi Party's] men" and commonly seen on the uniforms of so many of its formations. However, the symbol that arguably came to be the most potent of all remained the double, silver-on-black lightning-flash of the SS runes. Adorning SS men's uniforms, their banners, and their units' heraldry, the runes called to mind "that twilight world of ferocious gods and desperate heroes [in] the German romantic imagination."[4] The SS runes also became perhaps the most feared symbol of Nazi Germany's minions, and by 1939 the men who wore them had earned a reputation of absolute obedience to Hitler. Theirs was obedience unto death as they proclaimed in their oath upon being sworn in as members of what their leader, *Reichsführer*-SS Heinrich Himmler, envisioned as a new order of chivalry. Sometimes described as the praetorians of the Nazi regime, the SS were also its latter-day berserkers, men who took fierce pride in their self-perception of peacetime discipline and honor but who would also remorselessly and without compunction kill enemy soldiers, civilians, prisoners of war, other Germans, and even their own SS comrades. All the while they would glory in the deed and, as they saw things, draw strength from it.[5]

The horse-mounted unit that was eventually to become the 8th *Waffen*-SS Cavalry Division *Florian Geyer* fully shared all of these traits. In that respect, it was hardly unique. It was unique, however, in being primarily a horse-mounted formation, even though it was not the only armed formation of the SS to employ horses. Notwithstanding the armed or *Waffen*-SS' reputation for typically receiving its full complement of tracked and wheeled vehicles, other SS units besides the SS cavalry also used horses.[6] The SS Death's Head (*Totenkopf*) Division, for example, a unit eventually elevated to the status of an armored formation, had regular difficulties before 1939, as did other early *Waffen*-SS formations, obtaining equipment owing to the army's resistance. In the case of the *Totenkopf* Division, these difficulties resulted in, among other things, its having to use horse-drawn, World War I–era field bakeries. Given the then-paucity of horses and the fact that the bakeries weighed nearly two-and-a-half tons apiece (they had to be taken off their rail cars by cranes), the latter were practically useless. Only on the eve of the invasion of France and the Low Countries in May 1940 did these difficulties begin to abate for this particular unit. By that time, the German army's own requirements were filled out sufficiently to allow the *Waffen*-SS divisions to receive surplus gear.[7] Nevertheless, another early *Waffen*-SS division, this one recruited from police personnel under Himmler's direct law-enforcement control as Chief of the German Police and therefore not subject to the army's recruiting demands, perennially found itself short of motorized and mechanized vehicles, at least until achieving its eventual rank as a *Panzergrenadier* division. As late as the invasion of France in 1940, this division, named *Polizei* because of its origins, "remained a marching unit, whose transport and artillery, like that of the bulk of the Wehrmacht, was horsedrawn."[8]

Horses' employment in the SS beyond the draft-animal role, however, had a particular place in the plans of the SS' leadership. Himmler saw a mounted combat unit of the SS providing a useful armed addition to the *Waffen*-SS while embodying a certain social cachet. The latter consideration had significantly influenced Himmler's thinking since well before the war began. Such a cachet in wartime would, in turn, bolster Himmler's long-standing efforts to attract a more elevated social type into the SS, efforts he'd undertaken even before the Nazis' accession to power in 1933. As early as 1931, for example, he'd raised a mounted SS detachment in Munich, the so-called "Capital of the Movement" (i.e., birthplace of the Nazi Party). In the course of 1932, that detachment was expanded and redesignated as an SS Mounted Company (SS-*Reitersturm*). From this early period, and with this nucleus of a mounted arm in hand, Himmler assiduously cultivated the task of recruiting more refined members into the SS, not least to raise his organization's profile ever further away from the plebeian identity of the brown-uniformed, street-brawling elements among the Storm Troopers (*Sturmabteilungen*; SA). Himmler found the prestige, leadership qualifications, and, not least, money that he needed to construct his Black Order in the worlds of commerce, finance, and the German nobility. Indeed, since 1933, the roster of new SS men's names sometimes read like a German version of *Debrett's Peerage*: the Prinz von Hohenzollern-Emden of the House of Sigmaringen; the Grand Duke of Mecklenburg; the hereditary Prince zu Waldeck und Pyrmont; the Princes Christof and Wilhelm of Hesse; Count von der Schulenburg; Count von Rödern; Count Strachwitz; and so on.[9] Just before the war's beginning in 1939, some 20 percent of the SS' nominal senior leadership and about 10 percent of its lower ranks would consist of titled nobility. Of particular relevance to this recruitment but also to the prewar mounted SS and, later, the SS Cavalry was Himmler's success in persuading "all the most important German horse-riding associations, preserves of upper-class sportsmanship and snobbish socializing, to enrol [sic] in the SS, irrespective of their political views . . . so that SS riders regularly won the German equestrian championships."[10] The equestrian associations of Germany's most important horse-breeding regions—East Prussia, Oldenburg, Holstein, Westphalia, Hannover—"put on SS uniform."[11]

While such enforced enrollment was first and foremost a public-relations exercise, it nevertheless helped create an impetus within the prewar SS toward a sort of cementing of the equestrian image within the organization. That image, in turn, would have further impelled Himmler toward the creation of a mounted SS combat unit as war approached, a natural extension, as it were, of the SS' prewar horse-mounted formations. A mounted SS combat unit would also constitute, at least in Himmler's eyes, a clear parallel to what was at that date still the army's 1st Cavalry Brigade. By 1934 the first SS Mounted Regiments (*Reiterstandarten* or *Reiter-SS*) had been established as successors to the original *Reitersturm*. By 1939 they numbered twenty-four and were stationed across the length and breadth of the Reich. Furthermore, in an effort to increase the equestrian proficiency of the SS' mounted personnel, an SS Main Riding School (*Hauptreitschule*) was established in Munich. In 1936 then–SS major (*Sturmbannführer*) Hermann Fegelein was assigned to command the school that happened to be located on his parents' property near the suburb of Riem, eventually the site of Munich's first major post-1945 airport. Not of noble birth himself, Fegelein rose rapidly through the ranks and during the same period became a successful equestrian competitor. His own career and that of the mounted SS combat troops would soon converge.

These combat units arose from early decisions by the Nazi government to elevate selected units of the SS from their original, ostensibly unarmed status to that of full-time, armed formations. As early as 1933, the Nazi regime had begun to establish such armed SS units, and they multiplied with confusing rapidity. First called Special Detachments (*Sonderkommandos*), these units guarded local Nazi bosses and their headquarters. If one of these headquarters guard-detachments grew to more than one hundred men, it could then be redesignated as a Political Readiness Squad (*Politische Bereitschaft*) possessing a military TOE. By 1934 the nationwide network of Political Readiness Squads had effectively been recognized by the Reich Ministry of Defense as a full-time, armed State Police force answering solely to Hitler or, at his discretion, to Himmler. Emerging, in turn, from this force came the SS Special Duty Troops (SS-*Verfügungstruppen*; SS-VT). Essentially the Nazi Party's standing army, the SS-VT took orders directly from Hitler or his designated lieutenant and remained subject to his exclusive disposition, hence the name. Not regarded by Hitler as belonging either to the army or to the police, they became the immediate organizational ancestors of the *Waffen*-SS. Arising roughly in parallel to the SS-VT—but initially separate from them organizationally—were the SS Death's Head Units (SS-*Totenkopfverbände*; SS-TV). The SS-TV drew personnel from among veterans of the army, active-duty or retired policemen, guard-detachments of the regime's concentration camps, and the General SS (*Allgemeine* SS). According to Hitler himself, the Death's Head Units comprised a full-time armed force of the SS for the resolution of "special internal political tasks" of a policing or security nature. As usual, he reserved this force to himself alone or to his appointed subordinate. Regardless of their original tasking, for all practical purposes the SS-TV would be informally incorporated into the *Waffen*-SS after 1939. Formal amalgamation followed in 1941–1942. It was through these Death's Head Units that many pre-1942 replacements for the SS cavalry would find their way into the larger *Waffen*-SS structure. Before wartime losses really began to manifest themselves, however, SS cavalrymen came from the pre-existing SS-*Reiterstandarten*. In the invasion of Poland in September 1939, SS horsemen trained and led by Fegelein and drawn from *Reiterstandarten* 15 (Munich) and 17 (Regensburg) would serve as security forces behind the front lines in the form of the SS Death's Head Horse Regiment (SS *Totenkopf-Reiter-Regiment* or *Reiterstandarte*). They would also participate in "actions" against Jewish and non-Jewish civilians (i.e., summary killings). When this regiment was reorganized as the 1st SS Cavalry Regiment in November and December 1939, Fegelein would be named its commanding officer.[12] When the 1st SS Cavalry Regiment was then assigned to serve as cadre (along with the 2nd Regiment that had been raised in the meantime) for a newly designated SS Cavalry Brigade in occupied Poland, Fegelein was once again assigned to command.[13]

As can be seen in Fegelein's case, as well as the cases of countless other SS men, non-noble birth meant little in terms of potential advancement. What really counted were fanatical loyalty, ruthlessness, and being a Nazi true believer. Still, noble status continued to carry weight in Himmler's and others' eyes. Of course, elevated social standing never really protected SS men, no matter their rank and background, from the murderous intrigue of the Nazi regime generally and within the SS as an organization. An early, aristocratic leader of the SS' mounted arm, Anton *Freiherr* (Baron) von Hohberg und Buchwald, presented a textbook example of extreme vulnerability despite his being of genuine noble birth. The leading SS horseman of East Prussia, von Hohberg was nevertheless cold-bloodedly gunned down in his own home by a rival in the purge known as the "Night of the Long Knives" in June 1934, ostensibly for having leaked SS secrets to the army.[14] Though he could not know it at the time, Fegelein himself would ultimately share Hohberg's fate in being summarily shot on Hitler's personal orders in the regime's final days in April 1945. Not even Fegelein's marriage to the sister of Hitler's mistress could prevent it.

Cold-blooded murder notwithstanding, Himmler viewed the men admitted to the SS as biologically and, therefore in his view, morally superior. As the best of the "Nordic race," they would be the supreme exemplars of that population's virtues. Like knights errant of old, the mounted SS units—indeed all SS units—were expected to uphold putative chivalric virtues. For his part, Himmler always remained convinced that they could and would do so, or at least could be made to. "Rectitude and chivalry," he said in a wartime speech to new officers of the Replacement Army's grenadier divisions, "were always best bound together in the 'germanic' German [*sic*] man."[15] While he was not here specifically addressing SS personnel, the sentiment most certainly applied to them. "Our *Volk*," he added emphatically, "has existed eternally, and the Aryan will go on into eternity. . . . As long as the Aryan lives, as long as our blood—Nordic German blood—lives, so long will there be order on the Almighty's globe."[16] When specifically addressing men of the *Waffen*-SS, he was even more emphatic; and Operation Barbarossa, the invasion of Soviet Russia in June 1941, would most effectively allow his SS men to exhibit their chivalric errantry.

In the first month of the invasion, Himmler spoke to reinforcements destined for the SS *Kampfgruppe Nord* fighting alongside the Finns on the northern extremity of the Russian Front. Though the men of *Kampfgruppe Nord* were not SS cavalrymen, their mission remained the same in Himmler's eyes. They were going, he said, to defend a Reich that was on the whole "a happy, beautiful world full of culture" whose essence was defined by a National Socialist ideology "based on the value of our Germanic, Nordic blood." On the other side, he went on, "stands a population of 180 million, a mixture of races, whose very names are unpronounceable, and whose physique is such that one can shoot them down without pity or compassion. These animals . . . you will see for yourself. These people have been welded by the Jews into one religion, one ideology, that is called Bolshevism, with the task: now we have Russia, half of Asia, a part of Europe. Now we will overwhelm Germany and the whole world."[17] And, in a throwback (unwitting perhaps?) to the exhortations made to the German cavalry and other soldiers who'd fought the Russians in 1914–1918, Himmler added for good measure, "When you, my men, fight over there in the East, you are carrying on the same struggle, against the same subhumans, the same inferior races, [as] at one time— 1,000 years ago at the time of King Henry and Otto I—under the name of Magyars, another time under the name of Tartars [sic], and still another time under the name of Genghis Khan and the Mongols. Today they appear as Russians under the political banners of Bolshevism."[18]

Facing this threat stood the SS man. In Himmler's fantasy world, the SS man, and the SS cavalryman most of all, was lofty of sentiment, knightly in carriage, and possessed of the grim, clear-eyed nature of the predator. As the Italian war correspondent Curzio Malaparte observed the preparations in Rumania for the invasion of the Soviet Union, he wrote that the German fighting man there "had the same clear, lustrous eyes. And there was in them a mysterious, timeless look—a look pregnant with a timeless, mysterious sense of the inexorable."[19] Though not describing the SS, Malaparte captured the precise ideal to which Himmler wanted his SS cavalrymen, indeed all SS men, to aspire. And in the east, the SS cavalrymen would find that domain whose rulers they of the Black Order would be: the same endless reaches from whose depths the feared invaders of World War I had come, the same eastern marches whose defense and expansion the German army had contested in 1914– 1918. Those vast spaces, what one recent work has so tellingly called the "bloodlands," would be at the SS' mercy.[20]

In this respect, Himmler was evoking a tradition antedating by decades the beginnings of Nazism. Not merely during World War I but as early as 1879, the renowned journal *Preußische Jahrbücher* had declared that the east had been Germany's promised land (*Land der Verheißung*) for as long as there had been a German history. The still–largely peaceful nineteenth-century struggle between Germanizing and Slavicizing tendencies had subsequently become open warfare in 1914. That war, in turn, had led inexorably to demands by prominent interest groups and individuals that the "face of Russia be turned back by force [away from Germany] to the East." Those same voices had demanded that Russia's Baltic provinces, along with Russian Poland and White Russia (Belarus), be partially or entirely absorbed into the Reich and Germanized, a process to be executed through the physical expulsion of the inhabitants if necessary.[21] Now, in 1941, the conquest would be driven forward with a ruthlessness and terror perhaps never yet witnessed in history, a ruthlessness necessary, so the Nazis proclaimed, to defend the west against not merely Slavs but "Tartars [*sic*] from the Crimea, the remnants of the Golden Horde; Kurds from Turkestan; and Mongols from the banks of the Don and Volga, from the shores of the Caspian, from the Kirgizian steppes, from the plains of Tashkent and Samarkand."[22]

In the Nazi phantasm, at once self-consciously exotic and malign, these creatures would be driven from all those lands destined to be ruled by the new aristocracy (*Hochadel*) of the SS, the fearless knights (*wehrhafte Ritter*) of a new order of men literally bred to racial purity—just like Hanoverian horses, mused Reich Peasant Leader (*Reichsbauernführer*) Walther Darré several years before. These men would weld together the Germanic peoples, indeed the whole of Europe. The bringing of German *Kultur* that had recommenced with the war of 1914–1918 after a centuries-long hiatus, but that had been so cruelly ended, as the Nazis saw things, by the reviled Treaty of Versailles, had already been re-initiated in the conquest of Poland in 1939, a country whose very existence had been enshrined in that hated document. Some 900,000 Poles would eventually be driven from their homes in the country's western regions. These areas had been annexed directly into the "Greater German Reich," while Stalin's Russia had gobbled up the eastern portion of the country at the same time under the terms of the Nazi-Soviet Non-Aggression Pact of August 1939. With some of these lands having been part of Germany before World War I, the Nazi government and many ordinary Germans saw their incorporation as a matter of course. The unwanted Poles, and most of all Polish Jews, had subsequently been dumped into a reservation including both Warsaw and the ancient coronation-city of Krakow called the General Government. Now, with the invasion of Russia, the bringing of *Kultur* and Hitler's drive for living space (*Lebensraum*) in the east would be completed.[23] Himmler's new chivalry would play its assigned part in this gigantic undertaking. "An idealized German *Drang nach Osten* was mentally spliced with an equally idealized [influence of the frontier]" in the view of many German nationalist writers and thinkers even before the racial ravings of Himmler and the Nazis took firm hold.[24] The result was "an emotion-laden narrative"[25] that had already overturned the verdict of World War I in the Treaty of Versailles, taken lands from Poland, sent the German army and the SS marching eastward, and set the stage for the extermination of whole peoples by the time Himmler unleashed his SS horsemen in Russia.

The SS Cavalry Brigade in Russia, 1941

As early as January 1941 the SS *Reiterstandarten* were in the process of yet another, and in this instance more overtly military-sounding, reorganization. In that month, orders came from Himmler's command that the old terminology of *Totenkopf-Reiterstandarten* would be dropped. Henceforth the SS' mounted regiments were to be officially designated as such, namely the 1st and, in the spring of that year, 2nd SS Cavalry Regiments. The change in designation indicated that the older, prewar SS nomenclature no longer quite fit Himmler's or the SS cavalry's own views of the mounted units.[26] The two regiments with all of their support elements continued to train throughout the period from January to the start of Operation Barbarossa in June. Unofficially they were apparently already being referred to collectively as the SS Cavalry Brigade (*SS-Kavallerie-Brigade*) in spring 1941. Orders from Himmler formally establishing the brigade, however, did not reach the regiments until August, by which time the SS cavalrymen had already been in Russia for some time. Depending on losses and other circumstances the brigade's combat-strength in 1941 averaged 3,300–3,500 men; 2,900 horses; and 375 vehicles of all types.[27] The principal maneuver elements of the brigade were the *Reiter* regiments and a Bicycle Reconnaissance Detachment (*Radfahrer Aufklärungsabteilung*; RAA). Essentially a battalion, the RAA consisted of three squadrons of bicycle-mounted infantry supported by several motorized reconnaissance vehicles. Other units organic to the brigade included a veterinary detachment, headquarters and headquarters platoon, logistics elements, and so on. Specifically, as of 3 August 1941, the brigade's combat-strength was 3,364. Its ration-strength was 4,114.[28] Despite the occasionally fierce political differences between the army and the Waffen-SS, the brigade's organization mirrored almost exactly that of the army's earlier 1st Cavalry Brigade in 1939–1940.

In Himmler's initial thinking, the SS Cavalry Brigade was not intended to be a frontline fighting formation, a fact that was crucial to its operational history both initially in Poland and subsequently in Russia and elsewhere. Instead, along with certain other units such as the 1st and 2nd SS Motorized Brigades, he envisioned the Cavalry Brigade as a fully militarized reserve formation to be employed in rear areas for pacification missions. "He had in mind such activities as capturing disorganized Red Army men behind the German lines, combating partisans, and, especially, the shooting of Jews—all in the name of German security."[29] These missions derived from the authority expressly granted to Himmler by Hitler in mid-July 1941 to conduct the "security policing of the newly occupied Eastern territories" (polizeiliche Sicherung der neubesetzten Ostgebiete).[30] For this mission, the SS cavalry were placed under the operational command of the Senior SS and Police Commander Center (Höhere SS und Polizeiführer; HSSPF) in the area behind Army Group Center or Russland-Mitte. At that time, the HSSPF Center was Erich von dem Bach-Zelewski.

The assignment of the SS cavalry to the HSSPF indicated what sort of actual duties the cavalrymen would have. The office of HSSPF had originated within the SS in 1937 with Himmler's intention to incorporate and further centralize the police and security functions of the SS into the overall defense of the Reich. By war's outbreak, the network of HSSPFs had spread across Germany. The number of HSSPFs had expanded with the invasion of Poland, and by the end of 1939 five additional HSSPFs had been assigned to the areas of Poland either annexed into Germany or otherwise occupied. Subsequently, three more HSSPFs, among them Bach, were appointed by Himmler to the occupied Russian territories as the invasion of the Soviet Union rolled forward in 1941.[31] While under Bach's command that summer, the SS cavalrymen would be operating in the area of the Pripet Marshes at roughly the same time as the army's 1st Cavalry Division. Some indication of the ruthlessness with which the SS cavalrymen would carry out their mission may be judged by their previous behavior. In occupied Poland on 6 October 1939, for example, men of the 4th Squadron of the *SS-Totenkopf-Reiterstandarte* had been ordered to a "special assignment" around Kutno. The phrase already meant the summary killing of Jews and/or suspected partisans or "looters." In November troopers of the 5th Squadron shot 440 of 1,000 prisoners, all of them "while trying to escape." On 14 January men of the 3rd Squadron captured a band of four "well-known thieves" in the town of Stoczek. Three of them were summarily shot. On 15 and 18 January men of the same squadron shot three Poles "while trying to escape" during searches for arms in the villages of Rossa and Russastara.[32] There were other such instances.

Specific orders concerning the SS Cavalry Brigade's mission in the context of Barbarossa arrived at the end of July 1941. On 28 July, over Himmler's signature, a Special Order spelled out which units would participate in the "combing through" of the marshes, those units' combat-performance expectations, and what specific actions those units were to take.[33] All arms would participate: mounted units, motorized detachments, and infantry. The brigade's mounted units were expected to cover twenty-five to thirty-seven miles per day (40–60 km) unless combat and/or local searches were being undertaken. The order acknowledged that the infantry would have a hard time keeping up with the horsemen. By contrast, motorized units might well range farther ahead of them. All villages were to be considered strongpoints, either for the enemy or for the Germans. As a consequence,

if the population serves as the enemy of Germany, is racially or humanly [*sic*] inferior, or indeed, as it often is in the marsh areas, made up of fleeing criminals, then all people that are suspected of helping the partisans are to be shot, while females and children are to be evacuated and cattle and food are to be apprehended and secured. These villages are then to be burned to the ground. Either the villages and settlements are a network of [friendly] strongpoints, whose residents kill partisans and pillagers and inform us of them, or they cease to exist. No enemy will be allowed to find support, food or shelter in these areas.[34]

To reinforce the intent, Himmler evidently met with HSSPF Bach personally on 31 July at the latter's headquarters at Baranovichi lying midway on the route between Brest-Litovsk and Minsk along the marshes' northern fringe, presumably to reiterate at least the order's sense if not also its words. The next day, 1 August, further orders went out via radio that "all Jews must be shot. Drive Jewish women into the marshes."[35] The SS Cavalry Brigade's commander, Hermann Fegelein, later reported that his men had killed 15,000 people between the towns of Pinsk and Baranovichi in the western reaches of the Pripet Marshes but that the water proved too shallow to drown the women.[36] At almost the same date that these orders were going out regarding operations in the marshes, namely on 2 August 1941, the notification came to Bach's headquarters at Baranovichi officially establishing the SS Cavalry Brigade.[37]

Between 29 July and 13 August 1941, the brigade was involved in its first clearing operation of the marshes in an area encompassing approximately the upper third of the triangle formed by the railways linking Brest-Litovsk, Minsk, and Gomel. Periodically, one element of the brigade, namely the Advance Detachment (*Vorausabteilung*), a sort of rapid-response unit, found itself attached to the army's accompanying 162nd ID. In these actions, the SS cavalrymen fought not only partisans but regular Red Army forces, both horse-mounted and infantry.[38] In one instance, for example—and in good cavalry fashion—an SS mounted patrol carried out a reconnaissance of more than 140 miles (230 km) in the four-day period of 28–31 July at the very beginning of the operation. On the basis of reports from the patrol's commander, a combat-engineer platoon leader (*Obersturmführer*) named Karl Fritsche of the 2nd *Reiter* Regiment, an encirclement of a large number of Red Army forces was accomplished by supporting German units. These included infantry from the 162nd ID, the SS Cavalry Brigade's Advance Detachment, and a German police unit. These troops successfully engaged the Russians, including Russian cavalry and infantry, and repeatedly prevented their breaking out of the pocket thus formed.[39] By the time the clearing operation ended on 13 August, the SS Cavalry Brigade's leaders were reporting great success. They indicated that their enemies had included two Red Army cavalry divisions (36th and 37th) and the 121st Rifle Division.

Further, they reported fully 15,878 enemy personnel killed in action and 830 taken captive at a cost of only 17 SS cavalrymen dead and 36 wounded. The brigade also listed 200 of its horses as having been killed. These, however, the brigade replaced from the haul of more than 800 horses captured.[40] The brigade's summative reports about a month later also recognized the fighting qualities of its opponents. Particular note was made of the Soviet soldiers' and partisans' effective defensive techniques and the concomitant difficulty the SS cavalrymen had in prying them out of their field fortifications even in the face of the Russians' certain death.[41] The relative lightness of the cavalry brigade's indirect-fire weapons might help explain these difficulties, a problem also faced by the army's 1st Cavalry Brigade / Division. The Soviet defenders' desperation might also be explained, however, by the SS men's already established reputation regarding the treatment of prisoners. Furthermore, the Red Army's own very harsh discipline almost certainly played a role in its soldiers' tenacity. It was at just this time, for example, that Soviet dictator Joseph Stalin issued his famous order for the immediate execution of any soldiers of the Red Army who attempted to remove their insignia and surrender. The soldiers' families would be arrested for good measure, with all that such arrest implied for the latter's fate. In addition, any Soviet troops finding themselves encircled and preferring to surrender rather than break out "are to be destroyed by any available means, while their families are to be deprived of all state allowances and assistance."[42] To the extent that Soviet soldiers hiding in the Pripet Marshes had radio contact with command elements farther east, they would presumably have learned of Stalin's directive. If fear of the SS cavalrymen didn't motivate them to fight to the end, fear of Stalin might.

Whatever the principal reason for continued resistance by Red Army soldiers and partisans, the two SS mounted regiments along with other units of the Cavalry Brigade were once again ordered out on a clearing operation after only several days rest and refitting. Between 17 August and 5 September the SS cavalrymen worked their way generally south-southeast through the Pripet Marshes via the town of Starobin, almost dead center in the triangle of roads surrounding the marshes (Starobin was secured by the 1st *Reiter* Regiment on 22 August), toward the southeastern corner of the triangle. Fierce fighting occurred at Turov on the banks of the Pripet River when other troopers of both *Reiter* regiments stormed the place on 21 August supported by anti-tank guns, light field artillery, and automatic weapons. Partisans and regular Red Army soldiers fighting from prepared defensive positions responded with heavy small-arms fire, anti-tank guns, and machine guns.[43] The towns of Petrikov and Mozyr, located farther east along the Pripet River, were occupied in the days leading up to 4 September.

In his comprehensive report written early in September, then–Colonel (*Standartenführer*) Fegelein noted that enemy forces were consistently "annihilated" when they comprised regular Red Army soldiers. Partisans posed a greater problem. Indeed, he wrote, they posed the greatest problem for German forces behind the front. They were "cold-blooded, brave until annihilated and asiatically [sic] cruel."[44] The SS men had to remain constantly on the alert because the partisans could appear anywhere, aided as they were by an apparently excellent communications network and their knowledge of the terrain. They exhibited calm in the difficult fighting in the marshes and continuously obstructed all roads and forest paths by laying mines, destroying bridges, and placing machine gun nests and bunkers at tactically important junctions.[45] Notwithstanding the irony of Fegelein's reference to Russian cruelty, it seems clear that the SS Cavalry Brigade and other German forces in the watershed of the Pripet knew clearly that their enemy was likely to stay there in spite of periodic "pacification" operations. They would have to fight that enemy again and again.

Between 7 September and 1 October, units of the brigade found themselves continuing to do just that. In this period operations were conducted in the marshes south of the road linking Brest-Litovsk and Gomel. The area of operations' western boundary was the Pripet River where that watercourse turned southeast at Mozyr. The River Dnepr formed the sector's eastern boundary. Throughout the period, the partisans' methods remained what they had been before: small-unit attacks on the SS horsemen; the mining and demolition of roads and bridges; and the disruption of German supply lines.[46] On 10 September, 38 Red Army soldiers were captured in fighting around the village of Krassnyi Ostrov. In that same engagement, however, 384 partisans were confirmed killed. Total losses to the SS Cavalry Brigade were 2 horses killed and 19 horses wounded.[47] Given the record of the brigade's personnel to that date, this very disparity (not to mention a complete absence of reported Red Army fatalities) smacks not so much of numerical inflation of enemy casualties but rather an effort to hide the genuine likelihood that most of the partisans in question were innocent civilians. Certainly, losses of some sort were being suffered by the cavalrymen, as 96 replacements arrived on 19 September. Nevertheless, the striking numerical disparities continued in most of the brigade's fighting during the period. On 25–26 September, for example, 280 more partisans and 87 "criminals" were reported shot by the brigade's troopers south and west of Gomel and several ammunition dumps were destroyed.[48]

As the clearing operation around Gomel came to end at the end of September 1941, the SS Cavalry Brigade found itself being eyed for redeployment to the north and east for a rear-area security mission in the forthcoming Operation Typhoon. This operation, it was hoped both in Berlin and German Army Group Center's headquarters, would be the final, successful drive to Moscow. The assault had earlier been postponed in the wake of the destruction of encircled Soviet forces in and around Smolensk in late July and early August. Following that victory, Hitler had ordered Army Group Center's drive on the Soviet capital suspended. To the frustration of many of his commanders, Hitler had the OKW divert significant German armored forces to the south to assist Army Group South in the conquest of Kiev and the western Ukraine. It had been as a small part of that much larger, and spectacularly successful, operational redeployment that the SS Cavalry Brigade itself had moved into the lower southeastern reaches of the Pripet Marshes and crossed the Dnepr in late September.[49] Now, as the Russian autumn came on in earnest, the forces of Army Group Center began preparations for a renewal of the great strategic advance on Moscow. As it had since June, the advance would continue roughly along the axis of the highway running eastward from Brest-Litovsk via Minsk to Moscow. Whether German armies could breach Soviet defenses and reach Moscow before the onset of winter may have troubled the minds of senior commanders. For the SS cavalrymen, as for hundreds of thousands of other German rankers, such larger questions made no difference. They may well have fretted about becoming cold—they and their horses would certainly be cold, bitterly cold, in less than two months' time—but they and their army counterparts would go where they were told for as long as they were told.

On 29 September, the brigade received orders to move to the town of Toropets which lay 124 miles (200 km) north of Smolensk and just above the road running eastward from Velikiye Luki to Rzhev. The redeployment entailed transporting men, horses, and equipment by rail from Gomel to Vitebsk, marching the brigade a further 111 miles (180 km) northward to Nevel, and then entraining again eastward to Toropets. In all, the brigade covered about 310 miles (500 km) and was essentially in place by 15 October. It was subordinated to the 403rd Security Division in the operational area of the German Ninth Army.[50] As the brigade moved closer to the front, operational command-authority for it shifted from the HSSPF to the army, even though the cavalrymen retained their own separate supply chains and replacement pools. By the time the brigade was ready to assume full operations, Typhoon had been under way for about a fortnight. The brigade's headquarters at Toropets and its area of responsibility lay not quite 100 miles (160 km) behind the front lines.[51]

As they had done in the Pripet Marshes, the brigade's troopers spread out in the region between Toropets and Rzhev and carried out security and anti-partisan operations. Rzhev had fallen to German troops on 14 October and was viewed as a likely staging point for a further German advance swinging to the north around Moscow as part of Army Group Center's massive projected encirclement of the Soviet capital. From time to time, the SS men were specifically assigned to guard the supply lines of particular units. In the second half of October, for example, the brigade's 1st *Reiter* Regiment received orders to guard the supply lines of the Army's 253rd ID while simultaneously executing anti-partisan missions.[52] In the same period, the brigade's Bicycle Reconnaissance Detachment carried out numerous patrols along the road linking Toropets and Yetkino and the railway connecting Velikiye Luki and Rzhev, this corridor being roughly the boundary between Army Group Center and Army Group North. "During these patrols, a combined total of 2,120 partisans and suspicious people were taken prisoner. Fegelein [still the brigade's commander] reported that these prisoners were 'handled in the general way,' although that was not elaborated upon. It is generally assumed that they were executed."[53] Also at this time the autumnal rains fell heavily. Consequently, the brigade's mobility was significantly hampered both for the vehicular units and for the mounted formations. The 1st *Reiter* Regiment soon reported that its horses had become exhausted by their exertions, particularly in light of the brigade's difficulties with supply lines stretching back, as they did, all the way to Warsaw. Despite such difficulties, however, the brigade's mounts held up fairly well under the prevailing conditions. Brigade-level reports listed a total strength of 3,183 horses in October. Of those, only 4 died of exhaustion between 25 and 31 October. Fifty-one were reported sick and unfit for service. Unfortunately, the more general situation for the army's horses in Russia at this time went from bad to much worse. The standard of equine care and horses' rates of survival in the SS Cavalry Brigade (and the army's 1st Cavalry Division) would presumably have been higher than in the German armies collectively. For the latter, the overwhelming majority of horses were draft animals, and their handlers were not always trained well enough or sufficiently motivated to provide good care. Those animals began to die from exhaustion, poor feed, disease, and wounds at truly alarming rates—as many as one thousand per day—as cold autumnal rains quickly turned Russian roads to bottomless, glutinous sloughs of mud. This was the famed *rasputiza*, literally the "time without roads." In a situation common to so many German units elsewhere in Russia in 1941, from 21 October all forward progress of the SS Cavalry Brigade as a whole completely stopped, albeit temporarily, owing to the mud, even though the first snows had already fallen before the brigade was actually in place in Ninth Army's area. Even if they weren't actually moving forward, however, the brigade's troopers continued unabated their wide-ranging security and anti-partisan patrols, sometimes reaching as far northwest as the city of Cholm.[54]

Nevertheless, as winter approached, the nature of the combat facing the brigade's troopers began to change. In early November certain units of the brigade began to find themselves in increasingly heavy fighting with regular Red Army forces. This situation was coincidental with three factors affecting the German offensive generally. First and foremost, the weather was rapidly growing colder. Secondly even as the temperatures dropped, German armies were reaching, or had already reached, the limits of their supply lines. Finally, Russian resistance was stiffening as the invaders approached the region immediately around Moscow, Rzhev being only about 130 miles (209 km) to the northwest. Famed armored commander General Heinz Guderian noted that "the bitterness of the fighting was gradually telling on both our officers and men. . . . It was indeed startling to see how deeply our best officers had been affected by the latest battles." The cavalrymen of the SS constituted no exception to Guderian's general assessment. They, too, were encountering ever stronger and more formal resistance, even in the rear areas. There also appeared a growing likelihood that they might be called upon by the army for frontline duty. Himmler, however, did not necessarily endorse such a development. As already indicated, the *Reichsführer-SS* had been entrusted by Hitler with ensuring the proper settling of the "special tasks" attending the "political administration" of the occupied territories of the Soviet Union, tasks recognized officially by the OKW as being entirely Himmler's own independent responsibility. In keeping with the views of the *Reichsführer*-SS noted earlier in his various addresses to SS men heading for Russia, these "special tasks" would "derive from the decisive struggle that will have to be carried out between the two opposing political systems [of Nazism and communism]."[55] Himmler believed that the war to be waged against partisans, Jews, and other undesirables—whether in the Pripet Marshes or, now, in what OKW touted as the final drive on Moscow—was just as important as the one being fought on the front lines. If his cavalrymen, as well as other SS units, could be kept to their "special tasks," that would be his and their signal contribution to Germany's victory and Europe's future. As early as 15 September, for instance, he had evidently rebuffed suggestions that the SS Cavalry Brigade be assigned to frontline combat.[56] The war's changing nature in late October and early November 1941, however, forced the SS Cavalry Brigade into ever-heavier fighting whether Himmler was comfortable with it or not. In the first week of November elements of the 1st *Reiter* Regiment fought in a major battle alongside the army's 102nd and 253rd IDs in stopping a Russian assault near the town of Yeltsy. The commander of the 253rd ID subsequently sent formal thanks to the brigade for the *Reiter* regiment's support.[57] Evidence also continued to indicate that larger and more competent Soviet forces were successfully infiltrating the brigade's area of responsibility. In mid-November, shortly after the 1st *Reiter* Regiment's battle, troopers of the RAA discovered a munitions dump at the rail junction of Olenino west of Rzhev. They secured almost 500 pounds of explosives, cases of detonators, more than 900,000 rounds of rifle ammunition, and 1,200 rifle grenades.[58] Despite such localized successes, however, the SS cavalrymen might nevertheless have concurred with the views of Army Group Center's commander, Field Marshal Fedor von Bock. In an entry dated 1 December he wrote in his diary: "The fighting of the past 14 days has shown that the notion that the enemy in front of the army group has 'collapsed' was a fantasy. . . . Halting at the gates of Moscow, where the road and rail net of almost all Eastern Russia converge, is tantamount to heavy defensive fighting against a numerically far superior foe. The forces of the army group are not equal to this, even for a limited time."[59] Somewhat farther south than Olenino, on 4 December, General Guderian recorded that the temperature was minus 32 degrees Fahrenheit. He wrote to his wife: "The enemy, the size of the country and the foulness of the weather were all underestimated, and we are suffering for that now."[60] The SS cavalrymen would suffer right along with the rest.

The Soviet Counteroffensive—Winter 1941–1942

In the first week of December 1941, Soviet armies launched a massive counterattack against Army Group Center and the southernmost elements of Army Group North. Advancing pincer-like, in a negative mirror-image of the "C" formed by the arms of the Germans' farthest advance around Moscow, the offensive's objective was to blunt and, if possible, drive the invaders back from the metropolis. Red Army commanders envisioned a convergence of the arms of their reverse "C" on the highway running westward from the Soviet capital. North and west of Moscow, the Red Army's Kalinin Front (i.e., army group) smashed headlong into the German Ninth Army along a line roughly parallel to, but north of, the area of the SS cavalrymen's earlier security operations between Velikiye Luki and Rzhev. The principal objective of the Fourth Shock Army, Kalinin Front's main force, was to break Ninth Army's lines of supply, the very lines that the SS Cavalry Brigade had spent

October and November helping to protect. This was the offensive about which the brigade's men had been getting apparent clues throughout November. An indication of the offensive's seriousness showed clearly in the directives that went out in mid-December to the brigade's rear-echelon elements. The brigade's combat engineer company was ordered forward from Warsaw, though why it was still there remains unclear. Even the brigade's rear-area veterinarians were ordered to the front.[61] As with the army at that desperate moment, the cavalry brigade was scouring its rear-echelon formations for all possible replacement personnel. Furthermore, the entire brigade was now placed under the direct operational control of Ninth Army. All security missions along Ninth Army's resupply lines were terminated, though some subsequently had to be resumed, and all available elements of the brigade found themselves in the front lines.[62]

In the first weeks of December the Soviet offensive made good ground. In temperatures of minus 15 degrees Fahrenheit (–26° C) and with snow up to 3 feet (1 m) deep, the entire frontage of Ninth Army along a line east, north, and west of Rzhev gave way. As early as 7 December, Soviet forces overran the headquarters of the LVI Panzer Corps outside Klin on the railway running northwest from Moscow to Kalinin. For a time it seemed that the entire northern wing of Army Group Center might collapse. When Bock soon thereafter recommended withdrawal, Hitler relieved him (Bock was seriously ill with stomach ulcers in any case) and replaced him with General Günther von Kluge. Rather than countenance Bock's suggested retreat, Hitler ordered "fanatical resistance." Gradually, in bitter fighting, the Germans succeeded in hanging on, but the Soviet offensive slowed only slightly. At the end of December elements of the SS Cavalry Brigade's Bicycle Reconnaissance Detachment, temporarily attached to the army's 253rd ID, were conducting patrols on the shores of Lake Volga to the northwest of Rzhev.[63] Attacked on 9 January 1942 by heavy Russian forces supported by tanks, the RAA fought its way out of the lakeside village of Peno where it had been assigned. For the next fortnight, the RAA fought and fell back to the southwest as part of a terrible defensive struggle by elements of Ninth Army trying to hold back the Red Army's attacks. On 17 January the detachment's survivors stumbled into the cavalry brigade's former headquarters town of Toropets. The RAA had suffered 75 percent casualties from its reported December combat-strength of more than six hundred officers and men. For all practical purposes, the Bicycle Reconnaissance Detachment had been destroyed.[64]

The RAA's destruction left the brigade with only two substantial, combat-effective elements, namely the two *Reiter* regiments. As was the case with the RAA, between 31 December 1941 and 20 January 1942, these regiments found themselves in almost constant combat with strong Russian forces advancing in the Red Army's larger attempt to encircle Rzhev from the northeast. Being forced to leave their horses behind in more sheltered rear areas, the men of the *Reiter* regiments fought largely as regular infantry during this period, a situation that would repeat itself in the winter of 1942–1943.[65] When they did employ their horses, losses could rise rapidly owing not only to the weather but also to the ferocity of the fighting. By the beginning of February, after nearly four weeks of continuous combat, the two mounted regiments had suffered almost 50 percent casualties in both men and horses.[66] Even as losses mounted alarmingly, the remnants of the brigade found themselves transferred to the XXIII Corps' 1st Panzer Division. They remained attached to that armored unit for most of March. During this period reinforcements of ethnic Germans (*Volksdeutsche*) arrived and brought the brigade's strength temporarily back up to 1,500 men.[67] Nevertheless, by early April, the cavalry brigade's strength had been so reduced that the staff recommended to the *Reichsführer*-SS that its designation be changed from a brigade to a "weak *Reiter* regiment" in order to reflect its actual condition.[68]

The designation soon became semiofficial. By April the brigade was being referred to as the SS *Reiter* Regiment. At about the same time, Ninth Army's new commander, General Walther Model, issued plans that the unit be refurbished (though not necessarily once again expanded to brigade-strength) with better horses to be brought forward from the remount depot at Warsaw. Himmler received notification of the proposal, but it could not be executed in part owing to the Russians' seizure in January of the brigade's principal forward supply base at Toropets. With the town's capture, the brigade lost its supplies of saddles and other equipment. A lack of adequately trained riders also put paid to the effort to re-establish the mounted units at that juncture.[69] By month's end, the SS Cavalry Regiment had been effectively reduced to battalion-strength, approximately seven hundred men. As Fegelein had already returned to Warsaw in anticipation of the unit's probable reorganization, the survivors' then-commander, Major (*Sturmbannführer*) Gustav Lombard, requested of General Model that the remaining elements also be entirely withdrawn from the front and returned to Warsaw. This process gradually occurred between the end of April and the end of May. Only a small, ad hoc battle group remained behind.[70]

As the fitful and rainy Russian spring began to take hold in April and May 1942, the worst of the winter fighting subsided. The SS Cavalry Brigade's former area of operations between Toropets and Rzhev had largely been lost to the Red Army. German forces, however, still held a deep bulge in the Russian lines. Shaped like a right-handed boxing glove, Rzhev lay at the knuckle and Olenino at the fingertips. The thumb was formed by a much narrower salient that German counterattacks had driven northeast from the town of Dukhovshchina to Belyy, which lay to the southwest of Olenino. Very large pockets of Soviet partisans and Red Army regulars, including paratroopers dropped earlier in the winter battles, lay cut off and surrounded east and southeast of Smolensk and stretching along the railway toward Bryansk.[71]

The winter battles had been ferocious, and the brigade's condition reflected in microcosm the exhaustion and losses suffered by the Ninth Army and other German forces. Reporting on the carnage along the Leningrad highway northeast of Moscow, CBS Radio's Larry Lesueur was one of a small group of American correspondents covering the war from the Soviet Union at that time. In his reportage, Lesueur depicted the scene on all the fields of what the Germans were calling the Battle of Rzhev, including those fought over by the SS cavalry: burnt-out villages whose buildings were "now only charred, smoking embers"; battered and blackened German and Soviet vehicles; forests literally stripped bare and blown down as though swept by vast hurricanes; and everywhere the dead—not only dead soldiers but their horses—occasionally covered with what Lesueur called the "merciful cleanliness" of newfallen snow. "The war," he wrote, "was [particularly] hard on horses. . . . All along the roadside their frozen bodies lay in snow-covered blasted chunks."[72] In the wake of such destruction of man and beast, it remained to be seen how and to what extent the SS Cavalry Brigade would recoup its losses.

CHAPTER 9

ₚALε HOℛ𝒮εϻεN

THE 8TH *WAFFEN*-SS CAVALRY DIVISION
FLORIAN GEYER, 1942–1943

As early as March 1942, even before the final cessation of the bitter winter fighting around Rzhev, the SS Operations Main Office (SS-*Führungshauptamt*) was considering the re-establishment of the now badly depleted SS Cavalry Brigade at its bases in occupied Poland. That idea, however, was stillborn. Instead, and in keeping with the expansion of the *Waffen*-SS as a whole throughout the war, the Main Office decided to enlarge the brigade while rebuilding it. The result was to be a full-fledged SS Cavalry Division. Cadre would be provided by the remnants of the SS Cavalry Brigade as they transferred off the line following the Battle of Rzhev. As so often happened in the German armed forces during World War II, the brigade commander's name had by now become attached to the unit. Thus, cadre was sometimes referred to as coming from the SS Cavalry Brigade *Fegelein*. Beginning with the shattered remnants of the RAA, the brigade's survivors began returning from Russia as early as January. In the spring months, what remained of the *Reiter* regiments also found their way back. As the units arrived, they were ordered to the SS training area at Debica, about seventy miles (112 km) due east of Krakow. There they were augmented by substantial numbers of replacements. In fairly short order but without much actual training time, the cavalry brigade's remnants incorporated the new arrivals. The new organization would be officially designated the SS Cavalry Division (SS-*Kavallerie-Division*) effective 21 June 1942.[1]

As the reorganization took place, the combat power of the division grew apace. In place of the earlier brigade's two *Reiter* regiments the division would now have three, though standing up the third evidently took considerable time and effort. Each of the three regiments received an extra staff platoon in addition to four mounted squadrons, a combined machine-gun and mortar squadron, and a motorized heavy squadron. A full artillery regiment was also added, including both horse-drawn and motorized batteries. Further punch was added through the inclusion of a mechanized assault-gun battery and an anti-tank "detachment" (i.e., battalion). The assault-gun battery was later expanded to battalion-strength but was eventually disbanded, its guns being incorporated in the anti-tank battalion. A fully motorized divisional logistics train was also established, along with smaller elements such as bicycle companies, motorized signals platoons, and the all-important veterinary company.[2] As it turned out, these paper arrangements were subject to extraordinarily frequent alteration during the division's lifetime. Just as in the case of the earlier SS Cavalry Brigade, however, subsequent experience saw various elements of the division repeatedly seconded for temporary duty with other formations.

Unfortunately for the new division, most of the incoming replacements were *Volksdeutsche* from Hungary. Deemed "racially acceptable" from the SS' point of view, they nevertheless brought with them certain problems. Divisional staff found that the new recruits spoke German only haltingly or not at all (*mangelhaft oder überhaupt nicht*). They had had little or no paramilitary training with Nazi formations such as the Hitler Youth, SA, or SS, and the bulk of them had not served with any foreign armed forces.[3] Therefore, even if they could understand their orders, they might not be able to execute them. Consequently, both enlisted men and their NCOs had to be trained simultaneously not only in the German language but also in their military duties. This dual training continued in the field right through the end of 1942 and included, for veterinary personnel, everything from equine first aid, diagnosis, and medicinal treatment to farriery, tacking up, and saddling.[4]

Regardless of the training they conducted, however, the division's officers and NCOs were strongly cautioned not to treat the *Volksdeutsche* as inferior to Germans from Germany proper (*Altreich*). This was an enduring problem, and the division's commander in April 1943, Colonel (*Standartenführer*) Fritz Freitag, would still be alluding to it more than a year after the division had been formed. Since *Reichsführer-SS* Heinrich Himmler continued to put great emphasis on ideological indoctrination along with SS cavalry troopers' regular training,[5] the replacements' treatment assumed greater significance than might otherwise have been the case. Thus, for example, the division's leaders were ordered to avoid insulting the Hungarian *Volksdeutsche* by calling them "gypsies." That would offend their honor, affect their morale, and lessen the ideological indoctrination's impact because gypsies were considered grossly inferior in the Nazis' racial hierarchy. Officers and NCOs using the term would be punished. On the other hand, if it were necessary for disciplinary purposes, a *Volksdeutsch* recruit could be criticized expressly as a "dirty pig" (*Dreckschwein*) or even a "sad sack of shit" or "limp dick" (*Schlappschwanz*), just not as a gypsy. All personnel from the *Altreich* were to be instructed in this regard so as to ensure that no mistakes were made.[6]

Seriously complicating the difficulties of incorporating ethnic German replacements was the matter of the new division's horses. Cadre at Debica discovered that the horses shipped to the division had not been sufficiently schooled in the remount system, a fact that could have direct, adverse operational consequences. To expedite the replacements' equestrian training, as well as to further the conditioning of remounts, an SS Cavalry School was established for the division at Zamosc, about fifty miles (80 km) southeast of Lublin. Nevertheless, divisional staff reported that the horses themselves remained "raw,"[7] a fact evidently made worse by difficulties in getting enough feed. On 19 September the division's operations section reported to LIX Corps' chief of staff that there were insufficient oats for the horses and no independent means of acquiring any in what was by then the autumnal rainy season. The operations section further reported that the division was short three

hundred mounts in any case and warned about the impending likelihood of heavy losses among those horses the division did have. Training difficulties thus multiplied considerably even as the division's units
began their deployments. Troopers not yet trained to ride (*reiterlich
nicht vorgebildete Männer*)—and who might not understand their commanders anyway—were mounted on horses that were not yet trained
themselves and that might well have been improperly nourished.[8] Given
the urgency of the division's anticipated anti-partisan mission and the
short time of only some two-and-half months allotted for the entire
training process, this situation remained a recipe for incomplete operational results, not to mention occasional cracked skulls and broken arms
and legs.

As it turned out, when the 1st and 2nd *Reiter* Regiments and the Bicycle Reconnaissance Detachment began their movement earlier than
planned, on 27 August 1942, they shipped out not only to fight partisans
as they'd been told they would but also to help plug a gap in the German
front lines near Vitebsk. They were placed under the command of the
330th ID of LIX Corps. As the last maneuver element to be raised, the
3rd *Reiter* Regiment, along with the anti-aircraft artillery detachment
and the division's combat engineers, remained behind to complete its
training. For the 3rd Regiment, this training included squadron versus
squadron combat exercises.[9] In the meantime, between 7 and 19 September, the 1st and 2nd *Reiter* Regiments engaged in regular anti-partisan
missions in the 330th ID's area of operations. Their war diaries recorded
numerous caches of munitions and other supplies seized, but despite
what was occasionally reported as heavy fighting earlier in the month,
they recorded only low numbers of casualties inflicted and sustained
before the last two weeks of September. The numbers, however, rose
fairly significantly in that last fortnight.

Losses of horses were also rather light during the period to 30 September though they, too, rose as the month ended. By that date, divisional veterinary staff recorded 36 horses killed in action and 6 dead
from exhaustion or sickness. A further 82 had to be sent to rear-area veterinary hospitals, while another 107 were transferred from the 1st *Reiter*
Regiment to the veterinary company because the horses had become
superfluous (*überzählig*) as a result of unspecified reductions, presumably combat casualties, in regimental personnel (*Mannschaftsausfall*).

These horses would be followed a month later by another 203 when, this time specifically on the basis of casualties sustained in October, the 1st *Reiter* Regiment's 1st Squadron was actually disbanded.[10] While it remains unclear how many of these transferred horses were subsequently sent back to combat units, the veterinary detachment reported to LIX Corps headquarters on 4 October that a total of 118 horses had been treated between the start of the division's operations and 30 September, that is, over a period of about four weeks.[11] Such rates of activity remained constant throughout the period to the end of 1942, with horses being shunted continuously back and forth through the division's veterinary system in numbers ranging from twos and threes to scores and hundreds. The pace of these veterinary transfers persisted well into 1943 and would prove a significant hindrance to the division's operational capability.

Nevertheless, whatever difficulties the troopers were encountering with their supplies of horseflesh, the 330th ID's staff reported that the SS cavalrymen executed their tasks with what it called "noteworthy passion" (*mit bewundernswerter Passion*).[12] Whether that passion was in any way inspired by the fact that the division was now an officially enumerated unit, formally designated as the 8th *Waffen*-SS Cavalry Division, remains unrecorded. It also remains needless to speculate, though the speculation is unavoidable, about what sort of malevolent excesses might be subsumed under that phrase. Equally chilling was the reported "cleansing" (*Säuberung*) of lines of advance and rear areas at about the same time in the division's area of operations east of Vitebsk, missions undertaken again later, in November 1942, in the region south and west of Smolensk. By that date, the division had been transferred to VI Corps, and that corps' headquarters ordered the division's troopers to clear out (*räumen*) all civilians from an area approximately two miles deep behind the front lines. If necessitated by numbers, the division was to evacuate them to rear areas. Accompanying the directive was the admonitory instruction from VI Corps' staff that proper accommodation would have to be planned in advance of any such evacuation. Otherwise, the "further growth of guerrilla bands (*Banden*) would be unavoidable."[13] The SS men's response to the admonition was not recorded. On the basis of their earlier behavior in Poland and Russia, however, their response may be imagined.

One of the problems encountered by the division in that early autumn of 1942 was the notorious condition of the Russian roads. As in 1941, the division's troopers struggled in the biannual rainy season. Repeatedly, divisional war diaries bemoaned the fact that units, and especially the motorized detachments, simply could not move in the sodden, pudding-like tracks that passed for Russian roads. On 22 September 1942, for example, the divisional war diary recorded that the movements of combat elements were being badly hindered by continuous rain and bottomless mud. Minefields and blown bridges only made matters worse.[14] For the division's supply columns, too, conditions often made motorized movement literally impossible. On 25–26 September, the division's quartermaster was reporting that one brigade had to bring gasoline forward in confiscated Russian *panje* wagons, presumably drawn by confiscated *panje* horses, because the supply column's trucks couldn't move in the mud.[15] At one point during the period to 30 September this particular *panje*-wagon column grew to as many as seventy-six vehicles. Shortly thereafter the tally fell to only thirty-five wagons, but only after the attached veterinary company determined that no more than 50 percent of the draft horses pulling them were deemed fit for service.[16] Initial war-diary entries for the period did not specify whether the division's horse-mounted units made better headway than motorized and mechanized elements. Nevertheless, part of the rationale for retaining horses at all in the Russian campaign was precisely the adverse climatic conditions in which these motorized and mechanized SS detachments were finding themselves forced to operate in 1941 and now again in 1942.

Of course, the difficulties in movement were only beginning; and insofar as the horse-mounted elements of the division were concerned, the coming of the Russian winter would once again make matters much more serious even though lower temperatures made for hardened footing. As early as 7 October, well before the real winter weather had even set in and before the cavalrymen's transfer to VI Corps, the division's veterinary unit had already requested that 80,000 horse-shoe cleats from LIX Corps' logistics be made ready (*bereitgestellt*) for the division's horses.[17] The threaded cleats were screwed into the horse' shoes for added traction in ice and snow. In addition, *panje* horses continued to be viewed as an increasingly important source of replacements for the approaching winter. A potential requisition of some 200 of them, for example, was discussed with VI Corps veterinary officers in mid-November. Of these, 182 were eventually requested for the formation of an ad hoc battalion of ski troops, most of whom were transferred from the Cavalry Division's artillery but who were further augmented with men from the *Reiter* regiments. Furthermore, in light of the increasingly severe winter weather, the division's troopers were being warned to ensure that exhausted horses of whatever sort, and specifically those affected by apparently widespread bacterial ailments, be transferred to the veterinary company early enough so that they didn't actually die in transport or immediately upon arrival at the hospital.[18] Though the divisional veterinary staff couldn't foresee it, these steps for the SS men's mounts were being taken mere days before the launching of the massive Russian counterattack far to the southeast at Stalingrad where so many former troopers of the army's 1st Cavalry Division, now 24th Panzer, would find their graves.

For the SS Cavalry Division's men, as well as for their horses, the winter of 1942–1943 would once more pose the fierce challenge that had confronted German troops on the Eastern Front in 1941–1942. Nevertheless, with that first season's experience already under their belts, VI Corps' headquarters confidently pointed out that further weather-related difficulties could be avoided. Experience, winter uniforms, training, and constant supervision by all commanders and among all troops themselves could ward off winter's effects. By contrast, if numerous cases of frostbite did occur, then corps-level commanders would have to draw "certain conclusions" about the effectiveness of the division's training and the level of its morale.[19] Despite the implicit threat of such questions being raised, the division continued to suffer losses to frostbite, combat, and illness. Things could hardly have been otherwise, and by mid-November 1942, the division had been designated as Army Group Reserve with the mission of conducting anti-partisan sweeps and countering any airborne landings. In these missions it operated in support of the 197th ID and the 2nd *Luftwaffe* Field Division. At that time, the divisional adjutant reported that while the Cavalry Division's ration-strength stood at 10,204 officers and men, its combat-strength was only 5,214.[20]

The adjutant's report made no mention of the status of the division's horses.

In mid-December, the division was assigned to yet more anti-partisan operations, this time in the region around the town of Baturino about sixty-two miles (100 km) north-northwest of Smolensk. Given the winter conditions and the resulting difficulties of supply, the division's operations officer (the billet's German designation was *Ia*) reported on both 19 and 26 December that most of the division's horses had been placed in unspecified winter quarters. Consequently, and at least temporarily, the SS Cavalry Division was now only as mobile as a regular army infantry division. It would move for the time being on foot. The *Ia* also reported that while the division was only "conditionally capable" (*bedingt geeignet*) of offensive operations, it remained "fully capable" (*voll geeignet*) on the defensive. As it turned out, at the very moment when the division was essentially without its horses, its units also received orders to begin painting the division's newly assigned insignia on divisional vehicles: a horse's head in profile facing the viewer's left with a drawn sword crossing the neck from lower left to upper right, point uppermost.[21]

For the rest of the month of December, in temperatures falling from freezing to about 15 degrees Fahrenheit (–9° C), the troopers of the SS Cavalry Division engaged in sporadic combat with partisans employing not merely small arms but artillery. Divisional reconnaissance elements estimated the combined strength of the partisan *Banden* to be nearly three thousand. Normally, however, the latter appear to have operated in much smaller groups against both the SS cavalrymen and other units in the area, the latter now including the army's 52nd ID and, once again, the 2nd *Luftwaffe* Field Division. Divisional daily reports also indicated that these partisans, who had come into the division's area of operations from the north, not only communicated with other Red Army forces via two clandestine radio stations but also had command of an airstrip through which supplies flowed and from which wounded were evacuated. Though the daily reports recorded no specific indication of the partisans' success with the evacuation of their own sick and wounded, the same documents did note at some length an "extraordinary number" (*ausserordentliche Fülle*) of cold-induced illnesses in the division's own three *Reiter* regiments. As had already occurred so frequently in Russia, these units had occasionally been seconded to other echelons during this period for anti-partisan operations, as had the division's artillery regiment. Ill or not, however, the cavalrymen could not be taken out of the line. Instead, they were treated in place owing to the division's reduced strength.[22]

Notwithstanding its depleted state, the division continued with its grim work of hunting down, capturing, and killing anyone considered a partisan. Some measure of the viciousness of the business is recorded in a "Special Directive to the Forces" (*Besondere Weisungen an die Truppe*) dated 24 December 1942. No civilians were to be "evacuated" from their homes and/or expelled from the division's area of operations without the responsible officers first notifying the divisional Enemy Intelligence Detachment (Ic), implicitly because such unauthorized action would simply create more partisans. More directly sinister ran the following warning: "Any arbitrary killing of partisan prisoners does not serve the interests of the division." Clearly they were being killed arbitrarily, and not only by *Waffen*-SS units. If for no other reason than to ensure a continued flow of useful tactical and operational intelligence, the Special Directive expressly ordered that prisoners be sent to the divisional Ic for interrogation.[23] What happened to them afterward was another matter.

Orders or no orders, however, the killings went on just as they had since the invasion of Poland in 1939. Indeed, Hermann Fegelein's report from 1941 regarding Himmler's order to shoot or drive into the marshes all the Jews the earlier SS Cavalry Brigade came across clearly bears out the fact that the SS cavalrymen had long been killing persons out of hand, in vast numbers, and on a regular basis. The division's daily activity reports, and occasionally the division's war diary, for the period throughout the first quarter of 1943 are replete with references to prisoners and civilians being shot while trying to escape, wounded prisoners dying after interrogation, and suspected partisans and civilians being shot when found carrying arms. Representative of all of these individual reports was the divisional summary that was eventually compiled in early February 1943 for these continuing anti-partisan operations (codenamed Operation Sternlauf). Concerning prisoners taken, the report noted 34 "bandits"; 153 presumably male "civilians"; and 547 women and children, a total of 734. Of persons killed, the report listed 580 "bandits"; 119 "civilians"; and 32 women, a total of 731.[24] The report recorded no figures indicating children who might have been killed during the period. As with all soldiers on the Eastern Front at this time, the SS cavalrymen were being encouraged from the highest levels to be cruel. Hitler himself made this perfectly clear in an Order of the Day of 1 January 1943. It was evident, he said, that the consequence of a victory by Germany's enemies in the east would be Germany's destruction. German soldiers and men of the *Waffen*-SS already knew that. What German armies were prepared to do to prevent that outcome, he countered, those enemies would soon learn to their sorrow.[25] In Russia, Germany's enemies were already learning it. This kind of encouragement, coming from the führer himself, would obviously override any orders such as the one mentioned above from a mere divisional staff officer urging restraint in the matter.

The bitterness of the resulting anti-partisan warfare was matched by the bitterness of the cold. By January 1943, true winter weather had settled in on the SS cavalry. Temperatures recorded that month in the division's war diary routinely hit as low as minus 15 degrees Fahrenheit (–25° C).[26] Yet the vicious, usually small-scale combats continued. The SS cavalrymen grimly acknowledged the Russian partisans' skill not only in effective daylight cover and concealment but also night fighting. In the vicinity of Simonowo near Baturino, for example, a small scouting party of one officer and twenty-four men from the 1st *Reiter* Regiment was ambushed and surrounded in the failing afternoon light of 17 January by as many as 180 partisans. In badly cut-up terrain covered in dense brush, the scouting party was smothered with heavy automatic weapons fire and overrun. Only six men, three of them wounded, escaped the hand-to-hand fighting that followed. Upon reaching their own lines, the survivors reported that many of the badly wounded SS men who'd been left behind shot themselves so as to avoid falling into Russian hands.[27] This result, said the division's war diary, was further proof that the 1st Regiment simply could not maintain security across its assigned front of nearly eleven miles (17 km), while at the same time confronting strong partisan bands who were not only fighting to cut the Germans' supply lines but who were also widely supported by the civilian population.

Therefore it was imperative that all logistics elements of the division be better trained to resist the partisans' rear-area attacks on the division's supply columns.

Those supply columns, in turn, were at the same time being ordered to make greater use of horse-drawn vehicles because an expected delivery of fuel for the division's vehicles had not arrived. Orders to that effect went out to all units on 23 January 1943.[28] Indeed throughout the entire area of the Army's XXX Corps, to which the division was at that time assigned, horse-drawn vehicles were only to be driven at the walk unless transporting the wounded. This would have to be done in order to spare the horses. Empty horse-drawn vehicles were allowed only one or two passengers besides the driver. Loaded vehicles were not allowed to carry any personnel at all nor were any horses pulling such vehicles to be ridden.[29]

These prevailing winter conditions and the almost constant contact with the enemy resulted in a steady stream of casualties suffered by the division in the first quarter of 1943, a situation reminiscent in its own way of the German cavalry's campaign against *francs-tireurs* in the bitter French winter 1870–1871. Now in 1942–1943, however, the figures for the numbers of casualties the division's troops inflicted on the enemy— whether partisans, "bandits," or mere civilians—were much higher for the simple reason that the SS cavalrymen had been trained to a level of fanaticism unknown in the German cavalry not only in 1870–1871 but also in 1914–1918. Comparing the numbers cited above, as well as the nature, of Russian prisoners of war and those killed, and even including the last ten days of December 1942, the division's own losses in the period to 4 April 1943, though steady, were relatively minor. They included 154 killed, 498 wounded (74 of whom were not evacuated), and 54 missing.[30]

Of course, whatever losses the division did suffer had to be replaced. The *Reiter* regiments were given first priority for replacements after the more or less continuous contact with the enemy since the preceding fall and winter. However, insufficient numbers of replacements were available from the division's supply units to bring the *Reiter* regiments up to their 100 percent wartime establishment (*Kriegssollstärke*).[31] Consequently, only 70 percent of the wartime establishment could be maintained. This stark fact dictated a reduction in the number of mounted squadrons in each *Reiter* regiment from four to three. Similar conditions also prevailed in several other divisional units. As they had in the winter fighting of 1941–1942, commanders again reached all the way back to the divisional supply detachment based in Warsaw to find the required personnel. In addition, command staff scoured the division's NCO training program for possible replacements. All possible sources found themselves culled of men for the *Reiter* regiments, the division's anti-tank company, and the pioneer battalion. As a result, the 1st and 3rd *Reiter* Regiments received some 788 replacements. At 70 percent strength, this meant, for example, that the total number of officers and men in the 1st Regiment fell from 1,416 to 991. By 1 April 1943, the entire division's combat-strength was listed as only 4,585 officers and men, its ration-strength 6,809.[32] Curiously, however, the relevant documents list no horses at all, though the instructions for filling the forms out specifically stated that a unit's horses were always to be included in the reported ration-strength.

Divisional Anti-Partisan Operations—April to August 1943

From early April until the first week of August 1943, the now officially designated 8th *Waffen*-SS Cavalry Division *Florian Geyer* was once again assigned to anti-partisan operations under the overall supervision of the same man who had supervised the then–SS Cavalry Brigade's operations in the summer of 1941, HSSPF Erich von dem Bach-Zelewski. Under the circumstances, the moniker *Florian Geyer* seemed fitting. The Franconian knight who was the division's namesake had been a leader in the Peasants' War (1522–1526). That association fit neatly the crude "blood and soil" ideology of the SS. So too did the fact that Geyer's sixteenth-century followers had traditionally been referred to as the "Black Bands" (*schwarze Haufen*). Black featured very prominently in the SS' uniforms and regalia. As it turns out, when possible divisional names were being solicited, at least one of the division's units, the 3rd *Reiter* Regiment, suggested that the name of the eighteenth-century Prussian cavalry commander Hans Joachim "Papa" von Ziethen be used. Ziethen's victorious exploits were very widely known, and he'd introduced a death's-head cap-badge similar to, but much larger than, the one worn by the SS.

The cruel, *condottiere*-like nature of the original Florian Geyer, however, seemed more appropriate than that of a Prussian aristocrat in the conditions prevailing in that perilous spring of 1943 on the Eastern Front. Stalingrad had been lost along with the German Sixth Army in one of the war's greatest battles. Hundreds of thousands of Hungarian, Italian, and Rumanian troops who'd fought the Red Army along the Volga had also been killed or captured. In the retreat that followed, the 2nd SS Panzer Corps had rallied brilliantly and had retaken Kharkov in bitter, close-quarters combat after having been earlier driven out of the city. Further withdrawal would occur only in September in the wake of the Germans' defeat at Kursk in July, Hitler having forbidden such a withdrawal before then. The eventual projected stop line would be the Dnepr. This major north–south waterway was expected to provide a defensible barrier for German forces. The river also happened to be part of the large drainage basin through which flowed the rivers Pripet and Berezina, along whose banks the SS Cavalry Brigade had hunted partisans in 1941. As in that year, so now in 1943 the SS cavalrymen would be under Bach's control. Serving until the end of 1942 as HSSPF–*Russland-Mitte*, Bach had in the meantime been appointed Chief of Anti-Partisan Combat Units. As such, he now had responsibility for all such tasks on the entire Eastern Front outside of the army's immediate operational areas.[33] Bach had always willingly served his *Reichsführer*-SS. Now on an even larger scale than in 1941, his primary concern was fulfilling Himmler's orders to ensure that no partisans operating behind German lines hindered the successful retention of the occupied territories or assisted the Red Army.

Unlike 1941, however, Soviet partisans were now better organized, outfitted, and logistically supported by rear-echelon Red Army forces. At this point in the war, Soviet partisans numbered about 250,000 at any given moment. They were potentially capable of severely disrupting German lines of communication and supply in a much more serious way than during the invasion's first year. In addition to appearing for the first time after Stalingrad in the northern Ukraine, large numbers of partisans infiltrated the vast forested areas around Bryansk. They also once again took up station in the middle reaches of the Dnepr watershed and reassembled in the eastern Pripet Marshes.[34] Most importantly, by 1943 partisans had much wider and committed popular support. This support derived not only from the partisans' own brutally successful coercion of Soviet civilians but also because of the invaders' own frightful record of oppression. Consequently, the SS Cavalry Division's efforts entailed an even more intensive effort than in 1941 at rooting out any real or suspected partisans in a given area. In early 1943 that area once more included the region of the eastern Pripet Marshes, but the division also operated far to the east of the River Dnepr in the forests approaching Bryansk as well as southward in the direction of Kursk and Kharkov. As the division's troopers had already experienced (and as had the army's 1st Cavalry Division), the Soviet Union's vast swamps and forests continued to prove, if not an unassailable redoubt, then at least a recurrent refuge for Soviet partisans. Despite recurrent security sweeps, the partisans destroyed rail lines with "clockwork regularity," and, as the German withdrawal began in late summer, in many places they successfully "anticipated the routes . . . and systematically destroyed every bridge" in the rear areas.[35]

These conditions made the division's anti-partisan operations even grimmer than before, if that were possible. In the view of the division's then-commander, Fritz Freitag, they also required a mental adjustment from the earlier frontline combat around Rzhev. Freitag issued his orders accordingly, even before the Battle of Kursk was fought (and lost) and the German tide in Russia began to run out.[36] All personnel had once again to be aware of the special malice of the partisans so as to avoid unnecessary losses. This was especially the case among troops seizing loot that could be booby-trapped or otherwise wired with explosives. Freitag therefore ordered trophy-hunting strictly prohibited. At the same time, a fundamental suspicion of all persons and places was required. Every civilian could be a "bandit." He cautioned his troopers that once again there would be no recognizable front lines. Partisans could appear anywhere, even in pacified areas. Consequently, precaution and attention to detail would be critical in all things at all times. The combing through of forests and villages would have to be undertaken with the greatest possible care, and even apparently impassable terrain would have to be controlled. The cavalrymen would have to reckon with ambushes everywhere, all the time. The division's personnel would therefore have to respond in kind. They did, and they would continue to do so for the rest of the division's time in Russia and, later still, in the Balkans.

The division's command center for the operations of spring 1943 lay initially at Staryye Dorogi in what is now Belarus about thirty-seven miles (59 km) west of the city of Bobruisk. The latter city was located on the railway linking Minsk and Gomel. The division's three *Reiter* regiments, as always the principal partisan-hunting units, were based at the village of Lapichi, slightly north and east of the same railway about midway between Minsk and Gomel.[37] Divisional staff reported that the entire area, implicitly all the way from Minsk to Gomel, was infested with "bandits" and that all roads could be traveled only under armed escort. The road linking the divisional headquarters at Staryye Dorogi and the regional SS supply command at Bobruisk, for example, was reported to be so badly threatened that staff orders went out mandating a standing escort of at least twelve riflemen (*Karabiner*) and three vehicles.[38]

Besides the immediate threat posed to the division's mobility by partisan activity, recurrent problems with the division's horses further complicated matters. Always critical to effective anti-partisan warfare in Russia, sound horses were lacking in the division in the spring of 1943. Quite apart from operational implications, for a unit such as the SS Cavalry Division whose honorific title *Florian Geyer* was now gaining wider circulation and whose commanders really did think of themselves as cavalrymen, lack of sound horses was a very serious problem.[39] It was discovered, for example, that those horses the division did possess had to be treated regularly for scabies-induced mange. Evidently common in Russia at that time, this debilitating ailment had first appeared among the division's mounts in October 1942.[40] At that time in the division's operational area north of Smolensk, mange had been reported as being widespread among civilian livestock. Stabling had been inadequate, and the division's troopers hadn't been able to build proper accommodations owing to constant relocations. Because the mass of the division's personnel had been ordered deployed as infantry that winter, too few qualified personnel had remained to look after too many horses. The situation worsened with the occasional impressment of divisional mounts into regular army units, many of whose men didn't know how to care for them. Horses not properly and regularly groomed were particularly susceptible. Dirty blankets or tack, matted coats left too long uncurried, close exposure to infected animals: all of these could contribute to a major outbreak among the division's horses and evidently did. In early spring 1943, as the division's parent unit, Ninth Army, moved to the rear, provisionally treated horses became reinfected so that by April the majority (*die Masse*) of the division's horses were unfit for service. In the 1st *Reiter* Regiment fully half of the assigned horses were deemed incapable of operational employment. In the 2nd Regiment every single one fell into that category. For each regiment's horses, the treatment and recovery time was estimated to be at least six weeks. To make matters worse, all three of the division's *Reiter* regiments were already below strength in horseflesh. Each one carried 1,453 horses on the division's TOE. In reality, the numbers were 1,201 and 933 for the 1st and 2nd Regiments, respectively.[41] Consequently, commanders determined that a fully "cavalry capable" operation at that moment was impossible. Troopers would instead have to be truck-mounted and therefore more or less confined to the region's poor roads. Crew-served weapons, ammunition, and other equipment would be brought along in pack-columns of requisitioned *panje* horses.[42] Only one full squadron in the 1st *Reiter* Regiment could remain horse-mounted for the time being. None could be in the 2nd *Reiter* Regiment. Horses left behind on these operations would be cared for by local volunteers (*Hilfswillige*). The veterinary company would remain at Lapichi to look after the horses but would designate a veterinary squad (*Staffel*) to accompany the troopers forward. Divisional commander Freitag understood the importance of horses in the anti-partisan mission: "It must be guaranteed," he ordered, "that by incorporating every means and making every effort the horses be made operationally effective as soon as possible."[43] Capturing Russian horses was also given a high priority, despite the earlier outbreaks of mange and the fact that *panje* horses were likely to be infected. Freitag's successor, Hermann Fegelein, who had once again assumed command after a stint in the rear, ordered that the division at least double the number of horses on its TOE through the simple expedient of having "every cavalryman take every horse he sees." This, he said, was a given.[44]

In this reduced condition, the SS Cavalry Division undertook anti-partisan operations between 9 and 17 May and between 13 and 16 June

1943 in Operations Weichsel I and II in the roughly triangular area north and south of the town of Rechitsa on the Berezina River extending to the confluence of the Pripet and Dnepr Rivers. For the purpose, it was incorporated in a battle group (*Kampfgruppe*) with the 10th and 11th SS Police Regiments and Assault Battalion "South." Orders indicated that the encirclement and total destruction of partisan bands constituted the standing operational objective. Simply driving them away would accomplish nothing because they would just reappear elsewhere. Partisans' escape through SS lines, especially to the north, was to be avoided under all circumstances.[45]

Until the beginning of June the division's elements operated both east and west of the Pripet River, fighting mostly small engagements and capturing and/or killing many suspected partisans. However, the division's reinforced reconnaissance detachment also fought a sustained, three-hour battle on 17 May near the village of Novoselki. At a cost of 3 dead and 18 wounded, the SS cavalrymen killed more than 150 members of a partisan band armed not only with small arms but also with anti-tank guns and mortars. Despite the heavy rains that followed in the second half of May—rains that, as usual, made the marshes impassable for vehicles—the operations continued until the first week of June. Once again, most engagements were small and losses to the division few. Recorded enemy dead were also relatively few, though numbers of those who were killed were often reported, yet again, as "shot while trying to escape," or, in the case of at least one woman, shot for refusing to answer interrogators' questions. In order to prevent the partisans from re-establishing themselves in the region, the division and its supporting elements "evacuated" all civilians and sent them to unspecified "labor duties." All livestock that could be rounded up was also confiscated. Finally, every village and all individual habitations were burned to the ground (*restlos niedergebrannt*).[46] Between 8 May and 4 June 1943, the division suffered thirty-five casualties, of whom only eleven were killed in action.[47] From the last week of June to the last week of July, similar operations occurred in the old area of activity from 1941 around the city of Mozyr. Interestingly, this latter operation, code-named Seydlitz and occurring between Weichsel I and II, took its name from one of the most famous Prussian cavalrymen of the eighteenth century, Friedrich Wilhelm von Seydlitz. As usual, the division's *Reiter* regiments and the reconnaissance detachment were the principal partisan hunters. Though riding and marching as much as thirty-seven miles (60 km) per day, the division's units fought only one major battle. Just as it had always done, however, the terrain proved a great difficulty, especially since the partisans had destroyed all the bridges and mined most of the tracks. Consequently, at one point during the operation the 2nd *Reiter* Regiment had to be resupplied entirely by air—using an airstrip captured from the partisans no less—because motorized logistics vehicles couldn't reach it in the "immense marshes and forests." Combat engineers and even air strikes had to be called in to destroy heavily fortified bunker complexes. All civilian habitations were once again burned down. In keeping with established practice, those civilians who could be rounded up were again dispatched to "labor duties," and all of their livestock was taken.[48] In the period between 25 June and 17 August, the division suffered 26 killed and 56 wounded.[49] The division's strength, not including the 3rd *Reiter* Regiment or the combat-engineer battalion, stood at 8,890 officers and men on 20 August. The division's horses were not included in the count, and records for the period do not indicate what the number of mounts was.[50]

The End in Russia—September to December 1943

It was at this stage, in the late summer of 1943, that the *Florian Geyer* Division's time in Russia began to approach its end. In the wake of the fierce fighting at Kursk in early July, German forces began a slow withdrawal to the Dnepr, the same river along whose upper reaches the division had periodically operated for some two years. In the second half of 1943, the division found itself transferred to the Ukraine for anti-partisan and defensive operations in the area south of the city of Kharkov and subsequently around Kremenchug on the lower Dnepr some 140 miles (225 km) to the southwest.[51]

Even as these operations continued, another reorganization of the SS cavalry was impending, one that would eventually and significantly increase at least the nominal strength of the division to some 13,000 men. The *Reiter* regiments were renumbered and a fourth one was added, so that their designations simultaneously changed from 1st through 4th to 15th through 18th. Furthermore, the assault-gun detachment was expanded to give the division greater punch.[52] This reorganization and expansion featured as part of the much larger expansion of the *Waffen*-SS as a whole in the war's last two years. Of the thirty-eight *Waffen*-SS divisions officially established during the war (thirty-nine if one counts an SS mountain division that was subsequently disbanded and its number reassigned), fully thirty of them, starting with the SS Cavalry Division's numerical follow-on, the 9th SS Panzer Division *Hohenstaufen*, were raised after December 1942.

This vast accretion of strength reflected several important factors. Firstly, Himmler's personal importance to Hitler had grown enormously. Because the SS remained the most ideologically committed arm of a Nazi regime now fighting a purely defensive and increasingly bitter war on all fronts against rising Allied power after July 1943, Himmler could successfully make ever-greater demands for men and equipment. Hitler didn't call Himmler his "Loyal Heinrich" for nothing. Nowhere was this more the case than on the Eastern Front. Secondly, the *Waffen*-SS constituted some of the most effective combat forces still at Germany's disposal, and it seems clear that the *Florian Geyer* Division saw itself in that light. Expanding the division would also fit the nature of the war in the region to which it would be transferred in 1944, namely the Balkans. There the war had been nothing but an anti-partisan campaign since the initial German and Italian victories in the spring of 1941. As an experienced and utterly ruthless anti-partisan force, the SS Cavalry Division would be a natural choice for assignment there; and until the division's eventual destruction in Budapest between December 1944 and February 1945, it would see no genuine large-scale combat against regular forces as it certainly had in Russia. Then, too, the extermination of Jews in the Balkans really only occurs during this same period, particularly in Hungary. The division could demonstrate its evil expertise in that enterprise as well. Finally, as a third factor explaining the *Waffen*-SS' large-scale expansion after December 1942, it should also be noted that the nature of the organization as a whole was fundamentally transformed in the course of 1943–1944 quite aside from numbers. That transformation encompassed the recruitment of very large numbers of personnel who earlier were regarded as strictly off-limits for ideological reasons. Danes, Norwegians, Dutchmen, Flemings—these had always been recruited as racially acceptable SS men. Now, however, in 1943 and 1944, the manpower pool was expanded to include not only "borderline Aryans" such as Latvians, Estonians, and Lithuanians but even Ukrainians and Bosnian Muslims. Hang-dog units these new SS formations may well have been. Evidently, most were. Nevertheless, they represented a radical departure from the perceived racial superiority that certainly still existed in the *Waffen*-SS when the *Florian Geyer* Division was established in early 1942, even if many of the division's veterans may have thought less than good things about *Volksdeutsche* as replacements. This larger environment thus further serves to place the SS Cavalry Division's service in 1944 in a light different from its earlier campaigns between 1939 and the end of 1943.

Ultimately, the *Florian Geyer* Division did not represent a continuation of any German cavalry tradition between 1939 and the end of 1943 insofar as its racially charged mission is concerned, even though its equipment and organization did actually place it well within the framework of what a German cavalry unit of the time was supposed to look like. Throughout its deployments in Poland in 1939–1940 and in Russia between 1941 and 1943, its primary task always remained rear-area security and anti-partisan warfare. This mission came to it from the very highest levels of the regime. Occasionally, of course, it fought pitched battles with those same partisans. Then, too, it participated in the fierce defensive battles of winter 1941–1942 against the Red Army near Rzhev and 1942–1943 near Smolensk. Nevertheless, the division's *Reiter* regiments and reconnaissance battalions hunted Jews and other civilians just as often, if not actually more often, than it fought organized enemy formations, whether partisans or otherwise.

This orientation arose directly from the *Waffen*-SS' origins in the internal security apparatus of the Nazi Party and reflected one of Himmler's most important concerns. Unlike certain other *Waffen*-SS divisions, that, for all of their murderous excesses, became primarily frontline combat units (e.g., the 1st and 2nd SS Panzer Divisions *Leibstandarte-SS Adolf Hitler* and *Das Reich*), the 8th *Waffen*-SS Cavalry Division never shed the original security function of its organizational antecedents. Those antecedents had been, and the division always remained, the mounted arm of a Nazi Party formation the enemies of which, real or imagined, were to be ferreted out and exterminated without mercy.

Fegelein, Freitag, and others may well have seen themselves as chivalric mounted warriors, but that fact is immaterial. The SS cavalrymen executed few of the modern horse-cavalry's missions that were still being actively trained for in the *Heer* in the late 1930s and some of which the army's 1st Cavalry Division itself undertook: long-range reconnaissance; turning the enemy's flank; the interdiction of the enemy's logistics and lines of communication; and force protection through screening. On the contrary, the SS cavalrymen, like all SS men, were very much "Hitler's army" to a degree that even the markedly politicized army was not.[53] As in Poland in 1939 and 1940, so too from first to last in Russia, the *Florian Geyer* Division participated in a war of extermination against largely civilian populations. In stand-up battles against regular troops of the Red Army or well-organized formations of partisans, its men appeared to have fought as tenaciously as any. That fact was in keeping with the cavalrymen's self-perceived warrior's ethos. It was also not uncommon in most units of the *Waffen-SS* raised before the end of 1942. Nevertheless, most of the division's operations, as well as those of its predecessor, the SS Cavalry Brigade, were conducted against persons who could offer little or no resistance. None of the mounted arm's tradition of true chivalry remained, notwithstanding Fegelein's and the division's aping of those same traditions. To that extent, *Florian Geyer's* troopers manifested the distinct reality of the *Waffen-SS* as political soldiers, ever willing to serve the murderous ideological imperatives of the Nazi dictatorship.

CHAPTER 10

LAST RECALL

THE 1ST CAVALRY CORPS, 1943–1945

The dissolution of the German army's 1st Cavalry Division in the autumn of 1941 seemed to mark the end of that army's formal cavalry tradition. True, the mounted squadrons of divisional reconnaissance battalions remained, but the presence of horse-mounted maneuver-units capable of independent action under the control of higher-echelon command appeared over for good. As things turned out, "for good" lasted for about twelve months. In fact, throughout the period from November 1941 to December 1942, various mounted units continued in existence in addition to, and sometimes amalgamated from, divisional reconnaissance squadrons. In July 1942, for example, an improvised cavalry brigade was authorized by the then-commander of Ninth Army, General Walther Model. It had the mission of helping eliminate Red Army forces, some 60,000 strong, still occupying a salient in the dense, swampy forests behind Ninth Army's lines, a result of the latter's near encirclement in the earlier winter fighting in the Battle of Rzhev. Comprised of elements of the reconnaissance battalions of the eight divisions under Model's command, the brigade included three cavalry regiments of one or two horse-mounted troops (companies) and three to four bicycle-mounted troops each.[1] There was also a combat-engineer company, a medical company, and one motorized and one horse-drawn logistics column. Each cyclist troop's immediate supplies were carried in a two-wagon detachment hauled, as usual in Russia, by the ubiquitous *panje* horses. For their part, the troopers in the mounted elements rode regular military horses. The brigade remained a light formation, however, in that tanks and anti-tank units were seconded to it as required. Its organic artillery consisted of six (per regiment) of the same 75-mm guns typical of the 1st Cavalry Division before 1941. In its one major combat operation, from 2–13 July, the "Cavalry Brigade Model" as it was unofficially known successfully maneuvered and fought its way through more than ten miles of seemingly impenetrable terrain while the tanks of the panzer division to which it was attached sometimes found themselves literally stuck in their tracks. And while postwar German analysis admitted that the operation would likely have been successful even without the brigade's presence, that same analysis concluded that the cost to Ninth Army in men, matériel, and time would almost certainly have been greater owing to the inability of either purely infantry or armored formations to move as effectively as the brigade had done.[2]

The Cavalry Brigade Model's example may also have served as inspiration for another effort to resurrect the mounted arm when, later in 1942, then *Rittmeister* Georg *Freiherr* (Baron) von Böselager managed to convince the commander of Army Group Center, Field Marshal Günther von Kluge, that horse-mounted cavalry might still be useful on a full-time basis, despite the 1st Cavalry Division's having been disbanded the year before. Given the terrible winter of 1941–1942 and the biannual rains, with all of the difficulties in maneuver that such weather always brought the German army on the Eastern Front, Kluge eventually agreed. Possessing a sort of provisional character, this "Cavalry Unit Böselager" was subsequently created by an army-group order in January 1943.[3]

Born in Hesse in 1915, Böselager came from a military family and in his youth became a successful competitive rider. In due course, he found his way into the army, and he became an enthusiastic cavalry officer even as he continued to compete in both show jumping and flat racing.[4] His original regiment, the 15th *Kavallerie*-Regiment, was one of those that became part of the infantry's reconnaissance forces. In this case, his regiment became the eyes of the 6th ID. It was in his capacity as a squadron commander of the resulting 6th Reconnaissance Battalion that he made his case to Kluge.

By the end of March 1943, this unit was expanded to the size of a regiment and designated, because of its army-group assignment, Cavalry Regiment Center. Army Groups North and South followed suit shortly thereafter.[5] Thus, even though the 1st Cavalry Division had earlier disappeared, the cavalry tradition lived on in at least an ad hoc fashion. That fashion, however, was soon formalized. The then–chief of staff of the army, Colonel-General Kurt Zeitzler, authorized a full-fledged cavalry corps under the initial command of Major General Oswin Grolig and, shortly thereafter, Lieutenant General Gustav Harteneck, former commander of the 9th Cavalry Regiment in 1939–1940 and chief of staff of Second Army in 1943–1944. Orders establishing the I Cavalry Corps were issued on 25 May 1944, and the corps was supposed to be ready for operations (*verwendungsbereit*) by the beginning of August.[6] Curiously enough, the Cavalry Corps first saw the organizational light of day in the very same region where both the 1st Cavalry Division and the 8th *Waffen-SS* Cavalry Division *Florian Geyer* had already served, namely in the neighborhood of Pinsk in the western reaches of the Pripet Marshes. It was here that the Corps received assignment of its principal maneuver elements from the German army: 3rd and 4th Cavalry Brigades (outgrowths of the earlier Cavalry Regiments North, Center, and South). Also assigned was the 1st Royal Hungarian Cavalry Division. That division still carried the designation "royal" in light of the fact that Hungary remained a nominal monarchy, though it had been ruled since the 1920s by a regent, Admiral Miklós Horthy de Nagybánya. It was at Pinsk, too, that General Harteneck assumed command of the Cavalry Corps on 22 June, the third anniversary of the beginning of Operation Barbarossa.[7]

More striking even than the bare fact of the Corps' establishment was the inclusion of an entire Hungarian division. The Hungarian division's heritage derived from the ancient Magyar tradition of the hussars. For centuries, Magyar light horsemen had enjoyed a reputation for dashing intrepidity and equestrian skill. They had even bequeathed the nineteenth-century accoutrement of the fur-trimmed, braid-covered pelisse worn rakishly over one shoulder of the fanciful hussar's dress. By the time of World War II, of course, much had changed. The Hungarian army, though officially fighting alongside Germany's since 1941, had frequently been regarded in Germany largely as an inferior force and, in truth, suffered from inferior equipment and logistics. Furthermore, relations in general between Germans and Hungarians had never been consistently cordial.[8] Nevertheless, the Cavalry Corps' open inclusion of Hungarian horsemen could not be more different from the treatment so frequently meted out not only to Hungarians themselves but also to ethnic *Germans* from Hungary serving with *Waffen-SS'* 8th Cavalry Division.

Whether enjoying brotherly relations or not, several of the Corps' units saw action even before its official date for initial operational capability. While the 4th Brigade and the Hungarians still found themselves in the process of establishment and training (with troopers of the 4th Brigade also being assigned the German cavalry's by-now-standard Russian-theater anti-partisan mission), elements of the 3rd Brigade were deemed sufficiently ready to be sent into combat against regular forces of the Red Army.[9] Their presence was sorely needed, as was that of every single German soldier available: June 1944 was the moment of the resumption of the great Soviet drive to the west through Belorussia. In fact the Red Army had opened its offensive the day after Harteneck assumed command of the Cavalry Corps.

At the end of June, troopers from the 3rd Brigade were dispatched to Slutsk, not quite 150 miles (241 km) northeast of Pinsk to help fend off advancing Soviet forces. Tellingly, they were sent without their horses, indeed without most of their supplies. In Slutsk, designated to be held as a sort of hedgehog position (*fester Platz*), the cavalrymen served as part of a blocking force along with an attached assault-gun battery and a company of pioneers.[10] Even though they were eventually reinforced by the bulk of the 4th Brigade and other noncavalry units (ultimately including 4th Panzer Division), and even though they inflicted occasionally heavy losses on advancing Soviet troops, the Germans could not hold out in Slutsk, not least owing to the insufficient defensive works constructed before the cavalrymen arrived. By 30 June the Corps' troopers had been driven out of the town by Soviet mechanized units. As July began, they were forced to retreat farther to the west so as to avoid encirclement. Interestingly enough, the Soviet troops driving them out included cavalry of their own. Part of Lieutenant General I. A. Pliev's cavalry-mechanized group consisting of the 4th Guards Cavalry Corps (including three cavalry divisions) and the 4th Mechanized Corps, the Soviet horsemen were executing the very sorts of reconnaissance and flanking missions, as well as dismounted combat, that the German horsemen themselves had so often conducted since 1940 but now on a much larger scale.[11] Some indication of the intensity of the fighting in the often swampy and heavily forested region west of Slutsk may be gained from the fact that the Corps' own headquarters were directly attacked on 4 July by Russian infantry covered by supporting fire from heavy mortars. Nine staff personnel were killed and wounded and fully nineteen reported missing, presumably taken prisoner, by the time the attackers were driven off. And the Russians very nearly managed to capture or kill the commander of the German Second Army, General Walter Weiß, who happened to be attempting to land at the Cavalry Corps' headquarters at that very moment.[12]

As the Corps slowly withdrew under intense Soviet pressure toward Baranovichi, located at the midpoint on the road linking Brest-Litovsk and Minsk, friction arose between German and Hungarian units. Various reports surfaced in early July that the Hungarian cavalrymen appeared to be folding under the admittedly heavy weight of the Soviet advance. The Hungarian Division had been brought up to the line on 4 and 5 July to support the 4th Cavalry Brigade that had been sent forward earlier. The Hungarians were immediately and heavily attacked by Soviet armored elements. These attacks shook (*erschüttert*) the Hungarians badly, and, as a result, divisional elements began to withdraw, evidently without orders. As the fighting continued on 6 July, the Hungarian Division's commander reported that his unit was, at least temporarily, combat-ineffective (*keine Kampfkraft mehr besitzt*). He said his troops had been without supplies and ammunition for three days, were physically exhausted, and had been unnerved by the Soviet tanks. By way of reply he was told that assault guns from the already hard-pressed German 4th Cavalry Brigade would be sent to support him.[13] Nevertheless, the 4th

Brigade's right flank was uncovered by the Hungarian troopers' movement, and the German cavalrymen were threatened with encirclement.
Harteneck therefore intervened personally. He went to the Hungarians'
command post and peremptorily ordered the Magyar horsemen to stand
fast. His mood can be imagined. He had already earlier intervened in a
much more formal fashion, writing a two-page letter to the Hungarian
divisional commander on 4 July and addressed to "Your Excellency." In
that missive, he had pointed out certain disciplinary deficiencies in the
Hungarians' logistics elements (the very ones whom the Hungarian
commander had said were missing), though he wished the Hungarian
cavalrymen well in their "first major action" (*ersten . . . einsatz im
Großkampf*).[14] Evidently that letter had not had the desired effect. For his
part, Hungarian commander General Vattay defended himself against
accusations of overly rash withdrawal. In a situation report he indicated
that because the Corps' headquarters had been temporarily out of communication owing to the attacks on it of 4 July, and beause he'd received
the approval of (*im Einvernehmen mit*) the commander of the 4th Brigade, he'd ordered his men back to a more defensible position. In the
same report he also incidentally requested rations for 17,000 men and
11,000 horses, as well as 16,000 gallons (60,000 L) of gasoline for his
vehicles.[15]

Though it remains unclear from the Corps' records how the Hungarians managed to get their horses forward when so many of the Germans'
mounts had initially been left behind, the Corps' defensive positions
around Baranovichi were to be defended by more than just horse-
mounted troopers. The Cavalry Corps now in fact represented, at least
in its TOE, what the commander of the 1st Cavalry Division, General
Kurt Feldt, had so consistently advocated in 1940 and 1941: a combined-
arms, corps-strength force. On 4 July 1944, just before the fighting around
Baranovichi began in earnest, the Corps included not only the 4th Cavalry Brigade and the 1st Royal Hungarian Cavalry Division (both minus
certain elements). It also temporarily included the 4th Panzer Division,
the 904th Assault Gun Brigade, the 447th Regimental [Combat] Group,
a security regiment, an additional field artillery battalion, an anti-aircraft
artillery battalion, a combat engineer battalion, an anti-tank detachment, and a separate assault-gun detachment of ten guns. It even

included two companies (five vehicles each) of Tiger tanks, the heaviest
armored vehicles then available in the German army.[16] Earlier in the war,
at the time of the then–1st Cavalry Brigade's campaign in Poland, Feldt
had maintained that at least divisional status for his unit would be necessary to prove whether horse-cavalry could still play an effective operational role. That status had been achieved by the time of the invasion of
the Low Countries and France in 1940. Subsequently, at the end of the
1st Cavalry Division's campaign in Russia in 1941, Feldt had argued that
even his by-then-successful division still didn't possess sufficient artillery
firepower and support elements, particularly combat engineers. Cavalry
could still be effective, he'd argued, but only if it operated at the organizational level of a corps. On that he'd insisted in his final report as divisional commander. Instead of being reorganized, however, the 1st Cavalry Division had been disbanded and its horses and men dispersed to
other formations. Now, in the form of the 1st Cavalry Corps, Feldt's
injunctions finally appeared to have been realized, even though he was
no longer present. In the great defensive battles that began in the summer of 1944, however, it remained to be seen whether the Corps could
hold its own in the face of a surging Red Army that had achieved all-
season operational superiority on the Eastern Front.

This superiority evidently continued to make itself felt, and so did
the resulting tension in the Corps' command structure. Both the 4th
Cavalry Brigade and the Hungarian Division received orders dated 5
July to hold off advancing Soviet forces so as to ensure that the roads
running westward from Slutsk through Baranovichi to Bialystok and
southwestward from Baranovichi to Brest-Litovsk wouldn't be cut.
These perennially important roads had always been critical to the passage of German forces through the northern expanse of the Pripet
Marshes. To help ensure that the roads stayed in German hands, all
commanders of the Corps' various elements were explicitly ordered by
Ninth Army's commander, General Nikolaus von Vormann, to personally lead operations to maintain the link between the Corps' own 4th
and the neighboring 12th Panzer Divisions. General Harteneck, in turn,
informed the Hungarian Division's General Vattay that Hitler himself
had ordered (*der Führer . . . ausdrücklich befohlen hat*) that Baranovichi's
road junction was so important to the situation on the Eastern Front

that it simply had to be prevented from falling into Soviet hands, period. Harteneck curtly said that he expected the Hungarians to hold their defensive positions south of the place regardless of their own situation (*unbedingt gehalten wird*).

General Harteneck reiterated these orders on 7 July, as well as similar ones for the 4th Cavalry Brigade but added for emphasis that 4th Brigade had to ensure that the road running southwest from Baranovichi had to be held open until the 4th Panzer Division could be withdrawn along it. He closed by alluding to Field Marshal Model's stated expectation that all commanders lead from the front.[17] As if he'd not said enough on the subject already, Harteneck then sent yet another two-page letter to Vattay on that same day, as well as several additional notes. Among other things, he observed that officers from the German cavalry and armored units felt that their Hungarian counterparts were not behaving in a manner routinely demanded of, and exhibited by, German officers. When properly led, he wrote, the Hungarian cavalrymen were just as worthy as the Germans. When Hungarian officers failed to act as combat leaders (*Vorkämpfer*), however, their troopers "failed immediately" (*sofort versagen*). He coldly pointed out that he'd found the Hungarians' entire 3rd Hussar Regiment in the town of Tartak without their ever having had contact with the enemy, indeed without their having conducted any reconnaissance. He rounded on Vattay for the lack of march discipline in the Hungarian columns and expressly forbade the withdrawal of any Hungarian unit without his (Harteneck's) prior concurrence. Under the enormous pressure of the continuing Soviet attacks, any sloppy behavior on the roads placed both Hungarian and German troops in danger.[18] There was plenty of that in any case, and Harteneck's orders couldn't deflect it: the Soviets succeeded in driving the Cavalry Corps out of the area surrounding Baranovichi by the next day, 8 July.

Harteneck thereupon reported to Second Army that his Corps was executing a fighting withdrawal under extreme pressure from heavy Soviet forces supported by tanks. He also reported "heavy losses" (*erhebliche Verluste*) but did not further specify. At the same time, General Vattay was reporting to him that his own division was "completely exhausted from eleven days' fighting and marching" (*durch die elf Tage hindurch andauernden hinhaltenden Kampf und Marsch*) and that it was momentarily

combat-ineffective. He further requested that the Hungarian cavalrymen be withdrawn from the front. As proof of the stress, he reported
that his two principal mounted regiments had been reduced from a combined combat-strength of 2,895 men on 24 June to a mere 404 on 8 July.
He did not indicate losses of horses.[19] It remains unclear how Vattay's
report was received at Harteneck's headquarters. Nevertheless, Vattay's
report may not have been exaggerated. Various communications had
earlier indicated that the main weight of the Soviet attacks in the Corps'
sector had landed squarely on the Hungarian Cavalry Division, so the
losses Vattay reported seem reasonable. Then, too, losses to the Corps'
German units appeared to be equally severe. For example, one squadron
of the 4th Cavalry Brigade's 41st *Reiter* Regiment was reduced to an
effective strength of only 82 men and no heavy weapons at all. The
entirety of the 4th Brigade's other mounted regiment, the 5th *Kavallerie*-
Regiment, numbered only 674 men, that is essentially one squadron.
Neither unit indicated how many horses, if any, they had at that moment.
Further, the 5th Regiment's entire complement of heavy weapons consisted of two 37-mm anti-tank guns, weapons that were virtually useless
against Soviet armor of vintage 1944. Absent effective anti-tank guns,
only German tanks or assault guns might ward off the Soviets' mechanized forces. Unfortunately, the Cavalry Corps' 4th Panzer Division was
equally hard-pressed. Its effective combat-strength on 10 July consisted
of only a number of Panzer IVs, four assault-guns, and two Tiger tanks.
For his part, General Harteneck nevertheless doggedly continued to
order "bitter resistance" by his troopers (*müssen . . . verbissenen Wider-
stand lesiten*).[20]

   He also attempted to instill an even greater will to resistance in his
cavalrymen, infantrymen, and tankers by evoking in them a desire to
fight for kith and kin. In a directive dated 11 July and sent to the commanders of the all of the Corps' major combat elements (the 4th Cavalry Brigade, the 4th Panzer Division, and the attached 129th ID that had
replaced the by-then-withdrawn 1st Royal Hungarian Cavalry Division)
Harteneck emphasized that the Corps had now crossed the borders of
the Reich in its westward retreat. This was the border between the former *Reichskommissariat Ostland*—consisting between 1941 and 1944 of
Soviet and Baltic territories overrun during the invasion of the Soviet

Union—and occupied Poland. In Berlin's view, and therefore Harteneck's, the latter constituted territory of the Reich proper. The Cavalry
Corps was now fighting on soil that was supposed to be settled by Germans. If officers, noncoms, and enlisted men failed to understand this
fact and accordingly do their duty as defenders of Germany, then the full
severity of military justice would be felt. "I expect," he went on grimly,
"that use will be made of armed force and courts-martial where that is
necessary" (*Ich erwarte, daß von Waffengewalt und Kriegsgericht da Gebrauch
gemacht wird, wo es notwendig ist*).[21]

Clearly, Harteneck deemed such encouragement necessary. The
Soviet offensive that had crashed into Army Group Center and the neighboring Army Group North Ukraine continued to roll forward despite
the bitter resistance urged by the Corps' commander. In the fighting
withdrawal of the Cavalry Corps and other German units, anti-tank
weaponry necessarily assumed ever-greater importance. Therefore, the
4th Panzer Division by its very nature, the anti-tank elements of the Cavalry Brigade, and the 129th ID were continually forced to meet advancing Soviet forces head on throughout the month of July. By contrast, references to the Corps' horsemen as horsemen, not to mention their
mounts, are almost entirely absent from daily reports in the Corps' war
diary for the period. This makes sense, however, in light of the overall
operational situation. The Red Army's summer offensive was grinding
its way steadily into occupied Poland with Germany as the ultimate
prize. In light of repeated orders to the Corps (and all other German
troops) to stand fast and hold positions, its cavalry troopers simply did
not have much opportunity to employ their mounted skills or their
horses against an enemy that was constantly coming straight at them.
Given those facts, and until the hold-at-all-costs orders changed, what
counted was straightforward defensive firepower as supplied by the cavalrymen's precious tanks, assault guns, and anti-tank guns. The cavalry
troopers themselves fought essentially as dismounted infantry. And ferocious though their resistance evidently often was, the Corps' daily reports
speak repeatedly, indeed almost every day, of the "retreat continuing."

In these reports, however, one also hears the old refrain, repeated so
many times in so many places since 1941, that the terrain over which the
Corps was now moving was unsuitable for either tracked or wheeled

vehicles beyond the few paved roads in the Corps' operational area. The 4th Panzer Division's headquarters, for example, reported just that condition on 13 July. It warned further that any vehicles that got stuck would likely fall into the Red Army's hands.[22] Such conditions, of course, were precisely one of the original justifications for retaining the cavalry in the first place. A more bitter pill for the German cavalrymen to swallow was the fact the advancing Soviet forces continued to employ their own cavalry for precisely the sorts of fixing-and-holding attacks that the German horsemen had so often undertaken in their own invasion of the Soviet Union three years before. General Harteneck apparently shared this frustration in that he recommended to his own superiors that a more mobile defense be undertaken. The 129th ID, he reported, was practically exhausted in any case and should be transferred to XXIII Corps, thus freeing the 4th Cavalry Brigade and the 4th Panzer Division to use their horses and vehicles, respectively, for the sort of mobile defense that he advocated. He seems to have felt, and implied, that if vehicles got stuck in the process and had to be abandoned, then so be it. He issued orders for just such a mobile defense to the Cavalry Brigade and 4th Panzer on 14 July, even though the 129th ID still remained part of the Corps. The wisdom of Harteneck's orders was borne out the very next day when the Corps' infantry division, weakened and stationary, was very nearly cut off by advancing Soviet forces. It was extricated only with great difficulty through the efforts of a detached armored reconnaissance battalion from the panzer division.[23]

Mobile or not, the Corps' fighting withdrawal continued, as did that of the entire German army on the Eastern Front. By the end of July, the cavalrymen had reached the line of the River Narew, the very stream that the 1st Cavalry Brigade had triumphantly crossed into Poland in 1939. Crossing points and fords were determined, and on 26 July the Cavalry Corps' headquarters requested permission for a withdrawal across the river. The necessary orders were issued two days later. For their part, the horsemen of the 4th Cavalry Brigade were to prevent at all costs (*mit allen Mitteln zu verhindern*) any Soviet breakthrough to the bridge over the Narew at Lapy, about fifteen miles (24 km) southeast of Bialystok. They also ended up defending another crossing point just upstream (i.e., to the south) of Lapy at Suraż against repeated Soviet attacks supported by tanks; and even though the Soviet troops managed to get across the river, subsequent reports commended the cavalrymen's "smartly executed counterattacks" (*schneidig geführten Gegenangriffen*) and their containment of the enemy's bridgehead on the western bank. Nevertheless, another defensive line was already being evaluated, a so-called blue line running partially along the Nurec River that lay another twenty miles (32 km) farther to the south and west. Positions along this river were incorporated into the Cavalry Corps' defensive line by 31 July.[24]

By that point the Cavalry Corps had been in nearly daily contact with advancing Soviet forces for more than five weeks. The fighting had frequently been severe, and the losses told. On the same day, for example, that the defensive positions along the Nurec were being occupied, General Harteneck reported that the 4th Cavalry Brigade had been "burned out by heavy losses" (*durch starke Verluste ausgebrannt*). These losses hadn't been made good with replacements. Consequently, the brigade now consisted really of only one full-strength regiment and assorted bits and pieces. Only the mounted elements specifically remained combat-effective (*kampfkräftig*), but they were short of men and weapons (*schwach an Zahl und Waffen*). The combat-support elements (pioneers, anti-tank units, etc.) were combat-ineffective at that moment. The 4th Brigade's entire strength that day totaled 1,369 officers and men. In other words, its strength represented only about 20 percent of the 1st Cavalry Brigade's numbers when that unit had ridden into Poland five years earlier. Similar conditions obtained for the 129th ID whose combat-effectiveness Harteneck described simply as "zero" (*gleich Null*).[25]

Unfortunately for the 4th Brigade, the Soviets had no intention of granting the horsemen a breathing space. Renewed armored attacks by an entire corps were launched against the cavalry troopers' positions on 3 August. Emerging from the Soviets' bridgehead at Suraż, the attacks inflicted heavy, though unspecified, losses on the brigade, and it should have been overrun. Nonetheless, the cavalrymen's defenses remained steadfast enough to warrant Harteneck's recommendation to Second Army that they be mentioned in OKW's official dispatches. The cavalrymen killed more than seven hundred Soviet troops and captured nearly eighty. Furthermore, they destroyed (among other things) six Soviet assault guns, seventeen anti-tank guns, thirty-nine machine guns, and eight *panje* wagons loaded with ammunition. In the process, however, the 4th Brigade had reached a stage at which, in Harteneck's assessment, it was "dissolving itself in the aggressive fulfillment of its mission" and was—he reiterated the phrase—"burning itself out" (*Die ihre Aufgabe stets angriffsweise lösende 4.Kav.Brig. brennt zunehmend aus*).[26] Barely three days later, however, the brigade repeated the accomplishment. This time they fended off an attack by a Soviet infantry division. In this battle, the commander of the 41st *Reiter* Regiment, Lieutenant Colonel Rojahn, and fifteen men of the regimental staff personally succeeded in bringing the entire Russian attack to a standstill (*den feind[lichen] Ansturm zum Stehen brachte*). Similarly, *Rittmeister* Count Plettenberg, the commander of the Brigade's Heavy Cavalry Detachment, which was essentially a small assault-gun battalion, distinguished himself. Despite having been wounded earlier, Plettenberg led from the front and helped plug gaps in the German lines, thereby re-establishing contact with the brigade's neighboring units. In this fierce fighting, the 4th Brigade's troopers killed another 750 Soviet soldiers. They also destroyed 9 tanks, 6 artillery pieces, and 36 anti-tank guns. For these actions, Harteneck recommended Rojahn for the Knight's Cross.[27] In a period of four days, the brigade's cavalrymen had inflicted casualties on the enemy totaling more than the entire strength of their own unit.

Of course, the 4th Brigade's own casualties also demanded redress. In light of the larger situation facing German armies on the Eastern Front, however, these replacements were increasingly hard to come by. Two hundred fifty stragglers (*Versprengte*) were ordered to be picked up from the rear-area train depot at Zichenau (Ciechanów), about eighty-five miles (137 km) northeast of Warsaw, and assigned to the 4th Brigade. The 69th Cavalry Replacement Detachment was to provide another fifty NCOs and men. A further forty-nine were assigned to the 3rd Cavalry Brigade that only now resurfaced in the Cavalry Corps' order of battle.[28] Interestingly, the Corps' daily reports for early August 1944 also began to note, at least indirectly and really for the first time since the Corps' establishment, the general situation regarding the Corps' horses. General Harteneck, for example, insisted that at least horse-mounted reconnaissance elements remained essential to the Corps' mobile defensive operations. Consequently, the 69th Cavalry Replacement Detachment received orders on 6 August to continue mounted training. Furthermore, horses were now being shifted around within the Corps as various units were cannibalized for personnel to serve as infantry. The 69th Field Security Battalion, for example, was ordered to turn over one hundred horses and their tack to a sister unit of anti-Soviet Cossacks before moving up to the Corps' forward area for frontline duty. To the extent that the Cavalry Corps' horses may at this point have been restricted primarily to the reconnaissance elements, it risked ending up looking like a mere armor-reinforced infantry corps. Again, however, in the defensive fighting on East Prussia's borders, the Corps' horses were not as essential as they would have been in offensive operations had an offensive been possible.[29]

What Harteneck most emphatically did not want, even as replacements, were more Hungarian troops. On 5 August he wrote to Second Army's commander, General Weiß, that his (Harteneck's) experience with the Hungarian troops was the "worst imaginable."[30] All of the Hungarian hussar regiments were failures, he said. They suffered constant shortages of ammunition because they always threw it away when they fled. And if they were equipped with German weapons and ammunition, they'd simply throw that away, too. While recognizing that the Cavalry Corps had been established precisely to bring together German and Hungarian cavalrymen, Harteneck wrote that he "view[ed] with dismay the day when the Hungarian Cavalry Division would once again be at the side of my brave German horsemen." He maintained that if the Hungarian division were again to fight alongside his men, then the Hungarians would not only have to be directly reinforced with German personnel but also be placed directly under German command. He did not, however, think that the Hungarians would agree to these conditions. "As I see it," he added, "the only correct solution is to send the entire Hungarian Cavalry Division, and any other Hungarian troops, back home."

Even as Harteneck was rejecting the possibility of adding more Hungarian troops, the Cavalry Corps underwent yet another reorganization. As August wore on and the Soviet offensive continued, the 4th Panzer Division was withdrawn and redeployed. In its place came two new infantry divisions. In an attempt to mitigate the loss of the armored division, additional miscellaneous mechanized units were assigned to the Corps. When the next push by the Red Army occurred in the cavalrymen's sector of the front on 22 August 1944, the Corps included the 3rd and 4th Cavalry Brigades; the already sorely tested 129th ID; the newly arrived 14th and 102nd IDs; and assorted assault-gun and panzer units, none at the divisional level, though there was evidently some thought of adding the 6th Panzer Division.[31] Interestingly, at this time the Corps' two mounted brigades were placed on the flanks adjoining the operational areas of the XXIII and LV Army Corps, in other words on the weak seams that had frequently been the targets of earlier Soviet attacks. This seems a clear indication of the cavalrymen's reliability, in this case with their being entrusted the crucial mission of maintaining contact with neighboring formations. Their placement also seems to have been a mark of General Harteneck's appreciation of their fighting qualities.

Such tenacity found itself in heavy demand. Throughout the last ten days of August, the Corps fought a series of defensive battles generally east and south of the Narew River and between that stream and the River Bug against large Soviet formations. The infantrymen and cavalry troopers bore the brunt of the bitter combat in the stretch of river running southwest from Łomża past Ostrolenka (renamed Scharfenwiese by the Germans in 1941), a town lying only about twenty-five miles (40 km) from the prewar border of East Prussia. The hard-pressed troops suffered accordingly, both physically and in their morale (*seelisch*). Their condition deteriorated rapidly under the pounding, particularly from the apparently massive preparatory barrages that the Soviets' artillery could bring to bear without fear of German counter-battery fire. Harteneck reported to Second Army headquarters that the result from this Soviet preponderance in uncontested artillery fire was "disproportionately large human and material losses" for his units.[32] The additional formations that had just been assigned to the Cavalry Corps were clearly inadequate to the task. Therefore, all of the Corps' staffs, logistics units, horse-handler elements, emergency reserves (*Alarmeinheiten*), and irreplaceable maintenance personnel were combed through for additional manpower. These troops were slotted into the front at every opportunity. Furthermore, all riding horses not absolutely required had been sent to rear-area veterinary companies not only to keep valuable horseflesh out of harm's way but also so that they wouldn't impede the defense. By 1 September, the fifth anniversary of the start of the war, the Corps' troops had destroyed fully 154 enemy tanks and self-propelled guns and 76 pieces of artillery in these river-line battles, and that day passed relatively quietly. Still, in Harteneck's estimation, the Cavalry Corps would simply not be able to prevent a major Soviet breakthrough much longer.[33]

Despite this continuing threat of a breakthrough, the Cavalry Corps earned highest recognition for its accomplishments between the Rivers Bug and Narew. On 2 September the commander of Second Army, General Weiß, forwarded to Harteneck a statement that he (Weiß) had received from the commander of what remained of Army Group Center, *Generaloberst* (Colonel-General) Georg-Hans Reinhardt. In the ten days preceding the end of August, Second Army had managed, according to Reinhardt, to hold off at least thirty Soviet infantry divisions; three armored brigades; and numerous independent armored and assault-gun regiments. The steadiness and bravery of the German horsemen and infantry was "above all praise" (*über jedes Lob erhaben*). Combat leadership had been excellent, and these qualities manifested themselves even more strongly in light of the fact that air support from the *Luftwaffe* had been minimal. The Cavalry Corps was therefore singled out for Reinhardt's "unreserved recognition" (*uneingeschränkte Anerkennung*) in that it had carried the heaviest burden of the defensive battles. Nevertheless, Reinhardt also made clear that further fighting awaited the cavalrymen and their comrades: "Inspired by this spirit," he wrote, "we can await the coming battles with confidence." But such confidence demanded a great deal of faith, for on the same day that Reinhardt issued his statement, the Cavalry Corps reported a total combat-strength of a mere 9,022. Fully one third of these (3,504 altogether) were the officers and men of the Corps' principal maneuver elements, the 3rd and 4th Cavalry Brigades.[34]

Following several days of relative quiet on the Corps' sector of the front, the Soviet advance resumed. In the meantime, the elements of the Corps had been withdrawn to "Defensive Position East Prussia II" hard by the Narew. As the name of the new positions indicated, the cavalrymen were now for all practical purposes defending the prewar German homeland. Furthermore, they were also defending the final redoubt of the Prussian-German cavalry tradition. The emotional significance of both facts was surely lost on no one. Not coincidentally, and in order to stoke the defensive effort, the specter was raised once again of threatening Asiatic hordes, a threat overlaid with the veneer of an all-devouring communist menace. On 12 September General Harteneck issued a directive to all commanders aimed at increasing the Corps' defensive effectiveness.[35] The Cavalry Corps now stood on the Reich's very borders in positions dug by German men and women, German boys and girls. They'd dug with the sure hope that Corps' soldiers would protect them and their homes from the Red Terror. Not one trooper or infantryman would be allowed to withdraw without orders, and only then if live enemy fire forced him from his position. Cowardice would be summarily punished with armed force if necessary. Commanders at every level would remain at their posts to the last possible moment, always leading from the front. Every position to a depth of six miles (10 km) behind the lines was to be dug in (*einzubunkern*) for protection from Soviet artillery fire. No man, no horse, no vehicle was to be without a foxhole or anti-shrapnel revetments. Furthermore, the Corps' horses, such as those of the 4th Brigade that Harteneck noted specifically, were to be kept hidden in woods and not kept in villages, evidently to protect them from aerial attack and long-range artillery-fire. But even as these preparations continued, so too did combat training for unit leaders and technical specialists such as combat engineers, radiomen, and machine-gunners. Almost incredibly, at the same time Harteneck also ordered that even riding, driving, and horse-feeding training was to continue, with 55 officers and men being ordered to Fordon near Bydgoszcz (Bromberg), 160 miles (257 km) in the rear for that purpose.[36]

No doubt surprisingly, the next several weeks passed with relatively little large-scale fighting, though regular and sometimes intense contact with Soviet troops continued. The Corps' positions along the west bank of the Narew came under regular artillery and light weapons fire from Soviet forces on the other side of the river, the latter's objective being to expand several bridgeheads that they'd managed to achieve on that stream's western bank. On the Germans' side, time was spent improving defensive positions and scraping together replacements from stragglers in the rear. In addition, yet another infantry division, the 292nd ID, was attached to the Corps on 22 September. This gave the Corps a total of three nominal infantry divisions on its TOE and brought its total combat-strength at the end of that month to 14,283 (a figure approximately representing the strength of a normal division of the German army in 1939). Since 29 June, the Corps' units had killed a reported total of 8,942 Soviet troops, almost 40 percent of whom had fallen at the hands of the troopers of the 3rd and 4th Cavalry Brigades.[37]

During the period roughly between 1 October and 31 December, the Red Army entered a time of regrouping and resupply following its crushing summer offensive against German Army Group Center. During the Soviets' operational pause, the Cavalry Corps was now at least able to catch its breath, even if replacements continued to be hard to come by. In that late fall of 1944, the Corps continued to hold its positions along a forty-odd-mile stretch of the Narew between Rozan and Nowogrod. Because of the continuing Soviet pressure and the inevitability of a renewal of the Red Army's drive toward Berlin, it also began another reorganization and redeployment of its various elements. One of the most significant of those reorganizations was the detachment of the 3rd Cavalry Brigade. It was moved to Fourth Army whose center of gravity at that moment lay to the east of the Masurian Lakes, the very lakes where Russian armies had come to grief in 1914.[38] This transfer was noteworthy not only in that it meant that the Red Army's forces had reached, and in many places crossed over, the borders of East Prussia. The transfer also meant that the Cavalry Corps had to temporarily relinquish fully half of that operational component that gave the Corps its very name and character, namely horsemen. With the 3rd Brigade's departure for duty with Fourth Army, the Corps retained the 4th Cavalry Brigade as its only dedicated mounted element. The remainder of the Corps' strength consisted in this period of four infantry divisions. They, of course, still had their horse-drawn logistics and artillery trains, along with various mounted reconnaissance elements. Before year's end, other formations, both infantry and armored, would also be assigned to the Corps for various and usually brief periods of time. These included a scratch force named "Combat Group Hannibal." About 1,400 strong, it comprised personnel from the 4th SS Police Regiment. The entire Corps would also be transferred briefly to the command of Fourth Army, even though its defensive positions remained the same.

Throughout the last half of October and the whole of November, Soviet artillery and aerial attacks continued as did ground combat, the latter sometimes intense and often at battalion strength. Though the widely anticipated, front-wide Soviet offensive did not occur, the Corps' units suffered from this near-constant contact. As they had in the fighting retreat to the Narew, the Cavalry Brigades recorded many of those casualties. Alone in the period from 15 to 27 October, for example, the Corps' two mounted brigades suffered 961 troopers of all ranks killed, wounded, and missing.[39] And these losses occurred in a period when the Corps' morning reports very frequently stated that the preceding day or night had passed quietly. The sacrifices in the mounted elements did earn another formal recognition. Second Army's commander explicitly commended the "outstanding service" (*hervorragende Bewährung*) of the 3rd and 4th Cavalry Brigades and wrote further to General Harteneck that the cavalrymen had delivered the "best proofs of the cavalry spirit" (*Beweise besten Reitergeistes geliefert haben*) in the defensive battles. Presumably the cavalrymen appreciated the sentiment. Such glowing praise, however, wouldn't provide the horsemen with fresh mounts or those mounts with feed (deliveries for the entire Fourth Army area had been stopped), much less gasoline for the Corps' vehicles or ammunition for its artillery. Neither could Hitler's ferocious order of 29 October to the *Ostheer*, which commanded every German soldier to do one of two things: "stand or die."[40] Perhaps, however, the troopers took greater comfort in the fact that dismal autumnal weather was now frequently grounding Soviet fighter-bombers. They certainly needed the respite. Both of the Corps' mounted brigades had been much reduced. By the end of November, the 3rd Brigade's combat-strength (2,054) was only about 41 percent of its total ration-strength (6,055). The 4th Brigade could show a slightly better percentage, namely about 50 percent (2,181 out of 4,350) even though its overall number of personnel was lower. Similar figures (approximately 50 percent) obtained in the Corps' other units such as the now-attached 558th *Volksgrenadier*-Division.[41]

Even as the Corps attempted to recoup the losses it had suffered since June, General Harteneck evidently attempted, and in keeping with

Army-level directives, to ensure that whatever training could be done was done. In one order, for example, he indicated that certain veterinary personnel and feeding specialists were supposed to attend a three-day school for instruction in winterizing the Corps' horses and care and maintenance schedules.[42] Attendees would subsequently act as training cadre for other soldiers. More significantly, he'd also issued a four-page directive entitled "The Basics of Cavalry Leadership" on 5 November.[43] In it Harteneck re-emphasized most of those doctrinal elements of the cavalry that had last been formalized in 1935 in *Truppenführung*, the same ones that General Kurt Feldt had stressed in his own repeated statements regarding the earlier 1st Cavalry Brigade/Division. Despite nearly six years of war and all of the vicissitudes that the war had brought to the German army's mounted arm, the cavalry's essential characteristics remained the same in Harteneck's view: mobility, flexibility, audacity, tenacity. True, the last physical vestiges of the cavalry's traditional weapons—sabers—had disappeared in 1940–1941. True, as well, at least since the invasion of the Soviet Union if not earlier, the German cavalryman was now essentially a dragoon. He rode to battle but fought dismounted. And now, in 1944, he just as often fought his battles alongside attached armored and infantry formations. Nevertheless, a stubborn cavalry spirit hung on, and Harteneck hammered it home in his directive, not only as regarded his men but also as regarded the Corps' horses. He also made it clear at the end that he expected his commanders to inculcate a National Socialist bearing in the Cavalry Corps. Whether his statement regarding this matter rested on personal conviction or expediency in the wake of the attempted assassination of Hitler on 20 July 1944 cannot be determined from the directive itself. Furthermore, the degree of subsequent Nazi indoctrination of the Corps' various formations after November 1944 cannot be reliably deduced from the documents at hand. Nevertheless, Harteneck's insistence in this regard sheds a disturbing light on the Cavalry Corps' leadership as it faced the chaotic last six months of the war. And in light of his repeated and fairly ruthless advocacy of summary courts-martial, his urging on of stringent political indoctrination at least seems consistent.

As December arrived, the Cavalry Corps received new orders, ones that took it far away from the Soviet avalanche that was to bury East Prussia beginning in January 1945. Unfortunately, those orders took the

Corps to Hungary. There a similar fate awaited the remaining horse-men. Between 18 and 23 December 1944, the Cavalry Corps' command elements and logistics units were loaded onto trains at Lyck in the south-eastern corner of East Prussia. From there they traveled south. The 4th Cavalry Brigade went as well. There followed a circuitous route by rail through Posen, Beuthen in Silesia, and western Slovakia. Upon arrival in Hungary—from Lyck an airline distance of some five hundred miles (800 km) and much more by train—the Corps was assigned to the area north of the eastern end of Lake Balaton (Plattensee). Orders arrived on Christmas Day placing the Corps under the command of Sixth Army and, shortly thereafter, Second Panzer Army. Three days later the Corps, in turn, received command of the 1st and 23rd Panzer Divisions.[44] From now on, the I Cavalry Corps was essentially an armored formation con-taining large horse-mounted and horse-drawn components. Its mission was to help stabilize the then S-shaped front stretching northward from Lake Balaton to the borders of prewar Czechoslovakia, to protect a vital oil refinery at Petfürdö and, possibly, to assist in the relief of Budapest, the Hungarian capital having been encircled by advancing Soviet forces on 24 December. By a curious twist of fate, the 8th *Waffen*-SS Cavalry Division *Florian Geyer* found itself trapped in the city with the remaining German garrison. It had ended up there following its anti-partisan cam-paign in the Balkans in 1944 after being earlier withdrawn from Russia. There was even a second, nominal SS cavalry division, the 22nd Volun-teer SS Cavalry Division (sometimes carrying the moniker *Maria The-resa*) in the city as well. In this last week of December, the Corps was in constant combat with Soviet forces attempting to solidify their lines while other Red Army units lay siege to Budapest, a siege that would continue until the city's fall in February. Though the combat was some-times heavy—regimental-strength attacks or better by Soviet forces—the cavalrymen and their sister armored divisions held, even though they had to do so without being able to call on reserves. At that moment, there weren't any. As it turned out, the Cavalry Corps and the other Ger-man units in Hungary were aided by the fact that Soviet forces there went over to the operational defensive throughout January, February, and into March 1945.[45]

In the meantime, and at that moment unbeknownst to the Corps, Hitler was planning what turned out to be his last operational offensive on the Eastern Front, code-named Operation Spring Awakening. Its objective would consist of the preservation of the oil fields north and south of Lake Balaton by Sixth SS Panzer Army (transferred from the Western Front) and Second Panzer Army, respectively. More airily, Hitler yet dreamed of the recovery of Budapest and the destruction of Soviet forces in Hungary. While the bulk of the offensive's armored strength was comprised of the Sixth SS Panzer Army, the Cavalry Corps also took part. Officially it remained an element of Second Panzer Army but also seems later to have been temporarily assigned to Sixth SS Panzer Army. At some point between January and March, the 3rd Cavalry Brigade—or elements of it—rejoined the Corps. Furthermore, at least on paper, both it and the 4th Cavalry Brigade were re-formed as cavalry divisions by order of OKH effective 23 February 1945. They did not, however, receive reinforcements to flesh out the redesignation.[46] Consequently, whether there would be enough men, equipment, vehicles, and horses for continued effective operations remained an open question. For instance, losses of horses by early 1945 were high enough to have drawn the attention of Hitler himself. In a conference with the head of Army Administration in the Army High Command, SS *Obergruppen-führer* (General) August Frank, on 29 December 1944, Hitler had been informed that the attrition specifically of horses and vehicles could no longer be sustained.[47] For the cavalrymen on the ground, the matter no doubt seemed clear enough, and though the Soviet forces facing them remained on the operational defensive, the fighting nevertheless continued.

For example, in an earlier effort to relieve the garrison encircled in Budapest, the Cavalry Corps' troops had been heavily engaged. On 7 January, in bitterly cold weather, they'd punched a ten-mile-wide (13 km) hole in the Russian lines southeast of the city and had fought their way forward about the same distance. Nevertheless, and despite several days of intense fighting, neither they nor their counterparts to the northeast of Budapest could force their way into the city itself, though unsubstantiated reports maintained that some of the Cavalry Corps' patrols reached the suburbs. By the end of January, the defenders remaining in the fortress of Buda on the Danube's western bank, like their French counterparts in Paris in 1870, were reduced to eating horsemeat and bread. In the final attempted breakout on 11 February, fewer than 700 members of the garrison reached German lines. Total German losses in the city amounted to some 51,000 killed and 92,000 taken prisoner.[48] The suitability of the cavalrymen for such a relief mission may be questioned, though the heavy armor of several of their formations (even if in depleted strength) now theoretically made their employment for such a task conceivable. Nevertheless, Harteneck and other commanders on the scene weren't the only ones wondering whether mounted formations might still be useful. Once again, Hitler and his most senior commanders in Berlin seriously discussed, on 2 March, the defensive use of cavalry on the eve of the spring offensive that began seven days later. Though the Cavalry Corps had clearly shown in occupied Poland and on the borders of East Prussia what the cavalrymen could do on the defensive, the specific suggestion at Hitler's conference—the employment of pro-German Cossacks—seems to have been more or less dismissed.[49]

Ultimately, Operation Spring Awakening began on 5 March. Initially it made headway but in appalling conditions. Hampered from the outset by cold rain and flurrying snow, mud, a serious lack of fuel, and stiffening Russian resistance, the offensive had stuck fast by the middle of that month. The Soviets then responded by launching their own spring counteroffensive in reply. It would roll forward inexorably, and the Germans would retreat just as inexorably until their final surrender. Indicative of the changing fortunes in Hungary, the OKW on 16 March no longer reported news of German attacks but rather news of a "successful defense" and "counterattacks" along Lake Balaton. In other words, Spring Awakening had been stopped, and the German troops in it had gone over to the defensive. By 19 March OKW was reporting a "bitter defense" by German troops in the region. On 24 March the high command's announcements indicated that "'the Bolshevists' forward attack groups had been brought to a standstill on both sides of Veszprém . . . after heavy enemy losses."[50] Lying just west of Lake Balaton's northern end and on the edge of the Bakony Forest, the city of Veszprém happened to be defended by none other than the now redesignated 3rd and 4th Cavalry Divisions of the Cavalry Corps. Just as had been the case in East Prussia, the cavalrymen's efforts in defense of Veszprém earned them notice, again at the highest levels. At a conference on 23 March, Hitler was specifically informed that the cavalry divisions, along with the

9th SS Panzer Division *Hohenstaufen*, had at least temporarily and successfully re-established "security" not only east of Veszprém but also along a nearby railway line. Successful or not, however, the Germans simply could not hold off the weight of the Soviets' forward movement. And as the German armies retreated, they began slowly to disintegrate. On 10 April 1945, the *New York Times*' war correspondent Hanson W. Baldwin reported that an unspecified number of German troops had effectively been isolated in a pocket around Vienna as the German army "melted away," and by the end of that month OKW would have to admit in a public statement that German troops had been forced to withdraw to the southeastern borders of the Reich. These events were accompanied by reports that the Red Army was "storming the last German defenses in Vienna." The city fell on 13–14 April, and the Soviet High Command reported 200,000 German troops killed or captured. Furthermore, other Soviet units had already begun their march up the valley of the Danube toward Bavaria.[51]

As the Soviets advanced and shifted the brunt of their efforts to the drive on Berlin, the German retreat continued and followed two general routes. The Sixth SS Panzer Army and related forces moved more or less to the northwest. The Second Panzer Army, including the Cavalry Corps, moved generally southwest. This route took the Corps through Lower Austria and into the province of Styria. The cavalrymen, like the rest of the Second Panzer Army, were trapped by Russian armies advancing into the eastern province of Burgenland and the British Eighth Army marching steadily northward toward the Italo-Austrian border. Here the Cavalry Corps found itself when Germany's unconditional surrender was signed on 8 May. On 10 May 1945, the Cavalry Corps also officially surrendered to British forces. Its reported total of 22,000 men and 16,000 horses—*The* (London) *Times* spoke of the "immense task" of collecting "vast hordes" of both men and horses from many different units—now went into Allied captivity.[52] The day of the German horseman was done.

WHITHER THE HORSES?

The day of the European military horseman appears gone for-ever. Done is the age when horses played a major, even central, role in Europe's wars and affairs of state. Except for ceremonial units in some European countries, many of which antedate World War II in one form or another—for example, the Queen's Household Cavalry in the United Kingdom, the Irish Defense Forces Equitation School, France's Republican Guard, or the King's Royal Guard in Spain—horses in large numbers have not had a significant military or political role for nearly three-quarters of a century. Never again will a monarch travel in a cavalcade requiring 30,000 horses, as Elector Frederick III of Branden-burg is said to have done in 1701 on his way to being crowned King Fred-erick I in Prussia. Never again will a ruler have 5,000 horses in one stable, as Louis XIV is reputed to have had at Versailles. And certainly never again will a fortress such as the Alcázar of Toledo be built with subterra-nean stables to house 2,000 cavalry mounts.[1] One might safely para-phrase Shakespeare and say that the horse has done his duty; the horse may go.

One also has to admit, however, that if the history of military equi-tation begins at a point five thousand or six thousand years ago somewhere on the Eurasian steppe, then ending that history's European progress in 1945 is not a bad run. As has been shown, the military horse was written off many times before he actually left the stage. The idea that the horse no longer had a useful place on the modern battlefield arose many times. In the 1890s, in 1918, and in the 1930s, critics dismissed the horse as a romantic obsolescence at best and, at worst, an actual hindrance to military effectiveness. Time and again horses nonetheless proved themselves useful, sometimes exceedingly so. In the case of the German army they were crucial to Prussia's victory over France in 1870, a victory sealing the establishment of a German Empire. In World War I, horses served in every theater where German and other troops took the field. Not least, between 1939 and 1945 they ended up being literally irreplaceable, and they materially helped secure many of the German army's victories before the end of 1942. This remained so throughout the war in the cavalry arm, the logistics trains, and more often than not for the artillery. Whether in Germany or elsewhere, technological promises regarding motorization and mechanization repeatedly showed themselves to be premature. Until vehicles of whatever sort became sufficiently numerous and sufficiently reliable the horse would stay. It made no real difference whether vehicles' deficiencies lay in faulty design, political leaders' ineptitude, military commanders' operational mistakes, combat losses, or domestic industrial bottlenecks caused by strategic aerial bombardment. Whatever the reason, as long as machines could not do the job, horses would have to. In Germany this meant not only that horses would continue to pull supply wagons, field kitchens, ambulances, and guns after 1939 but also that horse-mounted cavalry would soldier on. In confronting this reality, Germany was by no means alone. Poland, France, Rumania, Hungary, Italy, and, most dramatically, Russia all employed horse-cavalry, though not always with the same results.

The military horse thus survived Europe's rapid nineteenth-century industrialization and went on to serve in huge numbers throughout the period from 1900 to 1945. Though their specific cavalry service largely disappeared on the Western Front after the First Battle of the Marne, horses (and mules) nevertheless served valiantly there and in every theater of World War I, particularly in East Prussia, Poland, the Baltic States, and Rumania. They carried on in the interwar period, and they served faithfully once again when a second war came in 1939. Between that year and 1945, approximately seven million horses saw active duty in the armed forces of European countries directly involved in World War II.[2] In the German armed forces alone, the number reached at least 2,800,000 during the same period. Of course, the vast majority was assigned to the army, but the *Luftwaffe*'s field units and even the *Kriegsmarine* used minimal numbers of horses as well.[3] But just as horses served in unprecedented numbers, so they died. The General Staff of the army reported that for the period between the beginning of the invasion of the Soviet Union on 22 June 1941 and 31 December 1944, the army's and *Luftwaffe*'s average monthly loss of horses to all causes was approximately 30,000, 90 percent of which were horses from the army's units on the Eastern Front, the *Ostheer*. According to the same report, by the latter date the armed forces' total losses in horseflesh amounted to 1,558,508 animals.[4] As demonstrated throughout this history, and particularly in the two world wars, losses could mount with frightening rapidity and in the most appalling fashion. Like their human counterparts, those horses not dying from exposure, illness, or malnutrition were killed and maimed by the bombs and bullets of machines whose triumph no horse-mounted or horse-drawn army could prevent.

In his *Victory Report* of 1 September 1945, General George C. Marshall, then chief of staff of the U.S. Army, alluded to this sort of technological supremacy when he wrote that "the greatest advantage in equipment the United States has enjoyed on the ground . . . has been in our multiple-drive motor equipment, principally the jeep and the 2½-ton truck."[5] In the U.S. Army, as well as in other armies (though not always to the same extraordinary degree), these mundane vehicles had given American forces unprecedented mobility. Especially once ashore in France after D-day, the mobility of these vehicles and the troops riding in them became "strikingly clear." The German army, continued Marshall, was "completely outclassed." He went on to observe that "the Germans discovered too late the error of the doctrine a member of their general staff expressed to General [Albert C.] Wedemeyer, then in Berlin, in the late thirties: "The truck has no place on the battlefield."[6] This was, of course, the very same attitude expressed so sharply to a young Heinz Guderian when he was told emphatically that trucks were supposed to carry flour, not troops. It was, however, these same very ordinary jeeps and trucks, possessed of an extraordinary cross-country capability, that spelled the real doom of the military horse in Europe.

The American automotive industry not only made the horse redundant for all practical purposes in the U.S. Army, it also helped complete the motorization and mechanization of the British ground forces and did a great deal to put Stalin's legions on wheels and tracks. Fully 76,737 jeeps and 98,207 trucks went to the British army and 28,356 jeeps and 218,888 trucks to the Red Army. Still more remarkable was the fact that, in addition to these deliveries and the outfitting of U.S. forces literally around the globe, "almost all of the equipment used by the revitalized French Army, which had 12 fully equipped divisions in action at the time of Germany's surrender, came from the United States."[7] As if such American production alone were insufficient, Great Britain also produced nearly a million wheeled vehicles during the war, not to mention 109,500 armored vehicles. In comparison to these prodigious Allied figures, Germany produced approximately 800,000 military trucks and automobiles of all types and perhaps 68,000 armored vehicles. Though by no means paltry figures, these numbers represent a German industrial base that simply could not keep pace, particularly when wartime attrition, normal wear-and-tear, resistance in the occupied countries, and the Allies' strategic bombing campaign are taken into account.[8] Consequently, even if sentimental attachment contributed to the German army's retention of the cavalry in 1939—and the evidence cited makes clear that this was not a dominant factor—keeping the horse in service after that date in both the combat and noncombat arms became ever more a matter of sheer necessity.

As a semblance of peace returned to the charnel house that was Europe in 1945, no serious thought appears to have been given to retaining the military horse beyond its ceremonial function, if that. Nevertheless, horses lingered on in an official military capacity after V-E Day and would remain on active duty beyond the parade ground in several European armies even at the beginning of the twenty-first century. Interestingly, the U.S. Army itself initially raised a small mounted force in the American Zone of Occupied Germany in the immediate postwar years.

As a part of what was called the U.S. Constabulary,[9] this force consisted of both horse-mounted and vehicle-mounted patrols for internal security missions. Furthermore, and more directly germane to the present subject, almost immediately after the Federal Republic of Germany established the Federal Armed Forces (*Bundeswehr*) in 1955, an equine pack-animal unit was raised for the *Heer*'s alpine troops at their training center at Mittenwald in the Bavarian Alps. Another such unit followed in 1960 at Bad Reichenhall near Berchtesgaden. Since 1981, Bad Reichenhall has been the only location where pack animals are based. In 2008 Mountain Pack Animal Company 230 (*Gebirgstragtierkompanie 230*) constituted the sole remaining unit in the *Heer* with horses and mules on its regular TOE. Training in the operational use and keeping of the animals, both mules and Haflinger horses, is the task of the Pack Animal Mission and Training Center (PAMTC), co-located at Bad Reichenhall and established in 1993. According to the *Bundeswehr*, all plans for the elimination of the animals from military service have long since been shelved for the same reasons that cavalry originally survived the advent of the first motorization of German armies at the beginning of the twentieth century: horses and mules can frequently go where vehicles can't roll and helicopters can't land, and they're cheaper than either. By the *Bundeswehr*'s current reckoning, each pack horse or mule can do the work of four soldiers. That fact only adds to equids' advantages as force multipliers.[10]

In 2009 the PAMTC included fifty-four mules and Haflinger horses. In a notable development, mounted training has also recently been reinstated for that unit's personnel. The mounted training's purpose is to provide better coordination with the reconnaissance elements of the Army's 23rd Mountain Rifle Brigade (*Gebirgsjägerbrigade* 23). Furthermore, and curiously reminiscent of the practice established during World War II, especially on the Eastern Front, German troops of the PAMTC purchased Bosnian "ponies" during their first foreign deployment involving the actual operational use of the animals. This deployment occurred in Kosovo between 2002 and 2004. Though the German troops did not take their own horses, the stock they purchased evidently rendered outstanding service in Kosovo supplying outposts over terrain and in weather conditions that made use of vehicles impossible.[11] This same expertise, though once again not the PAMTC's own animals themselves, subsequently found its way to northern Afghanistan as part of the *Bundeswehr's* contribution to NATO's International Security Assistance Force (ISAF) operating in that troubled country.[12]

Other European armed forces also recognized the horse's continuing potential utility in the period after 1945. When the Austrian Federal Army (*Bundesheer*) was established in 1958, for example, horses were called upon to outfit three pack-animal companies whose initial missions were planned to be entirely combat service support. As with their German counterparts, these missions included keeping alpine troops equipped with weapons, ammunition, and other supplies.[13] Even though the three companies were eventually reduced in the 1970s to four platoons based at Hochfilzen, Landeck, Lienz, and Spittal/Drau, horses were retained for these tasks. Furthermore, a remount station was established in 1983 to keep the units supplied with trained stock. In 2005 these numbered 47 remounts and foals in training out of a total of 116 horses in the *Bundesheer* overall. As in the Federal Republic of Germany, the Austrian horses and their handlers also regularly received mounted training. They put this training to use for the first time between fall 1994 and summer 1999 when they executed mounted patrols along Austria's eastern borders, a mission they replicated in 2004 and 2005.[14] Both the German and Austrian armies' employment of horses in such missions, whether in Kosovo or along Austria's own frontiers, were in keeping with what are called the "Petersberg Missions": tasks undertaken by the member States of the Western European Union, a defense association of a number of European countries, to use their armed forces for crisis management, peacekeeping, and humanitarian assistance in loose conjunction with, or even wholly outside of, NATO.

While it may in retrospect seem absurd for any army to have retained horses in the face of motorization and mechanization in the early twentieth century, technology could not always and everywhere fulfill its promise. Such would be the case even at the beginning of the twenty-first century. Interestingly enough, modern technology's limitations in at least one instance were put precisely in equine terms: the aerial Thermal Imaging Airborne Laser Designator (TIALD) pod on the Royal Air Force's Tornado GR4 attack aircraft used in Iraq in 2006–2007 found itself up against certain interesting difficulties in the counterinsurgency campaign there. The TIALD pod, said one RAF officer, could easily designate big, static targets like bunkers, but it couldn't be used "to try to spot a man on a horse with a gun."[15] The point is merely, but importantly, that high-tech systems cannot always surmount challenges presented by decidedly low-tech alternatives, whether in 2007 or circa 1940. And of course everyone is also now familiar with the image of U.S. Special Forces riding into combat against the Taliban in Afghanistan in 2001 alongside as many as two thousand Northern Alliance horsemen.[16] Perhaps not so familiar is the U.S. Army's related horseback training program for Special Forces troops at Ft. Carson, Colorado.[17]

Beyond such technical considerations, any discussion of the German cavalry between 1870 and 1945 must also bear in mind that attitude called the "cavalry spirit," an attitude stressing a commander's initiative, independence, speed, flexibility, and audacity. One noted authority, Robert M. Citino, convincingly maintains that by 1939 that very spirit had been an integral element of a "German way of war" for very nearly three hundred years.[18] In the latter year, it still survived in the concept of *Auftragstaktik*, the ability of commanders to employ their forces essentially on their own without interference from higher command as long as they accomplished the mission. While implicit at almost every level of command, *Auftragstaktik* assumed particular importance at corps-level echelons and particularly in the armored forces.

Just as technology spelled the eventual doom of the horse-cavalry, Hitler's stultifying dictatorship did the same for a concept owing so much to the cavalry's traditions. Shortly after becoming chancellor, Hitler issued a "fundamental order" requiring all higher commands to submit a regular blizzard of reports on troop dispositions, supplies, movements, combat actions, status reports, and so on. These higher commands in turn had to request the same of their immediate subordinates, they of theirs, and so on down the line. In this effort, according to Citino, Hitler was aided and abetted by the army's then–chief of staff, General Franz Halder. Such paper-based micromanagement was poison to *Auftragstaktik*. Furthermore, *Auftragstaktik* by its nature was incompatible with the totalitarian character of Hitler's very much personalized regime, and his "stand fast" order in the Russian winter of 1941 inflicted a mortal wound to what was left of the tradition. His subsequent direct assumption of operational command was the coup de grace. "The dash, the impetuousness, the ability to roam free, away from higher control—all these belonged to a bygone era."[19] The reference here is to an operational concept, but the statement could just as well serve as the German cavalry's epitaph.

In the main, the German army's cavalry in the modern age, including during World War II, fought not only valiantly but honorably, though the latter simply cannot be said of the cavalry of the *Waffen*-SS. Between 1939 and 1945, the horsemen also fought about as effectively as one could expect in a conflict that came to be dominated ever-more completely by titanic masses of machines. As with so many other formations of the German army, however, the cavalrymen's legacy was fouled by the evil nature and conduct of the régime they served in those years. The horsemen endured much. They and their mounts suffered greatly. But they also willingly inflicted much suffering in Hitler's name. The Nazis' cause condemned them. What was said of another cause eighty years before and an ocean away thus might also apply to that of the German horsemen of World War II: it was one of the worst for which a people ever fought.[20]

*   *   *

Once, some years ago, the author was asked in an interview whether he could name a horse that he regarded as the most famous horse in history. He replied by asking in turn whether he might choose an anonymous one. If so, then he felt compelled to say that the most famous horse in history would have to be the horse of the mounted warrior, whether Scythian, Sarmatian, Hun, Magyar, Mongol, Turk, European knight, U.S. Dragoon, Native American horseman, samurai, or modern cavalryman. This horse carried the fate of empires on his back. Sometimes he carried the fate of civilization itself. One would like to think that he did so largely without complaint. Without doubt, he did so while all too often improperly fed, watered, or cared for. He risked his own life and paid it in full more frequently than did his rider. This horse should be remembered.

> Under the western horizon, far below where radiant Venus
> Arises, meander pastures that nurture the stallions of lustrous
> Sol, not by letting them graze themselves, feeding on grass throughout
>   the night,
> But with Ambrosia, restoring strength to legs, setting them aright . . .

Ovid, *Metamorphoses* IV.260–263
(translation by Cheri S. Dorondo)

COPY[1]

Army High Command 4
(Fourth) Army Headquarters 18.9.1941
Abt. Ia/IVc[2]

ARMY ORDER
Re: Sparing of Horses (*Pferdematerial*).

During the advance to date, it has been observed that completely worn out (*heruntergekommen*) horses and horses reduced to walking skeletons by weight-loss have been delivered to the Army's field veterinary hospitals. That fact, in addition to the marked difference between the numbers of horses dropping out on the march and the total number of horses available in the various units, indicates that understanding of proper horse-management is largely absent.

In view of the increasing demands placed upon the Army's horses, the following is ordered for the sparing and maintaining of same:

1.) *March and driving discipline*, especially uniform draft-horse usage, is to be constantly observed by all commanders and subordinates.

---

1. NARA Microfilm Publication T-315, Roll 78, Frames 53–54. Translation by the author. A marginal note by the Cavalry Division's commander ordered the transmission of this directive to all squadrons, though cavalrymen presumably felt no need to be instructed in the matter of horsemanship, much less riding and driving.

2. Operations and Veterinary Staffs.

2.) *Uniform march-tempo at all gaits.* The length of distance marched does not tire horses as much as irregular and unreasonable tempo. All unnecessary trotting is forbidden. Coldbloods [i.e., heavy draft horses] are to be trotted only in exceptional circumstances.

3.) *Sufficient rest.* Whenever possible, the march should initially be paused after one-quarter hour to check the fit of saddles, tack, and harness. Thereafter, a 5–10-minute rest every hour. After the first half of the march, a rest of 1–2 hours. Remove saddles and tack during these rests whenever possible.

4.) To *lighten draft loads*, it is ordered: a) frequent dismounting of riders and drivers; b) only drivers to sit in the driver's seat (*Bock*); other persons permitted only under special *circumstances*, for a limited time, and by express order of the unit's commander; c) artillerymen and machine-gunners to dismount on uphill inclines and on difficult surfaces (e.g., sand); d) riders and drivers driving from horseback to dismount at every halt, even when the column is simply delayed (*Marschstockungen*).

5.) On steep inclines, brief and preplanned halts. Chock wheels at every halt. Wheel-chocks to be carried.

6.) Use every rest to check *saddles, tack, and shoes.* Loosen girths.

7.) As the march begins, *feed supplies are to be arranged in advance by designated personnel (Vorkommandos)* so that horses can be fed sufficient amounts immediately upon arrival or when at a rest-halt. Extended distances from feed supplies or difficulties in acquiring same will not be allowed to result in horses' receiving reduced rations. If necessary, motor vehicles or local transport will be employed [to transport feed]. *Scythes and sickles* will be carried in vehicles. For the march, hay or green feed will be carried in feedbags. *Horses are to graze at every opportunity.* Clover and alfalfa can be substituted occasionally for hay and oats; in emergencies they can replace them. *Oats on the stalk* are not dangerous. At every feeding with green feed, water horses beforehand or at most an hour later. In general, *water* horses as often as time and conditions permit. The warmer the weather, the more frequent the watering. As the march begins, ensure that sufficient numbers of *feedbags, mangers*, and buckets with feed are carried so that they can be employed immediately [at the halt] and not only after large numbers are collected. Allow sufficient time for horses to feed, especially the heavy breeds (*Schlage*).

8.) *No use of horses to extreme limits (bis zum Äussersten).* Horses showing signs of exhaustion are to be removed from service in a timely manner. Longer rest periods and timely replacement with fresh horses (*Vorspann*) are to be provided, especially when only two horses are hitched to heavy vehicles.

9.) *No overloading of vehicles.* [There must be] ruthless reduction of loads.

10.) *Distribution of personnel for assisting with haulage (Zieh- und Schiebekom-mandos).* Drag-ropes are to be carried and personnel employed in a timely manner to assist draft horses with haulage. The number of horses dropping out on the march, the number of horses lost, horses' capacity for work (*Lesitungszustand*), and thereby the mobility of the forces depend upon the personal intervention of line officers, as well as veterinary officers and noncoms.

I will observe the execution of the foregoing order throughout the Army's area of operations.

> *Signed,*
> [Günter] von Kluge
> *Field Marshal*

Results of SS Cavalry Division's Operations Weichsel I and II May–June 1943[1]

[Matériel and persons captured, confiscated, and/or destroyed]

Civilians "evacuated": 10,422.

Villages destroyed: 61.

Bandits and suspected bandits "dealt with" (*erledigt*, i.e., killed): 1,114.

Bandits and suspected bandits captured: 16.

Forest camps: 12.

Bunkers: 46.

Panje vehicles taken: 162.

Mines discovered: 21.

Explosives: 50 kg + 1 satchel charge [?] (*Beutel*).

Saddles: 5.

Enemy operation center(s): 1 + various medical facilities.

Axes: 15.

Spades: 20 + various hand tools.

Machine-gun ammunition drums: 3 with rounds + large amounts of other ammunition and rifles.

---

1. *Zusammenstellung Über* [sic] *Beuteergebnis im Zuge der Unternehmen "Weichsel" im "Nassen Dreieck."* NARA Microfilm Publication T-354, Roll 642, Frame 1190. Translation by the author.

[Livestock taken]

Cattle: 5, 676.
Calves: 1,073.
Sheep: 3,153.
Horses: 1,223.[2]
Foals: 40.
Swine and piglets: 1,398.

Chickens: 1,588.

Geese and ducks: 633.

Large quantities of rye and flax also seized.

2. In the general withdrawal of German forces to the Dnepr following the Battle of Kursk in July 1943, more than 150,000 horses, 200,000 head of cattle, and 270,000 sheep were driven ahead of the retreating armies. See Earl F. Ziemke, *The Soviet Juggernaut* (New York: Time-Life Books, 1980), 74.

Order of the Day to the SS Cavalry Division
Brigadier-General (*Oberführer*) Hermann Fegelein
14 May 1943[1]

Men of the SS Cavalry Division!
Men of the *Waffen*-SS!

By order of the Führer I assumed command of the SS Cavalry Division on 20 April 1943.

The tradition of this division is grounded in the very beginnings of the Guard Echelons (*Schutzstaffeln*; SS) of the N.S.D.A.P. The cornerstone was laid in Munich in 1929 by order of the *Reichsführer-SS* with the establishment of the 3rd Company, 1st Battalion of the 1st Regiment. It was by way of the *Reiter* companies that the *Reiter* regiments and *Reiter* districts (*Abschnitte*) of the General SS were developed following the assumption of power in 1933. With the beginning of this great conflict in September 1939, the first 400 cavalrymen of the reinforced SS-Death's Head Units advanced into Poland and subsequently formed the basis of the 1st SS *Reiter* Regiment. Disbursed in thirteen garrisons across the General Government,[2] this regiment supplied cadre for the formation of the 2nd SS *Reiter* Regiment and thereby for the SS Cavalry Brigade.

1. Translation by the author.
2. The General Government was the rump Polish State administered by, but not annexed to, Germany.

The brigade's march of more than 6,000 kilometers, its renowned engagements and battles, and the crowning achievement of the closing of the gap near Rzhev in the winter battles of 1941/42 are a unique witness to the heroism and bravery of all of the blood-related Reich- and ethnic-German units of the Greater German Reich.[3]

On the basis of trials in the bitterest offensive and defensive battles, in winter as well as summer, the Führer approved the establishment of the SS Cavalry Division. Once again, in the second winter battles of 1942/43, near Smolensk as well as Orel, the division added imperishable fame to its flags. All of that was accomplished through the efforts of the troops whose bravery, determination, and surpassing heroism overcame even the direst crises. A skilled leadership and the instinct for success in war allowed for an avoidance of severe losses.

Even though we were only established during the course of the war, we proceed from the principle that we are the equal of the other regiments and divisions of the *Waffen*-SS. It is good when every unit desires to be the best. It is good when regiments strive with one another in their accomplishments. No one need maintain that we suffer from presumption when we say that we-constituted as we are from all of the pedigrees (*Stämme*) of the Reich—desire to be the best men of the whole of Greater Germany. If only others would say the same! Therefore we hold fast to our company (*Verband*) and because of this pride we lay the greatest worth on a doctrine (*Erziehung*) that appropriately meets our objectives. Therefore we know nothing of conceit and presumption, because presumption is merely a disputing over one's lack of worth. The great man is always a natural man; he doesn't forget whence he comes.

Our love is Germany's treasure, our loyalty its protection and security. Manly virtues, with loyalty first of all, must determine the course of how we lead our lives.

The tasks the division now faces have been ordered by the Führer because they help protect and strengthen the entire front in the East. It is an honor for us to prove through superior leadership and hard-bitten effort in marching and fighting that we can exterminate the dangerous enemy who opposes us. Our

3. "... *aller reichs- und volksdetuschen Stammes-Einheiten des Grossdeutschen Reiches.*"

will to exterminate the enemy must be inexorable, without mercy or compassion. Every weakness means a prolonging of the war.

With exactly the same drive and determination with which I commanded the first *Reiter* Company of the Guard Echelon, I now assume command of the only cavalry unit of the Greater German Army.[4] To you I want to be a good superior and comrade.

We have the holy obligation to continue a tradition of the cavalry stretching back thousands of years, one expressed in the words of the Führer:

Let us more strongly close the ring of our great community in the trust of our *Volk*, filled with the belief in our mission, ready for any sacrifice that the Almighty might demand of us. Then will Germany—the National Socialist Third Reich—pass through the time of distress and trouble, armed with that metal that alone can preserve the knight, unsullied and fearless, in the battle with death and the devil.

Just as we have withstood our many battles and just as so many of us have calmly looked death in the eye, so too do we love the struggle and thereby life.

Long live the Führer![5]
Fegelein

4. The Army's 1st Cavalry Division had been officially disbanded in 1941. Ad hoc Army cavalry units, later somewhat more formalized, were nevertheless starting to reappear by the late spring and early summer of 1943.
5. Fegelein did not use the more typical *"Sieg heil!"*

The Basics of Cavalry Leadership[1]

5 November 1944

1. *Be quick! Speed saves blood!* Speed frequently substitutes for strength! Make decisions quickly. Hesitation and waiting is always bad. Even the best reconnaissance can't provide a completely clear situation in war. Your own action provides the most rapid clarification of the situation.

Give orders quickly. Short, clear, thorough orders to saddle up have always been the tools of a good commander of mounted troops. The quicker you give orders, the quicker they'll be executed, and that execution occurs most rapidly in the cavalry. Whoever wants to give orders quickly, however, has to "speak the same language" as his subordinates and be well acquainted with them. Therefore, practice (*übt*) giving orders.

Transmit orders quickly. If an old woman (*Botefrau*) can get to the objective first, I don't need a mounted courier. If the radio message takes too long, then a rider or motorcyclist can transmit the information quicker than over the airwaves. Therefore keep your command and control route in mind. Organize it. Accelerate it. Always choose the fastest route, and keep several options open for simultaneous use in difficult conditions.

1. *Grundsätzliches über Kavallerieführung*. NARA Microfilm Publication T-314, Roll 27, Frames 499–503. 5 November 1944. Translation by the author. The German familiar form of "you" was used throughout the original. Ellipses indicate omissions of generic statements not specific to the cavalry's ethos, training, or organization.

Execute orders quickly. If a *Volkssturm* battalion can execute orders just as rapidly, then the cavalry has no reason to exist.[2] An average march-tempo of five miles per hour (8 km/h) must be maintained in the mounted regiments. Rest periods and enforced halts due to aerial attack or artillery-fire have to be taken into consideration. Speed in assembly hinders, or at least shortens, enemy countermeasures. From the assembly point the mass of troops—not merely reconnaissance and attack elements—moves simultaneously; otherwise the troops are incorrectly assembled. Speed in the attack exposes troops to enemy fire for a shorter time and helps avoid losses.

Speed of execution is limited by the unavoidable fact that all arms must operate together in order to achieve success. But the cavalry commander must be able to organize this coordination with complete thoroughness. That's why his heavy weapons are mobile and move quickly. However, they also require the first orders since they take the longest to prepare to fire.

2. *Be complete (Sei ganz)*. Only complete men (*Männer*) make it through. Only complete men (*Kerle*) are equal to every situation. Only complete leaders make suitable mounted commanders.

Make complete decisions. Whoever tries to cover everything covers nothing. Whoever tries to do everything accomplishes nothing. Collect the strengths you have. Determine a center of gravity (*Schwerpunkt*). Determine it in space and in time. Determine it by combining the fires of all weapons and collecting your entire offensive capability (*Stosskraft*).[3] The former is more important than the latter [in light of the defensive battles]. Don't be clumsy (*klotzen*) in approach marches, assembly, or dealing with personnel. That costs blood. Make the enemy your objective (*Bilde Deinen Schwerpunkt im Feinde*). The less you have, the more important the center of gravity becomes. Don't avoid the risk of making yourself weak where you have to in order to build a necessary center of gravity elsewhere. Accomplish one task after another rather than trying to do many things at once. You can do it because on the battlefield the cavalry is always quick and nimble.

Don't divide your heavy weapons. Instead, collect them in a "block" to maximize their effect (*klotze damit*). Since you control decision making, you can always move your center of gravity to the enemy's weak spot.

Be completely clear in your orders. Don't push your own responsibilities onto your subordinates.

2. The *Volkssturm* constituted largely useless, scratch formations of over-age civilians raised by the Nazi authorities in a desperate effort to fend off the Soviet invasion of Germany.

3. Nearly illegible in the original, but *Stosskraft* perfectly fits the context.

[. . .]

3. *Be flexible*. Your speed and your mobility give you the ability to do this. Use them! A cavalryman who can't should join another branch of the service.

[. . .]

Only troops who reconnoiter and report properly make flexible command possible. In the cavalry "reconnaissance" is written in capital letters.

[. . .]

4. *Stay mobile*. The strength of the cavalry is in its mobility over difficult terrain and on the battlefield.

Keep yourself mobile and lead from the front, so far forward that you can quickly and securely make use of your knowledge of the enemy and the terrain. Only then can you lead correctly and flexibly. If you don't do this, you'll be overtaken by events.

Keep your troops mobile. Rapid alteration between fire and maneuver is the essence of cavalry combat. Therefore, keep the led horses[4] only as far away as the enemy's fire dictates. Even when you're displacing by truck-transport, bring all horses—or as many as possible—forward so as to keep the reserves and reconnaissance elements mobile.

Stay mobile on the defensive, too. If you have to send your led horses [further] to the rear, at least keep your reserves mobile. The reserves' led horses have to be kept as far forward as possible so that the reserves remain mobile even if the dismounted troops are dug in. If led horses can't be kept standing close by, then arrange truck-transport to take troopers to their horses so that they [horses and riders] can be made mobile as quickly as possible. Led horses should also march at five miles per hour. If they lag, drive vehicles through their columns if necessary (*Fahre dazwischen, wenn sie bummeln*).

5. *Take care* [of your men]. If you don't think ahead about caring for the men, your troopers will quickly lose their edge.

[. . .]

Ensure that your men have rest whenever there's an opportunity. In addition to combat and marching, a cavalryman can easily be overloaded by the further, required horse-care. A basic rule is that in combat and on the

---

4. *Handpferde* were horses held slightly to the rear by a cavalryman (traditionally every fourth one) while his dismounted comrades were in action. *Handpferd/e* can also apply to the leading horse(s) in a team.

march, every trooper up to and including the platoon leader sees to his own horse. This applies especially to the led horses in the rear.

[. . .]

Take care of your horses. They must be watered and fed *in a timely manner.* Be rigorous about this. Never let them stand idle with tight girths. That causes compression in the gut. Saddles that are kept on but not tightly cinched don't cause problems, and they lend themselves to rapid use. Keep horses dispersed in assembly areas and provide dirt revetments or stone/block stalls for shrapnel protection. Otherwise you'll suffer avoidable losses. A horse can live without oats but not without fodder. It takes time for him to eat the amount he needs, so give him something at every rest-halt. Give him straw if nothing else is available. When green fodder is growing, scythes belong in every squadron, battery, and column so that fodder can be provided at every rest-halt.

6. *If you're attached to other units, then*:

Ensure that you carry the day (sich durchsetzen). Not just anyone can lead and employ cavalry. You're responsible for appropriate and effective operations. Let yourself take orders, but how you execute them is your concern.

Ensure that you don't let your forces be divided absent an emergency.

[. . .]

Ensure that you lead. You have learned how to command cavalry. When combat groups (*Kampfgruppen*)[5] are formed, strive to be appointed to overall command or at least make sure that your cavalryman's influence isn't ignored by the commander.

7. *Train.* Cavalry training is the most difficult of all arms. Training saves blood.

[. . .]

Train for combat. The horse is your means of getting to the fight. Your troopers and horses don't need to know anything more than this fact demands. You fight on foot. The bulk of your training time belongs here.

8. [. . .]

9. Don't just command and train your unit, educate it. Without a clear and tireless National Socialist leadership, you won't have your unit well in hand. Political instruction by the CO (*der Chef*) comes before every other instruction.

Signed,

Harteneck

---

5. *Kampfgruppen* were composite formations of varying strength and usually operational for temporary periods.

Chapter 1: The Day of the Horseman

1. Norman Davies, *Europe: A History* (Oxford: Oxford University Press, 1996), 1038. For a general overview of mounted warriors in antiquity, see John Keegan in the video series "War and Civilization."

2. Benno Hubensteiner, *Bayerische Geschichte* (Munich: Süddeutscher Verlag, 1985), 46.

3. *The Revelation to John*, VI: 1-4, *The New American Bible* (Wichita, KS: Catholic Bible Publishers, 1994–1995), 1234; G. Ronald Murphy, S.J., trans., *The Heliand: The Saxon Gospel* (Oxford: Oxford University Press, 1992), xiv. For the role of cavalry in the age of classical Greece, see Victor Davis Hanson, *The Wars of the Ancient Greeks and Their Invention of Western Military Culture* (London: Cassell, 2000). On Roman cavalry see Lawrence Keppie, *The Making of the Roman Army From Republic to Empire* (Norman: University of Oklahoma Press, 1998).

4. Brian M. Fagan, *People of the Earth: An Introduction to World Prehistory*, 9th ed. (New York: Longman, 1998), 469.

5. John Keegan, *A History of Warfare* (New York: Alfred A. Knopf, 1993), 181–182.

6. Andrew Jacobs, "Police Turn to the Stable for Crime-Fighting Clout," *New York Times*, 18 April 2006, 1. See also Steven D. Price, "On Patrol With the NYPD," *Equus*, 398 (November 2010): 45–48.

7. Ann Hyland, *The Medieval Warhorse From Byzantium to the Crusades* (Stroud: Sutton Publishing, 1996), xi–xii.

8. Keegan, *A History of Warfare*, 213, 387.

9. Hyland, *The Medieval Warhorse*, 11–12. Not all historians agree that Western European cavalry truly acted as a shock force. See Carroll Gillmor, "Cavalry, Ancient and Modern," in Robert Cowley and Geoffrey Parker, eds., *The Reader's Companion to Military History* (Boston: Houghton Mifflin, 1996), 74–75. On the horse-people's style of

warfare see the eloquent description by Marco Polo in his *The Travels of Marco Polo*, Bk. 1, Ch. 49.

10. Hyland, *The Medieval Warhorse*, 57–58.

11. Gillmor, "Cavalry, Ancient and Modern," 74–75.

12. Robert L. O'Connell, *Soul of the Sword: An Illustrated History of Weaponry and Warfare from Prehistory to the Present* (New York: The Free Press, 2002), 123.

13. Andrea Brady, "Dying With Honor: Literary Propaganda and the Second English Civil War," *The Journal of Military History*, 70, no. 1 (January 2006): 14–15, 18.

14. Ben Cassidy, "Machiavelli and the Ideology of the Offensive: Gunpowder Weapons in *The Art of War*," *The Journal of Military History*, 67, no. 2 (April 2003): 392 and note 50 there.

15. Ibid., 394 and note 55.

16. Ibid., 393 and notes 51–53.

17. Louis A. DiMarco, *War Horse: A History of the Military Horse and Rider* (Yardley, PA: Westholme, 2008), 205–206.

18. Jeremy Black, *European Warfare, 1494–1660* (London and New York: Routledge, 2002), 208.

19. Ibid., 207.

20. Michael Roberts, "The Military Revolution 1560–1660," in Clifford J. Rogers, ed., *The Military Revolution Debate: Readings on the Transformation of Early Modern Europe* (Boulder, CO: Westview Press, 1995), 14.

21. David A. Parrott, "Strategy and Tactics in the Thirty Years' War: The 'Military Revolution,'" in Rogers, *The Military Revolution Debate*, 238.

22. Ibid., 237–239.

23. Vladimir Littauer, *Horseman's Progress: The Development of Modern Riding* (N.p.: The Long Riders' Guild Press, n.d. [1962]), 92; Louis A. DiMarco, *War Horse*, 183–190.

24. Littauer, *Horseman's Progress*, 93.

25. DiMarco, *War Horse*, 191.

26. Williamson Murray, "Cavalry, 1500–1945," in Cowley and Parker, *The Reader's Companion to Military History*, 75–76.

27. Ibid. Murray writes that precisely one prepared infantry square was overrun by cavalry attack in the Napoleonic era, and that only because horse and rider were killed before they could turn away. They consequently crashed headlong into the square and broke open its side. It should be noted, however, that the 1st and 2nd Dragoons of the (British) King's German Legion successfully destroyed two French infantry squares at Garcia Hernandez on the day after the Battle of Salamanca.

28. Jeremy Black, "The Military Revolution II: Eighteenth-Century War," in Charles Townshend, ed., *The Oxford Illustrated History of Modern War* (Oxford: Oxford University Press, 1997), 41.

29. Alan Forrest, "The Nation in Arms I: The French Wars," in Townshend, *The Oxford Illustrated History of Modern War*, 59.

30. Cf. Martin van Creveld, "Technology and War I: To 1945," in ibid., 181–182, 188.

31. Ibid., 181.

32. The following is drawn from D. R. Dorondo, "Review of *Noble Brutes: How Eastern Horses Transformed English Culture*, by Donna Landry," *Itinerario*, no. 2 (2009).

33. Cf. DiMarco, *War Horse*, 217.

34. Ibid.

Chapter 2: The Legacy of 1870

1. Cf. Lucian K. Truscott Jr., *The Twilight of the U.S. Cavalry: Life in the Old Army, 1917–1942* (Lawrence: University Press of Kansas, 1989), ix–xx.

2. Hugh Trevor-Roper, *The Rise of Christian Europe* (New York: Harcourt, Brace, 1965), 77.

3. See general references in G. Ronald Murphy, S.J., trans., *The Heliand: The Saxon Gospel* (New York: Oxford University Press, 1992). Here see specifically xiv and 135 with the footnote there.

4. Trevor-Roper, *The Rise of Christian Europe*, 95–98; John Keegan, *A History of Warfare* (New York: Alfred A. Knopf, 1994), 189.

5. Wolfgang J. Mommsen, *Imperial Germany 1867–1918: Politics, Culture, and Society in an Authoritarian State*, trans. Richard Deveson (London: Arnold, 1995), 124. See also Koppel S. Pinson, *Modern Germany: Its History and Civilization*, 2nd ed. (Prospect Heights, ILL: Waveland Press, 1989), 255–273.

6. Michael Howard, *The Franco-Prussian War: The German Invasion of France 1870–1871* (New York: Dorset Press, 1961), 7–8.

7. Ibid., 60, 350, and note 3 on the latter page. Most of the more than 700 Bismarck memorials built after 1870 loosely depicted the Reich Chancellor either as a knight or in his cuirassier's uniform. See Heinrich August Winkler, *Der lange Weg nach Westen: Deutsche Geschichte* (München: C. H. Beck Verlag, 2002), I:278–279.

8. Vezio Melegari, *The World's Great Regiments* (New York: G. P. Putnam's Sons, 1969), 100.

9. On Langensalza and Königgrätz, see Robert M. Citino, *The German Way of War: From the Thirty Years' War to the Third Reich* (Lawrence: University Press of Kansas, 2005), 153-170. On Moltke's memorandum, see Michael D. Krause, "Moltke and Origins of the Operational Level of War," in Michael D. Krause and R. Cody Phillips, eds., *Historical Perspectives on the Operational Art* (Washington, D.C.: Center of Military History, 2005), 124–125.

10. A. L. Wagner, ed., *Cavalry Studies from Two Great Wars. Comprising the French Cavalry in 1870 by Lieutenant-Colonel Bonie, the German Cavalry in the Battle of Vionville–Mars-la-Tour by Major Kaehler and the Operations of the Cavalry in the Gettysburg Campaign by Lieutenant-Colonel George B. Davis* (Kansas City, MO: Hudson-Kimberly Publishing Company, 1896), 5–6.

11. Ibid., 6.

12. Mary Lee Stubbs and Stanley Russell Connor, *Armor-Cavalry*, part I: *Regular Army and Army Reserve* (Washington, D.C.: Office of the Chief of Military History Unites States Army, 1969), 4.

13. Edward J. Katzenbach, "The Horse Cavalry in the Twentieth Century: A Study in Policy Response," *Public Policy: A Yearbook of the Graduate School of Public Administration*, Harvard University, 1958, 128.

14. Bonie cited in Wagner, *Cavalry Studies from Two Great Wars*, 9. These regulations were presumably the same ones studied by U.S. Cavalry officers sent to France by Secretary of War Joel Poinsette in 1839–1840.

15. Ibid., 12.

16. Cf. Gerhard von Pelet-Narbonne, *Cavalry on Service: Illustrated by the Advance of the German Cavalry Across the Mosel in 1870*, trans. D'Arcy Legard (London: Hugh Rees, 1906), viii. Pelet-Narbonne's text is a very detailed account of German small-unit cavalry operations from the battles at Wörth and Spicheren to the eve of the clash at Mars-la-Tour. He illustrates clearly the moral superiority of the German cavalry over its French counterparts, particularly at the junior-officer level. He does, however, provide instances of the French cavalry's effective use of firearms, particularly among the dragoons and freely admits (282; see the note there) that their chassepot carbine was "far superior" to the German troopers' weapon. French cavalrymen, he writes, "were much more accustomed to use it than the German cavalry, both on foot and on horseback."

17. Ibid., 15; see the note there.

18. Bonie cited in Wagner, *Cavalry Studies from Two Great Wars*, 23–28.

19. Geoffrey Wawro, *The Franco-Prussian War: The German Conquest of France in 1870–1871* (New York: Cambridge University Press, 2003), 132–133.

20. Ibid., 133; Bonie cited in Wagner, *Cavalry Studies from Two Great Wars*, 23–28; Howard, *The Franco-Prussian War*, 112.

21. Bonie cited in Wagner, *Cavalry Studies from Two Great Wars*, 28.

22. Howard, *The Franco-Prussian War*, 73, 100–101.

23. Pelet-Narbonne, *Cavalry on Service*, 265. Order from Prussian Royal Headquarters dated 13 August 1870. The original order had the passage underlined.

24. Wawro, *The Franco-Prussian War*, 141.

25. Ibid., 143.

26. Ibid., 249.

27. Howard, *The Franco-Prussian War*, 131; Denison, *A History of Cavalry From the Earliest Times*, 404–407.

28. Pelet-Narbonne, *Cavalry on Service*, 287–314.

29. Wawro, *The Franco-Prussian War*, 156; Howard, *The Franco-Prussian War*, 157; Kaehler as cited in Wagner, *Cavalry Studies from Two Great Wars*, 167–189. In addition to preparatory fire before a charge, the other principal tasks of the horse-artillery were to prevent enemy cavalry's rallying; to provide a rallying point for one's own cavalry if necessary; and to help secure specific defensive positions.

30. J. F. C. Fuller, *The Conduct of War, 1789–1961* (New York: Minerva Press, 1968), 105.

31. Ibid., 119.

32. Gordon A. Craig, *The Battle of Königgrätz: Prussia's Victory Over Austria, 1866* (Philadelphia and New York: Lippincott, 1964), 21.

33. Geoffrey Wawro, *The Austro-Prussian War: Austria's War with Prussia and Italy in 1866* (New York: Cambridge University Press, 1996), 16–20.

34. Ibid., 17.

35. Ibid., 19.

36. Ibid., 269, 271.

37. Howard, *The Franco-Prussian War*, 2–4.

38. Ibid., 3.

39. Ibid., 4.

40. P. H. Sheridan, *Personal Memoirs*, intro. Jeffrey D. Wert (New York: Da Capo Press, 1992), 534.

41. Jonathan M. House, *Towards Combined Arms Warfare: A Survey of 20th-Century Tactics, Doctrine, and Organization* (Ft. Leavenworth: U.S. Army Command and General Staff College, 1984), Prologue. No page reference in the online edition.

42. Michael Howard, *War in European History* (Oxford: Oxford University Press, 1976), 104.

43. David Johnson, *Napoleon's Cavalry and Its Leaders* (New York: Holmes and Meier, 1978), 13.

44. Z. Grbasic and V. Vuksic, *The History of Cavalry* (New York: Facts On File, 1989), 243.

45. Andrew Roberts, *Waterloo: June 18, 1815. The Battle for Modern Europe* (New York: HarperCollins, 2005), 66–67, 80.

46. Craig, *The Battle of Königgrätz*, 17; Katzenbach, "Twentieth Century Horse Cavalry," 122–123; Pelet-Narbonne, *Cavalry on Service*, 21. See Pelet-Narbonne, 244–246, for use of ferries near Metz in mid-August 1870. In September 1939, horsemen of the German 1st Cavalry Brigade (redesignated 1st Cavalry Division after October 1939) covered as much as forty-five miles per day, fully equipped, in the invasion of Poland.

47. Major F. Maurice, "The Franco-German War (1870–1)," in A. W. Ward et al., eds., *The Cambridge Modern History*, vol. XI: *The Growth of Nationalities* (Cambridge: Cambridge University Press, 1969), 580.

48. Geoffrey Wawro, *The Franco-Prussian War: The German Conquest of France in 1870–1871* (New York: Cambridge University Press, 2003), 86; Bonie, "The French Cavalry in 1870," in Wagner, *Cavalry Studies from Two Great Wars*, 35–36.

49. Howard, *The Franco-Prussian War*, 65.

50. Ibid. By way of comparison, in the last sustained cavalry war before 1870, the American Civil War, the Union Army was requiring approximately five hundred remounts *per week* by mid-1863, a number that could be met only with a remount service that had been operating for more than two years. See Phil Livingston and Ed Roberts, *War Horse: Mounting the Cavalry With America's Best Horses* (Albany, TX: Bright Sky Press, 2003), 43–45. In the next major European war featuring large numbers of horses, World War I, the French Government was able, but only with greatest effort

given its own supreme needs over four years, to supply the American Expeditionary Forces, with some 63,000 equids during the course of 1918. "Final Report of General John J. Pershing: Part III—Supply, Coordination, Munitions, and Administration—'Remounts,'" in Francis J. Reynolds, *The Story of the Great War: History of the European War From Official Sources* (New York: P. F. Collier and Son Company, 1920), vol. 8, Appendix, xlviii.

51. Howard, *War in European History*, 84; Bonie, "The French Cavalry in 1870," in Wagner, *Cavalry Studies from Two Great Wars*, 40.

52. Waitman Beorn, "'Heads Up, By God!' French Cavalry At Eylau, 1807 and Napoleon's Cavalry Doctrine." www.napoleonseries.org/articles/wars/eylau.cfm. 25 January 2005. Beorn also provides examples from Austerlitz, Borodino, and suggests that even at Waterloo the French cavalry's action was not born merely of desperation.

53. Johnson, *Napoleon's Cavalry and Its Leaders*, 12. See also Grbasic and Vuksic, *The History of the Cavalry*, 243.

54. Pelet-Narbonne, *Cavalry on Service*, 248–249, 251.

55. Jay Luvaas, *The Military Legacy of the Civil War* (Chicago: University of Chicago Press, 1959), 119, 123.

56. Ibid., 124.

57. Ibid., 136. Luvaas does note the exceptions to this way of thinking in the likes of General Friedrich von Bernhardi and the civilian novelist and military writer Karl Bleibtreu.

58. Ibid., 130ff.

59. Howard, *The Franco-Prussian War*, 8.

60. Grbasic and Vuksic, *The History of Cavalry*, 250; George T. Denison, *A History of Cavalry From the Earliest Times: With Lessons for the Future* (London: Macmillan, 1913), 411.

61. Howard, *The Franco-Prussian War*, 190–194.

62. Ibid., 195, 197–198. Explicit instructions coming from Paris also kept French Marshal MacMahon from ordering a withdrawal away from the Germans.

63. Denison, *A History of Cavalry From the Earliest Times*, 410-411.

64. Ibid., 411–412. Howard, *The Franco-Prussian War*, 215, indicates that even before the reserve cavalry's attacks, two squadrons of French lancers had been destroyed attempting to halt the advancing German infantry at nearly the same spot on the same day.

65. Wawro, *The Franco-Prussian War*, 221.

66. Ibid., 231.

67. Ibid., 241.

68. Ibid., 248.

69. Ibid., 265.

70. Howard, *The Franco-Prussian War*, 329.

71. Ibid., 379–381; Wawro, *The Franco-Prussian War*, 279.

72. Wawro, *The Franco-Prussian War*, 288.

73. Denison, *A History of Cavalry from the Earliest Times*, 412–413.

74. Sheridan, *Personal Memoirs*, 495.

75. Luvaas, *The Military Legacy of the Civil War*, 122–123.

76. Ibid., 123.

77. Ibid., 125.

78. Ibid., 146–151.

Chapter 3: Not Quite Sunset

1. Hew Strachan, *The First World War*, vol. 1 (Oxford: Oxford University Press, 2001), 231.

2. See Friedrich von Berhardi, *Germany and the Next War*, trans. Allen H. Powles (n.p., 1912). Here Chapter X. http://www.gutenberg.org/files/11352/11352-8.txt

3. Van Michael Leslie, "French, John Denton Pinkstone, Earl of Ypres," in Spencer C. Tucker, ed., *The European Powers in the First World War: An Encyclopedia* (New York: Garland, 1996), 271.

4. John Ellis, *Eye-Deep in Hell: Trench Warfare in World War I* (New York: Pantheon Books, 1976), 84.

5. John Keegan, *A History of Warfare*, 187–188. Here Keegan cites the Marquess of Anglesey's *A History of the British Cavalry*.

6. Ibid., 224.

7. Strachan, *The First World War*, vol. 1, 232. On British cavalry doctrine after 1902, see Stephen Badsey, "The Boer War (1899–1902) and British Cavalry Doctrine: A Re-Evaluation," *The Journal of Military History*, 71, no. 1 (January 2007): 75–97.

8. Jean Bou, "Cavalry, Firepower, and Swords: The Australian Light Horse and the Tactical Lessons of Cavalry Operations in Palestine, 1916–1918," *The Journal of Military History*, 71, no.1 (January 2007): 102, and Gervase Phillips, "Scapegoat Arm: Twentieth-Century Cavalry in Anglophone Historiography," in ibid., 39. According to this British analysis, "mounted rifles" differed from "mounted infantry" in that the latter were not expected to use horses for any real purpose other than moving from one position to another. The articles cited do not specify the mounted infantry's training requirement for equitation. Note, however, that novice infantrymen astride anything other than "dead broke" horses would run a very real risk of multiple, and potentially dangerous, falls.

9. Phillips, "Scapegoat Arm," 43–44.

10. Norman Davies, *Europe: A History*, 902.

11. Keegan, *A History of Warfare*, 271; Lawrence Keppie, *The Making of the Roman Army: From Republic to Empire*, 26–32.

12. Keegan, *A History of Warfare*, 221–234, notes the importance of tradition in helping shape the organization and function of armed forces.

13. Ellis, *Eye-Deep in Hell*, 84.

14. Henderson had observed the South African campaign from the headquarters of the British commander, Lord Roberts. He is quoted in Peter Paret, ed., *Makers of Modern Strategy from Machiavelli to the Nuclear Age* (Princeton: Princeton University Press, 1986), 516.

15. Ibid., 519.

16. Keegan, *A History of Warfare*, 307–308.

17. Edward Spiers, "The Late Victorian Army 1868–1914," in David Chandler, ed., *The Oxford Illustrated History of the British Army* (Oxford: Oxford University Press, 1994), 212. The British campaign in Palestine is excluded from this discussion merely because of its extra-European geographic context. The British army's use of cavalry there, as well as the Ottomans' both there and in eastern Anatolia and the Caucasus Mountains, remains nonetheless noteworthy.

18. John Keegan, *The First World War* (New York: Alfred A. Knopf, 1999), 73. Though the British figure seems remarkably low, it is estimated that the British equine population was at least 3.3 million as early as 1901. Monthly averages of 165,000 horses and mules were imported by Great Britain from the United States over the duration of the war. Figures from R. H. C. Davis, *The Medieval Warhorse: Origin, Development and Redevelopment* (London: Thames and Hudson, 1989), 46.

19. Davis, *The Medieval Warhorse*, citing a passage from F. Nagle, *Fritz* (Huntington, WV: n.p., 1981), 15–19. *Bundesrat* decrees cited in *The Times* of 1 August 1914 under "A State of War." These decrees applied also to animal products; oil, coal, and their by-products; automobiles; spare parts, etc.

20. John Singleton, "Britain's Use of Military Horses 1914–1918," *Past and Present*, 139 (May 1993): 182.

21. Christian Freiherr von Stenglin, *The Hanoverian*, trans. Christina Belton (London: J. A. Allen, 1990), 36; Eberhard von Velsen and Erhard Schulte, *The Trakehner*, trans. Christina Belton (London: J. A. Allen, 1990), 12.

22. "The Battle of Big Nations for Thoroughbred Horses," *New York Times Magazine*, 3 May 1914, SM9 at http://query.nytimes.com/gst/abstract.html (18 March 2009).

23. Ibid.

24. Daniel David, *The 1914 Campaign: August–October, 1914* (New York: Wieser and Wieser, 1987), 19.

25. Ibid.

26. Hew Strachan, "Military Modernization, 1789–1918," in T. C. W. Blanning, ed., *The Oxford Illustrated History of Modern Europe* (Oxford: Oxford University Press, 1996), 80.

27. "France Invaded"; "Franco-German Fighting"; "Franco-German Encounters"; *Times*, 2–6 August 1914.

28. Cf. Dennis E. Showalter, "World War I," in Robert Cowley and Geoffrey Parker, eds., *The Reader's Companion to Military History* (Boston: Houghton Mifflin, 1996), 523. See John Keegan, *The First World War*, 33–36 for the implications of such density of personnel on the ground. On the flanking mission of the German cavalry see Paret, *Makers of Modern Strategy*, 513.

29. Robert A. Doughty, "French Strategy in 1914: Joffre's Own," *The Journal of Military History*, 67, no. 2 (April 2003): 436.

30. Ibid., 437.

31. David, *The 1914 Campaign*, 122–123, 142,148; Keegan, *The First World War*, 20, 77,

129; *Handbook of the German Army (Home and Colonial)* (London: Imperial War Museum, 1914; Nashville, TN: The Battery Press, 2002), 51–52, 130, 142–143; for cavalry-horse paces, see 239.

32. Keegan, *The First World War*, 81. For the entire campaign on the Western Front to the end of 1914 see Maximilian von Poseck, *The German Cavalry: 1914 in Belgium and France*, trans. Alexander C. Strecker et al., ed. Jerome Howe (Berlin: E. S. Mittler und Sohn, 1923). This translation was commissioned by the U.S. Cavalry Association. Poseck held the rank of lieutenant general and Inspector of Cavalry.

33. Doughty, "French Strategy in 1914," 446, 449, 451; Keegan, *The First World War*, 84; Francis J. Reynolds, ed., *The Story of the Great War* (New York: P. F. Collier and Son, 1916), ii, 9.

34. Doughty, "French Strategy in 1914," 452; Keegan, *The First World War*, 92.

35. Reynolds, *The Story of the Great War*, ii, 18–19.

36. S. L. A. Marshall, *World War I* (New York: American Heritage Press, 1971), 61.

37. Reynolds, *The Story of the Great War*, 25; "British and French Join," *New York Times* (1857–Current file), 10 August 1914; ProQuest Historical Newspapers, *New York Times* (1851–2002), 2. On the fear of a German cavalry attack on Brussels see ibid. On Haelen and Donck, see Poseck, *The German Cavalry*, 22–28.

38. "Belgian Peasants Panic," *New York Times* (1857–Current file), 21 August 1914; ProQuest Historical Newspapers, *New York Times* (1851–2002), 1.

39. "Save Ostend From Uhlans," *New York Times*, 26 August 1914; ProQuest Historical Newspapers, *New York Times* (1851–2002), 2.

40. John Keegan, *The First World War*, 107; Richard Holmes, "The Last Hurrah: Cavalry on the Western Front, August–September 1914," in Hugh Cecil and Peter Liddle, eds., *Facing Armageddon: The First World War Experienced* (London: Leo Cooper, 1996), 286.

41. Poseck, *The German Cavalry*, 53.

42. Keegan, *The First World War*, 113; Strachan, *The First World War*, vol. 1, 254.

43. Strachan, *The First World War*, vol. 1, 254.

44. Ibid., 232, 254, 258.

45. Ibid., 259–260; Martin Gilbert, *The First World War: A Complete History* (New York: Henry Holt, 1994), 74. British lieutenant quoted in Holmes, "The Last Hurrah," 290. Holmes, 280, 288, further notes that the French alone retained large numbers of breast-plated cuirassiers in 1914; and, given the fact that breastplates were not bulletproof and could be seen for several miles on sunny days, their utility in 1914 was unclear.

46. Trevor N. Dupuy, *1914: The Battles in the West* (New York: Franklin Watts, 1967), 71.

47. Poseck, *The German Cavalry*, 160–161.

48. Ibid., 175–176.

49. Ibid., 177.

50. Ibid., 210, 212–213.

51. Ibid., 213.

52. Martin Gilbert, *The Somme: Heroism and Horror in the First World War* (New York: Henry Holt, 2006), 21–22.

53. Ibid., 27–28; David T. Zabecki, "Somme, Battle of (1 July–19 November 1916)," in Spencer C. Tucker, ed., *The European Powers in the First World War: An Encyclopedia* (New York: Garland, 1996), 649.

54. Gilbert, *The Somme*, 27.

55. Ibid., 112–113.

56. Both quotations from ibid., 92–94.

57. Ibid., 228–229.

58. Gilbert, *The First World War*, 235, 255.

59. Andrew N. Liaropoulos, "Revolutions in Warfare: Theoretical Paradigms and Historical Evidence—The Napoleonic and First World War Revolutions in Military Affairs," *The Journal of Military History*, 70, no. 2 (April 2006): 377–384.

60. Robert M. Citino, *The German Way of War*, 223.

61. Keegan, *The First World War*, 141–142.

62. Ibid., 140; Strachan, *The First World War*, vol. 1, 316.

63. Davies, *Europe: A History*, 902.

64. Keegan, *The First World War*, 83.

65. Citino, *The German Way of War*, 225. On Prussian / German identification, see Christopher Clark, *Iron Kingdom: The Rise and Downfall of Prussia, 1600–1947* (Oxford: Oxford University Press, 2006), 607–608. Tukhachevsky quoted in Adam Zamoyski, *The Battle for the Marchlands*, East European Monographs, No. LXXXVIII (New York: Columbia University Press, 1981), 12, see also 28; "Deutsches Kulturland," in Norman Stone, *The Eastern Front 1914–1917* (New York: Charles Scribner's Sons, 1975), 49.

66. Gilbert, *The First World War*, 48–49; Vejas Gabriel Liulevicius, *War Land on the Eastern Front: Culture, National Identity, and German Occupation in World War I* (Cambridge: Cambridge University Press, 2000), 15. A distinctly pro-Russian account of the Eastern Front is contained in Alexis Wrangel, *The End of Chivalry: The Last Great Cavalry Battles 1914–1918* (New York: Hippocrene Books, 1982). Wrangel, 70, clearly states that Russian cavalrymen helped themselves in gentlemanly fashion to the relative "affluence" of East Prussian farms, while follow-on forces came "like a swarm of locusts" burning farms and turning villages to wilderness. Wrangel's ancestor, Baron Peter Wrangel, a captain of the Russian Imperial Horse Guards Regiment, fought in East Prussia. Interestingly, Alexander Solzhenitsyn, *August 1914*, trans. Michael Glenny (New York: Farrar, Straus and Giroux, 1971), 218, has the German general Hermann von François write in an order of the day to the German I Corps of the "Russian hordes who, in defiance of international law, are burning the towns and villages of our homeland." By contrast, Imanuel Geiss, "The Civilian Dimension of the War," *Facing Armageddon*, 18, says bluntly that stories of Russian depredations were mere German propaganda. The Russian eyewitness account reproduced above is in Vladimir S. Littauer, *Russian Hussar: A Story of the Imperial Cavalry, 1911–1920* (London: J. A. Allen & Co., 1965; Long Riders' Guild Press, 2007), 138–139, 143–144.

67. Citino, *The German Way of War*, 227. "Frog stickers" and references to

intelligence failures are in Dennis E. Showalter, *Tannenberg: Clash of Empires* (Hamden, CT: Archon Books, 1991), 189. Intra-service derogation was not unique to the Imperial German Army. British cavalrymen in 1914–1918 were sometimes referred to, not least by ANZAC troops, as "donkey wallopers."

68. Citino, *The German Way of War*, 229. For the Russian cavalry's encounter with German infantry near Kaushen, see Wrangel, *The End of Chivalry*, 23–38.

69. Showalter, *Tannenberg*, 151.

70. Ibid., 210; Citino, *The German Way of War*, 229.

71. Strachan, *The First World War*, vol. 1, 321, 327; Littauer, *Russian Hussar*, 142.

72. "Hindenburg--Falkenhayn," *Vossische Zeitung* (Berlin), 30 August 1916. http://www.zld.de/projekte/ millenium/original_html/vossische_1916_3008.GIF.html (9 March 2007).

73. T. Dodson Stamps and Vincent J. Esposito, eds., *A Short Military History of World War I With Atlas* (West Point: USMAAG Printing Office, 1950), 123–128.

74. Ibid.

75. Marshall, *World War I*, 216–218; Stone, *The Eastern Front 1914–1917*, 171–172, 188–189; Liulevicius, *War Land on the Eastern Front*, 19. On the German cavalry in Courland, see *The Story of the Great War*, vol. III (New York: P. F. Collier and Son, 1916), 337–339.

76. For this discussion, see Stamps and Esposito, *A Short Military History of World War I*, 198–203.

77. David Christian, *A History of Russia, Central Asia, and Mongolia*, vol. 1: *Inner Eurasia from Prehistory to the Mongol Empire* (Oxford: Blackwell, 1998), 13–16. The Great Hungarian Plain (the *Alföld* or *puszta*), though separated from the Black Sea Steppe by the Carpathian Mountains, constitutes the westernmost extremity of the Eurasian grasslands. The *Alföld*'s area is some 30,000 square miles.

78. Singleton, "Britain's Use of Military Horses 1914–1918," 189.

79. Ibid.

80. Stamps and Esposito, *A Short Military History of World War I*, 5.

81. Holmes, "The Last Hurrah," 286.

82. Stamps and Esposito, *A Short Military History of World War I*, 4.

83. See, for example, those noted throughout by Poseck, *The German Cavalry*.

84. Wrangel, *The End of Chivalry*, 105–153.

85. Holger Herwig, "The German Victories, 1917–1918," in Strachan, *The First World War*, 260–263. Herwig also notes that the Germans possessed only 23,000 trucks as against the Allies' 100,000 vehicles.

86. See the useful examination of the armistice's development and final terms in Bullitt Lowry, *Armistice 1918* (Kent, OH: The Kent State University Press, 1996), here particularly chapters 7 and 8.

87. Poseck, *The German Cavalry*, 206.

88. Holmes, "The Last Hurrah," 287.

Chapter 4: False Dawn

1. *Peace Treaty of Versailles. Articles 231–247 and Annexes. Reparations.* http://www.lib.byu.edu/~rdh/wwi/versa/versa7.html (5 June 2003). The Fourth Hague Convention on the Laws and Customs of War on Land (1907) had earlier reflected the horse's continuing military importance at the beginning of the twentieth century by specifying in Chapter II, Article 4 that all horses, if taken along with POWs, automatically ceased to be the property of enemy individuals or States.

2. John Ellis, *Eye-Deep in Hell*, 84. This constituted a reiteration of the British army's 1907 *Cavalry Manual*'s assertion that the rifle "cannot replace the effect produced by the speed of the horse, the magnetism of the charge, and the terror of cold steel." Ibid.

3. Carlo D'Este, *Patton: A Genius for War* (New York: HarperCollins, 1995), 139,162, 334.

4. Quotation in Alexander M. Bielakowski, "General Hawkins's War: The Future of the Horse in the U.S. Cavalry," *The Journal of Military History*, 71 (January 2007): 137.

5. For the argument over mechanization within the U.S. Cavalry as a whole, see ibid., 127–138.

6. Zamoyski, *The Battle for the Marchlands*, 44–46.

7. Ibid., 58–61; David M. Glantz and Jonathan House, *When Titans Clashed: How the Red Army Stopped Hitler* (Lawrence: University Press of Kansas, 1995), 6.

8. Norman Davies, *Europe: A History*, 935; Zamoyski, *The Battle for the Marchlands*, 163–174.

9. "Strength of German Army in World War I" in Charles E. Heller and William A. Stofft, eds., *America's First Battles, 1776–1965* (Lawrence: University Press of Kansas, 1986), 155.

10. Text of the Treaty of Versailles at http:www.FirstWorldWar.com (19 September 2006). See also Wilhelm Deist, *The Wehrmacht and German Rearmament*, foreword A. J. Nicholls (Basingstoke: The Macmillan Press, 1981), 4. Overview of command structure of the *Reichsheer* of the Weimer period and the *Heer* after 1935 at http:www.bundesarchiv.de/php/bestaende_findemittel/bestaendeuebersicht (16 February 2007).

11. Initially each squadron was approximately the size of a U.S. Army infantry company of that period. Later reorganizations increased the size of squadrons to a level comparable with those of the U.S. Cavalry, i.e., roughly the size of U.S. Army battalions. For the German cavalry division's TOE of 1919, see James S. Corum, *The Roots of Blitzkrieg: Hans von Seeckt and German Army Reform* (Lawrence: University Press of Kansas, 1992), 207 and 46. See also Robert M. Kennedy, *The German Campaign in Poland (1939)*, Department of the Army Pamphlet No. 20-255 (Washington, D.C.: Department of the Army, 1956), 11. Unlike their infantry counterparts, the cavalry divisions drew personnel from beyond their immediate regional military area (*Wehrkreis*). The 3rd Cavalry Division, for example, though headquartered in Weimar in Thuringia, included a Bavarian mounted regiment. See Kennedy, *The German Campaign in Poland*, 11.

12. Corum, *Roots of Blitzkrieg*, 31–32.

13. Von Seeckt, from his *Thoughts of a Soldier* (London: Ernest Benn, 1930) as quoted in ibid., 32. See also Army Service Regulation (*Heeresdienstvorschrift*) 487, here Part 1, 47 as quoted in ibid., 42. Poseck, *The German Cavalry*, 231. In the present text, "motorized" refers throughout to armored and unarmored wheeled vehicles; "mechanized" refers to tracked vehicles. On "operational" versus "tactical" see the very useful work by Bruce W. Menning, "Operational Art's Origins," in Michael D. Krause and R. Cody Phillips, eds., *Historical Perspectives of the Operational Art* (Washington, D.C.: Center of Military History, 2005), here 8–9; note particularly the influence of Soviet thinkers in the 1920s and 1930s. On von Moltke, see Michael D. Krause, "Moltke and the Origins of the Operational Level of War," in Krause and Phillips, here 124–125.

14. Seeckt, *Thoughts of a Soldier*, 84–86.

15. Ibid., 84, 91–92.

16. Ibid., 92, 95, 99–100; Poseck, *The German Cavalry*, 233–234.

17. Seeckt, *Thoughts of a Soldier*, 101–106.

18. Klaus Christian Richter, *Cavalry of the Wehrmacht 1941–1945* (Atglen, PA: Schiffer, n.d.), 23. The numbers of hours of equitation training would drop dramatically in the wake of the army's rapid expansion beginning under Hitler in 1934–1935. Under the Nazi régime's conscription regulations, the initial term of service was only one year. That fact, when combined with the stipulation that only 10 percent of cavalrymen could be volunteers, meant that the overwhelming majority of horsemen were short-term draftees who had to be taught hurriedly to ride well and shoot accurately. See Richter, *Cavalry of the Wehrmacht*, 23. Limiting volunteers to 10 percent of the whole would seem to indicate that the army did not want to allow for a disproportionate share of highly motivated young men going to the mounted arm. Comparisons of volunteer totals for other *Waffengattungen*, if available, would be useful in this context. The present work draws no conclusions on this point.

19. Ibid.

20. Ibid., 199. In the *levade* the horse rears to an angle of about 40–45 degrees with the hind feet planted firmly and square. The Horseman's Badge depicted the horse at a somewhat lower degree of inclination.

21. Poseck, *The German Cavalry*, 226, 229.

22. Corum, *The Roots of Blitzkrieg*, 46; cavalry's divisional TOE of 1923 on 209; Poseck, *The German Cavalry*, 227.

23. Ibid., 47, 79, 123–124; http://www.neufahrland-online.de/seite6.htm *Chronik des Dorfes Krampnitz* (7 February 2007).

24. On Hans Joachim von Ziethen, cf. Theodor Fontane, *Wanderungen durch die mark Brandenburg. Erster Band. Die Grafschaft Ruppin*, ed. Edgar Gross (München: Nymphenburger Verlagshandlung, 1963), 15–25. While "Hannover" is the spelling of the German city's name, the widely accepted (but not universal) English rendering of "Hanoverian" is used throughout to indicate the breed.

25. Corum, *The Roots of Blitzkrieg*, 69.

26. Matthew Cooper, *The German Army 1933–1945* (London: Scarborough House, 1978), 135.

27. Ibid., 136.

28. Corum, *The Roots of Blitzkrieg*, 66. See 55–66 for the various schools of thought in the army regarding the most appropriate form of warfare for Germany. For offensive and defensive war plans, see 172–174.

29. Zamoyski, *The Battle for the Marchlands*, 25–26; Poseck, *The German Cavalry*, 231.

30. Corum, *The Roots of Blitzkrieg*, 71.

31. Ibid.

32. Ibid.

33. Corum, *The Roots of Blitzkrieg*, 184.

34. Ibid., 186.

35. Ibid., 187.

36. Ibid., 177.

37. Deist, *The Wehrmacht and German Rearmament*, 10.

38. Ibid., 12–17; Corum, *The Roots of Blitzkrieg*, 193–194, 196–197.

39. Corum, *The Roots of Blitzkrieg*, 197.

Chapter 5: The Field of Mars

1. Paul Louis Johnson, *Horses of the German Army in World War II* (Atglen, PA: Schiffer, 2006), 125. Johnson reproduces the U.S. Army Military History Institute's postwar publication MS#P-090 on horses in the German army. Various period illustrations indicated that the officer's saber had a less dramatic curvature to the blade than the enlisted man's.

2. See the illustration and caption in Klaus Richter, *Weapons and Equipment of the German Cavalry 1935–1945* (Atglen, PA: Schiffer, 1995), 3. Bayonet in author's collection and illustrated in ibid., 126.

3. Ibid., 5. See also Ian Hogg, "Small Arms," in I. C. B. Dear and M. R. D. Foot, eds., *The Oxford Companion to World War II* (Oxford: Oxford University Press, 1995), 1013–1016.

4. Richter, *Weapons and Equipment of the German Cavalry 1935–1945*, 6; Corum, *The Roots of Blitzkrieg*, 104; Zamoyski, *The Battle for the Marchlands*, 27. On the MG 01, see *Handbook of the German Army (Home and Colonial) 1912 (Amended to 1914)*, 118. The all-up weight of the earlier weapon, with water jacket and mounting sledge, was fully 176 pounds. Thus the MG 08 still weighed in at nearly 150 pounds, not including the limber, ammunition, and other ancillary equipment.

5. Corum, *The Roots of Blitzkrieg*, 104.

6. On the MG 34 and MG 42, see Hogg, "Small Arms," as in note 3 above. Transport details and supporting illustrations in Richter, *Weapons and Equipment of the German Cavalry 1935–1945*, 7–8.

7. Charles B. MacDonald, *Company Commander*, intro. Dennis Showalter (New York: History Book Club, 2006), xiv. The quotation is from Showalter.

8. Http://www.lexikon-der-wehrmacht.de/Waffen/Infanteriegeschütze-R.htm (30 January 2007).

9. Ibid.; Richter, *Weapons and Equipment of the German Cavalry 1935–1945*, 18; David Stone, *Fighting for the Fatherland: The Story of the German Soldier From 1648 to the Present Day*, foreword Richard Holmes (Washington, D.C.: Potomac Books, 2006), 321. "Gypsy artillery" in Klaus Christian Richter, *Cavalry of the Wehrmacht 1941–1945* (Atglen, PA: Schiffer, 1995), 114.

10. Ibid. On the cavalry's reorganization, see below.

11. Richter, *Weapons and Equipment of the German Cavalry 1935–1945*, 18–19.

12. As demonstrated below, bicycle-mounted formations would also become integral to the later cavalry formations of the *Waffen*-SS. The SS Cavalry Brigade and the subsequent SS Cavalry Division would include an entire bicycle-mounted battalion officially tasked with reconnaissance duties.

13. Table XIII, "Livestock and Dairy Production," in "Germany," *Encyclopedia Britannica* 10 (Chicago: University of Chicago Press, 1947), 245; Richter, *Cavalry of the Wehrmacht 1941–1945*, 202. Richter indicates no source for his cited figure of 3,800,000.

14. Velsen-Zerweck and Schulte, *The Trakehner*, 5–6.

15. Ibid. See also Hans Graf von Lehndorff, *Meschen, Pferde, weites Land: Kindheits- und Jugenderinnerungen* (München: Verlag C. H. Beck, 2002), 63–64. Reference to Frederick the Great in David Blackbourn, *The Conquest of Nature: Water, Landscape, and the Making of Modern Germany* (New York: W. W. Norton, 2006), 5, 30. For the reference to 30,000 horses, see Clark, *Iron Kingdom*, 67. Another translation for "Trakehnen" is "burnt earth," as in land that has been cleared for farming by being burnt over.

16. Lehndorff, *Menschen, Pferde, weites Land*, 64.

17. Remount progression and Trakehner breeding objectives at *Bundesarchiv* (hereafter BA), *Pferde im Einsatz bei Wehrmacht und Waffen-SS. Pferderassen: Ostpreuße. Vorschrift: Das Truppenpferd von 1938*. www.bundesarchiv.de/aktuelles/aus_dem_archiv/galerie (3 October 2008).

18. Von Velsen-Zerweck and Schulte, *The Trakehner*, 15, 38. These heights are somewhat less than those preferred for both stallions/geldings and mares for the breed in the post-1945 period.

19. Sometimes referred to as the *Niedersachsenroß* ("Lower Saxon Horse"), the Hanoverian's history is so deeply intertwined with the region that, after 1945, it was made the heraldic animal of Lower Saxony. It appears as a white horse rampant on a red field.

20. Stenglin, *The Hanoverian*, 13.

21. Ibid., 15.

22. Ibid., 34.

23. Ibid., 35–36. Because of its relatively small size of 13–14 hands, the Haflinger was also well-suited as a packhorse for infantry and mountain troops. It would, for example, find a place (along with mules) in the post-1945 armies of the Federal Republic of Germany and Austria. On the Hanoverian's qualities relative to the Trakehner, see BA as in note 17 above.

24. Richter, *Cavalry of the Wehrmacht*, 23.

25. Stefanie Albrecht, "Prof. Dr. Hans Jöchle (1892–1968)—Ein Leben für den

Hufbeschlag. Quellen und Materialien zur Geschichte der tierärztlichen Fakultät der Universität München" (DMV diss., Tierärztliche Hochschule Hannover, 2006), 88. Hereafter *Ein Leben für den Hufbeschlag*; Johnson, *Horses of the German Army in World War II*, 55.

26. Johnson, *Horses of the German Army in World War II*, 55. In reality the total number of horses and mules actually used by the German armed forces of all arms during the course of World War II approached some three million. See the figure in Richter, *Cavalry of the Wehrmacht*, 202.

27. Johnson, *Horses of the German Army in World War II*, 55.

28. Ibid, 53. See the chart there.

29. Ibid.

30. Albrecht, *Ein Leben für den Hufbeschlag*, 166, 168.

31. Richter, *Cavalry of the Wehrmacht*, 202; Johnson, *Horses of the German Army in World War II*, 65.

32. Johnson, *Horses of the German Army in World War II*, 65, for numbers purchased/requisitioned. See Richter, *Cavalry of the Wehrmacht*, 202, for the latter figure and Johnson, 40, for horses' rations. For the figure of 25,000 Hungarian horses see R. L. DiNardo, *Mechanized Juggernaut or Military Anachronism? Horses and the German Army of World War II*, foreword Williamson Murray (New York: Greenwood Press, 1991), 12. On the *panje* horse, see Johnson, 13–14.

33. Cf. excerpts of speech of 3 February 1933 in Jeremy Noakes and Geoffrey Pridham, eds., *Documents on Nazism: 1919–1945* (New York: Viking, 1974), 508–509. See also Heinrich August Winkler, *Der lange Weg nach Westen* (München: Verlag C. H. Beck, 2002), 2:50–53; and Deist, *The Wehrmacht and German Rearmament*, 23.

34. Ian Kershaw, *Hitler 1889–1936: Hubris* (New York: W. W. Norton, 1998), 490–495.

35. Bruce Condell and David T. Zabecki, eds. and trans., *On the German Art of War: Truppenführung* (Boulder, CO: Lynne Rienner Publishers, 2001), 5, hereafter *Truppenführung*. Deist, *The Wehrmacht and German Rearmament*, 36, indicates that Hitler actually decided on the expansion in May 1934 with an effective date of October.

36. Condell and Zabecki, *Truppenführung*, 5; Deist, *The Wehrmacht and German Rearmament*, 37.

37. For this discussion, see Deist, *The Wehrmacht and German Rearmament*, 36–53, and 86–101.

38. Ibid., 38, quotation on 91.

39. *Truppenführung*, 1–3.

40. "The German way of war" is taken from Robert Citino, *The German Way of War: From the Thirty Years' War to the Third Reich* (Lawrence: University Press of Kansas, 2005). Throughout his work, Citino maintains that the enduring thought in Prussian and German military history is that those campaigns succeed best that are "short and lively" (*kurz und vives*) and led by the bold.

41. *Truppenführung*, 184, 187. Subsequent references to the numbered sections of *Truppenführung* are found in the main body of this text, indicated in parentheses.

42. Brain Bond and Martin Alexander, "Liddell Hart and De Gaulle: The Doctrines

of Limited Liability and Mobile Defense," in Peter Paret, ed., *Makers of Modern Strategy from Machiavelli to the Nuclear Age* (Princeton: Princeton University Press, 1986), 608.

43. Ibid., 606.

44. Ibid., 600.

Chapter 6: Bucking the Trend

1. Editorial by Paul Albert in *Western Horseman*, November–December 1939, cited in *Western Horseman*, 71, no. 1 (January 2006): 32. The November–December 1944 (!) issue of the same magazine featured an advertisement depicting the new Model M-5 Type Gas Mask for cavalry use.

2. Matthew Cooper, *The German Army, 1939–1945* (London: Scarborough House, 1978), 107–108.

3. Cf. P. M. H. Bell, *The Origins of the Second World War in Europe* (London: Pearson, 2007), 185.

4. See, for example, his remarks to assembled *Wehrmacht* officers of 22 August and 23 November 1939 in Ian Kershaw, *Hitler 1936–1945: Nemesis* (New York: W. W. Norton, 2000), 206–208, 276.

5. Michael Geyer, *Deutsche Rüstungspolitik 1860–1890*, ed. Hans-Ulrich Wehler (Frankfurt am Main: Suhrkamp Verlag, 1984), 125.

6. Ibid.

7. Jeremy Noakes and Geoffrey Pridham, eds., *Documents on Nazism 1919–1945* (New York: Viking Press, 1975), 375.

8. Ibid., 375–376.

9. Paul Kennedy, *The Rise and Fall of the Great Powers: Economic Change and Military Conflict From 1500 to 2000* (New York: Random House, 1987), 305. Figures for unemployment and GNP on 306.

10. Noakes and Pridham, *Documents on Nazism 1919–1945*, 380.

11. Ibid., 381.

12. Kennedy, *Rise and Fall*, 304–305.

13. Stone, *Fighting for the Fatherland*, 320. As it has done to this point, the present work treats the army's (and *Waffen-SS*') maneuver-unit cavalry formations and their various organic elements (brigades, regiments, and other subordinate formations) exclusively. The numerous mounted reconnaissance units of the army's infantry regiments and divisions, though drawn in 1939 from the prewar cavalry regiments, require and deserve a freestanding historical investigation.

14. Noakes and Pridham, *Documents on Nazism 1919–1945*, 390.

15. Ibid.

16. Ibid., 399.

17. Ibid., 401–412.

18. Louis L. Snyder, ed., *Hitler's Third Reich: A Documentary History* (Chicago: Nelson-Hall, 1981), 328.

19. Noakes and Pridham, *Documents on Nazism*, 413.

20. Gervase Phillips, "Scapegoat Arm: Twentieth-Century Cavalry in Anglophone Historiography," *The Journal of Military History*, 71, no. 1 (January 2007), 51; Keith Sword, "Poland," in I. C. B. Dear and M. R. D. Foot, eds., *The Oxford Companion to World War II* (Oxford: Oxford University Press, 1995), 900. The Polish army was authorized fourteen cavalry brigades, eleven of which were active in September 1939. See Kennedy, *The German Campaign in Poland (1939)*, 51–54.

21. Karl-Heinz Frieser, *The Blitzkrieg Legend: The 1940 German Campaign in the West*, ed. John T. Greenwood (Annapolis: Naval Institute Press, 2005), 17.

22. Richard Overy, *Why the Allies Won* (New York: W. W. Norton, 1995), 200.

23. Cf. Wilhelm Deist, *The Wehrmacht and German Rearmament*, 36–53, 91.

24. R. J. Overy, "Transportation and Rearmament in the Third Reich," *The Historical Journal*, 16 (June 1973), 391.

25. Cf. Martin van Creveld, *The Changing Face of War: Lessons of Combat From the Marne to Iraq* (New York: Presidio, 2006), 7–8.

26. Overy, "Transportation and Rearmament in the Third Reich," 392.

27. Ibid., 402, 405 and note 89 there.

28. Ibid., 409.

29. DiNardo, *Mechanized Juggernaut or Military Anachronism?*, 9-10; Gerhard Rempel, *Hitler's Children: The Hitler Youth and the SS* (Chapel Hill: The University of North Carolina Press, 1989), 22. Interestingly, the Nazi Party also had a formation called the National Socialist Mounted (*Reiter*) Corps (NSRK). It was intended to "train young men to the standard of cavalry recruits of six months' service before they join the army." See *Handbook of the German Army* (Nashville, TN: The Battery Press, 1996), 216–217. First published in 1940, this source indicates no degree of effectiveness of the NSRK.

30. Frieser, *The Blitzkrieg Legend*, 23.

31. Ibid., 22.

32. Deist, *The Wehrmacht and German Rearmament*, 108–109; Geyer, *Deutsche Rüstungspolitik*, 154.

33. DiNardo, *Mechanized Juggernaut or Military Anachronism?*, 16–17.

34. Guderian's reminiscence as quoted in Frieser, *The Blitzkrieg Legend*, 33–34.

35. Richard Overy, "Total War II: The Second World War," in Charles Townshend, ed., *The Oxford Illustrated History of Modern War* (Oxford: Oxford University Press, 1997), 121.

36. Frieser, *The Blitzkrieg Legend*, 31–38.

37. Ibid., 33 and the useful diagram there. On reconnaissance detachments' TOEs see BA *Pferde im Einsatz bei Wehrmacht und Waffen-SS. Reiter Schwadron der Aufklärungs-Abteilung 157: Rast auf dem Vormarsch in Kapucany, östliche Slowakei 1939. www.bundesarchiv.de/aktuelles/aus_dem_archiv/galerie/oo172/index. html?index=0&id=3&nr=1. Handbook of the German Army 1940*, 43, 50. Overall, each infantry division's TOE carried approximately 1,743 saddle horses, 3,632 draft horses, and 1,133 horse-drawn vehicles. For these figures see, Johnson, *Horses of the German Army in World War II*, 148.

38. On the "German Weekly Newsreel" see Robert Edwin Herzstein, *The War That*

Hitler Won: The Most Infamous Propaganda Campaign in History (New York: G. P. Putnam's Sons, 1978), 223–258. See also *Signal: Years of Triumph 1940–42. Hitler's Wartime Picture Magazine*, ed. S. L. Mayer (New York: Prentice-Hall, 1978).

39. Mayer, *Signal: Years of Triumph 1940–42*, no page-numbers indicated.

40. See Kennedy, *The German Campaign in Poland (1939)*, 11, 23–25 for divisional comparisons. See the brigade's table of organization for September 1939 in Fowler, *Axis Cavalry in World II*, 7.

41. Kennedy, *The German Campaign in Poland (1939)*, 61 and the chart, as well as the brigade's initial mission, at 74–75.

42. Ibid., 79–82 for dispositions of the Polish cavalry on Third Army's front.

43. Citino, *The German Way of War*, 261; Kennedy, *The German Campaign in Poland (1939)*, 81.

44. Kennedy, *The German Campaign in Poland* (1939), 98.

45. On this tradition's continuity see Isabel V. Hull, *Absolute Destruction: Military Culture and the Practices of War in Imperial Germany* (Ithaca: Cornell University Press, 2005), here 163.

46. F. W. von Mellenthin, *Panzer Battles: A Study of the Employment of Armor in the Second World War*, trans. H. Betzler (Norman: University of Oklahoma Press, 1956), 3. Mellenthin served with the Seventh Cavalry Regiment from 1924 to 1935 and occupied the Intelligence billet in the German Third Corps during the invasion of Poland. He eventually rose to the position of chief of staff of Fourth Panzer Army and was captured by American troops on the Western Front in 1945. Hans von Luck, *Panzer Commander: The Memoirs of Colonel Hans von Luck*, intro. Stephen A. Ambrose (New York: Dell, 1989), 29.

47. M. K. Dziewanowski, *War At Any Price: World War II in Europe, 1939–1945*, 2nd ed. (Englewood Cliffs, NJ: Prentice Hall, 1991), 62, 68 and note 11 on the latter page. For a recent example of the story of the Polish cavalry's putative charge against the panzers, see Frieser, *The Blitzkrieg Legend*, 19. Frieser cites Heinz Guderian's memoirs. On the encircled Polish cavalry, see Norman Davies, *No Simple Victory: World War II in Europe, 1939–1945* (New York: Viking, 2006), 77–78.

48. See Citino, *The German Way of War*, 364, note 57. Interestingly, this Polish arrangement would later be echoed in the SS Cavalry Division's retention of an assault-gun detachment on its own TOE.

49. "Germans Cut Off Polish Corridor," *New York Times*, 5 September 1939, 12.

50. On the Polish 18th Lancers, see Citino, *The German Way of War*, 259 and note 57 on 364.

51. Heinz Guderian, *Panzer Leader*, foreword B. H. Liddell Hart, trans. Constantine Fitzgibbon (Costa Mesa, CA: Noontide Press, 1988), 71. Guderian reports (72) that the *Pomorske* Brigade had attacked German tanks "with lances and swords" and "in ignorance of [the tanks'] nature." He does not, however, cite any source from any unit for this information in the English edition of the work. In many subsequent retellings of Polish cavalry charges against tanks, Guderian's own remarks are cited as the source of the story.

52. Ian Kershaw, *Fateful Choices: Ten Decisions That Changed the World 1940–1941* (New York: Penguin, 2008), 64.

53. *Erfahrungsbericht der 1. Kavallerie-Division über den Einsatz in Holland und Frankreich, 13 August 1940*, in NARA Microfilm Publication T-315, Roll 83, Frame 336. Coincidentally, Friesland was the Dutch portion of the ancestral northwestern European breeding area for the Friesian horse. The Friesian was also bred in the adjacent German region of Ostfriesen. Friesians were not unheard-of as light draft horses in the *Heer* during the World War II.

54. Ibid.

55. Ibid., Frame 337. The division's records do not indicate whether the dive-bombers at Kornwerderzand were Junkers Ju-87 *Stukas* or Henschel Hs-123 biplanes. The 88-mm gun detachment was not part of the cavalry division's establishment.

56. Ibid., Frame 338.

57. Ibid. The records consulted included no copies of communications from higher echelons criticizing the division's actions in the Netherlands.

58. Ibid., Frame 339.

59. Ibid.

60. Ibid.

61. Ibid., Frame 340. As the *Erfahrungsbericht* makes no mention of a mounted charge against the heights, the final assault presumably occurred on foot. No German casualties are recorded. *Reiter* (i.e., "rider" or "horse") regiments were those originally attached to the 1st Cavalry Brigade prior to the outbreak of war. *Kavallerie* (i.e., "cavalry") regiments were ones normally assigned to provide the mounted reconnaissance squadrons to the army's infantry divisions as per the army's prewar reorganization. Though both types rode, and though both certainly thought of themselves as true cavalrymen, the term *Reiter* carried a more traditional cachet and can be traced back at least as far as seventeenth-century Prussia. As noted in the previous chapter, the mounted reconnaissance elements of the army's infantry divisions merit a separate history and are not treated in the present work.

62. Ibid., Frame 341.

63. Ibid., Frames 341–342.

64. Ibid., Frame 342.

65. Ibid., Frames 342–343.

66. Ibid., Frame 343.

67. Ibid., Frame 344.

68. Ibid., Frame 345. The division's reports do not mention any resistance being offered by the French cavalrymen or whether any French horses were taken.

69. Ibid., Frame 346.

70. Ibid. The context of Feldt's emphasis in the original might reflect either defensiveness in the face of criticism or simply a cavalryman's enthusiasm. As above, the records consulted include no communications criticizing the division's performance.

71. Ibid.

72. Charles B. MacDonald, *The Last Offensive, United States Army in World War II-- The European Theater of Operations*, ed. Maurice Matloff (Washington, D.C.: Center of Military History, 1973–1993), 22.

73. Ibid. For German nationalists on the Ardennes, in this case Ernst Moritz Arndt, see Winkler, *Der lange Weg nach Westen*, I:64–65.

74. *NS Archiv, Dokumente zum Nationalsozialismus: Tagebuch Generaloberst Ritter von Leeb*, 3 October 1939. http://www.ns-archiv.de/krieg/1939/leeb/ (12 May 2008).

75. Robert A. Doughty, "French Operational Art 1888–1940," in Krause and Phillips, *Historical Perspectives on the Operational Art*, 95, 100–101. See the table of organization of the French 5th Light Cavalry Division in Frieser, *The Blitzkrieg Legend*, 128.

76. Quoted in Alistair Horne, *To Lose a Battle: France: 1940* (New York: Penguin, 1969), 270–271.

77. Ibid., 271.

78. Ibid., 294–295.

79. Frieser, *The Blitzkrieg Legend*, 133–136, here specifically 136.

Chapter 7: Barbarossa

1. A very useful general examination of Operation Barbarossa is to be found in Earl F. Ziemke and Magna E. Bauer, *Moscow to Stalingrad: Decision in the East* (Washington, D.C.: Center of Military History, 1987).

2. Blackbourn, *The Conquest of Nature: Water, Landscape, and the Making of Modern Germany*, 251. Renderings of "Pripet" are many and varied, "Pripyat" being also commonly used in English.

3. Ibid. See also *Terrain Factors in the Russian Campaign*, facsimile ed. (Washington, D.C.: Center of Military History, 1982, 1986), 4–5, 28–43; reference to numbers of bridges at 29.

4. National Defense University, "Military Geography for Professionals and the Public: 6. Regional Peculiarities." http://ndu.edu/.../milgeoch6.html (29 October 2008).

5. Ibid.

6. *Terrain Factors in the Russian Campaign*, 9, 29.

7. Ziemke and Bauer, *Moscow to Stalingrad*, 14.

8. *Rear Area Security in Russia: The Soviet Second Front Behind German Lines*, "Chapter 5: The Front Behind the Front." Department of the Army Pamphlet 20-240 (Washington, D.C., 1951). http://www.history.army.mil/books/wwii/20240/20-2403.html (4 November 2008).

9. Glantz and House, *When Titans Clashed*, 66. On the general state of the Red Army in 1941, see Ziemke and Bauer, *Moscow to Stalingrad*, 7–13.

10. Ibid. Stalin could and did allow his soldiers' lives to be thrown away even more recklessly than Hitler. In a latter-day Charge of the Light Brigade, the 44th Mongolian Cavalry Division attacked the German 106th Infantry Division across an open, snow-covered field near Klin on 16 November 1941 during the Soviet counteroffensive against

German forces threatening Moscow. Two thousand cavalrymen and their horses were killed. The Germans suffered no recorded casualties. See ibid., 83.

11. From German translation, dated 15 August 1941, of Timoshenko's *Order to the Troops of the West Front No. 0109* in NARA Microfilm Publication T-315, Roll 78, Frame 47.

12. Glantz and House, *When Titans Clashed*, 56.

13. Ibid.

14. Ziemke and Bauer, *Moscow to Stalingrad*, 3.

15. *Tätigkeitsbericht* 22–29 June 1941 in NARA Microfilm Publication T-315, Roll 82, Frames 1397–1399. See also the report dated 27 June 1941 at Frame 36. The SS Division *Das Reich* and the Army's 10th ID (Motorized) were operating in the same area and further added to the traffic congestion on the *Panzer-Rollbahn*. Reference to marching infantry's difficulties in *Terrain Factors in the Russian Campaign*, 29.

16. *Kurzer Bericht über Aufträge der XXIV.Pz.Korps an 1.K.D. u. ihre Durchführung in der Zeit vom 22.6.–30.6.1941*. NARA Microfilm Publication T-315, Roll 82, Frames 80–87. Subsequent reports hereafter labeled simply *Kurzer Bericht* or *Bericht*, as appropriate, with dates and Frame numbers.

17. Ibid.

18. Ibid. Losses among the division's horses were not indicated.

19. Undated [June 1941?] veterinary circular. NARA Microfilm Publication T-315, Roll 82, Frames 1256–1257.

20. *Erfassungskommandos*. 5 July 1941. NARA Microfilm Publication T-315, Roll 82, Frame 1266.

21. Ziemke and Bauer, *Moscow to Stalingrad*, 14; *Terrain Factors in the Russian Campaign*, 6–7.

22. *Kurzer Bericht*, 1. – 31.7.1941. NARA Microfilm Publication T-315, Roll 82, Frames 185–197. Bobruisk lies on the northeastern edge of the Pripet Marshes. The surrounding forests in 1941 were thus frequently boggy and subject to localized flooding.

23. Ibid. The cavalrymen readily acknowledged the close-air support (CAS) provided—without being ordered—by the 51st Fighter Wing whose airfield the horsemen had earlier guarded. The troopers noted that such CAS was very useful in suppressing Soviet artillery. Their crossing of the Dnepr was slightly in advance of the one made by XLIII and LIII Infantry Corps farther downstream near Rogachev. On that crossing, see *Terrain Factors in the Russian Campaign*, 21–27. On 2nd Panzer Group at the Dnepr, see Glantz and House, *When Titans Clashed*, 58–59.

24. *Kurzer Bericht*, 1. – 31.7.1941. NARA Microfilm Publication T-315, Roll 82, Frames 196–197.

25. *Bericht*, 1.8.–2.9.1941. NARA Microfilm Publication T-315, Roll 82, Frames 324–343. All details of divisional horses' status on 10 August 1941 taken from Frame 340. Curiously, the *panje* horses are referred to as having been "hired" (*ermieteten*) before the campaign started. The record does not make clear whether the *panje* horses in

question were from occupied Poland or, much more likely, ones acquired between the operations in the Pripet Marshes and crossing of the Dnepr.

26. Ibid., Frame 324.

27. Ibid.

28. Ibid., Frame 325.

29. Ibid., Frame 327. See note 23 above. The so-called Gomel Pocket had been formed by the combined pressure of XLIII and LIII Infantry Corps attacking eastward across the Dnepr at Rogachev while XIII Corps, now the 1st Cavalry Division's parent formation, drove south and east from Mogilev. Thus Soviet forces were caught between the river, Rogachev, and Gomel.

30. Ibid., Frame 328.

31. Ibid., Frames 329–331. Just as the German cavalrymen were executing this striking advance, so Soviet cavalry were doing the same at about the same time but in the opposite direction. The very Twenty-First Army whose staff the German troopers almost bagged near Gomel had earlier ordered a deep cavalry raid northwesterly across the Denpr in an attempt to disrupt German forces around Bobruisk. See Glantz and House, *When Titans Clashed*, 59.

32. Ibid., Frame 331.

33. Ibid., Frame 332.

34. Ibid., Frame 334.

35. Ibid., Frames 334–337. The division's reassignment to 2nd Panzer Group was its seventh in total since 31 July.

36. Ibid., Frame 337.

37. All of the following after-action figures and assessments of the division's personnel, horses, equipment, status, and so on, from ibid., Frames 338–343. The report from which this material comes had what appears to have been an unusually large distribution list including, among others: Army High Command (OKH); the OKH's operations staff; Army Group Center; Fourth Army; 2nd Panzer Group; and the School for Rapid Deployment Troops (*Schule der schnellen Truppen*) at Krampnitz. "*Schnell*" in this case refers to fast-moving, mobile troops, usually motorized or mechanized. Cavalry had been administratively regarded as *schnelle Truppen*. "Winning themselves to death" in Glantz and House, *When Titans Clashed*, 60. The panzer division in question here was same 18th Panzer that the Cavalry Division had earlier relieved.

38. Feldt wrote specifically of the "East Prussian horse" (*Ostpreuße*) in the singular, but clearly seems to have been referring to all of the division's horses bred there. The division would naturally have drawn most of its mounts and draft horses from the province and *Wehrkreis* in which it was based.

39. All march-order details dated 13 September 1941 and taken from *Anordnungen für das Überholen und Kreuzen von mot.—und berittenen—Verbänden!* NARA Microfilm Publication T-315, Roll 78, Frames 4–5. On the larger situation regarding horses' condition on the Eastern Front and efforts to spare them, see the Fourth Army Order of 18 September 1941 in Appendix A.

40. *Tagesbefehl*. 13 September 1941. NARA Microfilm Publication T-315, Roll 78, Frame 13.

41. Untitled report of the divisional IIa (Adjutant) dated 15 September 1941 citing Felber's commendation of 26 August. NARA Microfilm Publication T-315, Roll 78, Frame 29. See Frame 45 for the following quotations regarding partisans and the report dated 18 September 1941.

42. See NARA Microfilm Publication T-315, Roll 78, various Frames from 76 to 171 unless otherwise specified. For general situation at the Desna and in Bryansk's environs, see *Terrain Factors in the Russian Campaign*, 18–20.

43. NARA Microfilm Publication T-315, Roll 78, Frame 171.

44. Ibid.

45. Ibid, Frames 61, 147–148.

46. Unless otherwise indicated, all of the following material regarding the Cavalry Division's capabilities and organizational fate are taken from *Umwandlung der 1.K.D. zu einer Panzer-Division* in NARA Microfilm Publication T-315, Roll 82, Frames 344–350.

47. In Directive 32, "Preparations for the Period After Barbarossa," issued 11 June 1941, Hitler had indicated that some sixty divisions would remain for security duty in what would have been former Soviet territory. That sort of static service would likely not have suited the temperament of the Cavalry Division's soldiers or their ethos. Directive cited in Ziemke and Bauer, *Moscow to Stalingrad*, 15.

48. One has to be careful to avoid reading a feeling of petulance into Feldt's comments at this juncture in the documents.

49. Feldt's advocacy of equestrian sport as effective military training for officers recalls quite similar sentiments regarding polo as expressed at various times before 1939 in the U.S. Army's *Cavalry Journal*.

50. Unless otherwise noted, references to divisional operations and prevailing conditions for the period are taken from *Kurzer Bericht 31.8.–21.10.1941*, NARA Microfilm Publication T-315, Roll 82, Frames 596–606.

51. Glantz and House, *When Titans Clashed*, 80, indicate that the weather not only deprived German forces of their vaunted mobility but also forced mechanized divisions (and, by extension, any other motorized or mechanized elements, as in the 1st Cavalry Division) to use up their fuel at three times the planned rate on average.

52. *Tätigkeitsbericht 8.11.1941–29.4.1942*. NARA Microfilm Publication T-315, Roll 83, Frame 217.

53. Ibid., Frames 218–219.

54. Ibid., Frames 237, 240.

55. Ibid., Frames 239–255. Strikingly, even after the division's reorganization as 24th Panzer Division, daily activity reports still regularly indicated nearly 150 horses on the division's ration-strength. These were presumably draft horses.

Chapter 8: Hell's Outriders

1. Ludwig Hollweck, ed., *Unser München: München im 20. Jahrhundert. Erinnerungen und berichte, Bilder und Dokumente von 1900 bis heute* (München: Süddeutscher Verlag, 1967), 256. For illustrations of the parade's horses and riders see any of the numerous extant video clips on-line. On the Nazi aesthetic, see Joan L. Clinefelter, *Artists for the Reich: Culture and Race from Weimar to Nazi Germany* (New York: Berg, 2005).

2. Frederic Spotts, *Hitler and the Power of Aesthetics* (New York: The Overlook Press, 2003), 173, 184, 364.

3. John Keegan, *Waffen-SS: The Asphalt Soldiers* (New York: Ballantine, 1971), 8.

4. Ibid.

5. On the bonding power of atrocity when collectively committed, see Dave Grossman, *On Killing: The Psychological Cost of Learning to Kill in War and Society* (New York and Boston: Back Bay Books, 1996), 195–227.

6. On the evolution of the mounted SS, the *Waffen-SS*, and the honorific *Florian Geyer*, see below.

7. Charles W. Sydnor, *Soldiers of Destruction: The SS Death's Head Division, 1933–1945* (Princeton: Princeton University Press, 1977), 43–45 and note 36, 69.

8. Keegan, *Waffen-SS*, 62.

9. Heinz Höhne, *The Order of the Death's Head: The Story of Hitler's SS* (New York: Ballantine, 1971), 152–153.

10. Richard Evans, *The Third Reich in Power, 1933–1939* (New York: Penguin, 2005), 418–419.

11. Höhne, *The Order of the Death's Head*, 156.

12. *BA Pferde im Einsatz bei Wehrmacht und Waffen-SS. Beiblatt zur Pferde-Einberufung für Gemeinden 1937* and *SS-Totenkopf Kavallerieregiment 1: Ergänzungs-Einheiten 8.12.1940* www.bundesarchiv.de/aktuelles/aus_dem_archiv/galerie/00172/index.html?index=0&id=2&nr=1 (3 and 8 October 2008). On the general history of the *Waffen-SS* see Höhne, *The Order of the Death's Head*, 493–545, here 495, 513ff. On Fegelein's service see BA *Pferde im Einsatz bei Wehrmacht und Waffen-SS. Beiblatt zur Pferde-Einberufung für Gemeinden 1937* (2 and 8 October 2008). Different sources provide different dates of the establishment of the *SS-Totenkopf-Reiterstandarte*. Its activation was in any case in the autumn of 1939. For Hitler's statement of the missions of the SS-VT and SS-TV, see Bernd Wegner, "SS," in Dear and Foot, *The Oxford Companion to World War II*, 1048.

13. See BA link, note 12 above, for Fegelein's service. The more "proletarian" Brown Shirts also had a mounted arm, the *Reiter*-SA. Before his murder on Hitler's orders in 1934, the SA's commander, Ernst Röhm, was frequently to be seen mounted when reviewing Storm Troopers on parade.

14. Evans, *The Third Reich in Power*, 3; Höhne, *The Order of the Death's Head*, 156.

15. *Rede des Reichsführers 26 Juli 1944*, NARA Microfilm Publication T-354, Roll 116, Frames 3750099ff.

16. Ibid.

17. John Keegan, *Waffen-SS*, 73.

18. Ibid.

19. Curzio Malaparte, *The Volga Rises in Europe*, trans. David Moore (Edinburgh: Birlinn Limited, 1951), 27.

20. Timothy Snyder, *Bloodlands: Europe Between Hitler and Stalin* (New York: Basic Books, 2010).

21. Heinrich August Winkler, *Der lange Weg nach Westen*, I:246, 253–254, 336–343.

22. Malaparte, *The Volga Rises in Europe*, 78.

23. John M. Steiner, "Über das Glaubensbekenntnis der SS," in Karl Dietrich Bracher, Manfred Funke, Has-Adolf Jacobsen, eds., *Nationalsozialistische Diktatur 1933–1945* (Bonn: Bundeszentrale für politische Bildung, 1986), 208, 217. Darré's comment in Hermann Rauschning, *Hitler Speaks* (London: Thornton Butterworth, 1940), 40. On Hitler's and the Nazis' long-standing ambitions in the East, see Kershaw, *Fateful Choices*, 55–59. Snyder, *Bloodlands*, xiv, notes a figure of some 200,000 Poles shot by German and Russian occupiers between 1939 and 1941. The figure of 900,000 cited in the text is taken from Nicholas Stargardt, "Hitler in the Driving Seat," *Times Literary Supplement*, 8 October 2008 at http://entertainment.timesonline.co.uk/tol/arts_and_entertainment/the_tls (13 October 2008).

24. Blackbourn, *The Conquest of Nature*, 295.

25. Ibid.

26. Mark C. Yerger, *Riding East: The SS Cavalry Brigade in Poland and Russia 1939–1942* (Atglen, PA: Schiffer, 1996), 73ff. Yerger's book provides an interesting examination, usually in tabular fashion, of the early evolution of the SS' mounted formations. The text itself, however, should be used with a certain caution in that it does not always contain the requisite citations of primary sources. Given that caveat, Yerger's work is helpful for the period prior to the actual formation of the SS Cavalry Division in early 1942.

27. Ibid., 88, 91, 94. Yerger refers to "operational strength." His numbers and their context, however, support the view that he is referring to combat-strength only and not ration-strength.

28. Raul Hilberg, Review of *Wegbereiter der Shoah. Die Waffen-SS, der Kommandostab Reichsführer-SS und die Judenvernichtung*, by Martin Cüppers. http://www.uni-stuttgart.de/hing/lb/lbrez_hilberg.pdf (29 October 2008).

29. Ibid.

30. Heinrich August Winkler, *Der lange Weg nach Westen*, II:88. Winkler, II:88–89, shows clearly the confused lines of authority among high-ranking Nazi officials in the administration of the occupied territories. He also shows, however, the unanimity of purpose among these same officials regarding the extermination of the Jews.

31. Charles W. Sydnor, "On the Historiography of the SS," Simon Wiesenthal Museum of Tolerance Multimedia Learning Center Online. http://motlc.wisenthal.com/site/pp.asp (29 October 2008).

32. Yerger, *Riding East*, 44, 47, 53.

33. Ibid., 98–100.

34. Ibid. Hilberg, Review of *Wegbereiter der Shoah*, note 27 above, points out the German verb *abzutransportieren* ("transport away") in contrast to Yerger's somewhat more benign "evacuate" in discussing the fate of captured women and children.

35. Blackbourn, *The Conquest of Nature*, 277. See also Hilberg, note 28 above. Winkler, *Der lange Weg nach Westen*, II:88, notes one of Himmler's meetings on 14–15 August in Minsk where he also referred explicitly to an order directly from Hitler for the shooting of all Jews ("einen 'Führerbefehl über die Erschießung aller Juden'"). On the evolution of Hitler's decision-making process culminating in the "Final Solution," see the excellent treatment in Kershaw, *Fateful Choices*, 431–470.

36. Ibid. Hilberg, note 28 above, attributes the observation about the marshes' depth to Major (*Sturmbannführer*) Franz Magill, the commander of the 2nd *Reiter* Regiment's horse-mounted battalion. It is entirely conceivable that Magill's own comment could have found its way up the line via brigade commander Fegelein's report to the *Kommandostab Reichsführer-SS*.

37. Yerger, *Riding East*, 91.

38. Ibid., 100–104.

39. Ibid., 101. The HSSPFs in the occupied territories of Eastern Europe often called up policemen in battalion-strength from both the Order Police (*Ordnungspolizei*; ORPO) and the Security Police (*Sicherheitspolizei*; SIPO). Himmler's authority over both the SS and all German police gave him unfettered access to huge manpower reserves. His place in the Nazi hierarchy close to Hitler also ensured a steady flow of supplies and equipment to SS units, particularly after his appointment in 1944 as Commander of the Replacement Army in the wake of the attempted assassination of Hitler. Hilberg, note 28 above, indicates that police personnel and sometimes local militia were also involved in mass shootings. In his estimation, therefore, it sometimes becomes difficult to determine precisely which members of which units were carrying out extra-judicial killings.

40. Ibid., 104.

41. Ibid., 105.

42. Andrew Nagorski, *The Greatest Battle: Stalin, Hitler, and the Desperate Struggle for Moscow That Changed the Course of World War II* (New York: Simon & Schuster, 2007), 71. According to Nagorski, 73, as many as 667,364 soldiers of the Red Army had been rounded up by 10 October 1941 for "escaping from the front," 10,201 were shot, and 25,878 were kept under arrest; 632,486 were formed into new units, many of which were penal battalions used for tasks such as clearing mine fields by being marched through them.

43. Yerger, *Riding East*, 107, 122.

44. Ibid., 126.

45. Ibid.

46. Ibid., 127.

47. Ibid., 126.

48. Ibid., 129.

49. Nagorski, *The Greatest Battle*, 107–109; Peter Young, ed., *Atlas of the Second World War* (New York: Paragon, 1979), 86–87. See Yerger, *Riding East*, 130–131, for illustrations of the barges and the occasionally ramshackle rafts used by the SS horsemen to ferry themselves and their mounts across the Dnepr. Retreating Russian forces had blown up the bridges spanning the river near Gomel.

50. Yerger, *Riding East*, 130–131.

51. See the map in Young, *Atlas of the Second World War*, 91.

52. Yerger, *Riding East*, 133. On Rzhev and its significance, see Nagorski, *The Greatest Battle*, 130, 134.

53. Yerger, *Riding East*. 134, and footnote 160 on that page.

54. Ibid., 132–133. Equine strength indicated on 141. See there also for the fact that, in the first week of November, the brigade lost another 3 horses dead while 102 were treated for sickness or wounds. Nagorski, *The Greatest Battle*, 130, notes that the first snows fell on the night of 6–7 October and, on 228, indicates the estimated mortality for draft horses at 1,000 per day. On *rasputiza*, see Glantz and House, *When Titans Clashed*, 80.

55. "Special Duties for the SS in 'Operation Barbarossa,' March 13, 1941." Documents of the Holocaust Part III. http://www.yadvashem.org/about_holocaust/documents/part3/doc169.html See Guderian's comments in Nagorski, *The Greatest Battle*, 130.

56. Yerger, *Riding East*, 128.

57. Ibid., 139–140.

58. Ibid., 142.

59. Nagorski, *The Greatest Battle*, 255.

60. Ibid., 254.

61. Yerger, *Riding East*, 150; Young, *Atlas of the Second World War*, 92–93.

62. Yerger, *Riding East*, 150, 157.

63. Glantz and House, *When Titans Clashed*, 89–90; Yerger, *Riding East*, 160.

64. Yerger, *Riding East*, 163–170.

65. Ibid., 171–172.

66. Ibid., 183.

67. Ibid., 193, 197. *Volksdeutsche* were recruited by the SS in areas of occupied Europe outside of Germany as defined by the country's borders of late 1938. Those borders encompassed both pre-1938 Austria and the Sudetenland. Consequently, *Volksdeutsche* were recruited in Hungary and elsewhere.

68. Ibid., 199.

69. Ibid., 199–201.

70. Ibid., 201. On battle-group (*Kampfgruppe*) "Zehender," see Yerger, 201–206.

71. Young, *Atlas of the Second World War*, 92.

72. Nagorski, *The Greatest Battle*, 287, 290–291. Farther to the northwest, the winter battles had also isolated 95,000 German troops and 20,000 horses in a pocket around the city of Demyansk. These forces included the SS Cavalry Brigade's sister unit, the

SS Death's Head Division, made up largely of former concentration-camp guards. See Sydnor, *Soldiers of Destruction*, 190–191.

Chapter 9: Pale Horsemen

1. *Vorgeschichte der SS-Kavallerie-Division*, NARA Microfilm Publication T-354, Roll 640, Frame 6. Hereafter *Vorgeschichte* with Frame number. The 3rd *Reiter* Regiment appears to have been largely absent from the division's operations throughout 1943. It would be used as cadre for a second, nominal SS cavalry division raised in 1944.

2. Yerger, *Riding East*, 208, shows the division's Order of Battle for September 1942.

3. *Vorgeschichte*, Frame 7.

4. *Tätigkeitsbericht zum Kriegstagebuch*, in NARA Microfilm Publication T-354, Roll 641, Frames 958–959, details instructional courses provided in the field to veterinary personnel.

5. "Special Instructions for the Area of Responsibility (*Arbeitsgebiet*) of Detachment VI," 22 April 1943, NARA Microfilm Publication T-354, Roll 642, Frames 913–920. *Abteilung VI* was the staff designation for the National Socialist Leadership Officer, essentially an indoctrination officer. This billet was set up only in March 1943.

6. Ibid.

7. *Vorgeschichte*, Frame 7. On the SS Cavalry School at Zamosc, see Yerger, *Riding East*, 207.

8. *Vorgeschichte*, Frame 7. Operations staff reports of 19 September 1942 in NARA Microfilm Publication T-354, Roll 641, Frame 6 under *Besprechungspunkte beim Chef des Stabes LIX Armee-Korps*.

9. NARA Microfilm Publication T-354, Roll 640, Frames 8–10.

10. *"Ausstellung der Pferdeausfälle seit Einsatzbeginn bis 30.9.42,"* NARA Microfilm Publication T-354, Roll 641, Frame 950. Horse transfers indicated by divisional veterinary staff in *Tätigkeitsbericht zum Kriegstagebuch* of 14 October and 1 December 1942 in ibid., Frames 952 and 958. Of the latter shipment, 183 horses had to be treated in gas tents (*Gaszellen*) for scabies-induced mange (*Räude*).

11. Ibid., Frame 951.

12. NARA Microfilm Publication T-354, Roll 640, Frame 16.

13. Ibid., Frame 64. VI Corps orders of 16 November 1942 in NARA Microfilm Publication T-354, Roll 641, Frame 466: *Generalkommando VI. A.K. Freimachung des Gefechtsgebietes*. The orders from VI Corps refer to a *K.L.* [*Kampflinie*; battle line].

14. NARA Microfilm Publication T-354, Roll 640, Frame 40.

15. *Kriegstagebuch. Die Quartiermeisterabteilung/Ib 11.9.1942 bis 20.12.1942*, NARA Microfilm Publication T-354, Roll 641, Frames 856–858.

16. Ibid., Frame 860.

17. *Tätigkeitsbericht zum Kriegstagebuch*, 14 October 1942 in ibid., Frame 951.

18. *Tätigkeitsbericht*, 15 November 1942 in ibid., Frame 957. See also ibid., Frame 958, *Tätigkeitsbericht* of 1 December 1942, for number of *panje* horses requested from

VI Corps. Regimental personnel transfers in *Aufstellung von winterbeweglichen Verbänden* in ibid., Frames 467–469. Interestingly, another major combat arm, the *Gebirgsjäger*, was also requisitioning large numbers of *panje* horses at about the same time for operations in the Caucasus Mountains. The Alpine Army Corps (*Gebirgs-Armeekorps*) had requisitioned some five-thousand *panje* horses in August 1942. These were in addition to the alpine troops' already assigned mules and Haflingers. See *Österreichs Bundesheer. Tragtiere im Einsatz*; www.bmlv.gv.at/truppendienst/ausgaben/artikel.php?id=375 (17 September 2008).

19. *Vermeidung von Kälteschäden*, in *Tätgkeitsbericht*, 15 November 1942, Frame 479.

20. *Gefechts- und Verpflegungsstärke SS-Kav.Division am 21.November 1942* in ibid., Frame 478.

21. *Zustandsmeldungen* to the Operations Officer of XXX Army Corps of 19 and 26 December 1942 in NARA Microfilm Publication T-354, Roll 642, Frames 422–423 and 430–431. Illustration of divisional emblem in ibid., Frame 428. A directive of 27 December 1942 noted that the divisional command would be requesting from *Reichsführer*-SS Himmler the awarding of a cuff band for the men's uniforms similar to those already worn by other *Waffen*-SS divisions. The cuff-title *Florian Geyer* would appear in 1943.

22. *Kriegstagebuch Nr. 2 SS-Kavallerie-Division* (hereafter *KTB*) of 22–29 December 1942, NARA Microfilm Publication T-354, Roll 642, Frames 10–20. *Terrain Factors in the Russian Campaign*, 42–43, notes that literally hundreds of thousands of German troops were tied down in anti-partisan operations, and that the partisans in some cases (as in the vicinity of Cholm) were not only able to conduct formal recruiting drives in their respective safe havens but also even live-fire artillery training exercises.

23. "Mit einem eigenmächtigen Umlegen solcher Gefangener ist der Truppe nicht gedient." *Besondere Weisungen an die Truppe*, 24 December 1942, NARA Microfilm Publication T-354, Roll 642, Frame 426.

24. *Gefangenen und Beute aus Unternehmen "Sternlauf,"* in daily activity reports to KTB in NARA Microfilm Publication T-354, Roll 642, Frame 758.

25. *Tagesbefehl an die deutschen Soldaten der Wehrmacht*, 1 January 1943, NARA Microfilm Publication T-354, Roll 644, Frame 538.

26. KTB, 15–17 January 1943, NARA Microfilm Publication T-354, Roll 642, Frames 54–59.

27. Ibid., Frames 54, 60–61.

28. Ibid., Frames 61–62, 73.

29. *Zur Schonung der Pferde, Kraft- und Pferdefahrzeuge*, 30 December 1942, NARA Microfilm Publication T-354, Roll 644, Frame 540.

30. *Verlustliste SS-Kav.Division (vom 21.12.1942–20.1.1943)*. This list actually records figures to 15 April 1943. NARA Microfilm Publication T-354, Roll 642, Frames 814–817.

31. *Divisionsbefehl zum Ordnen der Verbände und Umgliederung*, 18 March 1943, NARA Microfilm Publication T-354, Roll 642, Frames 639–656.

32. *Gefechts- und Verpflegungsstärke der SS-Kav.Division*, 1 April 1943, NARA Microfilm Publication T-354, Roll 642, Frames 818–819.

33. Michael R. Marrus, *The Nuremberg War Crimes Trial 1945–56* (New York: Bedford/St. Martin's, 1997), 165.

34. Heinz-Dietrich Löwe, "Resistance," in Dear and Foot, *Oxford Companion to World War II*, 1241.

35. *Terrain Factors in the Russian Campaign*, 42–43.

36. All of the following references come from the *Divisionsbefehl für die Vorbereitung des Einsatzes zur Bandenbekämpfung*, 18 April 1943, NARA Microfilm Publication T-354, Roll 642, Frame 903.

37. *Tätigkeitsberichte* and divisional orders of 16–17 April 1943 and 17 April 1943, respectively. NARA Microfilm Publication T-354, Roll 642, Frames 900–903.

38. *Stabsbefehl* of 17 April 1943, NARA Microfilm Publication T-354, Roll 642, Frame 898.

39. See Fegelein's Order of the Day of 14 May 1943 in Appendix C regarding the division's mounted traditions.

40. *Zustandsbericht*, 26 April 1943, NARA Microfilm Publication T-354, Roll 642, Frames 942–943.

41. Ibid. The 3rd Regiment was still not yet fully organized. Furthermore, its personnel would also subsequently be drawn upon for cadre for other SS units. On the veterinary threats to the division's horses see letter to the author of 20 November 2008 from Ms. Francine Ann Luker. At the time of writing, Luker served as Supervisor of Equine Management at Balsam Mountain Preserve in Jackson County, North Carolina and has more than forty years' experience in equine care.

42. *2. Divisionsbefehl zur Vorbereitung des Einsatzes zur Bandenbekämpfung*, 24 April 1943, NARA Microfilm Publication T-354, Roll 642, Frame 921. On treating mangy horses, see veterinary staff directives as indicated in note 10 above.

43. Ibid., Frames 922, 924–925.

44. *Divisionsbefehl*, 25 April 1943, NARA Microfilm Publication T-354, Roll 642, Frame 1093.

45. *Divisions-Befehl* [sic] *für das Unternehmen "Weichsel I,"* 11 May 1943, NARA Microfilm Publication T-354, Roll 642, Frames 996–999. Two *Einsatzgruppen* from the *Sicherheitsdienst* (SD) were also later attached for these operations. Units of the SD and the Security Police (SIPO) had routinely been assigned to shoot Jews ever since the beginning of Barbarossa. The SS Cavalry Division's records do not always indicate numbers of persons shot by the attached *Einsatzgruppen* or provide complete details of their operations. On the *Einsatzgruppen*, see Helmut Krausnick and Hans-Heinrich Wilhelm, *Die Truppe des Weltanschauungskrieges. Die Einsatzgruppen der Sicherheitspolizei und des SD 1938–1942* (Stuttgart: n.p.,1981).

46. See various after-action reports, divisional war-diary entries, etc., for the period in NARA Microfilm Publication T-354, Roll 642, Frames 1096–1188 and specifically the operational summary dated 10 June 1943 at Frame 1188.

47. *Verlustmeldung* of 10 June 1943 in NARA Microfilm Publication T-354, Roll 642, Frame 1191.

48. *Gefechtsbericht über den Einsatz der SS-Kav-Division im Unternehmen "Seydlitz" vom 25.6. bis 27.7.1943*, NARA Microfilm Publication T-354, Roll 643, Frames 27–29. For persons and material taken during Weichsel I and II, see Appendix B. The Operation Seydlitz noted here should not be confused with a similarly named operation undertaken by regular army units southwest of Rzhev in July 1942. See *Military Improvisations During the Russian Campaign*, facsimile ed. (Washington, D.C.: Center of Military History, 1983/1986), 11–17, 107.

49. *Verlustliste der SS-Kavallerie-Division für die Zeit vom 16.4. bis 18.8.1943*, NARA Microfilm Publication T-354, Roll 643, Frames 282–284.

50. *Tätigkeitsbericht vom 16.4. bis zum 18.8.1943*, NARA Microfilm Publication T-354, Roll 643, Frame 281. The document was dated 3 September 1943.

51. The division's records for the period from August to December 1943 are curious. While abundant, they lack the degree of completeness shown for similar records covering earlier periods. This is particularly the case regarding after-action reports.

52. See Wenger, "SS," in Dear and Foot, *The Oxford Companion to World War II*, 1046–1049, and the chart there of all of the *Waffen*-SS divisions, including units' national composition. The original 3rd *Reiter* Regiment of the *Florian Geyer* Division was actually used as cadre for a new SS cavalry division, the 22nd SS Volunteer Cavalry Division *Maria Theresa*. It was ultimately trapped and annihilated in Budapest along with most of the *Florian Geyer* Division in early 1945.

53. The phrase is Omer Bartov's. See his *Hitler's Army: Soldiers, Nazis, and War in the Third Reich* (New York and Oxford: Oxford University Press, 1992). On the chivalric presumptions, overlaid with Nazi fervor, of the SS Cavalry's wartime leaders see Appendix C.

Chapter 10: Last Recall

1. All details of the brigade's composition and operations from *Military Improvisations During the Russian Campaign*, 11–17.

2. Ibid. The brigade's losses in men and horses are not recorded. However, Russian losses included some 50,000 prisoners (approximately 83% of Soviet troops engaged), 230 tanks, 760 artillery pieces, and thousands of small arms. See ibid., 16.

3. Richter, *Weapons and Equipment of the German Cavalry 1935–1945*, 40. Other sources date the unit's establishment to 12 February 1943.

4. Böselager was killed in action in 1944. During the Cold War, the German *Bundeswehr* instituted The Boeselager [*sic*] Cup, an annual, later semiannual, competition among NATO armored reconnaissance units. See Lionel Ortiz and Brian Butcher, "Winners! U.S. Cavalry Squadrons Win and Place in Grueling NATO Reconnaissance Competition," *Armor* (November–December 1987), 21–24. http://www.benning.army.mil/armor/armormagazine/content/Issues/1987/ArmorNovemberDecember1987web.pdf

5. Richter, *Weapons and Equipment of the German Cavalry 1935–1945*, 40–42.

6. *Kriegstagebuch Nr. 1, Kav. Korps*. NARA Microfilm Publication T-314, Roll 25, Frame 7. Records of German Field Commands: Corps.

7. Ibid., Frame 9. The 3rd Cavalry Brigade would not officially be assigned to the Corps until August 1944.

8. By late 1943, the Operations Staff of OKW had drawn up plans for Operation Margarethe calling for the occupation of Hungary by German forces in the event that the country tried to desert the Axis. See Earl F. Ziemke, *Stalingrad to Berlin: The German Defeat in the East* (Washington, D.C.: Office of the Chief of Military History, 1968), 208, 287–288.

9. *Kriegstagebuch Nr. 1, Kav. Korps*. NARA Microfilm Publication T-314, Roll 25, Frame 9. Records of German Field Commands: Corps.

10. Ibid., Frames 10–11.

11. Ibid., Frames 11–17. On Pliev's forces, see David M. Glantz, *When Titans Clashed*, 190–191, 208. Pliev's combined cavalry-mechanized force would once more be in the 1st Cavalry Corps' area of operations during the Germans' failed attempt to relieve Budapest in January 1945.

12. *Kriegstagebuch* as in note 4 above, Frames 41–42.

13. Ibid., Frame 47.

14. Letter of 4 July 1944 in *Anlagen [sic] A zum Kriegstagebuch Nr. 2 Gen.-Kdo. Kav.-Korps* in NARA Microfilm Publication T-314, Roll 25, Frames 360–361.

15. Ibid., Frame 363.

16. Ibid., Frame 362.

17. Ibid., Frames 364–376, 415.

18. Ibid., Frames 423–424. Reference to 3rd Hussar Regiment at Frame 426.

19. Ibid., Frames 455, 461–462. Vattay's desire for his troops' withdrawal may well have been influenced not only by the more or less effective implementation of Operation Margarethe (see note 8 above) but also by the impending Soviet invasion of his country. On Margarethe's activation, see Ziemke, *Stalingrad to Berlin*, 287–288.

20. Ibid., Frames 508, 598, 600. The Panzer IV, a remarkably versatile prewar design, remained the workhorse of the panzer arm well into 1944.

21. Ibid., Frame 602.

22. Ibid., Frame 658.

23. Ibid., Frames 660–661, 688, 718. *Beurteilung der Lage am 13.7.44.* Orders for mobile defense at Frame 688.

24. Ibid., Frame 893, 920, 937, 948–949.

25. Ibid., Frame 954. Table of combat-strength for the Cavalry Brigade and the rest of the Corps at Frame 944.

26. *Anlagen zum Kriegstagebuch, Kav Korps, Ia. 1 Aug 1944–30 Sep 1944.* NARA Microfilm Publication T-314, Roll 25, Frames 986–988.

27. Ibid., Frame 1023.

28. Ibid., Frame 992.

29. Ibid. and Frames 996, 1001, 1011, 1020.

30. All of Harteneck's comments from his memo of 5 August 1944 in ibid., Frames 1009–1010.

31. *Korpsbefehl für 26.8.44*. NARA Microfilm Publication T-314, Roll 26, Frames 11–12.

32. Ibid., Frames 62–63.

33. Ibid. and Frame 77.

34. Ibid., Frame 88. *Abschrift Fernschreiben An Kav.Korps. 2.9.44*. Combat-strength for 2 September 1944 at Frame 90.

35. All of the following references from *Hebung der Abwehrbereitschaft*, 12 September 1944, in ibid., Frames 180–185.

36. Reference to equestrian training in ibid., Frame 186. Reference to 4th Brigade's horses at Frame 271.

37. Combat-strength and casualty figures in ibid., Frames 342 and 356, respectively.

38. *Kriegstagebuch Nr.3 mit Anlagen. Generalkdo.Kav.Korps/Ia mit Abt. IIa*. NARA Microfilm Publication T-314, Roll 27. Here Frames 4, 8.

39. Ibid., Frame 621.

40. Ibid., Frames 602–603. Commendatory order of 26 October 1944. For pointed requests for artillery ammunition (none was available) and for statements that units couldn't move for want of fuel, see Frames 18–20. Hitler's order of 29 October 1944 at Frame 578. Reference to feed cutoff at Frame 343.

41. Ibid., Frame 361. Cavalry and infantry strengths as of 20 November 1944.

42. Ibid., Frame 364. Directive of 20 November 1944.

43. See Appendix D.

44. Ibid., Frames 49–50.

45. Ibid. Frames 50–53, 137; Dear and Foot, *The Oxford Companion to World War II*, 448. The Cavalry Corps' records in the National Archives end 31 December 1944.

46. See date of OKH's orders in Richter, *Weapons and Equipment of the German Cavalry, 1933–1945*, 42.

47. Helmut Heiber and David M. Glantz, *Hitler and His Generals: Military Conferences 1942–1945* (New York: Enigma Books, 2003), 581 and note 1570.

48. Ziemke, *Stalingrad to Berlin*, 435, 448–449. German casualty figures at Budapest in Dear and Foot, *The Oxford Companion to World War II*, 169.

49. Heiber and Glantz, *Hitler and His Generals*, 685.

50. Ibid., 1117, note 1968.

51. Ibid., and page 700; Hanson W. Baldwin, "West Front Vanishes," *New York Times*, 10 April 1945, 6. ProQuest Historical Newspapers The *New York Times* (1857–2006). http://0-proquest.umi.com.wncln.wncln.org. See also "Round-Up in the Reich" and "Soviet Armies Link Up for Push on Prague as Vienna Falls," *New York Times*, 11 and 14 April 1945, 22 and 1, respectively, at the same site (2 December 2009). Ziemke, *Stalingrad to Berlin*, 452–465.

52. Richter, *Weapons and Equipment of the German Cavalry*, 42; "Cleaning Up In Austria," *The* (London) *Times*, 17 May 1945, 4. http://0-infotrac.galegroup.com.wncln.wncln.org (3 December 2009). The records consulted do not indicate the Cavalry

Corps' strength at the time of the surrender and are somewhat fragmentary. A nonscholarly source provides the figures noted in the text. At first glance, the number of horses seems high. Nevertheless, the totals correspond to last-ditch efforts to reinforce the southern armies for Operation Spring Awakening. Civilian reportage is corroborative, and Ziemke, *Stalingrad to Berlin*, 498, notes that German troops in May 1945 still totaled 430,000.

Epilogue

1. Clark, *Iron Kingdom*, 67; Jan Morris, *Spain* (New York: Oxford University Press, 1979), 132.

2. "Tragtiere im Einsatz." *Truppendienst*, Folge 287, Ausgabe 5/2005 (Wien: Bundes-ministerium für Landesverteidigung, 2005). www.bmlv.gv/truppendienst/ausgaben/artikel.php?id=375 (17 September 2008). Hereafter "Tragtiere im Einsatz."

3. "Pferde im Einsatz bei Wehrmacht und Waffen-SS." www.bundesarchiv.de/aktu-elles/aus_dem_archiv/galerie/00172/index.html (17 September 2008).

4. Ibid.

5. George C. Marshall, *Victory Report On the Winning of the War in Europe and the Pacific* (Washington, D.C.: War Department, 1945), 98.

6. Ibid.

7. Ibid., 99–100.

8. Overy, "Transportation and Rearmament in the Third Reich," 406.

9. Shelby L. Stanton, *Anatomy of a Division: The 1st Cav in Vietnam* (New York: Warner Books, 1987), 7.

10. "Die Gebirgstragtiere der Bundeswehr." www.bundeswehr.de/portal/a/bwde/streitkraefte/heer (16 September 2008).

11. Letter to the author of 7 July 2009 from the PAMTC's Public Affairs Officer.

12. Ibid.

13. "Tragtiere im Einsatz."

14. Ibid.

15. Douglas Barrie, "Tornado Watch," *Aviation Week and Space Technology*, 26 February 2007, 68.

16. See Doug Stanton, *Horse Soldiers: The Extraordinary Story of a Band of U.S. Soldiers Who Rode to Victory in Afghanistan* (New York: Scribner, 2009), here 55.

17. Lance Benzel, "Ft. Carson Special Forces train on horseback," *Army Times*, 8 September 2010. www.armytimes.com/news/2010/09/ap-special-forces-train-on-horseback-090710/

18. Citino, *The German Way of War*, 302–303.

19. Ibid., 303.

20. The reference is, of course, to General Ulysses S. Grant's observation on the Confederacy. See E. B. Long, ed., *Personal Memoirs of U.S. Grant* (New York: Da Capo Press, 1952/1982), 555–556.

Primary Sources

Divisionsbefehl zur Vorbereitung des Einsatzes zur Bandenbekämpfung. 24 April 1943. NARA Microfilm Publication T-354, Roll 642.

Albrecht, Stefanie. "Prof. Dr. Hans Jöchle (1892–1968)—Ein Leben für den Hufbeschlag. Quellen und Materialien zur Geschichte der tierärztlichen Fakultät der Universität München." DMV diss., Tierärztliche Hochschule Hannover, 2006.

Anlagen [sic] *A zum Kriegstagebuch Nr. 2 Gen.-Kdo. Kav.-Korps.* Letter of 4 July 1944 in NARA Microfilm Publication T-314, Roll 25.

Anlagen zum Kriegstagebuch, Kav Korps, Ia. 1 Aug 1944–30 Sep 1944. NARA Microfilm Publication T-314, Roll 25.

Anordnungen für das Überholen und Kreuzen von mot. —und berittenen —Verbänden! NARA Microfilm Publication T-315, Roll 78.

"Ausstellung der Pferdeausfälle seit Einsatzbeginn bis 30.9.42." NARA Microfilm Publication T-354, Roll 641.

Bericht, 1.8.–2.9.1941. NARA Microfilm Publication T-315, Roll 82.

Besondere Weisungen an die Truppe. 24 December 1942. NARA Microfilm Publication T-354, Roll 642.

Besprechungspunkte beim Chef des Stabes LIX Armee-Korps. (Staff reports of 19 September 1942). NARA Microfilm Publication T-354, Roll 641.

Deutschland Lexikon. Organizationsstruktur der SS. SS und die Wehrmacht and *Umstrukturierungen nach 1941.* http://lexikon.umkreisfinder.de/organizationsstruktur_der_ss

Die Gebirgstragtiere der Bundeswehr. www.bundeswehr.de/portal/a/bwde/streitkraefte/heer

Divisions-Befehl [sic] *für das Unternehmen "Weichsel I."* 11 May 1943. NARA Microfilm Publication T-354, Roll 642.

Divisionsbefehl für die Vorbereitung des Einsatzes zur Bandenbekämpfung. 18 April 1943. NARA Microfilm Publication T-354, Roll 642.

Divisionsbefehl zum Ordnen der Verbände und Umgliederung. 18 March 1943. NARA Microfilm Publication T-354, Roll 642.

Erfahrungsbericht der 1. Kavallerie-Division über den Einsatz in Holland und Frankreich, 13 August 1940. NARA Microfilm Publication T-315, Roll 83.

Erfassungskommandos. 5 July 1941. NARA Microfilm Publication T-315, Roll 82.

Gefangenen und Beute aus Unternehmen "Sternlauf." NARA Microfilm Publication T-354, Roll 642.

Gefechtsbericht über den Einsatz der SS-Kav-Division im Unternehmen "Seydlitz" vom 25.6. bis 27.7.1943. NARA Microfilm Publication T-354, Roll 643.

Gefechts- und Verpflegungsstärke der SS-Kav.Division. 1 April 1943. NARA Microfilm Publication T-354, Roll 642.

Generalkommando VI. A.K. Freimachung des Gefechtsgebietes. (VI Corps orders of 16 November 1942). NARA Microfilm Publication T-354, Roll 641.

Grundsätzliches über Kavallerieführung. 5 November 1944. NARA Microfilm Publication T-314, Roll 27, Frames 499–503.

Kriegstagebuch. Die Quartiermeisterabteilung/Ib 11.9.1942 bis 20.12.1942. NARA Microfilm Publication T-354, Roll 64.

Kriegstagebuch Nr. 1. Kav. Korps. Records of German Field Commands: Corps. NARA Microfilm Publication T-314, Roll 25.

Kriegstagebuch Nr. 2 SS-Kavallerie-Division. 22–29 December 1942. NARA Microfilm Publication T-354, Roll 642.

Kriegstagebuch Nr. 3 mit Anlagen. Generalkdo.Kav.Korps/Ia mit Abt. IIa. NARA Microfilm Publication T-314, Roll 27.

Kurzer Bericht über Aufträge der XXIV.Pz.Korps an 1.K.D. u. ihre Durchführung in der Zeit vom 22.6.–30.6.1941. NARA Microfilm Publication T-315, Roll 82.

Kurzer Bericht 1.–31.7.1941. NARA Microfilm Publication T-315, Roll 82.

Kurzer Bericht 31.8.–21.10.1941, NARA Microfilm Publication T-315, Roll 82.

Military Improvisations During the Russian Campaign, facsimile ed. Washington, D.C.: Center of Military History, 1986.

National Defense University, "Military Geography for Professionals and the Public: 6. Regional Peculiarities." http://ndu.edu/.../milgeoch6.html

NS Archiv, Dokumente zum Nationalsozialismus: Tagebuch Generaloberst Ritter von Leeb, 3 October 1939. http://www.ns-archiv.de/krieg/1939/leeb/

Order to the Troops of the [Red Army's] *West Front No. 0109* in NARA Microfilm Publication T-315, Roll 78.

Österreichs Bundesheer. Tragtiere im Einsatz. www.bmlv.gv.at/truppendienst/ausgaben/artikel.php?id=375

Overview of command structure of the *Reichsheer* of the Weimar period and the *Heer* after 1935. http:www.bundesarchiv.de/php/bestaende_findemittel/bestaendeuebersicht

Pferde im Einsatz bei Wehrmacht und Waffen-SS. www.bundesarchiv.de/aktuelles/aus_
dem_archiv/galerie/00172/index.html

*Pferde im Einsatz bei Wehrmacht und Waffen-SS. Beiblatt zur Pferde-Einberufung für
Gemeinden 1937* and *SS-Totenkopf Kavallerieregiment 1: Ergänzungs-Einheiten
8.12.1940* www.bundesarchiv.de/aktuelles/aus_dem_archiv/galerie/00172/
index.html?index=0&id=2&nr=1

*Pferde im Einsatz bei Wehrmacht und Waffen-SS. Pferderassen: Ostpreuße. Vorschrift: Das
Truppenpferd von 1938.* www.bundesarchiv.de/aktuelles/aus_dem_archiv/galerie

*Pferde im Einsatz bei Wehrmacht und Waffen-SS. Reiter Schwadron der Aufklärungs-Abteilung
157: Rast auf dem Vormarsch in Kapucany, östliche Slowakei 1939. www.bundesarchiv.
de/aktuelles/aus_dem_archiv/galerie/oo172/index.html?index=0&id=3&nr=1*

Rear Area Security in Russia: The Soviet Second Front Behind German Lines, "Chapter
5: The Front Behind the Front." Department of the Army Pamphlet 20-240.
Washington, D.C., 1951). http://www.history.army.mil/books/wwii/20240/20-
2403.html

Rede des Reichsführers 26 Juli 1944, NARA Microfilm Publication T-354, Roll 116.

Reichsheer and *Heer.* http:www.bundesarchiv.de/php/bestaende_findemittel/
bestaendeuebersicht

"Special Duties for the SS in 'Operation Barbarossa,' March 13, 1941." Documents
of the Holocaust Part III. http://www.yadvashem.org/about_holocaust/
documents/part3/doc169.html

"Special Instructions for the Area of Responsibility (*Arbeitsgebiet*) of Detachment VI."
22 April 1943. NARA Microfilm Publication T-354, Roll 642.

Stabsbefehl. 17 April 1943. NARA Microfilm Publication T-354, Roll 642.

Tagesbefehl. 13 September 1941. NARA Microfilm Publication T-315, Roll 78.

Tagesbefehl an die deutschen Soldaten der Wehrmacht. 1 January 1943. NARA Microfilm
Publication T-354.

Tätigkeitsbericht 8.11.1941–29.4.1942. NARA Microfilm Publication T-315, Roll 83.

Tätigkeitsbericht vom 16.4. bis zum 18.8.1943. NARA Microfilm Publication T-354, Roll
643, Frame 281.

Tätigkeitsbericht zum Kriegstagebuch. NARA Microfilm Publication T-354, Roll 641.

Tätigkeitsberichte (and 8th Waffen-SS Cavalry Division orders of 16–17 April 1943 and 17
April 1943, respectively). NARA Microfilm Publication T-354, Roll 642.

Terrain Factors in the Russian Campaign, facsimile ed. Washington, D.C.: Center of
Military History, 1982/1986.

"Tragtiere im Einsatz." *Truppendienst.* Folge 287. Ausgabe 5/2005. Wien:
Bundesministerium für Landesverteidigung, 2005. www.bmlv.gv/
truppendienst/ausgaben/artikel.php?id=375

Umwandlung der 1.K.D. zu einer Panzer-Division. NARA Microfilm Publication T-315, Roll
82.

Untitled report of 1st Cavalry Division IIa (Adjutant) dated 15 September 1941. NARA
Microfilm Publication T-315, Roll 78.

Verlustliste der SS-Kavallerie-Division für die Zeit vom 16.4. bis 18.8.1943. NARA Microfilm
  Publication T-354, Roll 643, Frames 282-284.

Verlustliste SS-Kav.Division (vom 21.12.1942–20.1.1943). NARA Microfilm Publication T-
  354, Roll 642.

Verlustmeldung. 10 June 1943. NARA Microfilm Publication T-354, Roll 642.

Veterinary circular. Undated [June 1941?]. NARA Microfilm Publication T-315, Roll 82.

Vorgeschichte der SS-Kavallerie-Division. NARA Microfilm Publication T-354, Roll 640.

Zur Schonung der Pferde, Kraft- und Pferdefahrzeuge[.] 30 December 1942. NARA Microfilm
  Publication T-354, Roll 644.

*Zusammenstellung Über Beuteergebnis im Zuge der Unternehmen "Weichsel" im "Nassen
  Dreieck."* NARA Microfilm Publication T-354, Roll 642.

Zustandsbericht. 26 April 1943. NARA Microfilm Publication T-354, Roll 642.

Zustandsmeldungen to the Operations Officer of XXX Army Corps of 19 and 26
  December 1942. NARA Microfilm Publication T-354, Roll 642.

Secondary Sources

Badsey, Stephen. "The Boer War (1899–1902) and British Cavalry Doctrine: A Re-
  Evaluation." *The Journal of Military History*, 71, no.1 (January 2007): 75–98.

Barrie, Douglas. "Tornado Watch." *Aviation Week and Space Technology*, 26 February
  2007.

Bartov, Omer. *Hitler's Army: Soldiers, Nazis, and War in the Third Reich*. New York and
  Oxford: Oxford University Press, 1992.

"The Battle of Big Nations for Thoroughbred Horses." *New York Times Magazine*. 3 May
  1914, SM9. http://query.nytimes.com/gst/abstract.html (18 March 2009).

Bell, P. M. H. *The Origins of the Second World War in Europe* (London: Pearson, 2007).

Benzel, Lance. "Ft. Carson Special Forces train on horseback." *Army Times*. www.
  armytimes.com/news/2010/09/ap-special-forces-train-on-horseback-090710/

Beorn, Waitman. "'Heads Up, By God!' French Cavalry at Eylau, 1807 and Napoleon's
  Cavalry Doctrine." www.napoleonseries.org/articles/wars/eylau.cfm. (25
  January 2005).

Berhardi, Friedrich von. *Germany and the Next War*. Translated by Allen H. Powles. N.p.,
  1912. http://www.gutenberg.org/files/11352/11352-8.txt

Bielakowski, Alexander M. "General Hawkins's War: The Future of the Horse in the
  U.S. Cavalry." *The Journal of Military History*, 71, no. 1 (January 2007): 127–138.

Black, Jeremy. *European Warfare, 1494–1660*. London and New York: Routledge, 2002.

———. "The Military Revolution II: Eighteenth-Century War." In *The Oxford Illustrated
  History of Modern War*, edited by Charles Townshend, 35–47. Oxford: Oxford
  University Press, 1997.

Blackbourn, David. *The Conquest of Nature: Water, Landscape, and the Making of Modern
  Germany*. New York: W. W. Norton, 2006.

Bou, Jean. "Cavalry, Firepower, and Swords: The Australian Light Horse and the
  Tactical Lessons of Cavalry Operations in Palestine, 1916–1918." *The Journal of
  Military History*, 71, no.1 (January 2007): 99–125.

Bracher, Karl Dietrich, Manfred Funke, and Has-Adolf Jacobsen, eds. *Nationalsozialistische Diktatur 1933–1945*. Bonn: Bundeszentrale für politische Bildung, 1986.

Brady, Andrea. "Dying With Honor: Literary Propaganda and the Second English Civil War." *The Journal of Military History*, 70, no. 1 (January 2006): 9–30.

Cassidy, Ben. "Machiavelli and the Ideology of the Offensive: Gunpowder Weapons in *The Art of War*." *The Journal of Military History*, 67, no. 2 (April 2003): 381–404.

Christian, David. *A History of Russia, Central Asia, and Mongolia*, vol. 1: *Inner Eurasia from Prehistory to the Mongol Empire*. Oxford: Blackwell, 1998.

Chronik des Dorfes Krampnitz. http://www.neufahrland-online.de/seite6.htm

Citino, Robert M. *The German Way of War: From the Thirty Years' War to the Third Reich*. Lawrence: University Press of Kansas, 2005.

Clark, Christopher. *Iron Kingdom: The Rise and Downfall of Prussia, 1600–1947*. Oxford: Oxford University Press, 2006.

Clinefelter, Joan L. *Artists for the Reich: Culture and Race from Weimar to Nazi Germany*. New York: Berg, 2005.

Condell, Bruce, and David T. Zabecki, eds. and trans. *On the German Art of War: Truppenführung* (Boulder, CO: Lynne Rienner Publishers, 2001).

Cooper, Matthew. *The German Army 1933–1945*. London: Scarborough House, 1978.

Corum, James S. *The Roots of Blitzkrieg: Hans von Seeckt and German Army Reform*. Lawrence: University Press of Kansas, 1992.

Craig, Gordon A. *The Battle of Königgrätz: Prussia's Victory Over Austria, 1866*. Philadelphia and New York: Lippincott, 1964.

Creveld, Martin van. *The Changing Face of War: Lessons of Combat From the Marne to Iraq*. New York: Presidio, 2006.

———. "Technology and War I: To 1945." In *The Oxford Illustrated History of Modern War*, edited by Charles Townshend, 175–193. Oxford: Oxford University Press, 1997.

David, Daniel. *The 1914 Campaign: August–October, 1914*. New York: Wieser and Wieser, 1987.

Davies, Norman. *Europe: A History*. Oxford: Oxford University Press, 1996.

———. *No Simple Victory: World War II in Europe, 1939–1945*. New York: Viking, 2006.

Davis, R. H. C. *The Medieval Warhorse: Origin, Development and Redevelopment*. London: Thames and Hudson, 1989.

Dear, I. C .B., and M. R. D. Foot, eds. *The Oxford Companion to World War II*. Oxford: Oxford University Press, 1995.

Denison, George T. *A History of Cavalry From the Earliest Times: With Lessons for the Future*. London: Macmillan, 1913.

Deist, Wilhelm. *The Wehrmacht and German Rearmament*. Foreword by A. J. Nicholls. Basingstoke: The Macmillan Press, 1981.

D'Este, Carlo. *Patton: A Genius for War*. New York: HarperCollins, 1995.

DiMarco, Louis A. *War Horse: A History of the Military Horse and Rider*. Yardley, PA: Westholme, 2008.

DiNardo, R. L. *Mechanized Juggernaut or Military Anachronism? Horses and the German Army of World War II.* Foreword by Williamson Murray. New York: Greenwood Press, 1991.

Dorondo, D. R. "Review of *Noble Brutes: How Eastern Horses Transformed English Culture* by Donna Landry." *Itinerario,* no. 2 (2009). http://www.let.leidenuniv.nl/history/itinerario/.

Doughty, Robert A. "French Strategy in 1914: Joffre's Own." *The Journal of Military History,* 67, no. 2 (April 2003): 427–454.

Dupuy, Trevor N. *1914: The Battles in the West.* New York: Franklin Watts, 1967.

Dziewanowski, M. K. *War At Any Price: World War II in Europe, 1939–1945,* 2nd ed. Englewood Cliffs, NJ: Prentice Hall, 1991.

Ellis, John. *Eye-Deep in Hell: Trench Warfare in World War I.* New York: Pantheon Books, 1976.

Evans, Richard. *The Third Reich in Power, 1933–1939.* New York: Penguin, 2005.

Fagan Brian M. *People of the Earth: An Introduction to World Prehistory,* 9th ed. New York: Longman, 1998.

Fontane, Theodor. *Wanderungen durch die mark Brandenburg. Erster Band. Die Grafschaft Ruppin.* Edited by Edgar Gross. München: Nymphenburger Verlagshandlung, 1960/1963.

Forrest, Alan. "The Nation in Arms I: The French Wars." In *The Oxford Illustrated History of Modern War,* edited by Charles Townshend, 48–63. Oxford: Oxford University Press, 1997.

Frieser, Karl-Heinz. *The Blitzkrieg Legend: The 1940 German Campaign in the West.* Edited by John T. Greenwood. Annapolis: Naval Institute Press, 2005.

Fuller, J. F. C. *The Conduct of War, 1789–1961.* New York: Minerva Press, 1968.

"Germany." *Encyclopedia Britannica,* vol. 10, 232–311. Chicago: University of Chicago Press, 1947.

Geyer, Michael. *Deutsche Rüstungspolitik 1860–1890.* Edited by Hans-Ulrich Wehler. Frankfurt am Main: Suhrkamp Verlag, 1984.

Gilbert, Martin. *The First World War: A Complete History.* New York: Henry Holt, 1994.

———. *The Somme: Heroism and Horror in the First World War.* New York: Henry Holt, 2006.

Gillmor, Carroll. "Cavalry, Ancient and Medieval." In *The Reader's Companion to Military History,* edited by Robert Cowley and Geoffrey Parker, 74–75. Boston: Houghton Mifflin, 1996.

Glantz, David M., and Jonathan House. *When Titans Clashed: How the Red Army Stopped Hitler.* Lawrence: University Press of Kansas, 1995.

Grbasic, Z., and V. Vuksic. *The History of Cavalry.* New York: Facts On File, 1989.

Grossman, Dave. *On Killing: The Psychological Cost of Learning to Kill in War and Society.* New York and Boston: Back Bay Books, 1996.

Guderian, Heinz. *Panzer Leader.* Foreword by B. H. Liddell Hart. Translated by Constantine Fitzgibbon. Costa Mesa, CA: Noontide Press, 1988.

Handbook of the German Army (Home and Colonial) 1912 (Amended to 1914). London: Imperial War Museum, and Nashville, TN: The Battery Press, 2002.

Handbook of the German Army 1940. Nashville, TN: The Battery Press, 1996.

Hanson Victor Davis. *The Wars of the Ancient Greeks and Their Invention of Western Military Culture*. London: Cassell, 2000.

Heiber, Helmut, and David M. Glantz. *Hitler and His Generals: Military Conferences 1942– 1945*. New York: Enigma Books, 2003.

Heller, Charles E., and William A. Stofft, eds. *America's First Battles, 1776–1965*. Lawrence: University Press of Kansas, 1986.

Herwig, Holger. "The German Victories, 1917–1918." In *The First World War*, edited by Hew Strachan. Oxford: Oxford University Press, 1998.

Herzstein, Robert Edwin. *The War That Hitler Won: The Most Infamous Propaganda Campaign in History*. New York: G. P. Putnam's Sons, 1978.

Hilberg, Raul. Review of *Wegbereiter der Shoah. Die Waffen-SS, der Kommandostab Reichsführer-SS und die Judenvernichtung*, by Martin Cüppers. http://www.uni-stuttgart.de/hing/lb/lbrez_hilberg.pdf

"Hindenburg —Falkenhayn," *Vossische Zeitung* (Berlin), 30 August 1916. http://www.zld.de/projekte/ millenium/original_html/vossische_1916_3008.GIF.html

Höhne, Heinz. *The Order of the Death's Head: The Story of Hitler's SS*. New York: Ballantine, 1971.

Hollweck, Ludwig, ed. *Unser München: München im 20. Jahrhundert. Erinnerungen und berichte, Bilder und Dokumente von 1900 bis heute*. München: Süddeutscher Verlag, 1967.

Holmes, Richard. "The Last Hurrah: Cavalry on the Western Front, August–September 1914." In *Facing Armageddon: The First World War Experienced*, edited by Hugh Cecil and Peter Liddle. London: Leo Cooper, 1996.

Horne, Alistair. *To Lose a Battle: France: 1940*. New York: Penguin, 1969.

House, Jonathan M. *Towards Combined Arms Warfare: A Survey of 20th-Century Tactics, Doctrine, and Organization*. Ft. Leavenworth: U.S. Army Command and General Staff College, 1984.

Howard, Michael. *The Franco-Prussian War: The German Invasion of France 1870–1871*. New York: Dorset Press, 1961.

———. *War in European History*. Oxford: Oxford University Press, 1976.

Hubensteiner, Benno. *Bayerische Geschichte*. München: Süddeutscher Verlag, 1985.

Hull, Isabel V. *Absolute Destruction: Military Culture and the Practices of War in Imperial Germany*. Ithaca: Cornell University Press, 2005.

Hyland, Ann. *The Medieval Warhorse From Byzantium to the Crusades*. Stroud: Sutton Publishing, 1994/1996.

Jacobs, Andrew. "Police Turn to the Stable for Crime-Fighting Clout." *New York Times*, 18 April 2006, 1.

Johnson, David. *Napoleon's Cavalry and Its Leaders*. New York: Holmes and Meier, 1978.

Johnson, Paul Louis. *Horses of the German Army in World War II*. Atglen, PA: Schiffer, 2006.

Katzenbach, Edward J. "The Horse Cavalry in the Twentieth Century: A Study in Policy Response." *Public Policy: A Yearbook of the Graduate School of Public Administration.* Harvard University, 1958.

Keegan John. *The First World War.* New York: Alfred A. Knopf, 1999.

———. *A History of Warfare.* New York: Alfred A. Knopf, 1993.

———. *Waffen-SS: The Asphalt Soldiers.* New York: Ballantine, 1971.

Kennedy, Paul. *The Rise and Fall of the Great Powers: Economic Change and Military Conflict From 1500 to 2000.* New York: Random House, 1987.

Kennedy, Robert M. *The German Campaign in Poland (1939).* Department of the Army Pamphlet No. 20-255. Washington, D.C.: Department of the Army, 1956.

Keppie, Lawrence. *The Making of the Roman Army From Republic to Empire.* Norman: University of Oklahoma Press, 1998.

Kershaw, Ian. *Fateful Choices: Ten Decisions That Changed the World 1940–1941.* New York: Penguin, 2008.

———. *Hitler 1936–1945: Nemesis.* New York: W. W. Norton, 2000.

Krause, Michael D. "Moltke and Origins of the Operational Level of War." In *Historical Perspectives on the Operational Art,* edited by Michael D. Krause and R. Cody Phillips. Washington, D.C.: Center of Military History, 2005.

Krause, Michael D., and R. Cody Phillips, eds. *Historical Perspectives of the Operational Art.* Washington, D.C.: Center of Military History, 2005.

Krausnick, Helmut, and Hans-Heinrich Wilhelm. *Die Truppe des Weltanschauungskrieges. Die Einsatzgruppen der Sicherheitspolizei und des SD 1938–1942.* N.p.: Stuttgart, 1981.

Legard, D'Arcy. *Cavalry on Service: Illustrated by the Advance of the German Cavalry Across the Mosel in 1870.* London: Hugh Rees, 1906.

Lehndorff, Hans Graf von. *Meschen, Pferde, weites Land: Kindheits- und Jugenderinnerungen.* München: Verlag C. H. Beck, 2002.

Leslie, Van Michael. "French, John Denton Pinkstone, Earl of Ypres." In *The European Powers in the First World War: An Encyclopedia,* edited by Spencer C. Tucker, 271–272. New York: Garland, 1996.

Liaropoulus, Andrew N. "Revolutions in Warfare: Theoretical Paradigms and Historical Evidence —The Napoleonic and First World War Revolutions in Military Affairs." *The Journal of Military History,* 70, no. 2 (April 2006): 363–384.

Littauer, Vladimir. *Horseman's Progress: The Development of Modern Riding.* Princeton, NJ: D. Van Nostrand, 1962. Reprint by The Long Riders' Guild Press, n.d. http://www.horsetravelbooks.com/others.htm.

———. *Russian Hussar: A Story of the Imperial Cavalry, 1911–1920.* London: J. A. Allen & Co., 1965. Reprint by The Long Riders' Guild Press, 2007. http://www.horsetravelbooks.com/others.htm

Liulevicius, Vejas Gabriel. *War Land on the Eastern Front: Culture, National Identity, and German Occupation in World War I.* Cambridge: Cambridge University Press, 2000.

Livingston, Phil, and Ed Roberts. *War Horse: Mounting the Cavalry With America's Best Horses.* Albany, TX: Bright Sky Press, 2003.

Long, E. B., ed. *Personal Memoirs of U. S. Grant.* New York: Da Capo Press, 1952/1982.

Lowry, Bullitt. *Armistice 1918.* Kent, OH: The Kent State University Press, 1996.

Luck, Hans von. *Panzer Commander: The Memoirs of Colonel Hans von Luck.* Introduction by Stephen A. Ambrose. New York: Dell, 1989.

Luvaas, Jay. *The Military Legacy of the Civil War.* Chicago: University of Chicago Press, 1959.

MacDonald, Charles B. *Company Commander.* Introduction by Dennis Showalter. New York: History Book Club, 2006.

———. *The Last Offensive, United States Army in World War II —The European Theater of Operations.* Edited by Maurice Matloff. Washington, D.C.: Center of Military History, 1973/1993.

Malaparte, Curzio. *The Volga Rises in Europe.* Translated by David Moore. Edinburgh: Birlinn Limited, 1951.

Marrus, Michael R. *The Nuremberg War Crimes Trial 1945–56.* New York: Bedford/St. Martin's, 1997.

Marsden, William, trans. and ed. *The Travels of Marco Polo the Venetian.* Garden City, NY: International Collectors Library, 1948.

Marshall, George C. *Victory Report On the Winning of the War in Europe and the Pacific.* Washington, D.C.: War Department, 1945.

Marshall, S. L. A. *World War I.* New York: American Heritage Press, 1971.

Maurice, Major F. "The Franco-German War (1870–1)." In *The Cambridge Modern History,* vol. XI: *The Growth of Nationalities,* edited by A. W. Ward et al. Cambridge: Cambridge University Press, 1909/1969.

Melegari, Vezio. *The World's Great Regiments.* New York: G. P. Putnam's Sons, 1969.

Mellenthin, F. W. von. *Panzer Battles: A Study of the Employment of Armor in the Second World War.* Translated by H. Betzler. Norman: University of Oklahoma Press, 1956.

Mommsen, Wolfgang J. *Imperial Germany 1867–1918: Politics, Culture, and Society in an Authoritarian State.* Translated by Richard Deveson. London: Arnold, 1995.

Morris, Jan. *Spain.* New York: Oxford University Press, 1979.

Murphy, G. Ronald, S.J., trans. *The Heliand: The Saxon Gospel.* Oxford: Oxford University Press, 1992.

Murray, Williamson. "Cavalry, 1500–1945." In *The Reader's Companion to Military History,* edited by Robert Cowley and Geoffrey Parker, 75–77. Boston: Houghton Mifflin, 1996.

Nagorski, Andrew. *The Greatest Battle: Stalin, Hitler, and the Desperate Struggle for Moscow That Changed the Course of World War II.* New York: Simon & Schuster, 2007.

New York Times, 5 September 1939.

New York Times, 10, 11, 14 April 1945. http://0-proquest.umi.com.wncln.wncln.org

Noakes, Jeremy, and Geoffrey Pridham, eds. *Documents on Nazism 1919–1945.* New York: Viking Press, 1975.

O'Connell, Robert L. *Soul of the Sword: An Illustrated History of Weaponry and Warfare from Prehistory to the Present.* New York: The Free Press, 2002.

Ortiz, Lionel, and Brian Butcher. "Winners! U.S. Cavalry Squadrons Win and Place in Grueling NATO Reconnaissance Competition." *Armor* (November–December 1987). http://www.benning.army.mil/armor/armormagazine/content/Issues/1987/ArmorNovemberDecember1987web.pdf

Overy, Richard. "Transportation and Rearmament in the Third Reich." *The Historical Journal*, 16 (June 1973).

———. *Why the Allies Won*. New York: W. W. Norton, 1995.

Paret, Peter, ed. *Makers of Modern Strategy from Machiavelli to the Nuclear Age*. Princeton: Princeton University Press, 1986.

Parrott, David A. "Strategy and Tactics in the Thirty Years' War: The 'Military Revolution.'" In *The Military Revolution Debate: Readings on the Transformation of Early Modern Europe*, edited by Clifford J. Rogers. Boulder, CO: Westview Press, 1995.

Peace Treaty of Versailles. Articles 231–247 and Annexes. Reparations. http://www.lib.byu.edu/~rdh/wwi/versa/versa7.html

Pershing, John J., General. "Final Report of General John J. Pershing: Part III —Supply, Coordination, Munitions, and Administration —'Remounts'." In Francis J. Reynolds, *The Story of the Great War: History of the European War From Official Sources*. New York: P. F. Collier and Son Company, 1920.

Phillips, Gervase. "Scapegoat Arm: Twentieth-Century Cavalry in Anglophone Historiography." *The Journal of Military History*, 71, no. 1 (January 2007): 37–74.

Pinson, Koppel S. *Modern Germany: Its History and Civilization*, 2nd ed. Prospect Heights, IL: Waveland Press, 1966/1989.

Poseck, Maximilian von. *The German Cavalry: 1914 in Belgium and France*. Edited by Jerome Howe. Translated by Alexander C. Strecker et al. Berlin: E. S. Mittler und Sohn, 1923.

Rauschning, Hermann. *Hitler Speaks*. London: Thornton Butterworth, 1940.

Rempel, Gerhard. *Hitler's Children: The Hitler Youth and the SS*. Chapel Hill: The University of North Carolina Press, 1989.

The Revelation to John, VI: 1–4. The New American Bible. Wichita, KS: Catholic Bible Publishers, 1994–1995.

Reynolds, Francis J., ed. *The Story of the Great War: History of the European War From Official Sources* . New York: P. F. Collier and Son, 1916.

Richter, Klaus. *Cavalry of the Wehrmacht 1941–1945*. Atglen, PA: Schiffer, [no date].

———. *Weapons and Equipment of the German Cavalry 1935–1945*. Atglen, PA: Schiffer, 1995.

Roberts, Andrew. *Waterloo: June 18, 1815. The Battle for Modern Europe*. New York: HarperCollins, 2005.

Roberts, Michael. "The Military Revolution 1560–1660." In *The Military Revolution Debate: Readings on the Transformation of Early Modern Europe*, edited by Clifford J. Rogers. Boulder, CO: Westview Press, 1995.

Sheridan, P. H. *Personal Memoirs*. Introduction by Jeffrey D. Wert. New York: Da Capo Press, 1992.

Showalter, Dennis E. *Tannenberg: Clash of Empires*. Hamden, CT: Archon Books, 1991.

———. "World War I." In *The Reader's Companion to Military History*, edited by Robert Cowley and Geoffrey Parker, 521–526. Boston: Houghton Mifflin, 1996.

Signal: Years of Triumph 1940–42. Hitler's Wartime Picture Magazine. Edited by S. L. Mayer. New York: Prentice-Hall, 1978.

Singleton, John. "Britain's Use of Military Horses 1914–1918." *Past and Present*, 139 (May 1993).

Snyder, Louis L., ed. *Hitler's Third Reich: A Documentary History*. Chicago: Nelson-Hall, 1981.

Snyder, Timothy. *Bloodlands: Europe Between Hitler and Stalin*. New York: Basic Books, 2010.

Solzhenitsyn, Alexander. *August 1914*. Translated by Michael Glenny. New York: Farrar, Straus and Giroux, 1971.

Spiers, Edward. "The Late Victorian Army 1868–1914." In *The Oxford Illustrated History of the British Army*, edited by David Chandler, 189–214. Oxford: Oxford University Press, 1994.

Spotts, Frederic. *Hitler and the Power of Aesthetics*. New York: The Overlook Press, 2003.

Stamps, T. Dodson, and Vincent J. Esposito, eds. *A Short Military History of World War I With Atlas*. West Point: USMAAG Printing Office, 1950.

Stanton, Doug. *Horse Soldiers: The Extraordinary Story of a Band of U.S. Soldiers Who Rode to Victory in Afghanistan*. New York: Scribner, 2009.

Stanton, Shelby L. *Anatomy of a Division: The 1st Cav in Vietnam*. New York: Warner Books, 1987.

Stargardt, Nicholas. "Hitler in the Driving Seat." *Times Literary Supplement*. 8 October 2008. http://entertainment.timesonline.co.uk/tol/arts_and_entertainment/the_tls

Stenglin, Christian Freiherr von. *The Hanoverian*. Translated by Christina Belton. London: J. A. Allen, 1990.

Stone, David. *Fighting for the Fatherland: The Story of the German Soldier From 1648 to the Present Day*. Foreword by Richard Holmes. Washington, D.C.: Potomac Books, 2006.

Stone, Norman. *The Eastern Front 1914–1917*. New York: Charles Scribner's Sons, 1975.

The Story of the Great War, vol. III. New York: P. F. Collier and Son, 1916.

Strachan, Hew. *The First World War*. vol. 1. Oxford: Oxford University Press, 2001.

———"Military Modernization, 1789–1918." In *The Oxford Illustrated History of Modern Europe*, edited by T. C. W. Blanning, 69–93. Oxford: Oxford University Press, 1996.

Stubbs, Mary Lee, and Stanley Russell Connor. *Armor-Cavalry*, part I: *Regular Army and Army Reserve*. Washington, D.C.: Office of the Chief of Military History Unites States Army, 1969.

Sydnor, Charles W. "On the Historiography of the SS." Simon Wiesenthal Museum of Tolerance Multimedia Learning Center Online. http://motlc.wisenthal.com/site/pp.asp

———. *Soldiers of Destruction: The SS Death's Head Division, 1933–1945.* Princeton: Princeton University Press, 1977.

The [London] *Times.* 17 May 1945. http://0-infotrac.galegroup.com.wncln.wncln.org

Townshend, Charles, ed. *The Oxford Illustrated History of Modern War.* Oxford: Oxford University Press, 1997.

Trevor-Roper, Hugh. *The Rise of Christian Europe.* New York: Harcourt, Brace, 1965.

Truscott, Lucian K., Jr. *The Twilight of the U.S. Cavalry: Life in the Old Army, 1917–1942.* Lawrence: University Press of Kansas, 1989.

Velsen-Zerweck, Eberhard von, and Erhard Schulte. *The Trakehner.* Translated by Christina Belton. London: J. A. Allen, 1990.

Wagner, A. L., ed. *Cavalry Studies from Two Great Wars. Comprising the French Cavalry in 1870 by Lieutenant-Colonel Bonie, the German Cavalry in the Battle of Vionville–Mars-la-Tour by Major Kaehler and the Operations of the Cavalry in the Gettysburg Campaign by Lieutenant-Colonel George B. Davis.* Kansas City, MO: Hudson-Kimberly Publishing Company, 1896.

Wawro, Geoffrey. *The Austro-Prussian War: Austria's War with Prussia and Italy in 1866.* New York: Cambridge University Press, 1996.

———. *The Franco-Prussian War: The German Conquest of France in 1870–1871.* New York: Cambridge University Press, 2003.

Western Horseman, vol. 71, no. 1 (January 2006): 32. Reprinted editorial by Paul Albert from the issue of November–December 1939.

Winkler, Heinrich August. *Der lange Weg nach Westen: Deutsche Geschichte*, vols. I and II. München: C. H. Beck Verlag, 2002.

Wrangel, Alexis. *The End of Chivalry: The Last Great Cavalry Battles 1914–1918.* New York: Hippocrene Books, 1982.

Yerger, Mark C. *Riding East: The SS Cavalry Brigade in Poland and Russia 1939–1942.* Atglen, PA: Schiffer, 1996.

Young, Peter, ed. *Atlas of the Second World War.* New York: Paragon, 1979.

Zabecki, David T. "Somme, Battle of (1 July–19 November 1916)." In *The European Powers in the First World War: An Encyclopedia*, edited by Spencer C. Tucker, 648–651. New York: Garland, 1996.

Zamoyski, Adam. "The Battle for the Marchlands." *East European Monographs*, no. LXXXVIII. New York: Columbia University Press, 1981.

———. *Warsaw 1920: Lenin's Failed Conquest of Europe.* London: HarperCollins, 2008.

Ziemke, Earl F. *The Soviet Juggernaut.* New York: Time-Life Books, 1980.

———. *Stalingrad to Berlin: The German Defeat in the East.* Washington, D.C.: Office of the Chief of Military History, 1968.

———, and Magna E. Bauer. *Moscow to Stalingrad: Decision in the East.* Washington, D.C.: Center of Military History, 1987.

ABOUT THE AUTHOR

D. R. Dorondo holds the degree of D.Phil. from the University of Oxford. He is professor of modern German and European military history at Western Carolina University.